THE TERROR COURTS

The Terror Courts

Rough Justice at Guantanamo Bay

■

JESS BRAVIN

Yale UNIVERSITY PRESS

New Haven and London

Yale University Press books may be purchased in quantity for educational,
business, or promotional use. For information, please e-mail sales.press@
yale.edu (US office) or sales@yaleup.co.uk (UK office).

Designed by Sonia Shannon.
Set in Minion type by Keystone Typesetting, Inc.
Printed in the United States of America.

Library of Congress Cataloging-in-Publication Data
Bravin, Jess.
The terror courts : rough justice at Guantanamo Bay / Jess Bravin.
pages cm
Includes bibliographical references and index.
ISBN 978-0-300-18920-9 (clothbound)
1. War crimes trials—United States. 2. Guantanamo Bay Detention Camp.
3. Military courts—Cuba—Guantanamo Bay Naval Base. I. Title.
KF7661.B73 2013
345.73'023170269—dc23
2012034913

A catalogue record for this book is available from the British Library.

This paper meets the requirements of ANSI/NISO Z39.48–1992
(Permanence of Paper).

10 9 8 7 6 5 4 3 2 1

To Anne Marie

"Shall the Souldier and Justice Sit on one Bench,
the Trumpet will not let the Cryer speak in Westminster-Hall."
—*Sir Edward Coke, 1628*

Contents

Prologue

NOVEMBER 24, 2001. AROUND NOON.

Checkpoints were common as potholes on the roads of Afghanistan. Salim Ahmed Salim Hamdan, driving north on Highway 4 in a Toyota hatchback, was not surprised to be stopped by a group of armed men as he approached the fortified town of Takht-e Pol.

Afghanistan was at war. It had been at war for decades. On October 7, less than a month after terrorist attacks obliterated the Twin Towers in New York and destroyed part of the Pentagon in Washington, the United States had become the latest entrant in the Afghan wars. American air strikes and Special Forces backed a loose confederation of militias hostile to the ruling Taliban movement, but here, in Kandahar province, the Taliban still dominated. The city of Kandahar, according to legend founded by Alexander the Great, was the home of Mullah Mohammed Omar, a half-blind cleric who led the Taliban with the aid of Pakistani intelligence. Highway 4 ran southeast from Kandahar to the frontier, into the Pakistani province of Baluchistan and its capital, Quetta. In recent decades, Quetta had been transformed by an influx of Afghan refugees and the elements that inevitably accompanied them: arms dealers, drug smugglers, factional cadre, intelligence agents. The city, which sat just outside the war zone, was a haven for various parties with an interest in Afghanistan. As the American-led campaign turned toward Kandahar, more Afghans would set out along Highway 4 seeking safety in Quetta.

But Hamdan was headed the other way: *to* Kandahar. And to his apparent surprise, the fighters at the checkpoint weren't Taliban but part of the enemy Pashtun militia. Hours before, American air strikes had blasted out Takht-e Pol's Taliban defenders, allowing fighters from the eight-hundred-man militia under the warlord Gul Sharzai to enter the town without firing a shot.[1] These fighters, nominally

1

loyal to the former king, Mohammed Zahir Shah, were clandestinely obliged to the Central Intelligence Agency.[2]

Sharzai's men had set up highway roadblocks north and south of Takht-e Pol, which would serve as a staging ground for a coming assault on Kandahar, after another American-paid Pashtun militia—this one headed by Hamid Karzai—arrived from the north. Traffic had been slight. Earlier, a white van had tried to blow past the checkpoint, prompting a shootout that left two Egyptian occupants dead and a third man captured, a Moroccan whose name would turn out to be Said Boujaadia.[3]

Hamdan was not so bold. He tried to flee, but the Afghans nabbed him and immediately identified him as an Arab. He was being dragged away to an uncertain fate when the American officer managing the Sharzai operation, Major Hank Smith, showed up to see what the shooting was about. The Pashtuns pointed to two SA-7 Grail surface-to-air missiles in battered, olive-drab carrying tubes. They said the missiles had been taken from the Arab's car.

With barely a dozen Americans on hand—soldiers and CIA—Smith hardly was equipped to deal with enemy prisoners of war. Still, Afghan militias were even less inclined to take prisoners, and summary execution of captured enemies was not unknown as a local tradition. Smith had his American soldiers take Hamdan and Boujaadia, hooded and bound, to a nearby shack.

A search of the Toyota turned up two passports, Yemen Airways tickets for Hamdan and a woman named Fatima, a handheld radio, brevity codes—a form of radio shorthand—and a folder with newspaper and magazine articles about al Qaeda. Plenty of cash was found —$1,900, plus about $260 in Pakistani rupees. There was a passport photo envelope from Razi's Portrait Inn Studio and Express Lab, located in Unit 44 of the Shalimar Shopping Center in Karachi, Pakistan. There were five photos of a baby girl. And there were letters. One, handwritten in Arabic on a page ripped from a small spiral-bound notebook, was addressed to "Brother Saqr."

"I hope you and all the brothers with you are well," it read. "If possible, please send me 25 to 30 original Russian Pikka"—a type of machine gun—"belts. Likewise, if you can find Pikka magazines. Most of the Pikkas we have do not have them and we are in urgent need of them. Even Grenav"—another Soviet-made weapon—"magazines will work. We cut them off and adapt them for the Pikka in the workshop. Please do whatever you can.

"Your brother, Khallad."

P.S. "Can you find three military compasses for us? They said there are a lot of them in Kabul."[4]

Major Smith looked at the SA-7s, now sitting on the tailgate of a blue pickup. By themselves, they were inoperable. No launchers or firing mechanisms had been found.

The Taliban had no air force. The only planes in the sky, the only possible target for a surface-to-air missile—the sort of weapon that in the 1980s, when supplied by Washington to the mujahideen, had proved so devastating to the Soviet military—was the American-led coalition air forces. After photographing the missiles to include in a future report, Smith ordered them destroyed. Not so Hamdan's car. He affixed an orange insignia to the hood, the signal to coalition air forces that the vehicle was friendly, and gave the car to one of his local interpreters. Smith considered it a form of "recycling."[5]

Small and swarthy, Hamdan sat on the dirt floor of a mud hut, his hands bound before him in flexicuffs. With a video camera running, a masked US Army interrogator questioned him in Arabic. An armed guard stood behind the prisoner, remaining silent as the interrogator struggled to make himself understood through his heavy American accent.

Hamdan spoke rapidly, his eyes bright, his smile and occasional nervous laugh suggesting he knew his number was up. He said he had come to Afghanistan as a relief worker for al Wafa, an Islamic charity. But with the recent fighting, he had borrowed a car to take his wife and daughter to safety in Pakistan. The car wasn't his—he had borrowed it from somebody named Abu Yasser—and neither were most of the items found in it. Sure, he knew there were SA-7s in the trunk, he said, but they must have belonged to Abu Yasser. Yes, he had heard of al Qaeda, but he knew little about it. "I heard that they train people who come to Afghanistan for training," he said. Perhaps he didn't expect ever to leave that hut. "I am not lying to you," he said.

"It's all finished for me, why should I lie?"

YEARS LATER, FROM A CELL at Guantanamo Bay, Hamdan recalled the events somewhat differently. He had been working in Kabul when the fighting began in October 2001, and feared for his wife and daughter in Kandahar. So he asked his boss, Osama bin Laden, for permission to go to them. "I decided to borrow a car to drive my family to Pakistan," he said.[6] After depositing them near the border, "I tried to return to Afghanistan to return the car to its owner," and to sell his belongings to raise enough money to get the family back to Yemen. But he was stopped by Afghans "looking for Arabs to sell to American forces. When they stopped me, they had already taken another Arab who they shot and killed. I tried to flee, but I failed and they captured me again. They tied my hands and feet behind me like an animal with electrical wire . . . so tight that the wire cut me."

He was taken to a house and then moved to another, "for seven days, where I was questioned by a man in a military uniform who spoke Arabic and said he was an American. The Afghan soldiers told me they had gotten $5,000 from the Americans for me," Hamdan said. He said he saw the money himself.

According to the account dictated from his jail cell in 2004, Salim Hamdan was born in 1969, perhaps, in the rural village of Khoreiba in the southeastern Yemeni region of Hadhramout. That was two years after the British pulled out of the country, which they had ruled as the protectorate of Aden. The newly independent state, following then-fashionable ideological fads, proclaimed itself the People's Republic of South Yemen and later the People's Democratic Republic of Yemen, a minor satellite in the Soviet orbit. In contrast, the adjacent Yemen Arab Republic, better known as North Yemen, independent since the collapse of the Ottoman Empire after World

War I, tilted more toward the West, despite its squabbles with adjacent Saudi Arabia. The rival Yemens, among the poorest countries in the Arab world, fought occasional battles that commanded little attention outside the region, until in 1990, in an equally overlooked event, the two states merged.

It was unclear what impact these political developments had on Salim Hamdan. Orphaned as a child, educated perhaps to a fourth-grade level, he spent the 1980s living with relatives in the port city of Mukalla, working odd jobs. At age twenty, he drifted westward to the newly unified Yemen's capital, San'a, "to seek better employment opportunities," he said. He drove a *dabbab*, a type of jitney, but fortune passed him by until 1996, when he met a man seeking recruits "to aid Muslims struggling against the communists in Tajikistan," he said. That former Soviet republic, on Afghanistan's northern border, was the next target for the international Islamic fundamentalist movement that had toppled the pro-Moscow regime in Kabul.

Traveling to Afghanistan via Pakistan, Hamdan proved less than a relentless *mujahid* for the Tajik struggle. "I met with other Muslims who were going to Tajikistan," he recounted. "We traveled by plane, then by car and then by foot until we got to Badashaw," on the Tajik border. But "the forces at Tajikistan wouldn't allow us to go further, and the weather in the mountains was bad." Rather than battle the elements or the border guards, "we turned around and left for Kabul." Hamdan said he just wanted to go home to Yemen, but a comrade named Muhammad reminded him there was no work to be found there. Besides, there was a better opportunity. Muhammad had gotten a lead on a suitable job for Hamdan. "He took me to a farm in Jalalabad, where I met Osama bin Laden," Hamdan said. The emir "offered me a job as a driver on a farm he owned, bringing Afghan workers from the local village to work and back again." As the year passed, Hamdan gained bin Laden's confidence. He "began to have me drive him to various places," Hamdan said.

Bin Laden's family also came from Hadhramout—his father Mohammed was born there—which perhaps explains the austere ideologue's affinity toward his barely literate driver.[7] Soon, bin Laden was functioning as a surrogate father, even arranging for Hamdan's marriage. Bin Laden sent Hamdan and another courtier recruited from the Tajik expedition, Nasser al-Bahri, to Yemen to marry sisters. Al-Bahri, a Saudi who adopted the nom de guerre Abu Jandal, had become one of bin Laden's chief bodyguards. He now was also brother-in-law to Hamdan, who would himself take an al Qaeda name of Saqr al Jeddawi, the Hawk of Jeddah.

HAMDAN'S RESISTANCE TRAINING proved somewhat deficient. After capture at the checkpoint, Hamdan later recounted, "I helped and cooperated with the Americans in every way," even though—or perhaps because—they "physically abused" him. "When I took them to the places I had driven Osama bin Laden, they would threaten me with death, torture or prison when I did not know the answers to their questions. One of their methods to threaten was to put a pistol on the table in front of me" and ask, "'What do you think?'"

Within weeks of September 11, the United States had orchestrated regime change in Afghanistan. Directed by intelligence units like the one Major Smith commanded and backed by coalition air power, the Northern Alliance and other anti-Taliban militias pushed out the black-turbaned Islamist foe. Prisoners, by the hundreds, were a dividend of this surprisingly rapid success. With US forces offering bounties for al Qaeda fighters, typically five thousand dollars or so, Afghan tribesmen turned over hundreds more, assuring the Americans that the prisoners were terrorists.

The US commander, General Tommy Franks, didn't want the small number of ground troops he had in Afghanistan tied up guarding enemy prisoners. That suited the Bush administration. It had developed plans to build a special kind of detention center in the Pentagon's own time zone, at the US naval base, Guantanamo Bay, Cuba. A new enemy would face a special kind of reckoning, trial by military commission, that could see prisoners prosecuted, convicted, and executed at President George W. Bush's command. Officials called it "rough justice." Guantanamo would be al Qaeda's Nuremberg, the end of the line for perpetrators of monstrous crimes.

Yet Guantanamo held no Mullah Omar, no Ayman al-Zawahiri, no Osama bin Laden. Al Qaeda's high command somehow had evaded the campaign the Pentagon called Operation Enduring Freedom.

A handful of real al Qaeda commanders *would* fall into American hands—Abdelrahim al-Nashiri, Ramzi Binalshibh, and the terrorist entrepreneur who conceived the 9/11 attacks, Khalid Sheikh Mohammed. The Bush White House, however, would decide that these men were far too important to put on trial. They were sent instead to years of secret detention and sometimes brutal interrogation within a clandestine prison network the CIA operated overseas. Despite pledging to bring the 9/11 conspirators to justice, President Bush hid them from prosecutors and even the abbreviated trial process he had prescribed for the alien enemy.

Pentagon prosecutors, ordered to create a justice system from scratch, scoured their prisoner lists for suitable defendants. Bin Laden had gotten away. But they had his driver.

Tater

AUGUST 2003.

Stuart Couch had been waiting nearly two years to start this job. He had been waiting since September 11, 2001.

Couch, a lieutenant colonel in the United States Marine Corps, was a military prosecutor. When President George W. Bush decreed that the 9/11 perpetrators would face trial by military commission, a form of martial justice last used against German and Japanese war criminals following World War II, Couch had volunteered for the mission. It was a matter of duty, not only to his country but to a fellow Marine.

Couch once had been a pilot, flying KC-130s out of the Marine Corps Air Station at Cherry Point, North Carolina. So had Michael Horrocks. While Couch moved on to law school, Horrocks—"Rocks" to his buddies in Marine Aerial Refueler Transport Squadron 252— kept flying after leaving the Marines.

On 9/11, Rocks was the copilot on United Airlines Flight 175. It struck the South Tower at 9:03:11 a.m. Couch had watched that footage a dozen times—or was it a thousand? As a pilot, a prosecutor, a Marine, Couch, a deeply religious man, believed he was called to seek justice for this unspeakable crime.

At the Pentagon, Couch was greeted by a Basic School classmate from Quantico, Kurt Brubaker, a fellow lieutenant colonel who had joined the prosecution staff nine months earlier. While Couch was preparing his move to Washington from Camp Lejeune, Brubaker had said that things were moving quickly at OMC-P, Pentagon short-hand for the prosecution unit at the Office of Military Commissions. By the time Couch arrived, Brubaker suggested, they likely would be in trial at Guantanamo Bay.

Not to worry, he had added. They were saving the best cases for Couch.

■

Voluble if slow-talking, Vernon Stuart Couch looked tired, perhaps older than his thirty-eight years, but his lidded face belied a churning, intensely reflective personality.

To avoid confusion with the passel of Vernons in his sprawling Southern family, Couch answered to his middle name and, by the time he reached college, to its first syllable alone.

When Couch spoke, the accent immediately betrayed his North Carolina origins. Despite missions on four continents, he never truly felt at home beyond the Tar Heel State. The Marine Corps, with installations at Camp Lejeune, Cherry Point, and New River, felt at home in North Carolina, too.

The youngest of three boys, Stuart Couch grew up in Asheboro, a struggling Piedmont town which, when not confused for the larger and livelier college center of Asheville, was best known for its furniture and hosiery industries. The former reached its peak after 1961, when President John F. Kennedy was photographed using an Asheboro-produced rocking chair in the Oval Office. The P. & P. Chair Company promptly renamed its flagship product the Kennedy Rocker, and it became a favorite for those, like President Kennedy, seeking relief from sciatica.[1] Otherwise, Asheboro took pride in being North Carolina's largest dry jurisdiction, a distinction it held through 2008, when voters reluctantly authorized the sale of beer and wine to help flagging downtown restaurants compete with their liquor-selling rivals outside the city limits.[2]

Stuart adored his mother, Kay, a Southern lady who nonetheless reflected the new thinking that reached even central North Carolina in the 1970s. Pulling together an alliance of white housewives and churchgoing blacks—two constituencies regularly ignored by the local establishment—she won a couple of terms on the city council, until the good ole boys regrouped to knock her off.

Stuart idolized men of courage, like the Antarctic explorer Sir Ernest Shackleton and James Stockdale, the naval aviator taken prisoner in North Vietnam. The brutal abuse Stockdale suffered made Stuart burn with anger. Like Stockdale, like his own father, Buck, a local dentist, Stuart wanted to be a pilot.

More personal examples of military heroism also inspired him, from a great-great-grandfather who served in the Confederate cavalry under J. E. B. Stuart to his dad, who had served as a corpsman to a Marine Reserve unit, and his uncle, Bob Biddle, a Marine officer and Vietnam veteran.

After Vietnam, Uncle Bob commanded a unit at the Marine Barracks in Washington. Known as Eighth and I, after its location on Capitol Hill, the installation was the Corps's ceremonial home, where the color guard, the President's Own Marine Band, and the Body Bearer Section were based. The 1970s marked a trough for the US military's reputation, and many kids would laugh at regimented performances like those at Eighth and I. But visiting his uncle, Stuart Couch was thrilled by the crisply uniformed men who executed precision maneuvers on the parade ground. Back home, Stuart already was on track to become an Eagle Scout. He resolved to be a Marine, too.

As a teenager, Stuart did odd jobs at an Asheboro hosiery factory but devoted enough time to plays and other activities to win his high school's nomination to the Governor's School of North Carolina, a summer honors program in Winston-Salem. Nominated on the performing arts track, Couch had to present a monologue for the admissions committee. He selected the opening speech from his favorite movie, *Patton.* The 1970 picture begins with the bemedaled protagonist declaiming his martial philosophy, an enormous American flag behind him.

"No bastard ever won a war by dying for his country," said seventeen-year-old Stuart, reciting lines made famous by George C. Scott. "He won it by making the other poor dumb bastard die for his country."

The teachers conducting the audition thanked Stuart for coming. Weeks later, he got a rejection letter. "Liberals," he figured. Instead, he signed up for an evangelical summer camp, away from home in the Colorado Rockies.

Years later, Couch would say he met two people during that summer: Jesus Christ. And Kimberly Wilder.

She was another teen from Asheboro, and Stuart Couch immediately developed a crush on her. After a hike to a Rocky mountaintop, she seemed to like him, too, he thought. Things between them fizzled out when they got home, but Stuart ended up spending time at the Wilders' house anyway. His own parents' marriage was breaking up and things were tense at home; Kim's father had been Stuart's scoutmaster, and the Wilders welcomed him, stepping up as almost a second family.

Stuart pursued Kim again after they both got to college—she was a nursing student at the University of North Carolina, just down the road from Duke, where Stuart, still fixed on becoming a Marine, had joined the Naval ROTC.

Couch was an "ROTC Nazi," as the nickname went, and his performance showed, winning him promotion to the program's top slot, battalion commander. It was at Duke that Couch first focused on Afghanistan, studying under the Afghanistan scholar Louis Dupree and, in his junior-year paper, comparing the Soviet invasion to America's experience in Vietnam. Still, Couch managed his share of Southern frat boy pleasures. Parties, Thursday night kegs, and Friday morning hangovers marked his time in Durham.

"Some people graduated *summa cum laude,* some people *magna cum laude,*" he joked, pronouncing it *law-dee.* "I graduated, *thank the good lawdy.*"[3]

Couch was a regular churchgoer, but that was social convention in towns like Asheboro, and he considered himself only nominally religious. Kim Wilder and her family, in contrast, put their evangelical faith first, and Couch, aiming to ingratiate himself with the pretty blonde, followed along. Over time, the strength and steadiness Kim drew from her faith took root in Couch, too.

Years later, he felt this change when Kim took him to the church her grandparents once attended, in Morehead City, near North Carolina's Outer Banks. The minister offered jokes and down-home wisdom, linking scripture to real life. "He had a Resurrection party on Easter Sunday, with two kegs up on his back porch," Couch said.[4] This was religion that spoke to him.

A DAY BEFORE THE DUKE graduation, in May 1987, Couch was commissioned a second lieutenant in the United States Marine Corps. He learned to pilot the KC-130, the Marine version of the Hercules cargo plane, from Cherry Point. Knowing Spanish, he hauled equipment for counternarcotics operations in Latin America. But he missed the career-making conflict of his generation, the first Persian Gulf War. When Saddam Hussein invaded Kuwait in 1991, Couch was in a five-week course training to be a squadron legal officer—a nonlawyer who advises the commander on basic legal questions. While more senior comrades were flying combat missions over Kuwait, Couch was stuck at Cherry Point, vying for flight time with other new pilots on the broken-down aircraft left behind. He was able to wrangle just one mission during Operation Desert Storm: a forty-eight-hour trip to retrieve materiel after Saddam abandoned Kuwait.

With the military drawdown that followed Desert Storm, flight hours were cut and Couch found himself spending more time at the base's legal center than in the cockpit. A colonel urged Couch to consider law school. There was a famous precedent for that path: in the 1950s, before getting his law degree, F. Lee Bailey had flown fighter planes out of Cherry Point.

Couch applied to five schools, including North Carolina's top programs, at Duke and Chapel Hill. All rejected him. The only place he got in was Regent University in Virginia, an evangelical law school Pat Robertson opened in 1986.

Just as Couch enrolled, conflict erupted over Robertson's dismissal of the founding dean. With Regent's accreditation uncertain, Couch tried to transfer to Campbell University, a small Baptist school in Buies Creek, North Carolina. Campbell had rejected Couch as a first-year applicant, but a personal appeal to the assistant dean won him a transfer admission. "You won't regret this decision," Couch promised.

Much as he wanted to become a lawyer, however, Couch hated law school. Without flight time, he took a pay cut to attend, and his studies siphoned attention from Kim, now his wife of nearly nine years and their two-year-old son, Stuart. But he persevered, was graduated in 1996, and returned to Cherry Point as a judge advocate—a JAG—the military term for its uniformed lawyers, assigned as a prosecutor.

It was a typical military caseload. Couch prosecuted Marines for brawling at bars, for falsifying travel claims, for rape. Then came Operation Longfuse, an investigation into a ring of Marines selling ordnance on the black market. Couch thought it significant that the scheme came to light when one of the conspirators confessed to his pastor, who told him that while he had God's forgiveness as a Christian, he also had a moral obligation to "make things right."[5]

Barely a year on the job, Couch received the biggest case on the Corps's docket.

In February 1998, a Marine pilot, about to end his assignment in Aviano, Italy, took his EA-6B Prowler out for some aeronautical antics over the Alps. Flying far below regulation altitudes as his navigator shot a souvenir video, the pilot clipped a ski gondola, sending it crashing to the ground and killing all twenty European tourists aboard.

Couch was the rare prosecutor with aviator's wings, and he

shared a home base, Cherry Point, with the Prowler. Newly promoted to major, he took the prosecution team's third chair.

Couch's job included serving as US government liaison to the victims' families. That made him a target for their hurt and anger. Yet instead of resenting their outbursts, Couch absorbed their sorrow and came to share it, even to view the survivors as an extended family of his own. Over the fourteen-month Aviano assignment, he spent so much time with the families that a superior complained about Couch's priorities.

But the case ended in acquittal. The chief investigator, Mark Fallon of the Naval Criminal Investigative Service, reached Aviano a day after the accident to find that key evidence—the navigator's videotape—had been destroyed. The Marine jury found the pilot, Captain Richard Ashby, not guilty. In the courtroom, Couch turned to the victims' families and mouthed the words: "I'm sorry."

Mark Fallon was no happier. He told himself it wasn't the prosecution team's fault. "It's difficult for Marines to convict Marines for killing foreigners," he said. Couch agreed. He called it "jury nullification." Three of the eight jurors were pilots themselves, and some of the junior officers obviously sympathized more with the air crew than the victims. Their loyalty to each other and to the organization overrode their duty to deliver a just verdict, Couch thought.

The prosecution tried to salvage a shred of victory by convicting Ashby and his navigator, Captain Joseph Schweitzer, of obstruction of justice. Schweitzer admitted tossing the tape into a bonfire, made a plea bargain, and was discharged from the Corps. Ashby pleaded not guilty.

Couch overprepared for trial. He retraced the defendants' backgrounds, even examining Schweitzer's course load at the Naval Academy. In a philosophy class, Couch found a passage from the stoic philosopher Epictetus that evoked the air crew's unethical choice.

"When you do anything from a clear judgment that it ought to be done, never shun the being seen to do it, even though the world should make a wrong supposition about it; for, if you don't act right, shun the action itself; but, if you do, why are you afraid of those who censure you wrongly?"[6]

Or, as Couch put it in his native "North Carolinese": "Don't be 'fraid to be seen doin' whatcher doin', 'cause if you're doin' whatcher s'possed to be doin', ya shouldn't have a problem with it." He planned to introduce the quotation to shame Schweitzer at trial but ultimately decided it was too esoteric. Nonetheless, the maxim stuck with Couch; years later, at the Office of Military Commissions, he taped it above his desk.

At his second trial, Ashby was convicted. The charges carried a maximum sentence of ten years. Couch asked only for two. He knew a Marine jury wouldn't consider anything harsher for one of its own.

"Captain Ashby needs to feel the sting for what he has done," Couch implored the court-martial.[7] "He doesn't deserve to wear a uniform." The jury returned with six months' confinement and dismissal from the Marine Corps. Couch was disgusted.

Most on the prosecution team swallowed their disappointment and moved on. Couch never quite could. He remained in touch with the victims' families, and in 2008 traveled at his own expense to Aviano for a commemoration on the accident's tenth anniversary.

DEMORALIZED BY THE AVIANO case, Couch wanted out of the military justice system. He left active duty for a local law firm, handling personal injury, medical malpractice, and similar civil cases.

Yet the tedious cycles of civil litigation only deepened his malaise. Criminal justice promised a greater redemptive potential. After fourteen months in private practice, Couch found a job as an assistant district attorney in Beaufort, across the Newport River from Morehead City. It was not a high crime district. He prosecuted drunken beachgoers, barroom brawlers, and, on occasion, a shrimp boat captain who clocked a fisheries inspector.

■

Things seemed to be looking up for America as 2001 began, Couch thought. George W. Bush would become president.

In his inaugural address, Bush acknowledged that Bill Clinton left him a nation at peace, a federal budget in surplus. It was, Bush said, "a time of blessing." He promised not to squander this inheritance but to confront the nation's "problems instead of passing them on to future generations." Without specifying his plans, he made a pledge: "I will bring the values of our history to the care of our times."

Couch recognized the religious imagery that salted Bush's speech, phrases evoking the faith he and the new president shared.

"The American story," Bush said, was "a story of flawed and fallible people, united across the generations by grand and enduring ideals.

"We are not this story's author, who fills time and eternity with His purpose," the president continued. "Never tiring, never yielding, never finishing, we renew that purpose today, to make our country more just and generous, to affirm the dignity of our lives and every life."

The dignity of every life. Couch choked up. That was a concept he affirmed each Sunday in church.

The next evening, however, Mike Wallace brought Couch back to earth.

"It's been a bad week for the United States Marine Corps," the CBS newsman said, opening a *60 Minutes* report on an accident-prone aircraft called the MV-22 Osprey.[8]

The brass loved the peculiar-looking, tilt-rotor plane, as did the congressman whose district produced it. Marines who flew the Osprey were less enthusiastic. The plane was chronically unreliable. In 2000, twenty-three Marines were killed in Osprey crashes. Couch knew one of the pilots who died.

One squadron found a way to meet the Corps's unrealistic expectations for the plane: falsify safety records. But an outraged mechanic taped a commander telling Marines to lie about the plane's readiness and sent the recording to *60 Minutes,* forcing officials to open an investigation.[9] Months later, the Corps geared up proceedings against the commander and several other officers.[10]

Again, the Marines had a serious case involving military aviation. Couch, who remained in the reserves, was asked to return to active duty for the prosecution.

He missed the Marines and was eager to accept. But Couch was a deliberative man. For advice, he called a judge advocate he admired, a colonel named Kevin Winters.

At Duke, an ROTC instructor had told Couch about Winters, who had been a tank commander before becoming a lawyer. When Couch attended the Basic School for new officers in 1988, Winters taught the course on military law. His confidence, accessibility, and sense of humor set him apart from the standoffish officers Couch often encountered.

Now, in the summer of 2001, he turned again to Winters. Apologizing for the out-of-the-blue phone call, Couch enthused over the idea of returning to uniform. He expected immediate affirmation from an officer who had devoted his own career to the Marines.

Winters didn't supply it. "Why in the world would you want to come back in?" he asked.

Couch paused. "You ever seen *The Shawshank Redemption?*" he said.

Winters had. Some considered the 1994 prison movie, based on a Stephen King story, a Christian parable.

"Remember the scene where they let Brooks out and he just can't handle it?" Couch continued. Brooks is an elderly trusty played by James Whitmore. Released after decades behind bars, he soon commits suicide. Red, a lifer played by Morgan Freeman, explains that Brooks was an "institutional man." He couldn't function on the outside.

"I feel like an institutional man," Couch said. The Marine Corps was a vast organization. But within it, Couch's place was clear.

"That makes a lot of sense," Winters said.

IN AUGUST 2001, THE MARINES activated Stu Couch for a temporary assignment on the Osprey prosecution. Careers were at stake. So was a forty-billion-dollar weapons program. Even as Couch readied the prosecution case, there was pressure from above to make the scandal go away.

Behind closed doors, a Marine general convened a pretrial hearing on September 7, 2001. The results were announced a week later. Five officers were cleared outright. One was found in dereliction of duty but received no punishment. The squadron commander got a reprimand and was allowed to retire.

There would be no court-martial. Stu Couch had suited up for nothing.

Between the hearing and its outcome, however, something significant had occurred.

■

On Monday, September 10, 2001, a junior prosecutor in Couch's office handed in a routine motion for a pending court-martial. Reading it, Couch grimaced. It was a terrible piece of work. It also was due that day at 5:00 p.m.

Couch got a one-day extension. He realized he would have to rewrite the motion himself.

Like a college student with an unwelcome assignment, Couch procrastinated into the evening, finally starting at 9:00 p.m. The delay meant he would have to pull an all-nighter. He fell asleep shortly before dawn. After a couple of hours' rest, he forced himself awake to finish the job.

At 9:30 a.m., Couch logged on to his computer. Under the tabs for auctions, shopping, and games, his Yahoo home page screamed about the World Trade Center. Hijacked airliners had crashed into the Twin Towers.

Couch flashed on his college roommate. An ROTC comrade and onetime Marine officer who left the Corps for a banking career, Chris Lozada worked in the World Trade Center. In the Marines, Lozada's morbid nickname was Death—a backwards construction from another nickname, Lozadeath. Where was Death?

Couch ran to the television. He watched the South Tower collapse at 9:59 a.m., the North Tower twenty-nine minutes later.

"Oh my God," he thought. "I'm sitting here watching Chris Lozada die."

The legal motion was due. Couch pushed aside his numbness and readied for work, shaving and donning his uniform, driving to the base where, with security suddenly tightened, he sat in an hour-long traffic jam before clearing the gate. All the while, he wrestled with the thought of his dead roommate.

Couch filed the motion and busied himself with office chores. Finally, he could suppress it no longer. He dialed Lozada's house in New Jersey.

A woman answered. Presumably Lozada's wife, whom Couch never had met.

"You probably don't know who I am, but I'm Chris's roommate from college," Couch said. "Uh, is Chris there?"

He closed his eyes and tensed.

"Sure, you wanna talk to him?"

Moments later, Lozada picked up the phone.

"Death! Death! Damn I'm glad to hear you're not dead," Couch said.

"Yeah, you wouldn't believe it," Lozada said. He had spent the morning surfing, before taking the ferry to Manhattan just before 9:00 a.m. He was walking down Wall Street to his office when the first plane, American Airlines Flight 11, passed overhead and struck the North Tower.

"Wow," Lozada thought. He continued toward work.

When the second plane, United 175, hit the South Tower, Lozada realized that this was an attack. He turned around, ran to the dock, and leapt aboard a ferry back to New Jersey.

THOUSANDS OF PEOPLE HAD been killed in the 9/11 attacks, but after talking to Lozada and checking the casualty lists from the Pentagon, Couch figured that people he knew personally had escaped the terrorists. He was wrong.

United 175's copilot was Mike Horrocks, Couch's buddy from Cherry Point. They had flown together, and lived nearby in Morehead City. Kim and Mike's wife had worked at the same hospital.

Couch's squadron nickname was Tater—derived from potato, as in couch potato. Horrocks had the tougher-sounding handle: Rocks. He was thirty-eight, with a nine-year-old daughter and a son, six. Before joining the Marines, Rocks had been a star quarterback at West Chester University, near Philadelphia. He was a popular and steady figure in the tight-knit world of KC-130 aviators.

Couch found out about Rocks in a phone call from a fellow pilot two days after 9/11. Then, on September 18, turning a page in *USA Today,* Couch froze on a photo. It was a familiar tableau, a military funeral. Receiving the folded flag was Horrocks's widow, her little son and daughter at her side.

He filed papers for a permanent return to active duty. Posted as chief prosecutor for Camp Lejeune, Couch watched as the military readied for war, looking for the mission that suited his skills. He found it on November 13, 2001.

On that day, President Bush issued a military order authorizing military commissions to try 9/11's perpetrators. In the world of military justice, nothing like this had been seen since World War II, the last time America had been so attacked.

Military Order

TWO OR THREE DAYS AFTER 9/11, Bill Barr, former attorney general of the United States and a prominent member of the conservative legal movement, placed a call to his former deputy, Timothy Flanigan, a senior lawyer in President Bush's White House.

Barr, now general counsel for Verizon Communications, was calling to remind Flanigan about the brass plaque outside Room 5235 at Main Justice, the department's headquarters in Washington.

It commemorated a trial that took place there in July 1942. Eight Nazi saboteurs, arrested after landing on American soil, had been convicted in a secret proceeding before a military commission appointed by President Franklin D. Roosevelt. The plaque summarized proceedings notable for their speed and severity:

> THE MILITARY COMMISSION APPOINTED BY
> PRESIDENT ROOSEVELT CONVENED ON JULY 8, 1942,
> AND ADJOURNED AUGUST 3, 1942.
> 6 EXECUTED ON AUGUST 8, 1942.
> 1 SENTENCED TO LIFE IMPRISONMENT.
> 1 SENTENCED TO 30 YEARS IMPRISONMENT.

That episode, unprecedented in American history, had intrigued Barr when he was working on a response to the 1988 bombing of Pan

Am Flight 103 over Lockerbie, Scotland. Like the Nazi saboteurs, the
suspects were agents of a foreign government: Libyan intelligence operatives, now back home and under Moammar Gadhafi's protection.
With the administration considering a covert operation to seize the
bombers, Barr concluded that a 1942-style trial would be the best way
to prosecute them.

Federal courts followed constitutional procedures intended to
protect the individual from being overwhelmed by the government's
vast resources through rules that bar prosecutors from using evidence
obtained illegally.

Barr believed that military commissions were a type of military
operation. They existed not to limit the government's advantage but
to maximize it. Erroneous convictions and constitutional violations,
anathema to civilian courts, were more tolerable in military commissions designed more for efficiency than for accuracy.

As warfare evolved, Barr imagined expanding the definition of
war beyond the conventional battlefield—and with it, the reach of
war's laws. By classifying the Pan Am bombing as an act of war rather
than a crime, the United States could treat the suspects as military
targets and seize them outside normal extradition procedures. A military commission could quickly prosecute and execute the defendants
without following elaborate rules of criminal procedure. The symbol-
ism would matter as much as the substance: resurrecting the military
commission, a nearly forgotten relic of war's rough justice, would
convey that the modern terrorist was no freedom fighter but, like the
pirate in ages past, *hostis humani generis*—an enemy of all mankind.

Barr then was head of the Office of Legal Counsel, the Justice
Department unit that advises the executive branch on the extent of its
own powers. Federal agencies considered OLC opinions conclusive
statements of law, unless the courts held otherwise. Since only a tiny
percentage of legal questions results in litigation, OLC effectively
functioned as an internal Supreme Court for the executive branch—a
secret Supreme Court, in most instances, as it never held open meet-

ings and only rarely released opinions to the public. Had the proposal progressed, Barr's conclusions would effectively have become law.

The Lockerbie capture operation never took place, however, and anyway Scotland rejected the military commission approach. Instead, in 1999, Libya, pressed by diplomatic and economic sanctions, surrendered the suspects for a special trial conducted by Scottish judges at a former US military base in the Netherlands.

Barr, however, never abandoned the idea of reviving the military commission. After 9/11, its time had arrived.

"You know," said Tim Flanigan, "that's real interesting." Even before Barr's call, David Addington, counsel to Vice President Dick Cheney, had decided that prisoners soon to be captured would be tried, convicted, and executed by military commission.

The White House already had declared the 9/11 attacks an act of war. The distinction sounded metaphorical, but lawyers like Barr, Flanigan, and Addington vested it with specific legal consequences. War, they believed, triggered extraordinary powers embedded within the presidency. The Constitution's list of presidential duties includes "Commander in Chief of the Army and the Navy," which had been interpreted as giving him operational command of the battlefield. Now the battlefield was everywhere.

IT WAS NO ACCIDENT THAT Barr called Flanigan, the deputy counsel, rather than the chief White House lawyer, Alberto Gonzales, who had followed President Bush from Texas. Like his patron, Gonzales brought little interest or experience in foreign affairs or national security, and certainly not in "separation of powers"—the constitutional abstraction that allots government functions among the legislative, executive, and judicial branches.

But the separation of powers long had animated the lawyers who filled the next several echelons in the new administration. They were not Texans hitched to George W. Bush but a fraternity of movement conservatives whose Washington roots reached back decades, to the ascent of Ronald Reagan, bolstered by a younger generation, mostly in their thirties, whom they had trained. Under Bush, the White House counsel's office would become "a Republican Camelot of sorts, a chance for a new generation of conservative intellectuals to put their theories into practice," *Washington Post* columnist Dana Milbank predicted in January 2001.[1] Gonzales would not lead his staff but follow it.

The administration's legal vision came instead from David Addington, a secretive, dour man who had been Cheney's legal muse for almost two decades. After beginning his career at the Central Intelligence Agency in the early 1980s, Addington moved on to work for Cheney, then a Wyoming congressman on the House intelligence committee, and later served as the Pentagon's general counsel after Cheney became defense secretary under President George H. W. Bush.[2] Their goal, said a Democratic congresswoman who worked with both, was "restoring the Nixon presidency"—the vision of an unrestrained executive that had collapsed under Watergate.

For these conservative lawyers, the executive stood as the nation's mighty trunk, with the legislature and judiciary small offshoots. The Constitution assigned the president "the executive power"—or, as another Reagan Justice Department veteran, Samuel Alito, stressed in a speech six years before President George W. Bush elevated him to the Supreme Court, "*the* executive power"—of the United States.[3]

These like-minded lawyers found little support in the spare words of the Constitution but saw emanations from the framers' text, forming legal penumbras that gave life and substance to the executive's military power. They seized on passages in the Federalist Papers that seemingly anticipated their views. "A feeble executive implies a feeble execution of the government," Alexander Hamilton wrote in Federalist No. 70. Hamilton craved "energy in the executive," something "essential to the protection of the community against foreign attacks." A "unitary" executive, replacing government by committee under the failed Articles of Confederation, would exhibit "decision, activity, secrecy, and dispatch," he predicted.[4] From these arguments modern conservative thinkers, in law schools, policy shops, and, during their long control of the presidency, the Justice Department and its Office of Legal Counsel, assembled their constitutional doctrine. It centered on a theory of presidential primacy they called the "unitary executive." This, Alito approvingly said, was "the gospel according to OLC." It held that national power resided indivisibly in the person of the president. The subdivisions of the executive branch, including cabinet departments, specialized agencies, and military services, were no more than extensions of the president himself.

People like Stuart Couch, the military and civilian professionals of the federal bureaucracy, preferred to see themselves as standing somehow apart from the president, part of an apolitical, nonpartisan institution that served the public regardless of any particular elected leader and his appointees. In the Bush administration's view, this fundamentally misstated the structure of government. It was the *president* who served the public, and the federal workforce was his instrument to do so. In a favorite phrase within the administration, officers of the United States served at "the pleasure of the president."

In the weeks after 9/11, Washington, now divided with bollards and checkpoints, felt at war. People stood more erect, more purposeful, more watchful. To the movement lawyers, the shock of the attacks had punctuated the legal stasis, like a crack in the continental shelf, opening the way to reshape the constitutional landscape to their liking.

With the nation angry and, at the same time, fearful of another attack, federal agents conducted sweeps for aliens from Arab and Muslim countries, convened secret hearings in the immigration courts, and locked up or deported foreigners for visa infractions. Treasury Department investigators put aside privacy standards to pore over bank records, searching for the financial stream that fed the terrorist network. As the Pentagon planned its assault on Afghanistan, the movement lawyers cleared away whatever reservations might linger over executive authority.

The hothouse of that effort was the OLC office of Deputy Assistant Attorney General John Yoo, a thirty-four-year-old law professor on leave from the University of California, Berkeley. He long had pondered the war power.

JOHN CHOON YOO CAME TO America as an infant in 1967, when his parents, both psychiatrists, emigrated from South Korea to Philadelphia.[5] In prep school, he read Caesar's *Conquest of Gaul* and Thucydides' *Peloponnesian War* in the original Latin and Greek. Next came Harvard College, where he would be graduated summa cum laude. But Yoo already was the kind of Harvard student who preferred to pass out grades of his own.

Musing in the *Harvard Crimson* before his 1989 graduation, Yoo complained that "the student body, like the vast majority of Americans, is essentially anti-intellectual."[6] Harvard students preferred to spend time "playing a sport, partying oneself into senselessness, or watching TV and gossiping the night away" instead of studying hard and being "a geek," he wrote. The university was partly to blame, for it no longer bothered "to tell undergraduates what they need to learn, believing they will somehow find the correct education on their own." He urged them not to contribute to the class gift.[7]

Sometimes, it was hard to tell Yoo's true beliefs from a pose. He was "kind of straight, yet, on the other hand, wholly irreverent, always laughing at different things that struck him as absurd," his freshman proctor, Louis Caldera, remembered. Yoo certainly partied, "he just wasn't stupid about it." Yoo admitted as much. "Other conservatives think college is too much drinking, too much smoking," he said.[8] "That certainly wasn't me at all."

Yoo already considered himself a conservative, something he would attribute to his family's immigrant values. Besides, tacking right in Harvard's sea of liberal orthodoxy was fun. The *Crimson*'s editorial board adopted a position urging the world's richest university to raise its cafeteria workers' pay, then barely at minimum wage. Yoo, just elected to the board, objected. "I got up and said, 'I don't see the reason for paying more than the market rate,'" he recalled.

His undergraduate thesis, "Three Faces of Hegemony: Eisen-hower, Kennedy and Johnson and the Multilateral Force," focused on the executive's use of power. Yoo took Kissingeresque stances in his *Crimson* columns, too, urging Harvard to seek research grants from the CIA, cheering the *contras* fighting Nicaragua's Sandinista govern-ment, and backing Iraqi dictator Saddam Hussein in his war against Iran.[9]

Yet there were hints that Yoo could have thrived even if the political climate had shifted to the left. Reagan, he felt, let him down. After the Iran-contra scandal and other revelations, a Yoo column took aim at "the most scandal-ridden administration in history, pre-sided over by a man who neither knows nor cares what his subordi-nates do in his name."[10] During the 1988 presidential primaries, Yoo endorsed Democrat Michael Dukakis, the Massachusetts governor whose "personal qualities of honesty, candor and integrity" seemed "attractive and refreshing" in light of the corruption that marred Reagan's second term.

Yoo's effort to find the right place politically and professionally led him toward journalism and a summer internship at the *Wall Street Journal*. But he decided that a newsroom career wasn't for him. "There was something about journalism that was very ephemeral. You write the story and then it's gone and nobody remembers it," he said.[11]

THE PRIVILEGE AND STABILITY of academe appealed to Yoo. But in his undergraduate field, history, jobs were few and competi-tion was tough. Legal academia was an easier nut to crack.

At Yale Law School, famous for producing law professors, he decided to specialize in war powers, a field largely dormant since the Vietnam era. Yoo was fascinated by the wielding of force—not in practice, as he had no interest in military service, but rather as an abstract, academic pursuit. Besides, with little competition in the field, it offered a way to stand out.

Then it was off to Washington for a judicial clerkship with Judge

Laurence Silberman, a revered figure within the conservative legal movement and a mentor to its brightest prospects, many of whom would take senior positions in the George W. Bush administration.

"I learned more in that one year than in three years of law school," Yoo said. Silberman, too, was fascinated by presidential power, and in 1988 had written a signal opinion spelling out the unitary executive theory, over the dissent of Ruth Bader Ginsburg, then a fellow judge on the United States Court of Appeals for the District of Columbia Circuit.[12] It was reversed by the Supreme Court, seven to one.

"This was an issue Silberman stood for," Yoo said. "He was the champion of the unitary executive."[13] In 2000, Silberman would officiate at Yoo's wedding to Elsa Arnett, his college girlfriend and daughter of war correspondent Peter Arnett, one of few Western journalists to interview Osama bin Laden.

Following his year with Silberman, a Supreme Court clerkship was the natural next step for Yoo. Stunningly, all three justices who interviewed Yoo—Anthony Kennedy, David Souter, and Clarence Thomas —turned him down. Disappointed, Yoo hit the academic market, finding a job at Boalt Hall, the law school at the University of California, Berkeley. Things got back on track the following year, when Justice Thomas decided to offer him a clerkship after all.

Clarence Thomas prided himself on applying the Constitution's text according to his view of its eighteenth-century meaning. He found that Yoo often did him one better. "We'd kid him sometimes that he was right there at the founding," Thomas said.[14] But Yoo's term, 1993–1994, brought no foreign affairs or executive power disputes, and he yawned at the Court's garden-variety work in criminal procedure cases. "Not my thing," Yoo said.

The next year Yoo worked for Senator Orrin Hatch, the Republican chairman of the Senate Judiciary Committee, then returned to Berkeley. Back in academia, he limited his political activity largely to writing occasional op-ed articles. One of those op-eds would shape the future.

ELECTION DAY 2000 BROUGHT the closest vote in American history. While Al Gore won the popular vote nationwide, in Florida, which held the deciding say in the Electoral College, initial results put George W. Bush a fraction of a percent ahead amid thousands of disputed ballots. Canvassing boards began reviewing ballots, and the Florida Supreme Court ordered a recount in disputed counties. That boded ill for Republicans, because the counties at issue were heavily Democratic. Under Florida law, voter intent took priority over technical compliance with ballot regulations, so if ballots that were overlooked the first time broke the same way as others in the jurisdiction, Gore seemed likely to win.[15] The only way to guarantee Bush's victory was to stop the votes from being counted.

In a November 16 *Wall Street Journal* piece, Yoo showed Republicans how to do just that. He argued that, by ordering a recount only in contested counties rather than statewide, the Florida court violated the Fourteenth Amendment's Equal Protection Clause.[16] It was a remarkable theory, because Republicans traditionally attacked equal protection claims for violating states' rights. But Yoo urged Republicans to invoke liberal milestones, like the US Supreme Court's 1964 "one person–one vote" decision and the 1965 Voting Rights Act, in suing to stop the recount. In short order, that would bring Bush's claim to the Supreme Court—where seven of nine justices were Republican appointees.[17]

The article catapulted Yoo into the Republican war room. Soon he was in Tallahassee meeting with the nominee's brother, Governor Jeb Bush, testifying before the state legislature and appearing on national news programs. The Supreme Court heard Bush's case on December 11, and its five most conservative members adopted Yoo's argument. The five-to-four ruling halted the recount, freezing the tally with George Bush ahead by 537 votes.

As the abbreviated transition to the Bush administration began, John Yoo was invited back to Washington. Alberto Gonzales, at this stage preparing to become White House counsel, wanted to discuss possible opportunities in government. David Addington, Dick Cheney's counsel, sat in. "He didn't say much," Yoo recalled.

But Yoo wasn't interested in the job offered—vetting judicial nominations, then the highest priority for an administration determined to neutralize eight years of Clinton appointments to the bench. The jobs that Yoo wanted, like counsel at the National Security Council, went to others with more connections or seniority. Finally, he got an acceptable offer—a deputy's slot at OLC, with a portfolio including executive privilege and foreign affairs.

Yoo was working at OLC on the morning of September 11, 2001, when his secretary rushed in to report that a plane had struck the World Trade Center. "It's a terrorist attack," Yoo assumed. He switched on the television, in time to watch Flight 175 crash into the South Tower. "It's certainly a terrorist attack," he concluded.

With the nation fearing another blow at any minute, things moved quickly. Yoo shuttled between the command center atop Main Justice and FBI headquarters across Pennsylvania Avenue. "I was not stunned, or at a loss," he said. Instead, "I started thinking about what we should do."

The Pentagon's general counsel, William J. Haynes II—he went by Jim—was a contracts attorney with no experience in laws of war. Yoo, however, was perfectly situated. Almost immediately, he became the fulcrum for the legal implications of 9/11, including the creation of military commissions.

IN 1996, WHILE STUART COUCH was studying law in Buies Creek, John Yoo published a comprehensive theory of his constitutional passion, the war power.[18]

Most scholars believed that the Constitution assigned Congress authority over military policy, including the decision to wage war.[19] The president executed those decisions, much as he did domestic laws. There was a textual rationale for congressional primacy. The Constitution declared the president "Commander in Chief of the Army and Navy of the United States" but said nothing further about the subject. Congress, meanwhile, held a panoply of war powers, from broad authority "to declare War" and "provide for the common

Defence" to writing "Rules for the Government and Regulation of the land and naval Forces." The American Revolution, after all, was sparked by outrage at the British king, a "tyrant," the Declaration of Independence said, who "has affected to render the Military independent of and superior to the Civil power." The Framers hardly seemed inclined to vest their new nation's president the same authority that had soured them on George III.

Wrong, said John Yoo. His 125-page article in the *California Law Review,* "The Continuation of Politics by Other Means: The Original Understanding of War Powers," argued that mainstream scholars misunderstood the Constitution's fundamental character. Rather than discarding the structure of the British monarchy, the Constitution largely *continued* it, Yoo insisted, by transferring the crown's powers to the president and Parliament's duties to Congress. Sure, the Framers "intended to alter certain aspects of traditional Anglo-American forms of government," Yoo wrote, but "we should resist the temptation to see innovation and novelty in every constitutional clause." British subjects looked up to the king as their protector. Likewise, Yoo wrote, "many Americans in a society still infused by hierarchical patterns of social, political, and economic relations would have viewed the President as, if not a King, at least a paternal figure vested with the duty of protecting his fellow citizens."

In the 1990s, Yoo had been an eccentric figure at the periphery of legal thought. Now, his views became binding authority within the United States government. Under John Yoo's Constitution, George W. Bush embodied a power tracing to the misty day in Albion when young Arthur drew Excalibur from the stone.

The White House asked Yoo if it should seek a declaration of war. Unnecessary, he explained. Nevertheless, the senators and representatives needed to show constituents how tough they were after 9/11, so Flanigan and Yoo drafted a resolution for them. It passed, on September 18, 2001. "They would have passed anything," Yoo said.[20]

Only one lawmaker voted no: Congresswoman Barbara Lee of Berkeley, California, Yoo's hometown representative.

AT FIRST GLANCE, THE 314-word joint resolution, titled "Authorization for Use of Military Force," seemed to acknowledge a congressional role in war-making.[21] In its sole operative paragraph, the 9/11 Resolution stated that "the President is authorized to use all necessary and appropriate force against those nations, organizations, or persons he determines planned, authorized, committed, or aided the terrorist attacks that occurred on September 11, 2001, or harbored such organizations or persons, in order to prevent any future acts of international terrorism against the United States by such nations, organizations or persons."

Neither *necessary* nor *appropriate* was defined, and the sweep of permissible targets essentially was unbounded; the plural "nations" that "harbored" those the president linked to the attacks presumably included more than Afghanistan, while "persons" subject to the president's force could be anywhere, in an allied country such as Britain or Canada—or, like the 9/11 hijackers, within the United States. "Even the Tonkin Gulf Resolution says it's limited to Southeast Asia," Yoo said, pleased that he had provided Bush more authority than even Lyndon Johnson obtained through the 1964 measure he took as carte blanche for the Vietnam War.[22]

Perhaps most significant was a preambular phrase that so seemingly stated the obvious, the eye rolled right past it: "Whereas, the President has authority under the Constitution to take action to deter and prevent acts of international terrorism against the United States." Appearing after a *Whereas* and before the *Resolved,* the sentence located Bush's source of power not in anything Congress did but rather as inherent to his office.[23]

As Yoo conceived it, no limits applied to the "action" the president could take. He could have prisoners summarily executed. Or first he could have them convicted by military commissions.

■

After the 9/11 Resolution passed, Yoo filed a secret opinion reiterating that the entire exercise was superfluous: no act of Congress "can place any limits on the President's determinations as to any terrorist threat, the amount of military force to be used in response, or the method, timing, and nature of the response," Yoo wrote. "These decisions, under our Constitution, are for the President alone to make."[24]

Yoo next turned to other concerns, writing a series of memos to justify what he called the "new paradigm" of executive primacy, from warrantless electronic surveillance at home to nullifying the Geneva Conventions abroad.[25] He ruled that the president could use the military instead of law enforcement to go after suspected terrorists within the United States and that he could disregard the Fourth Amendment, which bars "unreasonable searches and seizures," when doing so.[26]

Immersed in so many matters, Yoo had an OLC deputy, Patrick Philbin, handle a simple opinion explaining that the "force" at the president's command included military commissions. Philbin, like Yoo a former law clerk to Judge Silberman and Justice Thomas, was unfamiliar with the topic. He typed "military commissions" into a legal database. Up popped *Ex parte Quirin*, the Nazi saboteur case.

EX PARTE QUIRIN WAS one of several Supreme Court rulings that affirmed vast executive powers during World War II, along with *Korematsu v. United States*, the case approving the internment of Japanese Americans. The Supreme Court had little occasion to revisit such exotic questions after World War II, so *Korematsu, Quirin*, and their sister cases technically remained valid precedents.

Where *Korematsu* was reviled because of its blatant ethnic prejudice, *Quirin* was notorious because it represented political manipulation of judicial process.

According to the plaque at Main Justice, "the submarine-borne Nazi agents who were landed on Long Island and Florida shores were apprehended by special agents of the Federal Bureau of Investigation within 14 days of their arrival." It omitted the fact that the FBI learned of the plot only because one of the saboteurs, George Dasch, turned himself in, traveling to Washington to offer J. Edgar Hoover his services as a double agent. The FBI met Dasch at the Mayflower Hotel, took down his story, and rounded up the other saboteurs.

Initial plans called for prosecuting the suspects in federal court, as had been done with an earlier group of German agents arrested in the United States.[27] But the government, having trumpeted the arrests as a triumph of FBI counterespionage skills, was determined to conceal the true circumstances of the saboteur ring's capture. Dasch was promised lenient treatment if he kept quiet.

The deal fell apart, however, and when Dasch made clear his plan to tell his story in open court, Roosevelt ordered the closed-door military commission. The president personally approved the seven generals who would sit on the commission, two colonels to defend the saboteurs, and the chief prosecutors, who conspicuously outranked the defense lawyers: Attorney General Francis Biddle and the Army judge advocate general, Major General Myron Cramer. In a note to Biddle, FDR indicated that the death penalty was "almost obligatory."[28]

Although Roosevelt's orders foreclosed appeal to the civilian courts, a defense attorney personally visited several Supreme Court justices to urge them to review the commission's legality. The Court agreed, although some justices had obvious conflicts of interest. Felix Frankfurter, for instance, already privately had suggested a military commission to the secretary of war, Henry Stimson.[29]

One day after the arguments, the Court issued a terse order approving the secret trial. Barely a week later, six of the eight defendants went to the electric chair. The Court took two months to issue an opinion explaining its rationale.

"The law of war draws a distinction . . . between those who are lawful and unlawful combatants," that opinion, by Chief Justice Harlan Fiske Stone, said. Both were "subject to capture and detention," but unlawful combatants also could face "trial and punishment by military tribunals for acts which render their belligerency unlawful."

John Yoo saw *Quirin* as a landmark statement of American constitutional values, validating a principle of national character the way most Americans looked to *Brown v. Board of Education* or the

Pentagon Papers case. After 9/11, he envisioned *Quirin* as a constitutional time machine that could teleport presidential powers dormant since the 1940s into the hands of George W. Bush.

Yet even the *Quirin* court left unresolved FDR's most extraordinary claim: that he held inherent power to convene military commissions. Stone's opinion said that since contemporary law included a passing reference to military commissions, it was "unnecessary" to determine whether "the president as commander in chief has constitutional power to create military commissions without the support of congressional legislation."

OLC had no such hesitation. In a November 6, 2001, memorandum citing John Yoo's 1996 *California Law Review* article as authority, it declared that Bush held "inherent powers as Commander in Chief" to use military commissions "to try and punish (even with death) offenders under the laws of war." And even though congressional authorization was unnecessary, Bush had it nonetheless, OLC said, thanks to the 9/11 Resolution Yoo and Flanigan had written. The resolution contained no reference to military commissions, and the topic never had been mentioned during any congressional proceedings, but OLC decided that the measure provided authority "for their use to the full extent permitted by past executive practice."[30]

The Bush administration treated the opinion as a state secret. It was transmitted to the Pentagon's general counsel, Jim Haynes, who kept it in his safe.

HAYNES GREW UP IN North Carolina, where he attended Davidson College through ROTC and then Harvard Law School. Haynes had an Army service commitment lasting through 1988, most of which he served at the Pentagon. He was about to leave active duty for a law firm job in Atlanta when superiors asked him to stay an extra two weeks as a staff aide for the transition from the Reagan to the George H. W. Bush administration.

The assignment lasted months, however, as the new president's nominee for secretary of defense, former Senator John Tower of

Texas, was rejected by the Senate amid allegations of drinking and womanizing. Over the extended stint, Haynes got to know another member of the transition team, David Addington, an adviser to the Wyoming congressman who soon would become defense secretary, Dick Cheney.

Haynes finally moved to Atlanta after the transition, but he had left an impression on the Cheney team. Several months later, he was offered a remarkably senior position: general counsel of the Army. Haynes, then thirty-one years old, had left active duty as a captain. He quickly accepted the invitation to return as a Senate-confirmed presidential appointee with the civilian rank equivalent of a four-star general. Back at the Pentagon, he reported to Addington, who soon became the younger man's mentor. At Haynes's wedding, Addington was best man.[31]

The Defense Department's legal apparatus is divided, and not quite comfortably, between the professional military, which operates the criminal justice system governing uniformed personnel, and civilian appointees, who advise the political leadership on policy decisions. The Defense Department, and separately, each of its three component military departments—the Army, the Navy (which includes the Marine Corps), and the Air Force—has its own presidentially appointed general counsel. But each military service also has its own chief uniformed lawyer, a general or admiral known as the judge advocate general who oversees his respective legal branch, or JAG corps.[32]

Operating in an insular legal world largely apart from the civilian justice system, JAGs like Stu Couch were proud, if not defensive, of their institutions. Many had been educated on the government's dime, often near military bases at lesser-known schools. In the status-conscious legal profession, JAGs knew they didn't rate very high. They were ready to rebut perceived slights by reeling off the improvements in courts-martial under the Uniform Code of Military Justice, which since World War II had transformed a blunt instrument of military punishment into a more sophisticated forum consistent with the Bill of Rights. By law, the judge advocates general were required to provide their independent judgment to Congress, even if it differed from the administration's official positions. If the UCMJ was the scripture of military justice, the JAGs were its priests and protectors.

Dick Cheney had no use for such independence, however, and as defense secretary sought to bring the JAGs to heel by placing them under the control of then–Army General Counsel Jim Haynes and his counterparts at the Navy and Air Force. Worried military lawyers called in favors on Capitol Hill to block the plan, and David Addington's own nomination as Pentagon general counsel stalled until Cheney backed down.[33] Bad blood remained when Cheney, Addington, and Haynes returned to government under George W. Bush, more powerful and ambitious than ever.

Haynes acted like a corporate counsel coming in after a hostile takeover. That meant imposing an iron grip over the JAGs. He made clear that he alone would speak for the department on any legal matter—not only to the public or press, but even within the administration. JAGs were not to consult with other agencies without authorization, and other agencies seeking their views should be directed to the general counsel's office. Even within Haynes's office, staff was kept guessing about what was really going on.

"It was not unusual for me to get a request from Jim Haynes," the deputy general counsel for intelligence, Richard Shiffrin, later said.[34] "And I'd find out just accidentally, two weeks later, that someone else was doing the same thing."

Many assumed that Haynes had been installed to do Addington's bidding, and the general counsel's office almost always took the same hard line that Addington did. In meetings and conversations, however, Haynes rarely indicated precisely where he personally stood on the legal issues consuming the Bush administration. He would listen rather than argue, ask questions instead of proferring answers. Sympathetic colleagues considered it a reflection of an open mind. Less charitable observers figured that Haynes was trying to avoid leaving fingerprints on questionable policies or, worse, that he simply didn't know enough to have an opinion.

"As many of his friends joke, he keeps things not only close to the vest but sewn inside the vest," said one colleague. "That's just Jim."

WHILE OLC HAD BEEN preparing its memo on military commissions, various entities within the Bush administration had been working on legal implications of 9/11. One was a small military group, a "tiger team" in Army parlance, assembled by the judge advocate general of the Army, Major General Thomas Romig, and his criminal law chief, Colonel Lawrence Morris. The two were excited by the prospect of reviving commissions, imagining they would provide military lawyers a central role in the war on terrorism. The tiger team pulled together both active duty officers and reservists called up from their civilian careers as law professors, prosecutors and public defenders.

But conflicts quickly emerged between the military lawyers and political appointees such as Yoo and Addington. Where the uniformed lawyers expected commissions to reflect military justice as practiced in the twenty-first century, the politicals envisioned a device to secure convictions by disregarding legal developments since the 1940s.

Yet the Bush administration was selective in the history it resurrected, ignoring records from the hundreds of US military commissions held overseas after World War II, files that documented the daily operations of a functioning trial system for enemy prisoners. Instead, it fixed on the singular case of *Quirin*, perhaps the least fair of the World War II–era trials. The Army and Navy both conducted commission trials after World War II, using a structure similar to that of courts-martial and providing a review of each conviction. The saboteurs trial, in contrast, was controlled politically, ordered up by the White House with every party clearly understanding the president's expectation of rapid convictions and executions. Haynes was fascinated by *Quirin*, so the tiger team retrieved the files from a National Archives facility in suburban Maryland, allowing the general counsel to touch the crumbling pages himself.

Then, in early November, Haynes summoned the top uniformed lawyers of the Army, Navy, Air Force, and Marine Corps for a secret meeting. He had a document for them to review. It was the draft military commission order, about to go to President Bush for his signature. The top JAGs would have thirty minutes with the document. No copies, no notes could leave the room.

The draft declared it "not practicable" for military commissions to follow "the principles of law and the rules of evidence" that defined American justice. Other than directing that trials be "full and fair," the eighteen-hundred-word order made no reference to basic elements of due process—proof beyond a reasonable doubt, presumption of innocence, the right to remain silent. The only standard was that evidence hold "probative value to a reasonable person"—a unisex updating of the FDR order's language, which referenced the "reasonable man." Instead of separating the roles of judge and jury, the order merged them into a single finder of law and fact, a commission headed not by a judge but a "presiding officer" who could be overruled by the other members.

There was no requirement that any member of the commission be a lawyer. Instead, lay officers from infantry, artillery, or other units would conduct a trial that could order a defendant executed.

"We all looked at the document, and looked at each other in disbelief," said Major General Thomas Fiscus, the judge advocate general of the Air Force.

"Insane," said General Romig.

The JAGs' objections weren't based solely on a sense of fairness. They feared that proceedings run by nonlawyers with no clear rules would collapse as defense lawyers hurled objection after objection, perhaps even provoking review by the federal courts.

Haynes thanked them for their comments. But the document tracked much of the language FDR had used for his *Quirin* trial. That had been upheld by the Supreme Court, so there was no need to deviate. Even the title—"Military Order," rather than "Executive Order"—aped the vocabulary of 1942.

In one fundamental way, however, the document exceeded even the powers President Roosevelt claimed during World War II. In 1942, the government unexpectedly found itself holding eight saboteurs who had infiltrated the country. Political and propaganda imperatives drove the White House to quickly and quietly dispatch them in a one-shot trial. In contrast, the Bush administration envisioned creating for the first time a permanent legal structure under the president's sole command.

ONE PERSON UNHAPPY WITH the developing military order was John Ashcroft, the attorney general. Ashcroft had been a solid religious conservative through his political career, but he was neither personally close to President Bush nor part of the circle of legal theorists who seized upon 9/11 to implement a vision of executive primacy. Whereas they imagined military commissions as key to establishing a new constitutional order, Ashcroft saw a threat to a core Justice Department function, as well as a risky legal gambit his department would be required to defend, ultimately, before the Supreme Court.

Before 9/11, the professional corps of federal prosecutors had a virtually unbroken record in convicting al Qaeda–linked defendants. The department had fully expected that would continue. In a September 26, 2001, draft memo, the criminal division reported it was ready to prosecute anyone involved in the 9/11 conspiracy, identifying federal crimes that covered the attacks, from murder to "malicious damage to a building used in interstate or foreign commerce by means of fire or explosive."[35]

To date, a civilian prosecutor, an assistant US attorney in New York named Patrick J. Fitzgerald, had notched the biggest victory against al Qaeda. In May 2001, Fitzgerald won convictions of four men for the August 1998 truck bombings of US embassies in Kenya and Tanzania. The trial raised legal issues that would be crucial to future al Qaeda prosecutions—and almost every one went the government's way. A December 2000 court ruling, for instance, held that the

Fourth Amendment ban on "unreasonable searches and seizures" did not apply to foreign intelligence investigations conducted overseas.[36] The case, named for the principal defendant, still at large, was *United States of America v. Usama bin Laden et al.*[37]

Now, however, the administration's informal "war council"—the self-appointed group of legal ideologues led by David Addington—was working to transfer the terrorism portfolio to one of Ashcroft's cabinet rivals, Donald Rumsfeld. In one early draft, the secretary of defense would select all the participants—the members of the commission, the prosecutor, and the defense attorney—and then would decide any appeals.

"You've got to be kidding me," said Ashcroft. The Justice Department's criminal and appellate experts said that even if such a structure could be set up, it was insane to expect the Supreme Court to uphold it.

Addington insisted, however, that defense attorneys had to be strictly controlled; unless the government chose the defense lawyer, there were sure to be leaks. Justice Department officials said the White House had it all wrong. Most of the time, defense lawyers actually proved helpful to investigators by persuading their clients to cooperate in exchange for a lesser punishment or detention privileges.

Ashcroft dialed his objections back to a single demand: that the Justice Department decide which defendants, if any, were turned over to military commissions.

For a time, it seemed he would get his way. Some versions of the commissions order gave the attorney general a veto over the defense secretary's decision to try a prisoner by military commission.

Later drafts, however, cut the Justice Department out entirely. And they had been approved by the war council's most precocious member, John Yoo. Although Yoo had become a favorite of Addington, Alberto Gonzales, and Jim Haynes, formally, he worked in the Justice Department. He had to explain the decision to his nominal boss, Ashcroft.

Yoo framed it as a simple matter of legal strategy. It would help the Justice Department defend the new system if it were defined as a purely military function, Yoo explained. If it looked too "civilianized," the federal courts might be tempted to muscle in.

Ashcroft asked few questions. Later, after realizing that the draft deleted the attorney general entirely, he exploded. His own subordinate, John Yoo, had been going behind his back, purporting to speak for the Justice Department while advocating positions that undermined the authority of the attorney general.

Ashcroft "didn't realize the implications of the advice we were giving," Yoo later surmised. The draft handed the defense secretary complete control over commissions, able even to remove any defendant from Justice Department custody.

Ashcroft complained to Gonzales, prompting Vice President Cheney to summon the principals to the White House on Saturday, November 9. Tempers were short, and manners unpleasant. In the Roosevelt Room, Cheney made clear that the decision was made; military commissions would proceed with or without the Justice Department's blessing. Ashcroft repeatedly interrupted Cheney, insisting the course was foolish and unnecessary. Using the federal courts, the Justice Department had obtained the death penalty for Timothy McVeigh, the domestic terrorist who blew up the Oklahoma City federal building and killed 168 people. How could the government argue that the only way to convict terrorists was to strip them of constitutional rights?

Tim Flanigan, the deputy White House counsel, later complained that Ashcroft had crossed the line, even for a cabinet officer, in his tone with the vice president. But Ashcroft wrung a small concession. Commissions defendants would be selected by the president, rather than the defense secretary, and could be moved to federal court if the president changed his mind.

Nevertheless, the final document, written by Addington with help from Flanigan and Yoo, presumed that the criminal justice system had failed. Unlike FDR's 1942 order, it made no mention of the attorney general or the Justice Department.

The order's terms extinguished all rights held by prisoners the president selected. It denied them "any remedy" from any "court of the United States," "any court of any foreign nation," or "any international tribunal."

ON TUESDAY, NOVEMBER 13, 2001, as the federal government restarted after the Veterans Day holiday, Vice President Cheney came for his regular luncheon with Bush, in the private dining room by the Oval Office. He brought the last draft of the military order.[38]

Bush had been little involved to date. White House Counsel Gonzales first raised commissions with Bush in late October—more than a month after Addington had begun setting the legal experiment in motion. Gonzales told the president how FDR used a military commission to take care of the Nazi saboteurs. "Strong move," Bush said. He told Gonzales to go ahead.[39]

When Cheney came with the final product, the president had other things on his mind. Later that day, Bush was scheduled to fly to his ranch in Crawford, Texas, with Russian President Vladimir Putin. Cheney made sure Bush would sign the commissions order before he left.

Normally, documents for the president's approval are filed with the White House staff secretary, who circulates the draft among key officials for last-minute comments or concerns. Staff Secretary Harriet Miers was traveling, so her deputy, Stuart Bowen, was on duty when Brad Berenson, an associate White House counsel, brought over the military order. Bowen said he would get right on it. It should be on the president's desk by Friday.

Berenson said this particular document was ready for Bush's signature immediately. There was no need for "staffing" it.

"We can do it on a quick turnaround"—maybe a day—"but it still needs to be staffed," Bowen said. That was the procedure.

Berenson said he would be right back. He quickly returned with Tim Flanigan, who told Bowen that Bush already had approved the military order at his lunch with Cheney and was waiting in the Oval Office to sign it.

Bowen now grasped the urgency. Accompanied by Berenson, he rushed the document over to the Oval Office, where Bush was standing impatiently. The presidential helicopter, Marine One, was on the lawn outside, rotor turning as it waited to take the president to his meeting with Putin.

"Is this it?" Bush said, and Bowen handed him the papers. Bush flipped to the last page, signed his name, and left.

The White House Press Office treated the signing as a minor event. Of ten press releases it posted that day on its website, the Putin meeting came first. "President Issues Military Order" was eighth, between "National Farm-City Week Proclamation" and "President Signs Reclamation Amendment."

But as news reports picked up the press release, there was shock —most of all among administration officials who discovered they had been cut out of the process.

Soon after 9/11, the National Security Council had set up an interagency group to do legal and policy research on the military commissions proposal, including alternative ways to prosecute suspected terrorists. Agencies including the Pentagon, the Justice Department, the State Department, the White House counsel's office, and the CIA sent representatives. The Office of the Vice President did not. David Addington "didn't do interagency," as one White House aide put it.

The White House counsel's office had expected the group to quickly provide bureaucratic approval for the commissions plan. Instead, it had been exploring options ranging from federal courts to courts-martial to an international tribunal in The Hague. Flanigan lost patience. "It had been decided it was going to be commissions. They were wasting their time," he said. "We were not going to have the Dutch deciding on what happened to Osama bin Laden."

Rather than risk further delay by confronting the interagency group, the war council simply finished the military order itself and obtained the president's signature. The fait accompli was intended to "send a message" to administration staffers who persisted in business as usual, Flanigan said. "This is war. Get it through your heads."

One such target was John Bellinger, counsel to National Security Adviser Condoleezza Rice and co-chairman of the interagency group. A career government lawyer, he had lost Addington's confidence soon after 9/11, when he advised Gonzales to make Bush stop saying things like he wanted bin Laden captured "dead or alive." Calling for an extrajudicial killing could expose the president to a future war crimes prosecution, Bellinger had warned. Addington considered such talk positively inane.

When an email popped up reporting that the presidential military order had been issued. Bellinger was dumbfounded. Minutes later, the phone rang. It was CIA lawyer John Rizzo. The military order had blindsided George Tenet, the director of central intelligence, and Rizzo was calling to convey his fury.

"John, what have you been doing to us?" he said, mistakenly assuming that the National Security Council would have been involved in such a momentous policy decision. Although the war council justified military commissions as essential to protecting intelligence, the CIA had not requested any alternative to the federal courts. To the contrary, the agency had great confidence in the federal prosecutors and judges in the Southern District of New York, which handled the biggest terrorism cases. They were expert in employing the Classified Information Procedures Act to protect CIA information, obtaining convictions that withstood appeal without a single intelligence leak. The agency was concerned that commissions would introduce legal uncertainties and untested personnel into its most sensitive operations.

Tenet wasn't the only senior official surprised by the military order. Bellinger's boss, Condi Rice, learned about it from a television report. So did the secretary of state, Colin Powell.[40]

Bellinger approached Stephen Hadley, the deputy national security adviser. Hadley's history with Dick Cheney dated from their days together in the Ford administration. Hadley said he didn't know anything about the order, either. He suggested calling Jim Haynes.

Haynes took Bellinger's call, but the courtesy went no further. He refused to discuss the commissions order. Go ask "your boss"—Al Gonzales—Haynes said, and he hung up.

Although Bellinger considered Condi Rice his client, the White House flow chart showed him reporting to Gonzales as well. Bellinger made his way over to the White House counsel's office. He "cried a river over it," Flanigan said.

Bellinger was just one of a parade of staffers who came through to complain about being sandbagged. "How could you do this to me?" said Hadley, his tone somewhere between sorrow and anger.

By day's end, Flanigan had been worn down by the gripes and discontent. When a reporter called to find out what was going on, the normally confident Flanigan sounded strangely defensive.

"The order's signed and nobody's ashamed of it," he said.[41]

THE NEXT DAY, WHILE Bush showed Putin around his ranch, Cheney attended the US Chamber of Commerce's quarterly board meeting.

"Mr. Vice President, welcome to an undisclosed, secure location," the chamber's president, Tom Donahue, said to wide laughter. "Once again it's a time of need, the country has called upon the vice president for his leadership and his experience, and we are all benefiting from that."[42]

In prepared remarks, Cheney laid out the administration's view that the war effort was best served by cutting business taxes. Then he took some questions.

"Assuming, I guess, that Osama was found alive, what's the difference between military tribunals . . . and The Hague?" was one.

Cheney ignored the part about The Hague, where the UN war crimes courts were based, and briefly summarized the military order.

"Now, some people say, 'Well, gee, that's a dramatic departure from traditional jurisprudence in the United States,'" Cheney said. "It is, but there's precedent for it." President Andrew Johnson convened a military commission for the plotters behind Abraham Lincoln's assassination in 1865, he observed. Then there were the Nazi saboteurs. "They were given a fair trial, prosecuted under this military tribunal and executed in relatively rapid order," he said.

Under the Bush administration, prisoners "will have a fair trial, but it will be under the procedures of a military tribunal, under rules and regulations to be established in connection with that," Cheney said. "We think it guarantees that we'll have the kind of treatment of these individuals that we believe they deserve."

■

As John Yoo and David Addington imagined it, dispensing rough justice to enemy prisoners was a true American tradition that had been lost in the postwar legal fetish for individual rights. They saw military commissions as a procedural incarnation of the executive power to subdue and slay the enemy, as intrinsic to the American way of war as the fife and drum corps. In public comments and secret memorandums alike, they claimed the blessing of George Washington himself, who as commander in chief of the Continental Army convened a military board and hanged a British spy, Major John André, days after his capture in September 1780.

But there were no comprehensive legal treatises regarding military commissions, nor had their decisions been indexed in the standard casebooks whose uniform system of citation allowed attorneys and scholars to find decisions from virtually any federal or state court, along with supporting and conflicting precedents. Legal and academic literature on military tribunals was anecdotal, tending to focus on specific episodes attractive for their rhetorical or narrative character rather than any consistent doctrine.[43] Unlike the federal judiciary or even courts-martial, military commissions had no contiguous path of historical development but rather were a collection of unrelated one-offs, sporadically appearing as ad hoc responses to moments of wartime peril, operating for a brief period, and then disappearing until officials of a later generation stumbled on them. They were the Brigadoon of victor's justice.

Under John Yoo's Constitution, the American president literally embodied the powers of a British monarch.[44] Those, Yoo explained to astonished JAGs and Justice Department officials, included putting enemy detainees to death. What about civilians? Could the president order them massacred? Could he have a village exterminated?

"Sure," Yoo said.[45] But the president could also act more modestly, such as ordering prisoners tried and convicted before their execution. Reaching such a legal conclusion, however, required not only a contrarian understanding of American history but a selective reading of British constitutional development as well.

To be sure, long ago the crown recognized few restraints in its treatment of enemy prisoners. After victory at Agincourt in 1415, Henry V issued instructions for his French detainees. "Cut the throats of those we have," he told senior officials, according to Shakespeare. "And not a man of them that we shall take / Shall taste our mercy."[46] But such glorious exceptions notwithstanding, the crown's powers had been on a downward trajectory at least since 1215, when the Magna Carta imposed limits on the king's authority. The royal prerogative took another severe blow in 1628 after Charles I, facing uprisings against his Thirty Years' War policies, imposed martial law, suspending habeas corpus and authorizing trials by military commission. In Parliament, Sir Edward Coke, a former chief justice and attorney general, pushed through the Petition of Right, rejecting the king's claim that his commander-in-chief powers permitted him to displace the civil courts for national security reasons.[47]

An insurgent "may be slain in the rebellion, but after he is taken he cannot be put to death by the martial law," Coke said at the parliamentary debate, because "when the courts are open martial law cannot be executed" merely because the king found it more expedient.[48] Coke refuted claims that military commissions were simply a more appropriate forum to dispense justice during wartime, given existential threats to the English state. If the crown alleged a crime, "bring it to a court of justice," he said. The army's job was crushing the enemy, not neutrally adjudicating his dispute with the commander in chief. As the Elizabethan jurist put it, "Shall the Souldier and Justice Sit on one Bench, the Trumpet will not let the Cryer speak in Westminster-Hall." In 1957, Justice Hugo Black recalled Coke's warning, using it to close an opinion restricting the jurisdiction of courts-martial to military personnel.[49]

When operating in overseas war zones, however, British commanders did on occasion make snap judgments regarding enemy detainees they considered unlawful combatants. One was Nathan Hale, captured in September 1776 when spying on British positions in New York for the American rebels. Hale confessed to General William Howe, who ordered him hanged the following morning.[50] Four years later, when Major André was apprehended after meeting with Benedict Arnold, General Washington reciprocated. But the process leading to André's execution was itself a Revolutionary War anomaly and not a military commission at all.[51] While Washington convened a "Board of General Officers" to review the evidence against André, it served only as an advisory panel. It was Washington himself, not the board after trial and conviction, who ordered the execution when the British refused to surrender Benedict Arnold in a prisoner exchange for André.[52] In contrast, more than two dozen courts-martial were held for alleged British spies under a Continental Congress resolution.[53]

During the jurisdictional uncertainty of America's revolutionary period—with newly independent states, a nascent federal government, and the residual force of English common law all in the mix—General Washington apparently turned to the same implicit authority as field commander Howe invoked to hang Nathan Hale. In 1789, however, the Constitution clarified the structure of national authority, and its war clauses assigned Congress, not the executive, the power to define violations of international law and "make Rules concerning Captures on Land and Water."

The rules on paper and the reality at the front did not always jibe. General Andrew Jackson was reprimanded by President James Madison for conducting military trials without congressional authorization during the War of 1812. During the Mexican War of the late 1840s, General Winfield Scott established military commissions to maintain law and order in occupied territory, after the collapse of the enemy government. But when the military set up a similar tribunal to adjudicate prizes—that is, the seizure of enemy vessels during armed conflict, a wartime tradition—the Supreme Court ruled that the executive had no such power.

"Every court of the United States therefore must derive its jurisdiction and judicial authority from the Constitution or the laws of the United States. And neither the President nor any military officer can establish a court in a conquered country and authorize it to decide upon the rights of the United States or of individuals in prize cases, nor to administer the laws of nations," the Court said in an 1851 case, *Jecker v. Montgomery.*[54] "The courts established or sanctioned in Mexico during the war by the commanders of the American forces were nothing more than the agents of the military power, to assist it in preserving order in the conquered territory and to protect the inhabitants in their persons and property while it was occupied by the American arms."

On the frontier, Native Americans usually faced the roughest military justice of all. After the Seminole War of 1818, a House committee rebuked General Andrew Jackson for having two captured Britons executed following a brief review by a military board, much as General Washington had done with Major André. The committee raised no objection to Jackson's summary hanging of two Creek Indians, as they were part of a "savage nation, which observes no rules," and therefore could be punished by "rigorous proceedings" that forced "them to respect the laws of humanity."[55] In 1862, an Army colonel convened a military commission to try 392 Dakota Indian captives, delivering 323 convictions, including 303 death sentences.

Some trials took only five minutes. President Lincoln personally intervened to blunt the rough justice, commuting all but 39 of the death sentences. To John Yoo, the episode simply demonstrated that detainees subject to military commissions would live or die at the president's discretion.

During the Civil War, the Lincoln administration suspended habeas corpus and held thousands of trials by military commission, often over the objection of the *Jecker* opinion's author, Chief Justice Roger Taney. Lincoln justified suspending habeas corpus as necessary to preserve the Union itself in the face of Southern perfidy. "Are all the laws but one to go unexecuted and the Government itself go to pieces lest that one be violated?" he said in a July 4, 1861, message to Congress.

These commissions, like General Scott's, were designed not so much to tilt the results but to extend military jurisdiction over enemy prisoners and civilians in occupied territory who were not normally subject to courts-martial. An 1862 general order directed that they be organized in a "similar manner" and follow "the same general rules as courts-martial in order to prevent abuses which might otherwise occur."[56] The Army turned again to military commissions in the Philippines after wresting the territory from Spain in 1898. Constituted both to hear routine cases and prosecute atrocities, the commissions operated under rules akin to those of courts-martial. Hearsay had to be corroborated by untainted evidence, confessions had to be proven as voluntary. All convictions automatically were reviewed by superior officers, and on several occasions were overturned.

In one such reversal, the Army reviewer invoked the definitive legal treatise of the Framers' generation, Blackstone's *Commentaries on the Laws of England*. "All presumptive evidence of felony should be admitted cautiously: for the law holds, that it is better that ten guilty persons escape, than that one innocent suffer," the English jurist explained in his 1783 compendium. Blackstone's ratio, as it was called, "is too well grounded in the administration of justice to pass unheeded by military commissions. So, too, it is better that no person, innocent or guilty, should be convicted unfairly, in violation of his legal rights and privileges, or in defiance of the well-established and equitable laws of evidence without which the evolution of [our] system of law and justice would be impossible," the 1901 Army ruling said. Although the evidence indicated a "strong presumption" of guilt, "the illegalities and irregularities" of the trial required reversal of the conviction.[57]

The Nazi saboteur trial of 1942 marked the return of commissions for World War II, but that event may have left President Franklin D. Roosevelt uncomfortable. Two years later, after a pair of German infiltrators was captured, Roosevelt, under advice from Secretary of War Henry Stimson, eschewed the direct control he had exercised over the *Quirin* trial and instead assigned the Army Judge Advocate General's Corps to handle the case. The defendants were convicted, but their death sentences were commuted, and both left prison by 1960.[58]

The vast majority of military commissions, however, were held after the war, when the United States again found itself occupying territory of a defeated adversary. Although Nuremberg and other postwar tribunals largely are remembered for prosecuting the Nazi leadership for crimes against humanity, the trials originated in the mistreatment of prisoners of war. It was the German practice of summarily executing downed Allied flyers that in 1944 led Washington to begin planning for war crimes prosecutions.[59] Of three hundred trials held by military commissions at Yokohama, 90 percent involved charges of prisoner abuse.

As in the Mexican and Spanish-American Wars, the quality of the proceedings varied, but they were administered by the regular Army hierarchy and mirrored contemporary court-martial procedures. On Guam, the Navy, for the only time in its history, conducted war crimes trials, attempting to one-up the Army with more rigorous standards of due process that largely excluded hearsay.[60]

By 1950, the United States had wound down its military commissions, with no expectation of making them a permanent part of the military justice system. During the Vietnam War, the United States left the disposition of enemy detainees to its ally, South Vietnam, rather than get back into the business of housing prisoners and punishing war criminals. The Pentagon did consider establishing at least one military commission to try an alleged war criminal that conflict produced, Lieutenant William Calley, who commanded the unit that massacred civilians at My Lai in 1968. Officials opted instead to court-martial Calley for murder, concerned that branding an American officer as a war criminal would needlessly hand the enemy a propaganda victory.

INITIAL REACTION TO BUSH'S military order was muted, at least within the mainstream of the legal community. Less than a week after the order was announced, Michael Ratner, president of the Center for Constitutional Rights, an advocacy group cofounded by the radical lawyer William Kunstler, wrote with astonishment that "a number of prestigious law professors (e.g. Laurence Tribe and Ruth Wedgwood) have accepted and even argued in favor of these tribunals."[61]

Yale's Wedgwood, a lapsed liberal who brought academic heft to the neoconservative movement, actually had been involved in developing military commissions, advising Rumsfeld's Pentagon on legal precedents and appearing in the news media as a public surrogate for the administration. Tribe was something else. Days after the November 13 military order, the Harvard professor mused that while indefinite detention was scary, "the idea that someone might be released and then go and blow up Cleveland is scarier still." Coming from the nation's best-known liberal legal scholar, Tribe's initial reaction seemed almost an endorsement: "I'm not entirely comfortable with it, but I don't see any better way."[62]

On reflection, Tribe came to view the military order more critically—"rife with constitutional problems and riddled with flaws," he said. In December 4, 2001, testimony before the Senate Judiciary Committee, Tribe urged Congress to draft rules for military commissions, said defendants must be entitled to appeal to the federal courts, and advised that the venue be reserved for al Qaeda's leadership. Rank-and-file terrorists should face normal criminal prosecution, he said.

Tribe's views jibed with those of Neal Katyal, a young George-town law professor he had met when both worked on Al Gore's legal team in the 2000 Florida election recount. Katyal had appeared before the Judiciary Committee the previous week, and a Senate staffer gave Tribe a copy of his statement. Soon the two professors were working together on a law review article distilling the flaws they saw in the military order. Tribe, who joined the Harvard faculty in 1968, was an elder statesman of the academy. His chances of appointment to high rank in government or the Supreme Court had faded during the Democrats' long exile from the White House.

Katyal, in contrast, could be seen as a Democratic answer to John Yoo. Confident, cerebral, and even icy behind designer rec-tangular eyeglass frames, Katyal too was a first-generation American. Fast behind Yoo, he had marched down the cursus honorum of the legal elite. But where Yoo turned hard right, Katyal tacked slightly left, maneuvering his way into the Democratic Party's brain trust at a time when it desperately needed a new generation of legal thinking.

The son of Indian immigrants who had moved to Chicago, Kat-yal, too, had attended a private prep school before heading to an Ivy League college. After his Dartmouth graduation, Katyal enrolled at Yale Law School, two years behind Yoo, clerked for Justice Stephen Breyer, and secured a teaching job at Georgetown. He had spent two years at the Clinton Justice Department working on national security issues for Deputy Attorney General Eric Holder, including justifica-tion for unilateral military moves, such as the air war Clinton launched to expel the Serb army from Kosovo.

Katyal joined the flock of lawyers battling over the Florida re-count in the 2000 election. But his candidate's defeat did little to harm his career. Like Yoo, he found the lifestyle, security, and prestige of academia a far better base from which to wield influence than the scrum of ground-level politics, the tedium of military service, or a lengthy apprenticeship as a trial attorney or prosecutor. On September 10, 2001, three weeks after the birth of his first child, Katyal returned to New Haven for a year as visiting professor.

Written through drafts emailed between New Haven and Cambridge, the article Katyal and Tribe published in the *Yale Law Journal,* "Waging War, Deciding Guilt: Trying the Military Tribunals," trundled forth in the burdened prose of academic writing. "A time of terror might not be the ideal moment to trifle with the most time-tested postulates of government under law," it began, leaving open when exactly the ideal moment for such trifling might be expected. But when they got to the point, the professors were clear: "The President's Order establishing military tribunals for the trial of terrorists is flatly unconstitutional," they wrote.

Katyal and Tribe examined much of the same history and precedent that John Yoo had but reached contrary conclusions. In sketching the weaknesses of the president's order, the article sometimes read like a mirror image of an OLC memorandum. To Katyal and Tribe, rather than a natural and necessary expression of the commander in chief's power, a military commission where "the executive branch acts as lawmaker, law-enforcer, and judge" defies the "Constitution's text, structure, and logic." The *Quirin* case was no landmark to celebrate but an embarrassment fit for "judicial confinement or reconsideration."

The professors did not reject military commissions per se but argued that Bush exceeded his power by issuing a unilateral decree authorizing trials that afforded defendants no rights or remedies. Perhaps military commissions were appropriate for certain "unlawful belligerents." But "the next steps require legislation if the administration hopes to use military tribunals and defend them from judicial invalidation."

Welcome to the Dungeon

WITH THE MILITARY ORDER signed, the JAG Corps had to supply staff for the commissions project. At Camp Lejeune, the legal services director went looking for Stuart Couch, the base prosecutor. He found him with his staff at the bowling alley bar.

Military personnel in the field knew nothing of the Bush administration's internal battles over commissions. What they saw was a president moving decisively against a virulent threat.

Mark Fallon, the federal agent who had headed the Aviano investigation, had been tapped to run investigations of Guantanamo prisoners for prosecution. He had floated Couch's name as a candidate for commissions work. Couch wanted in. In this war, he realized, his only chance to see action might be arguing in a courtroom.

It was nearly Halloween before he heard back. On the line was Lieutenant Colonel Bill Lietzau, a Marine officer working on the commissions project for Haynes at the Pentagon.

Couch had heard about Lietzau. He was the rare Marine with a law degree from Yale, a former military judge, an expert on the laws of war. During the Clinton administration, Lietzau had been part of the US delegation to the diplomatic conference that established the International Criminal Court. Although the United States ultimately did not join the court, Lietzau helped draft the legal code of war crimes the new tribunal was chartered to enforce.

Beyond his legal acumen, Lietzau was a skilled bureaucratic infighter who made himself essential to successive administrations of different parties. When the Bush administration repudiated President Clinton's efforts to strengthen international law, Lietzau suddenly popped up as the point man on designing military commissions that defied international norms.

As an adviser to Haynes and his staff, Lietzau would become "the most powerful Marine lieutenant colonel since Ollie North," Mark Fallon later quipped. Lietzau not only drafted the de facto criminal code for commissions, he also was the acting chief prosecutor, assembling the staff and working with Fallon to select defendants.

In the telephone interview Couch told Lietzau that he saw himself as a trial lawyer, a hands-on prosecutor who could deal with people—jurors, victims, witnesses, investigators. Legal research and writing weren't his strong suits.

"My thing is being in court. That's my *schtick*," Couch said, rolling the Yiddishism in his Carolina twang.

Lietzau had his hands full with policy issues in Washington. He told Couch to sit tight.

■

Donald Rumsfeld considered himself an independent thinker who transcended contemporary partisanship. Over the years, he had collected scores of influential friends, even some Democrats.

One was Newton Minow, a fellow Chicagoan who was serving in the Kennedy administration, as chairman of the Federal Communications Commission, when Rumsfeld first was elected to Congress in 1962. They had remained friends ever since.

Rumsfeld had called Minow during a visit home before Thanksgiving 2001, asking for help with a "big problem": military commissions. Rumsfeld said he wanted some of his well-set friends—"people who don't want anything from me," he explained—to make sure the project didn't embarrass him. Minow's only experience with enemy combatants came during World War II, when he was an eighteen-year-old soldier guarding German and Italian POWs on garbage duty. Nonetheless, he said he'd be happy to help. Minow, then seventy-five, expected to be the oldest guy there. Far from it. "It turned out to be the AARP," he said.

The group numbered several veterans of the Ford administration, when Rumsfeld first ran the Pentagon, including former Transportation Secretary William Coleman, eighty-one, and Rumsfeld's Princeton roommate, Marty Hoffman, a former secretary of the Army. Two had participated in World War II war crimes trials: University of Chicago professor Bernard Meltzer, eighty-seven, who had served on the Nuremberg prosecution force, and eighty-four-year-old Lloyd Cutler, White House counsel to two presidents, Carter and Clinton. As a young Justice Department lawyer in 1942, Cutler had helped prosecute the *Quirin* defendants.

The Sages, as Pentagon staffers called them, joined Rumsfeld for a Saturday luncheon. Cutler observed that the Uniform Code of Military Justice already provided for trials in war zones. What exactly were commissions supposed to accomplish that existing law couldn't, he asked.

"I don't know," Rumsfeld said. "I'm taking orders here from the White House."

Cutler vented his misgivings in a *Wall Street Journal* op-ed, where he recounted his *Quirin* experience.[1] "Although FDR's use of a military commission was sustained by the Supreme Court, our prosecuting team made a number of debatable decisions that the Bush team would be well advised to remember this time around," he wrote. In private, Cutler was more direct. Sure, he told Jim Haynes, the Supreme Court during World War II upheld a politically controlled military commission. *But we never held one again.*

Other Sages, however, were enthusiastic about the project. Bill

Coleman recalled discussing wartime cases with Justice Felix Frankfurter, for whom he clerked in 1948. The Supreme Court's World War II decisions weren't "as bad as people said," Coleman said, "because after Pearl Harbor, we really thought the Japanese would occupy part of the United States."

To Pentagon staff, the Sages created another nebulous layer of authority as various questions regarding commissions procedures were hashed out. Each Sage got his own line on the policy matrices that Rumsfeld loved, alongside those of David Addington and Alberto Gonzales. Rumsfeld, however, didn't care about legal details. He had just one question, in an old-fashioned phrase that perplexed some of his subordinates: If you dropped a plumb line through it, would it be a fair trial?

But no consensus existed on what the concept meant to President Bush. With comments coming from different agencies, and continuing disagreements between career military and political appointees, implementing documents went through more than a hundred drafts in an effort to find a workable structure. Even then, fundamental questions remained for Rumsfeld himself to resolve: Should defendants be permitted to hire civilian lawyers? Would an appeals panel reviewing verdicts be military or civilian? And this: Would the defendant be presumed innocent?

No one in uniform opposed presumption of innocence. Not so the civilians.

"Why should we presume them innocent? They should have to prove themselves," said one Sage. Jim Haynes refused to answer when, at a congressional hearing, Senator Carl Levin asked whether he considered presumption of innocence essential to a "full and fair" trial. Military lawyers included presumption of innocence in draft regulations sent to Gonzales and Addington at the White House; the provision would be deleted when the draft returned to the Pentagon.

"Presumption of innocence" is not mentioned in the Bill of Rights, the White House counsel's office argued, and Guantanamo inmates had no constitutional rights, anyway. Military lawyers working on the project were incredulous. Bill Lietzau, with just a few hours to return a draft, reached beyond the small circle working on commissions to the No. 2 lawyer in the Marine Corps, Colonel Kevin Winters—the same officer Stu Couch looked to for discreet advice. If it wasn't in the Constitution, Lietzau asked, where did presumption of innocence come from?

Winters pointed him to a dusty Supreme Court opinion called *Coffin v. United States*.[2]

The 1895 ruling reversed several embezzlement convictions, citing the trial judge's refusal to instruct the jury that defendants are presumed innocent "until they are proven, by competent evidence, to be guilty." The Court observed, with apparent surprise, that there were few relevant precedents. The reason, it suggested, was that presumption of innocence is so "axiomatic and elementary" to the administration of justice that no one really questioned it.

The Court traced the principle to the biblical book of Deuteronomy, through the laws of ancient Greece and Rome, canon law, and seventeenth-century England and its New World colonies. Several US states explicitly required presumption of innocence, including Texas, under an 1876 court decision called *Black v. State*.[3] Perhaps that would influence Al Gonzales, who preferred being addressed as "Judge," recalling the two years he spent as a Governor Bush appointee on the Texas Supreme Court.

Lietzau went to Haynes. "We need to fax these over to the White House," he said, handing him the *Coffin* and *Black* opinions. Soon Haynes came back with the answer: "Okay, okay, they say go ahead and stick it in there."

OTHER EFFORTS TO IMPROVE what Lietzau called the "optics" of military commissions were less successful. Trying to harmonize the Bush administration project with humanitarian law, Lietzau proposed including "crimes against humanity" among punishable offenses. John Yoo, however, wanted them out—for the very same reason. He chafed when drafts included notations asserting that various provisions were "consistent" with particular treaties and covenants, for fear of lending credibility to the concept of international law. Haynes, typically, declined to take a position. He called Lietzau into his office, where he had an open phone line to Yoo at Main Justice.

"All right, guys, fight it out," Haynes said. He sat silently while Lietzau, in front of him, and Yoo, over a speakerphone, conducted an impromptu debate.

The idea of crimes against humanity first appeared in the 1907 Hague Convention, one of the early treaties codifying the laws of war. It was a catchall category for offenses not specifically anticipated by the treaty but obviously running afoul of "the principles of the law of nations, as they result from the usages established among civilized peoples, from the laws of humanity, and the dictates of the public conscience." The concept was elaborated after each cataclysm of the twentieth century, by an Allied commission following World War I, in the charters of the Nuremberg and Tokyo tribunals after World War II, in the statutes of the UN tribunals for the former Yugoslavia and Rwanda, and, permanently, in the Rome Statute of the International Criminal Court. The precise meaning remained obscure. A crime against humanity apparently was worse than a mere war crime but not as bad as genocide.

Lietzau saw no harm, and a likely benefit, to including crimes against humanity in the military commission code. The November 13 military order had been purposely vague in defining the commissions' jurisdiction, including not only "violations of the laws of war" but also undefined "other applicable laws." War crimes could only be committed, and therefore prosecuted, in the context of armed conflict. Crimes against humanity could—and had—taken place regardless of whether a war was on. They seemed exactly the kind of "other applicable law" that fit alongside war crimes.

Allied governments in Europe and Canada still hoped that the Bush administration's war on terrorism could be aligned with the international framework for humanitarian law. Adding crimes against humanity would painlessly promote international credibility while doing exactly what the administration wanted—expanding the executive's military powers into a field beyond traditional laws of war. These were "good, conservative reasons, right-wing reasons," Lietzau said.

Yoo considered Lietzau, like him a Yale Law School graduate, a cut above other JAGs he was dealing with. But even Lietzau seemed to have been infected by the State Department affliction, the desire to appease and please foreign intellectuals. The military commissions were to try enemies of the United States for crimes against the United States; humanity could find its own champion. Yoo's opposition boiled down to discomfort with nomenclature he considered more suited to The Hague than the Pentagon. It wasn't that important to him. After forty-five minutes of argument, he gave in.

"Well, Jim, I don't feel that strongly about it," Yoo said. "If Bill really wants it in there, I can live with that."

Haynes turned to Lietzau. "Okay, put it in." Discussion turned to other matters. Before wrapping up, Haynes wanted to clarify the decision on crimes against humanity. "You're uncomfortable with it, right, John?"

Yoo was.

Haynes turned to Lietzau. "Well, we can always put it in later, right?"

"Technically, we can," Lietzau said.

"All right, keep it out. Keep it out," Haynes said. Yoo had, and not for the first time, somehow worked his sorcery to win a legal argument.

"Damn," Lietzau thought. "I just wasted forty-five minutes arguing with this guy, and I won. And he still wins."

After more than a hundred drafts, the administration settled on a sixteen-page document to frame implementation of Bush's military order, under the confusingly similar name of Military Order No. 1. The commissions would have from three to seven members, and only the presiding officer would be a lawyer. A two-thirds vote could convict and sentence, except for the death penalty, which required the unanimous vote of a seven-member commission.

The language was inflected to hasten verdicts. "The Presiding

Officer shall ensure the expeditious conduct of the trial. In no circumstance shall accommodation of counsel be allowed to delay proceedings unreasonably," it stated. The commission would "proceed impartially and expeditiously, strictly confining the proceedings to a full and
fair trial of the charges, excluding irrelevant evidence, and preventing
any unnecessary interference or delay." Once confirmed, sentences
"shall be carried out promptly," in contrast to the eleven years an
average American civilian spent on death row before execution.[4]

One word was conspicuously absent. Haynes, at Addington's direction, had told Lietzau to avoid using the word *rights*—except to state,
as the document did, that the order conferred none. Instead of rights,
those selected for military commissions would have, in the phrase Lietzau ultimately settled on, "Procedures Accorded to the Accused."

AT A PENTAGON PRESS conference, a reporter asked Rumsfeld how
the public could be sure commissions would be "impartial and fair and
not, sort of, kangaroo courts with predetermined outcomes?"

"There's that word," Rumsfeld said, irritated. "You had to get that
'kangaroo court' in there so that people would have that in their minds."
He left the briefing room, referring further questions to subordinates.[5]

■

At Camp Lejeune, Stu Couch had continued along as a base prosecutor, hearing nothing from commissions while receiving word that he
would be part of the Marine forces assembling to invade Iraq. Couch
was thrilled—at last, a chance to do what Marines sign up for. Then he
got a break in a case.

In September 2002, a lieutenant and two other paratroopers on
a training flight had jumped from a C-17, pulled their rip cords—and
nothing happened. Their lines had been cut. The men survived only
because their reserve chutes opened in time.[6] Ten other parachutes
were similarly sabotaged.

DNA testing matched a skin cell on a cut cord to disgruntled lance corporal named Antoine Boykins. Four weeks from deployment to the staging area in Kuwait, Couch was ordered to remain at Camp Lejeune to handle the prosecution. He hoped to wrap things up in time to join his unit. A preliminary hearing went well, when the military judge ordered Boykins to stand trial.

The following night, March 20, 2003, President Bush read an address to the nation. War had begun.

"To all of the men and women of the United States armed forces now in the Middle East, the peace of a troubled world and the hopes of an oppressed people now depend on you," Bush said. "The people you liberate will witness the honorable and decent spirit of the American military."

Couch frowned. History had bypassed him again.

"THIS IS A CASE ABOUT treachery," Couch argued at Boykins's court-martial. "We know from English literature, from William Shakespeare in his play about Julius Caesar, and how Caesar uttered the words 'Et tu, Brute?' as a knife was planted in his back by Brutus on the Ides of March," he continued. "And perhaps, the worst example of treachery of all, in the history of the world, when Jesus Christ was betrayed by his friend and disciple, Judas, with a kiss.

"And today we find ourselves, the United States Marine Corps, an organization that prides itself on tradition, on its 227-year history, and today it finds itself confronted with an incident of treachery of its own. Treachery, not with a kiss, not with a knife blade to the back, treachery with scissors in the hands of a skilled parachute rigger; a parachute rigger that was an honor graduate from the parachute rigger's school, Lance Corporal Boykins."

Less than a month later, Couch wrapped up the case with a plea bargain for a twenty-year sentence. He was promoted to lieutenant colonel. And a call finally came from Washington. It was Fred Borch, the Army colonel who was taking over as chief prosecutor for military commissions.

"We're ready for you," Borch said.

■

Bill Lietzau had been Jim Haynes's preferred choice for chief prosecutor, but as a lieutenant colonel, he was too junior in rank to run the new office.

Other candidates had been floated, notably Rudolph Giuliani. Nobody better symbolized America's response to 9/11 than the steady mayor of New York, a man who first rose to fame as the gang-busting US attorney in Manhattan. Appointing such a high-profile figure with genuine legal and political credentials would evoke President Harry Truman's selection of Robert Jackson, the Supreme Court justice and former attorney general, as Nuremberg prosecutor.

Some feared, though, that Giuliani was too big a personality to take orders from a bland patronage appointee like Haynes. Moreover, this was a *military* commission, and Giuliani's main experience with the armed forces had been obtaining a series of draft deferments during the Vietnam War.

Colonel Fred Borch was a safer choice. He not only shared Haynes's alma mater, Davidson College, he also was an old Army buddy of Haynes's chief deputy.

And Borch was excited by the potential of Bush's military commissions. An amateur historian, he had written several books on obscure military topics, such as *The Silver Star: A History of America's Third Highest Award for Valor.* In commissions, he saw a chance not just to write military history but to make it.

Over their phone conversations, Couch immediately liked Borch, a fellow North Carolinian. When Couch proposed taking a one-year temporary assignment in Washington, Borch told him to make a permanent move. Commissions, he said, would run for two years, maybe three; the entire project would probably wrap up in 2006.

"You got it," Couch said. He already had staked out the congregation he would join, the Falls Church in Northern Virginia. The pastor came from Asheboro, Couch's hometown.

Arriving at the Pentagon, however, it became clear that Borch

was a distant manager. It was Kurt Brubaker, the other Marine prosecutor, who greeted Couch and escorted him to the prosecution office. It was down in the Pentagon basement, a dilapidated, windowless space stuffed with surplus desks. There was no sign of Borch. The
deputy chief prosecutor, a Navy commander named Scott Lang, introduced himself.

"Welcome to the Dungeon," Lang said.

YEARS EARLIER, WHEN COUCH had gone for training at the
Naval Justice School in Rhode Island, Lang had been one of his instructors. But there was no warm reunion. A former surface warfare
officer, Lang still embodied the strict discipline enforced on warships.
He came from New Jersey's Philadelphia suburbs, and to Couch, his
impatient, Northeastern speech, relatively rare in a military dominated by backslapping Southerners, seemed cold and all-business.
"Not a Southern Comfort and barbecue guy," Couch thought.

The Dungeon, as commissions staff called it, had been the prosecution home for nearly a year. It had no Internet connection and just
one telephone line. Prosecutors had to take turns either making calls
or using a dial-up connection to check email or go online. In a bureaucracy like the Department of Defense, office assignments often
carry a message; this one was hard to square with the historic significance of a presidential military order.

Brubaker next brought Couch to the E-Ring, the Pentagon's
outer corridor, where the secretary of defense and senior staff had
their offices. Historical displays and portraits of previous department
secretaries decorated hallways leading to large and handsomely appointed suites, some with views of the shimmering Potomac River.
It was here that Fred Borch had managed to secure an office for
himself. In an effusive, if brief, meeting, Borch kidded Couch about
the Dungeon.

"Man, that place is a hole," Borch said. Fortunately, he added, he
had obtained better accommodations for the team. They soon would
relocate to the Crystal City office complex, about a mile from the

Pentagon, where the department leased overflow space. Couch nodded appreciatively.

The last stop was the Office of the General Counsel. Couch followed Brubaker when he swung into a conference room. A group of civilians, apparently political appointees, seated around a table, halted their discussion when the two Marines entered.

"Mr. Cobb, I hate to interrupt, but I wanted to bring our new prosecutor by," Brubaker said.

Paul W. Cobb Jr. was the deputy general counsel overseeing the commissions project. Known as Whit, for his middle name, Whitlock, Cobb was a small, thin-haired man who always seemed slightly annoyed.

"Stuart, good to see you," Cobb said. He addressed the group. "This is Stuart Couch. Stuart graduated from Duke."

The other civilians murmured their greetings, and Brubaker led Couch out.

Cobb and Couch, in fact, had been classmates at Duke and counterparts in ROTC—Couch commanded the naval contingent, while Cobb led the Army unit. Their paths diverged after college. While Couch went to flight school, Cobb headed to Yale Law School. After getting his degree, Cobb completed his military commitment in the Department of the Army's general counsel's office—then headed by Jim Haynes. The two men's lives seemed to overlap. Cobb's father had been a legendary athlete at Davidson, which Haynes attended as an undergraduate, and both Haynes and Cobb went from Army ROTC to law school, then served out their military obligations in Pentagon desk jobs. Neither seemed particularly comfortable in uniform, nor had either any intention of a military career. When Haynes went from the Pentagon to do defense contracting work at Jenner & Block, he brought Cobb with him.

People who knew both considered Cobb the smarter student and the better lawyer. But Haynes was tall and handsome, with a shock of dark hair and, occasionally, a roguish stubble on his cheek. The bespectacled, pale-faced Cobb was short and plain, as if born to play Haynes's sidekick. When Haynes became Pentagon general counsel, he brought Cobb on to manage the litigation docket.

"Whit is a real workhorse," Haynes said. "He's able to produce work of a very high quality." After 9/11, it was natural for Haynes to entrust commissions to his loyal protégé. That made Cobb the political official who dealt most directly with the career military staffing the project.

Although they had not been particularly close in college, Couch was looking forward to seeing Cobb. At home that night, he told Kim it seemed odd that Cobb hadn't mentioned they were classmates, instead simply announcing to the other politicals that Couch had attended an elite college.

"It was like he was telling them, 'Hey, he's almost one of us,'" Couch said.

IN THE PROSECUTION OFFICE, Couch was given command of the Planners and Financiers Team, one of four trial teams for different categories of suspects. He was thrilled; it was the most important work he ever had done.

His targets were al Qaeda's midlevel cadre, the men who moved the money and recruited the muscle for terrorist operations. Reading through case files, several detainees looked promising.

One, Juma al-Dossari of Bahrain, was an alleged al Qaeda talent scout who recruited a group of young Arab Americans from upstate New York, the so-called Lackawanna Six. Another, a Saudi named Ahmed al-Darbi, had been tied to an al Qaeda plot to blow up oil tankers in the Persian Gulf.

The worst, however, was a Mauritanian detainee named Mohamedou Ould Slahi. He was considered the most important prisoner at Guantanamo. Military intelligence had assigned a "special projects" team just for him.

WESTERN SECURITY SERVICES HAD been monitoring Slahi since the late 1990s, when he was identified in an intercepted phone conversation with an al Qaeda leader in Sudan who turned out to be Slahi's cousin. Slahi was moving money around at his cousin's request, and the timing suggested a link to the 1998 al Qaeda attacks on US embassies in Kenya and Tanzania.

Slahi had made his way from Mauritania to Germany and then to Canada, where he joined the Montreal mosque frequented by Ahmed Ressam, the Algerian later convicted of plotting to blow up Los Angeles International Airport on New Year's Eve 2000—the Millennium Plot. Authorities suspected that Slahi had come from Europe to activate Ressam's Montreal cell.[7]

Slahi's name surfaced again in 2002, after terrorists bombed a synagogue in Tunisia, killing twenty-one.[8] Just before the explosion, the suicide bomber telephoned both Khalid Sheikh Mohammed and one of Slahi's associates in Germany.[9]

But there was a more damning allegation. Slahi was said to have recruited members of al Qaeda's Hamburg cell, including three of the 9/11 suicide pilots: the ringleader, Mohammed Atta, who flew American Airlines Flight 11 into the North Tower; Ziad Jarrah, at the controls of United Airlines Flight 93 when it crashed in Pennsylvania; and Marwan al-Shehhi, who slammed United 175 into the South Tower after seizing the controls from the pilots and, the FBI believed, slashing their throats.

United 175 was Mike Horrocks's plane.

IN EARLY 2002, THE Defense Department set up a detective squad for Guantanamo Bay, assigned to gather evidence for military commissions. Based south of Washington at Fort Belvoir, Virginia, the Criminal Investigation Task Force was where Mark Fallon, the naval investigator whom Couch met on the Aviano case, was now deputy director in charge of investigations. Couch visited for an orientation.

CITF—pronounced *sit-iff*—was housed by an old warehouse, in a nondescript, windowless building surrounded by a chain-link fence. Couch felt as if he was in a spy movie; to enter, he had to place his palm against a touch-sensitive codepad. Rows of cubicles were inside, while the walls were covered with blow-ups of 9/11 scenes and photos of CITF teams in the field. The investigative piece clearly had ramped up far more quickly than the prosecution staff.

Mark Fallon looked like the star of a 1970s television detective show—specifically *Cannon,* the thickly mustached, heavyset private eye played by William Conrad. The son and grandson of cops, Fallon now had a management job but still strapped a gun to his ankle, just in case.

Fallon came from Harrison, New Jersey, a tiny working-class town on the Trans-Hudson subway line from Newark to the World Trade Center. After his 1974 high school graduation, he joined the US Marshals Service in Newark. But guarding courthouses was boring, and after two years he transferred to the naval investigative service. In the early 1990s, an investigation into stolen military surplus helped make Fallon one of NCIS's top counterterrorism specialists. The purchasers were followers of the blind sheikh Omar Abdel Rahman. A Fallon informant infiltrated the terror cell, providing evidence that would help convict the sheikh and other extremists for plotting to blow up the United Nations, the Holland Tunnel, and other New York City landmarks.[10]

More recently, Fallon led the Navy contingent investigating the attack on the USS *Cole* during its October 2000 refueling stop at the Yemeni port of Aden. A pair of suicide bombers had piloted a motorboat alongside the destroyer and, after standing to mock their victims with a smile and a wave, detonated their explosives. They blew a forty-foot hole in the warship's port side, killing seventeen sailors.

Bin Laden was the obvious suspect. Yemeni authorities picked up a couple of al Qaeda associates, but American officials believed they were shielding more senior operatives.[11] When the Bush administration took over in January 2001, however, it dropped the *Cole* case into bureaucratic purgatory, packed away with the rest of the Clinton era's unfinished business. "We really thought that the *Cole* incident was past," said Condoleezza Rice, Bush's national security adviser.[12] After 9/11, Fallon was a natural choice to run the Guantanamo investigations.

The big Jersey cop greeted his old friend Stu with a bear hug. But he seemed slightly evasive in describing the state of affairs. When Couch pressed, Fallon suggested that he visit Guantanamo Bay as soon as possible and see for himself.

■

"All in all, it's been a fabulous year for Laura and me," President Bush told a December 2001 press conference, reflecting on his "first-year accomplishments." But, he said, the fighting in Afghanistan, under way for two months, had produced some unanticipated problems.

"Today, I was briefed that there are hundreds of al Qaeda fighters being held hostage," Bush said, meaning prisoners in US or Northern Alliance custody in Afghanistan. "And by the way, we're in the process of developing a system to deal with each and every fighter, depending upon the nature of the fighter—how to deal with them, legally." Soon, he said, "we'll be able to brief the country as to how we're going to deal with these people."

Military planners briefly considered sending them to Leavenworth, or even reopening Alcatraz, but the administration's lawyers ruled out any location within the United States. If on American soil, they feared, the prisoners might have recourse to American courts.

Some suggested Diego Garcia, a flyspeck island in the Indian Ocean that housed an American base. It was relatively close to Afghanistan, only 2,900 miles away. But the lawyers nixed the idea, pointing out that because the atoll was a British territory, activities there could be vulnerable to political currents or legal actions in the United Kingdom. The Pentagon turned its attention to sparsely inhabited US possessions in the far Pacific, like Midway, Tinian, and Wake Islands, about twice the distance from Afghanistan.[13]

"Jim, why on earth would you put something like that way out there?" General Tom Romig asked Haynes at one of their early meetings. Conducting trials there would be difficult, requiring constant travel from Washington to the middle of nowhere. Romig had another idea, eight thousand miles from Afghanistan.

"Have you thought about Guantanamo?" Romig said. "There's a Navy base there. We housed the Haitian refugees there."[14]

"We did?" said Haynes.

GUANTANAMO BAY CAME INTO America's possession as the spoils of another war, now barely remembered, which originated in a shocking blow to the national psyche. On February 15, 1898, the USS *Maine* exploded in Havana harbor, killing 260 sailors. By April, the United States was at war with Spain, Cuba's colonial ruler.

The young and vigorous United States quickly defeated the wheezing remnants of the Spanish Empire. A December 1898 treaty ceded Guam, the Philippines, and Puerto Rico to the United States. Cuba was to become independent, but American forces remained in control, effectively rendering the island a tributary state. Washington directed Havana's external relations, reserved the power to intervene militarily "for the preservation of Cuban independence," and obtained authority to build "coaling and naval stations" at the place US Marines first landed in 1898: Guantanamo Bay.

The forty-five-square-mile territory, at the island's southeastern corner, would rent for two thousand dollars annually, paid to the new Cuban government "in gold coin of the United States."[15] American forces occasionally left the base to put down local rebellions, but their main impact was economic—particularly during Prohibition, when thirsty sailors could dash across the line into a country flowing with lawful beer and rum.

In 1934, President Franklin Roosevelt agreed to end most of the formal powers the United States claimed over Cuba. But Washington insisted on keeping the Guantanamo base. A revised treaty required both countries to agree before the lease could be terminated, guaranteeing that the Americans could remain as long as they wished.

A test came during the Cuban Missile Crisis, when Nikita Khrushchev told President Kennedy to "liquidate" the outpost. "The base in Guantanamo is only a burden for your budget, and what is the main thing, it is a great burden of a moral nature for political leaders in the USA," the Soviet leader said.[16] The idea appealed to Adlai Stevenson, JFK's ambassador to the United Nations, but "the President sharply rejected the thought of surrendering our base at Guantanamo in the present situation. He felt that such action would convey to the world that we had been frightened into abandoning our position," White House minutes say.

Attorney General Robert Kennedy suggested a different approach: "We should also think of, uh, uh, whether there is some other way we can get involved in this through, uh, Guantanamo Bay, or something, er, or whether there's some ship that, you know, sink the *Maine* again or something," a meeting transcript says. Defense Secretary Robert McNamara liked the idea. He later advised that "a Cuban attack on Guantanamo, even one inspired by us, might create a situation which we could exploit and thus justify courses of action adequate to overthrow Castro," records say.

Ultimately, however, the missile crisis proved irrelevant to the base's future. Instead, the turning point was a fishing dispute.[17] After the United States arrested thirty-six Cuban fishermen off Florida, Castro retaliated by cutting off Guantanamo's water supply, sparking what an official Navy history called the "Water Crisis" of 1964. President Lyndon Johnson decided to double down on Guantanamo, shipping a desalination plant to the base and launching a building program that covered the installation with low-slung bungalows, stucco apartment blocks, and a drive-in movie theater. Bob Hope filmed his 1971 Christmas special at Guantanamo, with special guests Jim Nabors and Charley Pride.[18]

Still, Guantanamo—or *Gitmo,* as sailors pronounced the military abbreviation GTMO—remained a backwater. *A Few Good Men,* the Aaron Sorkin play titled after a Marine Corps recruiting slogan, gave the base a toehold into popular culture. In it, a Marine colonel accused of covering up a homicide on Guantanamo insists that actions on the island are beyond the law.

"I have neither the time nor the inclination to explain myself to a man who rises and sleeps under the blanket of the very freedom that

I provide, and then questions the manner in which I provide it," sneers the colonel, played by Jack Nicholson in the 1992 film version. "I want the truth," demands Navy prosecutor Tom Cruise. Nicholson's reply: *"You can't handle the truth."*

After the Soviet Union's fall, however, military planners began to view Guantanamo as a costly relic. Cut off from the rest of the island by seventeen miles of fence line and a Cuban minefield, everything had to be made on base or brought by air or sea. Even moving within the base was difficult, as it comprised two separate shores, Leeward and Windward, split by the bay itself. Ferries continuously made the twenty-minute voyage between Windward, the larger side housing most of the base's population and activities, and Leeward, where the main airstrip was.

Unrest in the Caribbean gave the base a new mission—and focused the White House on Guantanamo's peculiar legal status. After a 1991 coup, tens of thousands of Haitians embarked on rickety rafts toward America. To stop them from making landfall in Florida and claiming rights under the international Refugee Convention, President George H. W. Bush directed the Coast Guard to intercept the boat people and hold them at Guantanamo. Later, waves of Cuban boat people were held there as well.

By September 1994, the base had become became a prison for tens of thousands of the migrants. They were held behind wire fences in tent cities designated by the radio alphabet, with names like Camp Juliet, Camp Lima, and, for troublemakers, Camp X-Ray.

Restive and frustrated, the migrants occasionally rioted, at one point prompting soldiers to ring the base McDonald's with concertina wire. It could take days to push the migrants back into their pens, diminishing what little sympathy the soldiers held for them. After one migrant uprising, a lieutenant colonel told his troops, "This is your chance for payback." At least two units were implicated in detainee abuse.[19]

Presaging post-9/11 practices at Guantanamo, some of the migrants were humiliated and beaten, or hooded, handcuffed, and left to swelter in the tropical sun, or held for extended periods in painful positions. In one detention unit, "migrants were placed under overturned wooden crates, pepper spray was sprayed inside the crate and then the crates were beat by two soldiers with poly-carbonate riot batons," said military police Sergeant John Bennett, who investigated abuse complaints in the 1990s.

"I thought that if this is my job, I don't have the mean streak in me to be in the Army," a female MP told Bennett, Army records say. In 1997, the Army inspector general concluded that "incidents of abuse did occur" and wrote that unspecified "corrective action was taken by the chain of command."

Activist lawyers challenged the migrants' detention, arguing that the Refugee Convention required the United States to review the Haitians' claims before deporting them. After lower courts split on the issue, a Yale law professor, Harold Hongju Koh, brought the migrants' case to the Supreme Court.

The justices rejected it by an eight-to-one vote. The migrants could claim treaty protections only after reaching American soil, the Court said, implying that Guantanamo lay outside the United States.

The case made an impression on Koh's student assistant at the time—John Yoo. It was on his mind in December 2001, when stressing Guantanamo's advantages as a laboratory for imprisoning, interrogating, and punishing enemy prisoners beyond the law's reach.

These men, captured after 9/11, hated and feared by the American public, had no political constituency to protect them. At Guantanamo, they would provide an ideal vehicle for establishing a new model of executive primacy. The only threat to administration plans came from the federal judiciary, where judges held life tenure to insulate them from political pressures in applying the law. For that reason, it was essential to prevent the courts from examining practices that would deviate from established legal standards for prisoner treatment.

Yoo explained it to Jim Haynes in a December 28, 2001, OLC memorandum.[20] Judicial review, he wrote, could "interfere with the operation of the system that has been developed to address the detainment and trial of enemy aliens." A judge might be tempted to examine the relevance of the Geneva Conventions and "whether and what international law norms may or may not apply to the conduct of the war in Afghanistan."

The perpetual lease between Washington and Havana gave the United States "complete jurisdiction and control" over Guantanamo Bay while reserving an undefined "ultimate sovereignty" to Cuba. This strange status left Guantanamo outside the orbit of both American and Cuban courts, Yoo reasoned. It was the "legal equivalent of outer space."[21]

Because it simultaneously fell under US control but outside American sovereignty, a Guantanamo prison would be perfect. "The great weight of legal authority indicates" that aliens held at Guantanamo would have no recourse, Yoo asserted.

The proposal went to President Bush himself. He didn't need to read a complicated legal opinion.[22] Neither did Donald Rumsfeld. At a press conference the day before the OLC memorandum was completed, he announced Guantanamo's selection.

"Mr. Secretary, we've gotten into trouble every time we've tried to use Guantanamo Bay in the past to hold people," a reporter asked. "Why use it? Why is it the best place?"

Rumsfeld gave no hint of the legal theorizing that was the true reason for selecting the facility.

"I would characterize Guantanamo Bay, Cuba, as the least worst place we could have selected," he said. "It has disadvantages, as you suggest. Its disadvantages, however, seem to be modest relative to the alternatives."

■

After Rumsfeld announced Guantanamo's new mission, personnel at the base beamed. "It's a little American town here," said Captain Robert Buehn, the Navy base commander.[23] "All of a sudden, we stepped on the world stage and can do something, and they are proud of that."

With the end of migrant operations in the 1990s, Guantanamo Bay had again receded to near oblivion. Facilities were mothballed, the mangroves grew, and the native fauna—tame iguanas that ate from the hand and oversized rodents the sailors called banana rats— roamed freely. About seven hundred uniformed personnel remained at the base, primarily to service counternarcotics missions the military was running in South America.[24] Another two thousand or so civilians worked there, too, mostly contractors. The military farmed out menial tasks, such as running the mess hall or cleaning the barracks, to companies that shipped in Filipinos and Jamaicans who worked long-term contracts for subminimum wages. The Fair Labor Standards Act, which since 1938 had guaranteed Americans a minimum wage, didn't apply at Guantanamo, either.

DIRECTED IN JANUARY 2002 to establish a new detention operation, commanders reactivated the task force that had run the migrant camps. With less than two weeks to prepare for the first detainees, the task force set up a rudimentary outdoor prison where troublemaking boat people once were held.[25] The location's name now took on an additional resonance, suggesting that the prisoners would keep no secrets: Camp X-Ray.

Certainly, they would have no walls to hide behind. As it had in the 1990s, X-Ray consisted of roofed wire cages, outfitted with a mat and a pail, exposed to the heat and, when the wind blew, the rain.[26] By January 9, 2002, a hundred outdoor cells were ready. A permanent facility was planned for a thousand or more.

"We have no intention of making it comfortable," the prison commander told reporters brought to tour the facility.[27] "It will be humane."

The first detainees arrived from Kandahar on Friday, January 11, 2002. Soon, Air Force cargo planes were in heavy rotation. The prisoners, shackled hand and foot, sedated and chained to their seats for the twenty-hour journey, were greeted with a display of force. Military teams surrounded the C-141 Starlifter when it landed at the Leeward airstrip. Behind them, four Humvees with mounted machine guns or rocket launchers and a forty-man riot squad were ready to move if the prisoners made any trouble. The unloading process followed the pecking order. Cargo came down the ramp first, then the plane's toilets were emptied, and then, finally, the prisoners were taken, one by one, into the thick Cuban air.

In bright orange jumpsuits that clashed with the island's Caribbean pastels, they looked shriveled and weak next to the burly American guards who gripped each arm. Clad in blacked-out goggles, they stumbled blindly. These tiny orange men were patted down, checked off a list, and placed on school buses with covered windows. The buses made a convoy to the Leeward dock and onto the ferry that crossed the bay. Arriving on the Windward side, the buses rumbled off the ferry, past the base's day care center, yacht basin, and pottery studio. Once through the gates of Camp X-Ray, the in-processing began.

Most prisoners arrived dehydrated. Some threw up. Others wept.

"They realized: This is the end of the line, this is it. No more airplane rides," said one guard, Private First Class Courtney Sletten.[28] "One guy was like, 'I'm not going to see my dad again,'" she said. "Well, think of all the others from the World Trade Center who aren't going to see their families, either." The prisoners "are just another number to us." Her Arabic consisted of four words: *yes, no, walk,* and *shut up.*

The military barred journalists from shooting photos, deciding instead that it alone would document the arrivals and decide which photos to release. In one picture the Pentagon posted on its website, the shackled, blind-goggled prisoners knelt in a double row within a fenced enclosure, a kennel for terrorists.

The American news media largely ignored the photo. But in London, tabloid editors immediately saw the shot's power. "TOR-TURED" read the *Mail on Sunday*'s Page One headline, above the

Defense Department photograph. "SHACKLED like wild animals, deprived of sight, sound, smell and touch, the Al Qaeda terrorists in our exclusive front page picture kneel before their American guards in the Guantanamo Bay prison camp," the story began.[29] "HANDCUFFED and blindfolded, they can see, hear, smell and feel nothing," declared the competing *Sunday Mirror*. "They cower on their knees as American guards stand over them in a scene which could have come straight from a horror movie. But this is not fantasy. These are captured Taliban and al Qaeda suspects, seen in the first pictures to show the use of sensory deprivation at Camp X-Ray in the US base at Guantanamo Bay, Cuba."[30] Combined with news that three British nationals were among approximately 150 men held at the prison, a rift appeared between Britain and the United States, the first since 9/11. In one of their frequent telephone conversations, Prime Minister Tony Blair urged President Bush to tread carefully around British and European sentiments on human rights.[31]

Donald Rumsfeld mocked concerns over the prisoners' treatment. "Henny Penny, the sky's falling, isn't this terrible what's happening?" he said.

Visiting Guantanamo soon after Camp X-Ray opened, Rumsfeld said he came simply to thank the soldiers who had to put up with the prisoners. "These are terrific young men and women doing an excellent job and I want to tell them that," he said.

It was a nostalgic day for Rumsfeld. On the ferry crossing to Windward, escorted by security boats mounted with .50-caliber machine guns, he reminisced about visiting Guantanamo when in the Princeton ROTC and later as a naval aviator. "That was back before they had air conditioning. It didn't even exist in those early days," he said. If he could handle the humidity, so could the terrorists.

Rumsfeld had brought four senators to tour Camp X-Ray with him. They echoed his satisfaction. Senator Dianne Feinstein, who had served on the California women's parole board in the early 1960s, marveled at the facility. "I'd rather be here in an eight-by-eight with the breeze than locked down in Folsom Prison," she said.[32]

NOT EVERYONE WAS SO enthusiastic about the emerging prisoner regime. Several European allies had expressed concern regarding Bush's military commissions order. Spain, which arrested eight suspected al Qaeda militants after 9/11, said it would not extradite them for "irregular" trials before US military commissions.[33]

Within the United States, activist groups that never trusted Bush immediately challenged the Guantanamo detentions. Days after the offshore prison opened, a group calling itself the Coalition of Clergy, Lawyers, and Professors went to federal district court in Los Angeles claiming the detentions were unlawful.[34] The next month, the Center for Constitutional Rights, Michael Ratner's group, filed a habeas corpus suit for one of the few Guantanamo detainees to be publicly identified, David Hicks, a young Australian captured among Taliban fighters in Afghanistan.

Initially, such challenges fared poorly in federal court. In Los Angeles, the judge dismissed the case, agreeing with the Bush administration that the Haitian migrant rulings foreclosed judicial relief. In Washington, DC, the judge hearing the Hicks case held that a 1950 Supreme Court decision, *Johnson v. Eisentrager*, required the same result.[35]

In *Eisentrager*, twenty-one German prisoners filed habeas claims after a US military commission in China convicted them of being, in effect, unlawful combatants; they were military advisers who continued to assist the Japanese army after Berlin surrendered in May 1945 but before Tokyo followed suit in August. By a six-to-three vote, the Court held that the Germans, then serving their sentences in a US military prison in occupied Germany, could not bring habeas corpus claims in federal court.

Slowly, however, critical views of the 9/11 prisoner policies began to gain traction. In academic journals and opinion pages, legal scholars disputed the legitimacy both of indefinite, unreviewable military detention and of military commissions as envisioned by the Bush administration—that is, ones in which defendants had no rights and judges answered to the president alone. International law authorities uniformly ruled against the American position, starting in March 2002, when the Inter-American Commission on Human Rights, an advisory panel of the Organization of American States, held that the Geneva Conventions covered the prisoners.[36]

Newspapers, meanwhile, began to report strikingly harsh American interrogation practices. Interrogation students at the Army intelligence school were being trained to deceive, humiliate, and inflict pain on prisoners, according to an April 2002 *Wall Street Journal* report.[37] In December 2002, the *Washington Post* detailed a global interrogation system that relied on beatings, sleep deprivation, and the transfer of prisoners to countries notorious for using torture.[38] After Khalid Sheikh Mohammed's March 2003 capture, US officials told the *Journal* that the suspected 9/11 planner would face an extensive ordeal of physical and psychological torment, including threats to harm his children and, it later was disclosed, 183 inflictions of waterboarding.[39]

The Bush administration's public statements, however, rejected criticism of its legal positions or allegations of prisoner abuse. Officials insisted that treatment of prisoners was "humane" and "consistent with" Geneva provisions. In June 2003, President Bush underscored those claims with a statement marking the United Nations International Day in Support of Victims of Torture.

"We are committed to building a world where human rights are respected and protected by the rule of law," the president said. "The Convention Against Torture and Other Cruel, Inhuman or Degrading Treatment, ratified by the United States and more than 130 other countries since 1984, forbids governments from deliberately inflicting severe physical or mental pain or suffering on those within their custody or control."

Bush condemned foreign countries for such practices. "Burma, Cuba, North Korea, Iran and Zimbabwe have long sought to shield their abuses from the eyes of the world by staging elaborate deceptions and denying access to international human rights monitors. Until recently, Saddam Hussein used similar means to hide the crimes of his regime," Bush said.

"We are leading this fight by example," he continued. "I call on all governments to join with the United States and the community of law-abiding nations in prohibiting, investigating and prosecuting all acts of torture and in undertaking to prevent other cruel and unusual punishment."[40]

More directly relevant to commissions, Jim Haynes, responding to a query from Senator Patrick Leahy, sent a letter stating that the United States conducted interrogations "consistent with" the Convention Against Torture and its implementing legislation. The Bush administration "does not permit, tolerate or condone any such torture by its employees under any circumstances," he wrote, and was determined "to prevent other acts of cruel, inhuman or degrading treatment or punishment which do not amount to torture." Any country receiving a prisoner from the United States had to promise "that it will not torture the individual," he added.

"In closing, I want to express my appreciation for your thoughtful questions," Haynes wrote. "We are committed to protecting the people of this Nation as well as to upholding its fundamental values under the law."

Survival, Evasion, Resistance, and Escape

WHEN STU COUCH VISITED Guantanamo in October 2003, the prison held about six hundred prisoners. The makeshift jail at Camp X-Ray had been replaced by a permanent facility called Camp Delta.

Couch trusted President Bush and the chain of command. To him, criticism from liberal activists, European governments, and the news media was suspect. While abuse allegations had dogged the Guantanamo prison, according to American officials al Qaeda trained its operatives to claim they were tortured, so the stories filtering out were no surprise.[1] Prisoner mistreatment was a possibility in any jail, but Couch assumed that any abuse was an aberration. Military interrogations, particularly after battlefield captures, could be tough—yet still, under the standards of military law, appropriate, humane, and lawful.

Still, Couch was concerned because nearly all prosecution evidence came from detainee statements—or, rather, summaries of detainee statements, paraphrased by an interrogator and edited by higher-ups. These were hearsay, and inadmissible in federal court or court-martial, where the Sixth Amendment provided defendants the right to confront prosecution witnesses.

But since the reports were "probative"—the only evidentiary requirement of Bush's military order—they were not automatically barred from commissions. For that matter, the rules did not prohibit use of statements taken through coercion or even torture.

Yet defense attorneys were certain to challenge interrogation summaries as unreliable and unfair. To respond, Couch felt he needed to know everything about a criminal investigation, including the conditions of confinement and how statements were taken. He wanted to see a detainee interrogation for himself.

Arriving at Guantanamo Couch learned that one of his target defendants, Ahmed al-Darbi, already was on the interrogation schedule. An Air Force reservist serving as base escort brought Couch to the interrogation control room to watch the Darbi session by video feed.

Awaiting Darbi's arrival, Couch was startled by an unlikely sound: grating, blasting, heavy-metal music. He went to look into the commotion. Perhaps some off-duty guards were fooling around with a boom box, he thought.

With his escort trailing behind, Couch followed the music toward an open door, where a strobe light's flash was spilling into the corridor.

Couch turned into the doorway. He froze.

On the floor, amid the flashing lights and the deafening metal sounds, was a shackled detainee, kneeling, mumbling, rocking back and forth. Praying. This man was in agony.

Let the bodies hit the . . . floor! the song roared. *Beaten, why for (why for).*[2]

Couch suddenly noticed that two men in polo shirts—apparently civilians, judging by their hair length—also were in the room. They planted themselves in the doorway, blocking his view.

"Can I help you?" one of the men shouted over the music. They looked to be in their late twenties or early thirties. Neither seemed particularly fit, nor were they groomed like military men. One wore hair mousse. The other, the fatter one, had a chin-beard.

"I'm Lieutenant Colonel Couch, and I'm trying to have an interview over here," Couch said. "You guys need to turn that down."

The men shut the door.

Walking back to the control room, Couch turned to his escort. "Did you see that?" he asked.

"Well, yeah," the escort said, noncommittally.

"Do you have a problem with that?"

"Uh, well, er—no. It's approved."

Couch flashed on the worst week of his life.

IN 1990, AFTER QUALIFYING as a Marine pilot, Couch received orders to report to the Naval Air Station at Brunswick, Maine. The installation ran a program called Survival, Evasion, Resistance, and Escape. The military pronounced it *seer*.

SERE school was designed for aviators, commandos, and others at risk of capture by enemy forces. "To Return with Honor" was the SERE motto, which meant resisting enemy efforts to extract intelligence or manufacture propaganda. To return with honor did not necessarily mean returning alive.

Couch had a general idea of what to expect: It would be tough, unpleasant, and effective. But prior graduates never discussed the specifics.

In Brunswick, Couch's class included students from the different uniformed services. The scenario involved being downed behind enemy lines, with rural Maine substituting for the countryside of Eastern Europe during a war with the Warsaw Pact. SERE school staff members portrayed enemy forces, even speaking with Russian accents.

Phase one involved avoiding capture. Make it to the safe house, and there would be a decent meal waiting. Fall into enemy hands, and what—or whether—the student ate depended on his captors.

For three and a half days, Couch and his classmates bivouacked through the backwoods, hunting small animals, drinking stream water they purified with iodine tablets, trying to angle their way past the enemy. Inevitably, like all the students, Couch was captured.

The scenario now changed significantly for the worse. Couch

was stripped and shackled. He was isolated in a cell, slapped and shoved, humiliated.

"Are you married?" an interrogator demanded.

"No," Couch said.

The interrogator smacked him. "Liar!" he yelled, pointing to Couch's left ring finger. Couch had removed his wedding band before the week's exercise began, but a callous and narrow tan line remained visible.

"You know what Kim's doing right now?" the interrogator asked, surprising Couch with his wife's name. "She's being fucked by a nigger."

The abuse, psychological and physical, was continuous. An interrogator lit up a pipe and blew smoke in Couch's face for what seemed like an hour, forcing Couch to repeat his name and his "war criminal number" as the smoke filled his lungs. Hacking, choking, suffocating, in the windowless cell, Couch lost track of time. In one cell, a strobe light flashed. In another, an endless tape loop blasted sounds of a rape scene, a child screaming for her mother, the roar of chainsaws. At other times, rock music blared, repeating over and over, blasting so loud he feared his eardrums would blow out. The song reinforced the Cold War scenario.

"Back in the U.S.S.R.," the Beatles sang.

ONE BY ONE, THE STUDENTS began to break, giving up information they were supposed to withhold from the enemy. Finally, Couch was roused from his cell and pushed down a hall to an assembly with the other captives. Shoved to the floor, they were forced to hold rigid positions. With a Bible in his hand, the commandant mocked America and ridiculed Jesus Christ, the god who couldn't help them now. The commandant lectured the captives, quoting from the Book of Acts to suggest that like America's enemies, Jesus and his disciples were socialists. After a five-minute tirade, he screamed, "This book is just a bunch of shit," ripped it in half, and threw it through the doorway, into a mud puddle outside.

Instinctively, one of the students let out a yell and leapt through the doorway to rescue the Bible. Guards rushed over, grabbed the student, and smacked him again and again. Couch felt sick.

The students then were ordered to the prison yard and put to menial tasks, hauling rocks and raking dirt. After an hour of forced labor, they were ordered to stand in formation.

"What happens to you next, you will never forget for the rest of your life!" the Russian-accented commandant said, with a sadistic chuckle.

Couch's heart raced.

"About face!" came the order.

The students spun around.

From a guard tower, a giant American flag unfurled. "The Star-Spangled Banner" boomed over loudspeakers.

With no order required, the students all sang the anthem. Tears streamed down their cheeks.

The commander congratulated the students for completing SERE training. Later, they were warned that everything they had experienced was a national security secret. Any disclosures would be punished by court-martial.

The SERE class went to downtown Brunswick for a steak dinner.

Years later, a Senate investigation would reveal that in December 2002, instructors from the Brunswick SERE school came to Guantanamo to train interrogators in breaking real prisoners the way they taught American service members to resist torture at enemy hands.[3]

AT GUANTANAMO, COUCH shook off his flashback and forced himself back into the present. In the control room, on the monitor, there was Darbi, the al Qaeda maritime operations planner he intended to prosecute, politely answering questions posed by a firm but courteous interrogator. Couch wondered if he was watching a real interrogation—or a performance.

On the return flight from Guantanamo, he decided he needed guidance. When the plane stopped in Raleigh, he telephoned Colonel Kevin Winters, the Marine judge advocate he long admired.

"Sir, I need to see you when I get back, talk about this commissions thing, if that's all right," Couch said.

"Whatever you need," Winters replied.

Days later, visiting Winters at the Washington Navy Yard, Couch unloaded his concerns. He wasn't sure exactly what was going on at Guantanamo. Winters, typically, listened more than he spoke. But when Couch said he suspected SERE tactics were being used "offensively" on Guantanamo detainees and that there could be big problems down the line for military commissions, Winters didn't contradict him. Couch took that as a signal.

"He was looking for a sanity check, asking: 'Am I crazy, or does this smell bad to you?'" Winters later recalled. But he had no specific advice for Couch. Instead, he ended with an elliptical suggestion.

"Do the right thing," Winters said.

BROWSING MAGAZINE RACKS at a bookstore, Couch stared at the *Atlantic Monthly*. The cover showed the back of a naked prisoner, head bowed, hands bound behind him. "The Dark Art of Interrogation," it read.

The sixteen-thousand-word story focused on the interrogation of Khalid Sheikh Mohammed, the al Qaeda commander captured the past spring in Pakistan. Writer Mark Bowden described KSM's experience at a secret prison the CIA called Hotel California.[4]

"Place and time, the anchors of sanity, were about to come unmoored," Bowden wrote. "He might as well have been entering a new dimension, a strange new world where his every word, move, and sensation would be monitored and measured; where things might be as they seemed but might not; where there would be no such thing as day or night, or normal patterns of eating and drinking, wakefulness and sleep; where hot and cold, wet and dry, clean and dirty, truth and lies, would all be tangled and distorted."

As Bowden relayed details of KSM's interrogation—"locked naked in a cell with no trace of daylight," "filled day and night with harsh light and noise," "kept awake cold and probably wet"—Couch recognized the SERE imprint.

The article said intelligence services had turned to "torture lite," tactics that were "excruciating for the victim" but left "no permanent marks" or "lasting physical harm."

"The history of interrogation by U.S. armed forces and spy agencies is one of giving lip service to international agreements while vigorously using coercion whenever circumstances seem to warrant it," Bowden wrote. Then he reached a perhaps startling conclusion:

"The Bush Administration has adopted exactly the right posture on the matter. Candor and consistency are not always public virtues. Torture is a crime against humanity, but coercion is an issue that is rightly handled with a wink, or even a touch of hypocrisy; it should be banned but also quietly practiced. Those who protest coercive methods will exaggerate their horrors, which is good: it generates a useful climate of fear. It is wise of the President to reiterate U.S. support for international agreements banning torture, and it is wise for American interrogators to employ whatever coercive methods work. It is also smart not to discuss the matter with anyone."

■

Army interrogators learned their craft at Fort Huachuca, the Arizona desert outpost that once housed the cavalry units chasing Geronimo and Pancho Villa.[5] Huachuca instructors taught thirty different "approaches" from Army Field Manual 34-52, Intelligence Interrogation. The "incentive" approach could involve offering a pack of cigarettes or improved conditions for a wounded buddy. Interrogators could say anything that might induce cooperation, and they didn't have to keep their promises, instructors taught. "Fear-down" was indicated for frightened prisoners, calming them, reassuring them, aiming to open them up by talking about their families and personal interests before slipping in the real questions. The approach "may backfire if allowed to go too far," the manual cautioned, by raising a prisoner's confidence enough to withhold critical information. "Fear-up," in contrast, involved "heavy-handed, table-banging violence," the manual explained. "The interrogator behaves in a heavy, overpowering manner with a loud and threatening voice" and may "throw objects across the room to heighten the source's implanted feelings of fear." The interrogator's last trick was "Pride and Ego Down," belittling the prisoner as worthless. It aimed to provoke a defensive reaction, getting the prisoner to prove his value by showing that he knows important information. Soldiers were taught to target the source's "loyalty, intelligence, abilities, leadership qualities, slovenly appearance or any other perceived weakness." But this was the end of the line. A prisoner who persevered against Pride and Ego Down likely had been hardened against cooperation.

The course included a day on the Geneva Conventions, but instructors emphasized how vague the treaty's terms were. In practice, they explained, Geneva's meaning varied according to the views of whatever JAG happened to be on duty when a question arose. "What we can get away with depends on them," Staff Sergeant John Giersdorf, a top Huachuca instructor, told a class preparing to join the war on terrorism in early 2002. "One JAG officer might say it's a go, another might say it's torture."

Geneva left interrogators plenty of options. "You can put a source in any position you want. You can chain his legs to the chair, you can handcuff his hands behind him," make him stand at attention, or have military police throw him to the ground, Giersdorf said. If a prisoner "says it hurts, is it torture?" he asked his class.

"Yes," students replied.[6]

"No, it's not," Giersdorf said. Several NATO armies used interrogation methods even harsher than America's, including forcing prisoners to hold painful "stress positions" until they talk. While this was not on Huachuca's official curriculum, "if you work with the Brits or the Dutch or the Germans, they can show you all about it," he said.

"While you're talking to a source, can you load a gun or sharpen a knife?" one student asked.

"Don't get caught doing it," Giersdorf said. "I mean," he said, grinning slightly as he corrected himself, "don't do it."

The class laughed.

Jim Haynes never visited Fort Huachuca during his years as an Army officer or Pentagon official. But even without reviewing the Army's interrogation training or speaking to its practitioners, he was certain that standard military methods were too soft for the post-9/11 world.

"There was widespread frustration that the existing doctrine was inadequate," Haynes said.[7] "As the chief legal officer of the Department of Defense, I was interested in that and concerned about it." He dispatched Richard Shiffrin, the deputy general counsel for intelligence, to find something better.

Shiffrin contacted the Defense Department's Joint Personnel Recovery Agency, which had been established in the early 1950s to train pilots and others at risk of capture to resist interrogation. The research the agency provided did not seem up to date. "It was real *Manchurian Candidate* stuff," he said, like studies of North Korean brainwashing techniques.[8] Pressing for more recent innovations, Shiffrin received the SERE protocols.

While the program was intended to teach resistance to brutal and abusive interrogation methods, it seemed "there might be some possibility of reverse engineering an effective SERE technique," Shiffrin said.[9] It was "just logical."

The agency's chief of staff, Lieutenant Colonel Dan Baumgartner, sent Shiffrin materials detailing the interrogation-resistance regimen. By "reversing this, an exploiter/interrogator has a plan for exploitation of [an] enemy detainee," Baumgartner wrote. Another memo, "Physical Pressures Used in Resistance Training and Against American Prisoners and Detainees," laid out twenty-five techniques. "Facial slap" meant striking the prisoner "midway between the chin and bottom of the corresponding ear lobe. The arm swing follows an arc no greater than approximately 18 inches." Proper application instilled "fear and despair." In the "block hold," the prisoner had to extend his arms out, palms up. The interrogator placed a ten- to fifteen-pound block on them. "The subject is required to keep their arms straight, told not to drop the block at risk of additional punishment," the directions read. "Stress position" instructions encouraged the interrogator to stretch his imagination. "There are any number of uncomfortable physical positions that can be used and considered in this category."

"Smoke" involved blowing "an extraordinary amount of thick, sickening smoke" from a pipe bowl into a prisoner's face, while "cramped confinement" meant forcing a prisoner "into a small box in a kneeling position with legs crossed at the ankle and having him [lean] forward to allow the door to be closed without exerting pressure on the back." Additional "tactics to induce control, dependence, compliance, and cooperation" included "isolation/solitary confinement," "degradation," "sensory deprivation," "manipulation of diet," "disruption of sleep and biorhythms," and "sensory overload."

Then there was the "waterboard." The "subject is interrogated while strapped to a wooden board, approximately $4' \times 7'$. Often the subject's feet are elevated after being strapped down and having their torso stripped. Up to 1.5 gallons of water is slowly poured directly onto the subject's face from a height of 12–24 inches. In some cases, a wet cloth is placed over the subject's face," the instructions read.

Baumgartner told the unit's psychology chief, Major Jerald Ogrisseg, that "some people were asking from above about the utility" of waterboarding enemy prisoners.

"Wouldn't that be illegal?" Ogrisseg said.[10]

Actually, the answer now was no.[11] A secret OLC opinion written by John Yoo determined that federal law making torture a crime did not apply to suspected terrorists.

■

At CITF, Mark Fallon had a different opinion regarding torture. Now that Couch had seen the way things worked at Guantanamo, Fallon let on that, for more than a year, he had been trying to get military intelligence to stop its brutal methods.

Soon after arriving at Guantanamo, CITF agents began reporting conflicts with military intelligence officers over interrogation techniques the investigators considered ineffective and illegal—and thus potentially fatal to the prosecution cases they were trying to build, Fallon said. The military, its inexperienced interrogators under extraordinary pressure to produce intelligence, seemed ready to push prisoners to the edge of death, Fallon's agents reported. Any doubts Fallon had vanished after he obtained the minutes of a meeting at Guantanamo in which a CIA lawyer named Jonathan Fredman briefed military intelligence officers on interrogation methods. Because the definition of torture was "subject to perception," Fredman said, there was only one sure way to know the limit: "If the detainee dies, you're doing it wrong."[12]

Fallon sent an urgent warning to the CITF legal adviser. Remarks by Fredman and the military intelligence officers "seem to stretch beyond the bounds of legal propriety," he wrote. "Talk of 'wet towel treatment' which results in the lymphatic gland reacting as if you are suffocating"—Fredman had discussed waterboarding—"would, in my opinion, shock the conscience of any legal body looking at using the results of the interrogations or possibly even the interrogators."

Shock the conscience wasn't Fallon's phrase—it was Justice Felix Frankfurter's. During a 1949 narcotics raid, a suspect swallowed two morphine capsules before Los Angeles County sheriff's deputies could seize them. The deputies handcuffed the suspect and brought him to a hospital, where a doctor forcibly pumped his stomach until he vomited up the capsules, which then were used as evidence to convict him. The Supreme Court unanimously invalidated the suspect's conviction. Frankfurter's majority opinion held that such "brutal conduct" violated the Fourteenth Amendment. Permitting the state to base a conviction on it "would be to afford brutality the cloak of law."[13] The ruling, which barred prosecutors from introducing evidence obtained by means that "shocks the conscience," remained the legal standard.

Fallon brought his concerns to Bill Lietzau, before he left military commissions, and Whit Cobb, the deputy general counsel. They seemed sympathetic, yet in the months since nothing had changed.

In this environment, Fallon realized, each man would have to draw the lines for himself. Fallon said he had already drawn his.

"You have no obligation to follow an illegal order," he told Couch. "I would be a greeter at Wal-Mart before I'd do that."

That conversation with Fallon was still resonating through Couch's mind when he met with his CITF investigator. The top priority was Slahi—the detainee, Couch concluded, with "the most blood on his hands."

Born around 1970, Slahi, a military interrogator later said, was "bright, capable, likable." Small, fair-skinned, and beardless, he could also come across as sly and, the interrogator said, "maybe a little effeminate." Slahi knew Arabic, French, and German when he arrived at Guantanamo and picked up casual English by his second year at the prison.

This sophistication was remarkable, given that Slahi came from simple circumstances in Mauritania, a poor and remote land at the western edge of the Sahara Desert. He was the eighth of a camel herder's thirteen children, twenty years behind his eldest sibling, twelve years older than his youngest. After his father died, Slahi's mother kept the family together. Mohamedou revered her.

In 1988, Slahi won a scholarship to study in Germany. He was the first in his family to attend university—or fly on an airplane.[14] He studied computers, electrical engineering, and microelectronics.

"He was supposed to save us financially," his younger brother Jahdih later said.[15] On a visit home, Slahi brought toys, cameras, and soccer balls.

But Slahi spent much of 1990 through 1992 in Afghanistan, one of many Arabs helping fight the Communist regime in Kabul. He trained at the al Farouk camp, took the alias Abu Masab, and pledged allegiance to Osama bin Laden.[16]

After the Communists fell, Slahi returned to Germany, where over the next six years he ran low-profile businesses that US intelligence later suspected were al Qaeda fronts to launder money and recruit fighters. After making the hajj, the pilgrimage to Mecca required of Muslims, Slahi moved to Canada and became a prayer leader at Ahmed Ressam's mosque in Montreal.

Slahi's arrival "signified the beginning of something," said Richard Clarke, then the White House counterterrorism chief.[17] Reading through the file, however, Couch realized that despite suspicious coincidences and obvious inferences, there was no solid evidence.

WESTERN INTELLIGENCE AGENCIES had been aware of Slahi before the Millennium Plot and moved against him immediately after Ressam's arrest in December 1999.

Canadian authorities questioned Slahi, sent officers to his mosque, and put a police car on his tail. One night, Slahi later said, he was awoken by agents drilling holes into his third-floor apartment to plant surveillance cameras.[18] He called the local police station, saying his neighbor was spying on him; the police suggested he cover the holes with glue.

"It was very clumsy," Slahi later said, "but they wanted to give the message that 'We are watching you.'" He moved to a room at the mosque, but the surveillance continued.[19]

Tired of constantly having "people right behind me, at the market, watching my butt," Slahi decided to return to Mauritania.[20] He left because of "the heat being placed on him," a spokesman for the Canadian Security Intelligence Service said with satisfaction.[21]

In New York, however, the US attorney's office was incensed that Slahi had been permitted simply to board a plane and disappear.[22] The FBI tracked his itinerary: flying via Brussels to Dakar, Senegal, where his brothers were to pick him up for the 270-mile drive north to Nouakchott, the Mauritanian capital.

At Washington's request, Senegalese police arrested Slahi when he landed.[23] He was questioned about the Millennium Plot and his jihadist past, but denied everything.[24] Four days later, the Senegalese put Slahi on a private plane to Nouakchott, where he was arrested again.

Despite denials from Mauritanian officials, word spread through the dusty capital that a suspect of intense interest to the United States had been seized. An Associated Press correspondent located Slahi's mother, Fatima, in what he described as "a crumbling apartment building in Bouhdida, just outside Nouakchott," where Slahi's once-nomadic family settled after droughts "ravaged the region in the 1970s."[25]

Surrounded in the cramped apartment by more than a dozen female relatives, Fatima insisted that Mohamedou "is not the kind of person who can kill." Her eighth-born child was sensitive and pious; he "cries when a member of the family has a simple injury," she said. The allegations against him were nonsense: "At the end, you will see that it all was a big lie."

An American team came to interrogate Slahi. He continued to deny wrongdoing, and after three weeks the Mauritanians released him. "The Americans keep saying you are a link," Slahi later said Mauritanian officials told him.[26] "But they didn't give us any proof, so what should we do?"

Once free, Slahi complained to reporters about his treatment.

"I have no links with the organization of bin Laden and defy anyone to prove the contrary," he declared.[27] He said he had returned home for a visit because his mother was ill.

Slahi's brother, Hamoud, said terrorism allegations against Mohamedou were preposterous, a "grand campaign of falsehood orchestrated by the West without foundation."[28]

Slahi then returned to Germany, only to be arrested again. The charge: welfare fraud. Slahi had been collecting benefits even though he had thirty-five thousand dollars in cash.[29] German counterterrorism agents used this pretextual arrest to solicit Slahi's cooperation.

"I said, 'Man, I don't know anything,'" Slahi recalled.[30] "If I am going to be roasted, then I am going to be roasted in my own freaking country."

He returned to Nouakchott, where, at American insistence, local officials confiscated his passport. Stuck in Mauritania, he launched several business ventures, including an Internet café and a computer wiring service. His clients included the presidential palace.[31]

Investigators later suspected that websites Slahi maintained for his businesses were al Qaeda portals.[32] The sites included secret back pages where users with passcodes could share information.

AFTER 9/11, AMERICAN AGENTS went back to question Slahi in Nouakchott.[33] One struck him with a plastic water bottle and threatened torture, Slahi said.

"I am going to bring in some black motherfuckers," he said the interrogator warned him. Slahi laughed at the thought that this threat would scare him. "Half of my country is black people," he said. Once again, he outlasted his interrogators and was released.

Freedom was brief. The next month, Mauritanian intelligence called Slahi in for more questions.

Why not flee?

"Maybe I'm stupid, I don't know," Slahi later said.[34] "I went to the police and said, 'Why do you want me?' They said, 'Please don't worry, it is just formalities.'"

Then he disappeared.

The file provided to Stu Couch didn't disclose what happened to Slahi between the Novermber 2001 arrest in Nouakchott and his July 2002 appearance at the Bagram prison, the way station before his transfer to Guantanamo.

THE INTELLIGENCE NARRATIVE stated that in 1999 Mohammed Atta, Marwan al-Shehhi, Ziad Jarrah, and Ramzi Binalshibh were on a train in Germany when they were approached by a fellow Arab who noticed their pious beards. They discussed Chechnya, and jihad.

Later, Binalshibh and Shehhi telephoned the man about joining the fight. He referred them to a Mauritanian in Duisburg called Abu Musab—the alias Slahi had adopted in the early 1990s, when he trained at al Farouk. It took several days, but when they finally got Slahi on the phone, he told them to come to Duisburg.

Binalshibh, Shehhi, and Jarrah made the trip. They told Slahi of their enthusiasm for the Chechnya jihad. They just had to find a way to get there.

Slahi had some advice. Avoid travel via the Republic of Georgia, a Christian country where they might arouse suspicion. Afghanistan was a much better route. Once there, they could meet other jihadists and obtain military training.

The Hamburg group was sold on Slahi's plan. He provided instructions on obtaining visas, contacts, and a connection in Karachi for travel to Afghanistan.

THE FILE DID NOT DISCLOSE the source of this recruitment narrative. But Couch had little trouble deducing it. Slahi, still uncooperative, could be ruled out. Same with Atta, Shehhi, and Jarrah. They had died with their victims on 9/11.

However, exactly one year later—September 11, 2002—Ramzi Binalshibh was captured in Karachi. President Bush himself had boasted of it. "One by one, we're hunting the killers down," he told reporters at Camp David. "We are relentless, we are strong, and we're not going to stop."

But Binalshibh was conspicuously absent from the roster of potential defendants under review by the Office of Military Commissions. The CIA had him, somewhere. Couch knew that from newspaper accounts; officially, the CIA would not confirm to the Office of Military Commissions that it held Binalshibh, much less whether prosecutors ever could hope to gain access to him. The agency had indicated that it also held eight volumes of information on Slahi. Couch's investigator requested a copy. Request denied.

Even under the minimal procedures of the military commission, Couch assumed that the intelligence summary—an unsourced hearsay statement—was problematic. Defense attorneys would challenge its reliability and insist that a "full and fair" trial required the opportunity to probe how the government got its information. Without corroboration, there was no case.

Couch and his investigator went over their options. They could try to squeeze Ahmed Ressam, already convicted in the Millennium Bomb plot. Facing 120 years in prison, Ressam had begun cooperating with the government in the hope of leniency.

Ressam still denied knowing any of the 9/11 hijackers, but he did testify against a co-conspirator in the Millennium Plot. Perhaps Ressam's memory of Slahi could be refreshed.

Foreign intelligence agencies were another possibility. The Germans had files on Slahi and wanted to interview him anew for their own investigation into the Hamburg cell. Perhaps some kind of arrangement could be made.

The best leads came from French intelligence, which had eyes throughout the francophone world and kept a close watch on former French colonies in Africa and the Middle East. In the 1990s, Paris had alerted Canada about the presence in Montreal of Algerian extremists like Ressam, only to have its warnings ignored.[35]

France, however, also had been Saddam Hussein's closest partner in the West, and the Bush administration remained furious at Paris for blocking a UN resolution authorizing the Iraq invasion in 2003.[36] When word got around that Couch's investigator had contacted French intelligence, he was reprimanded. To deflect suspicion, Couch reverted to code when discussing France. He called it "the place where they make fries and toast."

Couch's only authorized source of information was US military intelligence, which continued to provide summaries from Slahi's interrogations. Slahi's responses varied little: No Millennium Plot. No al Qaeda. No 9/11.

One day, however, Slahi suddenly began admitting the allegations against him. The intelligence reports started getting better and better. He described his central role in enlisting, organizing, and financing jihadists from Muslim communities in the West. He named names. Soon, Slahi was spilling so much that Couch couldn't keep up.

Something had changed.

UNLIKE RAMZI BINALSHIBH, Slahi was held at Guantanamo by the same Department of Defense that President Bush had ordered to conduct prosecutions. Couch assumed he would have access to personnel and records related to his case.

The Defense Intelligence Agency, the Pentagon unit overseeing Slahi's interrogations, saw it differently.[37] It refused to let Couch near Slahi.

Couch learned that the official running Slahi's interrogations wasn't even a career intelligence officer. It was a reservist from Chicago, a cop in civilian life named Dick Zuley. He was a Navy lieutenant—two ranks below Couch.

Couch's investigator asked a supervisor at Guantanamo to contact Zuley about Slahi.

"Zuley called, he was rather upset over my 'demanding' e-mail," the CITF officer reported back. Zuley said that Slahi is "a 'special projects' detainee, they don't need to coordinate anything with us, and 'you know all that,'" he wrote. "My impression was that Zuley seems as though he doesn't care about CITF, and he's not going to coordinate with anyone—he's got his green light so to hell with us."

The officer closed with a drop of sarcasm.

"Please let me know if you need any more information from him," he wrote. "It'd be my pleasure to speak with him again."

Hitting this stone wall, Couch decided to go around it. He and his investigator set up an intelligence operation of their own, targeting their fellow military personnel.

Guantanamo was a small world. There was one bowling alley, one officers' club, one tiki bar. The investigator began working his intelligence and law enforcement contacts, getting documents slipped to him, assembling a picture of what happened to Slahi.

"It was like Hansel and Gretel, following bread crumbs," Couch said.

TWO YEARS EARLIER, IN November 2001, Mohamedou Ould Slahi had voluntarily reported to police headquarters in Nouakchott for questioning.

Just "formalities," the police told him.[38] After a week in jail, however, he learned he was being sent to Jordan. This was disturbing, Slahi thought, because "the Jordanians have [a] very bad reputation when it comes to treatment of detainees."[39]

"Can you turn me over to the United States?" he asked. "What do I have to do with Jordan? Turn me over to America."

"The United States wants you to be turned over to Jordan," he was told.

"Then, man," Slahi said, "what happened to me there is beyond description."

Jordanian agents pressed him on the Millennium Plot. One "struck me twice in the face on different occasions and pushed me against concrete many times because I refused to talk," Slahi said. "He threatened me with torture" and pointed out another prisoner, "this guy who was beaten so much he was crying, crying like a child." As the months dragged on, Slahi said, he lost so much weight that he looked "like a ghost."

In July 2002, US agents showed up to retrieve him.

"They stripped me naked like my mom bore me, and they put new clothes on me," Slahi said. Aboard the plane, he was chained in place and fitted with a diaper. "I had to keep my water for eight hours straight," he recalled. "Psychologically, I couldn't [urinate] in the diaper. I tried to convince myself that it was okay, but I couldn't and I was exploding [on the inside]."

Slahi figured he would be returned to the Germans. "I was happy, because [I] know Germany and I think Europe is a lot more liberal than America," he said. "I thought they were going to ask me a few questions and then I would go to jail and I will be all right."

Blindfolded and shackled, he was taken from the plane to a helicopter and, after a ten-minute flight, placed in a truck. He heard voices in an unfamiliar language, and later surmised it was Tagalog; this must be the Philippines, he figured. Actually, it was Bagram, the US interrogation center in Afghanistan. There, as at many of America's overseas bases, Filipinos on long-term contracts performed low-skill labor.

Slahi said his time at Bagram was unpleasant but not unbearable. One MP, frustrated that the shackled Slahi wasn't moving fast enough, dragged him over concrete stairs. "I think he may have just had a bad day or maybe was clumsy or something," Slahi said, forgivingly.

The next month, Slahi learned he was being transferred to Guantanamo.

"I was very happy because it was American territory," he said. "I thought, This is America not Jordan, and they are not going to beat you."

WHEN SLAHI ARRIVED AT Guantanamo, the FBI insisted on taking charge. For several months, he was questioned exclusively by FBI and CITF investigators, who generally followed their law enforcement training.

"The FBI guy said, 'We don't beat people, we don't torture. It's not allowed,'" Slahi said. "I was, every once in a while, taken to interrogation. Okay, so far so good."

Up until this point, Slahi was considered an al Qaeda operative linked only to the Millennium Plot. Then, in Pakistan, Ramzi Binalshibh was captured. At Guantanamo, things "changed drastically," Slahi said.

Like Slahi before him, Binalshibh had been rendered to Jordan, where he was interrogated with "electric shocks, long periods of sleep deprivation, forced nakedness, and made to sit on sticks and bottles," the latter being "a form of sexual violence," according to another former Jordanian detainee.[40]

After Binalshibh disclosed the Duisburg meeting, Slahi suddenly became "the highest value detainee" at Guantanamo, "the key orchestrator of the al Qaeda cell in Europe," a brigadier general later testified.[41]

"The FBI and DoD speculated that . . . I sent [Binalshibh] to Afghanistan, called Osama bin Laden on the phone and said, 'A guy is going to come there. Recruit him,'" Slahi said, sarcastically. On the list of high-value Guantanamo detainees, the FBI said "I was—guess which number—Number One!"

Slahi's interrogators were under pressure. Stop "playing games," the FBI man told Slahi. "I am advising you to just tell the truth." But Slahi stuck to his story.

On May 22, 2003, the FBI interrogator "said this was our last session. He told me that I was not going to enjoy the time to come," Slahi said. It sounded less like a threat than a lament. Once military interrogators take over, you won't "be invited to tea and snacks," the agent said.[42]

"I don't care," Slahi said.[43]

"Goodbye, good friend," the agent said.

A FEBRUARY 2003 FBI memorandum stated that agents had "successfully established a high level of rapport" with Slahi.[44] The "investment in a long-term strategy of building rapport with the detainee will continue to pay off with higher quality dialogue," it predicted.

Military intelligence disagreed.

"We watched five months of FBI interrogations," said one military intelligence officer. FBI agents kept insisting, "'we're almost there,'" the officer said. "But they were not in control"—Slahi was. The most information they got out of Slahi was "his favorite color," the officer scoffed.

DIA interrogators could not understand the "friendly tenor," as one put it, of FBI and CITF interviews.[45] "FBI agents have not been willing to offend detainee or push him . . . because of the desire to maintain rapport," another intelligence officer complained.[46]

The DIA had its own plan for Slahi. A January 2003 agency memorandum listed "interrogation tools" that included yelling, strip searches, shaving the head and beard, and twenty-hour days. Water could be poured on Slahi's head to "enforce control."[47] He could be ridiculed, placed in a mask, made to wear signs with Arabic labels like "liar," "coward," or "dog." Dogs could be brought in "to bark and agitate" him. Slahi himself could be forced to act like a dog—collared, barking, and performing tricks.

He could be treated as a woman and forced to wear a burka or confronted with a female interrogator in "close physical contact." The plan called for preventing Slahi from praying or, alternatively, forcing him to worship a stag idol. Violating such "religious taboos" would "reduce the detainee's ego and establish control," the plan explained. He could be kept in a completely white room "to reduce outside stimuli and present an austere environment," or have light filtered through "red plastic to produce a stressful environment." Interrogators could question Slahi while using a strobe light to "disorient [him] and add to [his] stress level." Or he could be hooded while being questioned, thus inducing "feelings of futility."

The plan evolved over the months as military officials impatiently waited to seize Slahi from CITF and the FBI. On July 1, 2003, the Guantanamo prison commander, Major General Geoffrey Miller, signed the DIA proposal.[48] It was designed, the document said, to "replicate and exploit the 'Stockholm Syndrome' between detainee and his interrogators." Successfully implemented, "the subject feels that he is about to be killed," the NCIS chief psychologist, Michael Gelles, wrote regarding a similar special projects plan.[49]

The proposal went next to General James Hill, who oversaw Guantanamo as head of the Defense Department's Southern Command in Miami, and then to the Pentagon, where Jim Haynes's office approved it as legal and recommended that Rumsfeld authorize the plan.[50] Deputy Defense Secretary Paul Wolfowitz added his okay on July 28.

Those approvals were a formality. By August 13, 2003, when

Rumsfeld himself signed off on the "special interrogation plan," military intelligence had been interrogating Slahi for six weeks.

THE DAY GENERAL MILLER approved the plan, July 1, Dick Zuley took over the Special Team, the group that conducted "enhanced" interrogations. Around Guantanamo, some called them the Varsity Squad.

"The single most important aspect of these techniques is the initial shock of the treatment," the plan said. Slahi "will have the perception that his situation has changed drastically and that life can still become worse than what he is experiencing." If the first few days didn't make Slahi compliant, the plan called for dramatic escalation.

Slahi was forced to stand, stripped naked, bent over; his anal cavity was searched. He was beaten—medical records later recorded "rib contusions" as well as bruises and cuts to his lip and head—placed in isolation, subjected to temperature extremes, including a room called the "freezer." He would be accused of breaking rules, of hiding things in his cell, then insulted and disciplined again. The "interrogation team will make detainee feel psychologically uncomfortable, emotionally uncomfortable, assert superiority over detainee, escalate stress, play loud music, and continue to condition detainee to menial tasks," the plan said.

Slahi was childless and divorced, and interrogators sought to exploit his presumed feelings of sexual inadequacy. One female interrogator adopted a "maternal role and said things to him like, 'I'm very disappointed in you.' When she eventually left for another assignment, Slahi cried," said one person familiar with the interrogations.

Other female interrogators removed their camouflage tops and rubbed their breasts against the shackled prisoner, fondled his genitals, insulted him, and laughed at him.[51] Photographs of the reproductive process, of vaginas and birth canals and babies, were plastered on the walls. A woman interrogator ridiculed him for failing to impregnate his wife.

By July 8, the shackling, strobe light, and rock music treatment had begun. Stripped and yelled at, Slahi was kept "awake and in a state of agitation," records say.[52]

That day, a masked interrogator called "Mr. X" visited. Mr. X would direct when Slahi was forced to stand or be shackled in place, when he would freeze under an overworked air conditioner or melt as the heater was turned up.

On July 17, Mr. X told Slahi about a recent dream. In his mind's eye, Mr. X said, he had seen four detainees "chained together at the feet. They dug a hole that was six feet long, six feet deep and four feet wide." Into that grave the detainees lowered "a plain, unpainted, pine casket with the number 760." It was Slahi's Guantanamo serial number, painted in orange, the color of detainee uniforms.

In case the implications weren't clear, Mr. X interpreted his dream. It meant that unless Slahi talked, he would never leave Guantanamo. He would grow old there and die alone, his corpse buried on "Christian" land, "sovereign American soil."[53] Perhaps Slahi was ready to die for his cause, Mr. X said. But what about his loved ones? Must they, too, pay for his recalcitrance?

Three days later, Mr. X informed Slahi that his family in Mauritania had been "incarcerated."[54] Later, Slahi was told that his mother and brother were taken from Mauritania. Placed aboard a cargo plane, they wept during the flight.

FOR MONTHS, SLAHI HAD been told that Washington considered him a prisoner of extraordinary importance. Now, he learned, one of President Bush's senior aides was coming to question him personally. On August 2, 2003, the White House adviser on detainee operations, a Navy officer named Captain Collins, arrived. At age fifty-seven, he had thirty years on most members of the Varsity Squad. His professional, confident manner bespoke experience and importance.

Collins was a busy man, and minced few words. The United States had taken custody of Slahi's family. Things looked particularly bleak for his mother, who might well be transferred to Guantanamo. Collins showed Slahi an official memorandum describing the "administrative and logistical difficulties her presence would present in this previously all-male prison environment."[55] Collins translated the bureaucratese: Camp Delta was stuffed with desperate men who hadn't seen a woman in years. Unfortunately, the United States couldn't guarantee her safety. How would Slahi feel if his mother were gang-raped? If that happened, Collins said, it would be Slahi's fault.

"Interrogation logs clearly indicate that the interrogation went well beyond the 'threat to detain' made in the letter, and in fact was a threat to [Slahi] and his family that violated the UCMJ," Defense Department investigators later found.[56] It was a threat to have his mother raped.

"Slahi had a special link to his mother, and that was used on him," a person familiar with the interrogation explained. In fact, "Captain Collins" was Dick Zuley. A lieutenant general who reviewed the incident, Randall Schmidt, later testified that Zuley was a "zealot" who loved tormenting his prisoner. Zuley "essentially was having a ball," the general said.[57]

Captain Collins offered Slahi a way out.

"You can be part of the solution or you can be part of the problem," he said. "We are two men here in this room. We can stop the killing and make the world a better place."

Collins gave Slahi an article about Wernher von Braun, the Nazi scientist who developed Hitler's V-2 rocket. Rather than prosecute von Braun for war crimes—his missiles, fired at London and other cities, were built by slave labor at concentration camps—the United States welcomed him to head its own rocket science program. Von Braun went on to make educational films with Walt Disney and oversee the Saturn rockets that sent Apollo 11 to the moon.

Sure, Wernher von Braun "was a war criminal," Captain Collins told Slahi. "But America will embrace its enemies if the enemy embraces America."

AFTER PLANTING THAT SEED of hope, the pressure was increased. An August 2, 2003, memorandum relates that the interrogator returned to Slahi's cell with a message.

"That message was simple," records say.[58] The interrogation team was "sick of hearing the same lies over and over and are seriously considering washing their hands of him. Once they do so, he will disappear and never be heard from again."

The interrogator told Slahi to imagine "the worst possible scenario he could end up in." Surely, "beatings and physical pain are not the worst thing in the world," the interrogator said. "After all, after being beaten for awhile, humans tend to disconnect the mind from the body and make it through." Instead, he urged, just focus on "what scares [you] more than anything else."[59] It was, according to General Schmidt, a "death threat."[60]

Sooner or later, Slahi would talk, the interrogator said. "Everyone does."[61] The only question was which horrors Slahi and his loved ones would suffer until that eventuality. Meanwhile, records say, Slahi was told "he will very soon disappear down a very dark hole. His very existence will become erased. His electronic files will be deleted from the computer, his paper files will be packed up and filed away, and his existence will be forgotten by all. No one will know what happened to him and, eventually, no one will care."

ON AUGUST 24, 2003, the plan called for military police in riot gear, accompanied by German shepherds, to hood Slahi, drag him from his cell, and put him on a helicopter that would fly in circles for hours before depositing him in another section of the prison compound. "Pre-planned deceptive conversation among other passengers" would be staged to trick Slahi into thinking he had been taken from Guantanamo to some place far worse.[62]

When the plan was executed, a boat was substituted for the helicopter—"General Miller decided that it was too difficult logistically to pull off, and that too many people on the base would have to know about it to get this done," a report later explained.[63] In blacked-out goggles and shackles, Slahi was beaten. Groaning in pain, he could hear discussions, in Arabic, about his fate. He was to be killed, his body dumped overboard. He urinated in his pants.

Instead, the boat made landfall and Slahi was pulled ashore. "I was moaning and I recognized a voice, and he was talking to two Arab guys, one claiming to be Egyptian and one claiming to be Jordanian," Slahi later said.[64] "They told him in Arabic that they were there to torture me." Soon "they were hitting me all over. They put ice in my shirt until it would melt," he said. Next a doctor came in, but he "was not a regular doctor, he was a part of the team. He was cursing me and telling me very bad things," Slahi said. "He gave me a lot of medication to make me sleep."

The sensory manipulation apparently worked. "Slahi told me he is 'hearing voices' now," an interrogator wrote in an email to Lieutenant Colonel Diane Zierhoffer, an Army psychologist on the special projects team.[65] "He is worried as he knows this is not normal . . . By the way . . . is this something that happens to people who have little external stimulus such as daylight, human interaction etc.???? Seems a little creepy," the interrogator wrote.

"Sensory deprivation can cause hallucinations, usually visual rather than auditory, but you never know," Zierhoffer responded. "In the dark you create things out of what little you have."

SLAHI ASKED TO SEE Captain Collins.

The "detainee had made an important decision," interrogation records said.[66] He "was not willing to continue to protect others to the detriment of himself and his family."

"They said to me, either I am going to talk or they will continue to do this," Slahi later said.[67]

The interrogator "congratulated [Slahi] on his decision to tell the whole truth," military records say.[68]

In weekly reports to Deputy Secretary Wolfowitz, General Miller said that Slahi "continued to be cooperative."

"After he broke, he gushed, he told us more than we could process," said a person familiar with the interrogations. "He wrote and wrote, he did homework every night. We gave him a computer, and he immediately wrote a long autobiography. Then he began to map out the structure of al Qaeda—each name with a hyperlink, showing who else he knew."

■

It would be months before Stu Couch got a fuller picture of the Slahi interrogation. But as he began to piece together the facts, he became increasingly alarmed. Each detail suggested a sustained, systematic regime of physical and psychological coercion that undermined the reliability of everything Slahi said. Defense counsel would learn these allegations from their client and demand government records documenting them. The trial could end up being more about what the government did to Slahi than what he did for al Qaeda.

Meanwhile, Dick Zuley, looking to cap his achievement, ordered a series of polygraph examinations for Slahi to confirm his statements. The Varsity Squad had no polygraphers of its own, so he commandeered them from CITF. The sessions began on Halloween.

"Did you plan with anyone to attack that airport?" Slahi was asked, about the Millennium Plot.

"No."

"Do you know of any al Qaeda members that have lived in the U.S. or Canada that you have not told us about?"

"No."

"Did you participate in any way in the 11 September 2001 attack on the U.S.?"

"No."

The results regarding his truthfulness: *No Opinion.*

"While in Canada, did you make plans with anyone to harm the U.S. or Canada?"

"No."

"Do you know of any future plans to harm the U.S. or Canada?"

"No."

The results: *No Deception Indicated.*

When Couch saw the polygraph report, he was livid.

"This is yet another example of the concerns we have" with military intelligence, he told Colonel Borch, the chief prosecutor, in an email. "They knew that Slahi is on CITF hold, yet they apparently disregarded that and have induced Army polygraphers to test him again." Couch included a report from a CITF agent who wrote that the polygraph examiners "were lied to" by Zuley and another DIA officer "and told that 760 was not on CITF-HOLD."

The polygraph results had created another obstacle for the prosecution, he wrote.

"My initial thought is that a polygraph with 'no deception indicated' is exculpatory, regardless of the relevance or validity of the test," Couch continued. "If we deem that information is discoverable, the defense counsel will have another issue to talk to [military intelligence] about on the stand."

"We need to get this issue resolved before [military intelligence] does more damage to an important case."

London Calling

DESPITE SCOTT LANG'S CURT personality, Stu Couch had grown to respect, and even like, the deputy chief prosecutor. The spit-and-polish naval officer was a precise and professional lawyer and shared with Couch an ethical code that transcended their regional differences.

Lang was the first staffer that Bill Lietzau, when serving as acting chief prosecutor, had brought on board to set up the Office of Military Commissions.

Lang, who held bachelor's and law degrees from Villanova University near Philadelphia, was the rare JAG who had stuck with courtroom work rather than rotating into management after a few years of trial experience. With almost eight years in the courts-martial and an advanced degree in trial advocacy, he prided himself as the Navy's most experienced litigator. One of his cases had been profiled on *The New Detectives*, a Discovery Channel program about forensic investigations.

As Lang grew more comfortable with Couch, he began to let slip some of the office's secrets. When he had first begun putting OMC-P together, Lang had run into a separate commissions group that already seemed far along in an identical mission. It was the Army tiger team, led by Colonel Larry Morris, that in the days after 9/11 had been pulled together to assist the political appointees who were developing the presidential military order Bush issued on November 13,

2001, and then to flesh out its details. Nearly a year later, that team was still on the job, having been led to believe that it would evolve into a permanent prosecution staff for commissions.

Morris's expectation was quite logical. Historically, military commissions, like courts-martial, were ad hoc panels convened by commanders to address criminal allegations that arose within the unit's field of operations. The commander who calls a court-martial or military commission into action is, in the legal parlance, its "convening authority" or "appointing authority." After World War II, commanders in Europe and the Far East activated military commissions to try Axis prisoners for war crimes, using the military justice structure already familiar for courts-martial. Morris and his boss, Major General Tom Romig, the Army judge advocate general, assumed that the Army would follow past practice and likewise run the new military commissions trials. That assignment naturally would fall either to Romig or to the commanders of the regional military organizations, such as Central Command, which oversaw Afghanistan and the Middle East, or Southern Command, which included Guantanamo Bay.

Initially, Jim Haynes himself shared that belief, and he arranged for Romig and Larry Morris to meet with Rumsfeld to discuss the project.

Rumsfeld was unimpressed; to him, the JAGs came across as career bureaucrats who failed to understand that commissions were intended as something wholly different from the established system of military justice. During the Clinton administration, Rumsfeld thought, JAGs had become far too powerful at the Pentagon, sitting alongside commanders to make targeting decisions, setting the rules of engagement for forces in the field. Rumsfeld was not going to let career military walk all over him. JAGs, who looked on the Clinton people as soft-headed liberals who had to be educated in the hard realities of military operations, suddenly found the ground had shifted around them.

"When the Clinton administration was in, we were the troglodyte conservatives," said Tom Fiscus, the Air Force judge advocate general. Under the Bush administration, "we found ourselves being the bleeding heart liberals in the room. The suits were all the hard guys."

On November 12, 2001, the day before Bush formally authorized military commissions, Haynes brought Rumsfeld a document to get the project moving immediately: an order appointing the Army to operate commissions. Larry Morris and Whit Cobb waited in the hallway outside.

Haynes emerged with the order unsigned. His expression was equally blank.

"He's not going to sign it right now," Haynes said. Apparently there was some technical or procedural reason for the holdup.

In fact, Rumsfeld would never sign the order. He, along with Addington and other top officials, were convinced that the Army, with its fealty to the Uniform Code of Military Justice, couldn't be trusted to administer the kind of rough justice envisioned for the Bush trials. Instead, the new permanent commissions system would be run by political appointees. The first "appointing authority" was not a commander who found it necessary to activate a commission as part of his field responsibilities but rather Paul Wolfowitz, the deputy secretary of defense. The commissions themselves would be run out of a presidential appointee's office—the Office of the General Counsel, headed by Haynes—rather than the JAG Corps, where rank-and-file officers would be insulated by several layers of the military establishment from the political leadership.

Scott Lang, innocent of this backstory when he arrived at the Pentagon, initially sought assistance from Morris's Army team. He received a brusque, unhelpful reply, which he took as a signal that a bureaucratic turf war was under way. Actually, Lietzau assured Lang, the war was over. The Morris tiger team could safely be ignored.

"They'll be gone," Lietzau said. "They don't know it yet, but they'll be gone." Several weeks later, they were. Morris wound up in Iraq, his team members dispersed to other assignments within the military.

SOON AFTERWARD, LANG SAID, Lietzau told him to begin preparing a case. Military commissions would start with the prosecution of Detainee 558, Moazzam Begg. Lang dived in.

On November 16, 2001, during the Afghan campaign, a British newspaper correspondent made his way into a training camp near Jalalabad that had been struck by US bombers and cruise missiles.[1] He discovered a weapons laboratory stocked with chemicals, gas masks, and instruction manuals downloaded from the Internet. Also found was a money order asking the London branch of a Pakistani bank "to credit an account in Karachi held by a man named Moazzam Begg."

Born in 1968 to Indian Muslims in Birmingham, England, Begg already was known to British authorities. During the 1990s, he had traveled to jihadist hot spots including Afghanistan and Bosnia, been arrested for schemes to funnel welfare funds to Islamic extremists, and attempted to attend a terrorism trial in Yemen.[2] Begg's name was in a US counterterrorism database by July 2001, when he moved his family to Afghanistan, ostensibly to open a school and work on charity projects.[3] After American bombs began falling, the Beggs fled to Pakistan, where he was arrested in early 2002.

In England, Begg's family and friends denied he was an Islamic extremist, pointing out he had attended a Jewish elementary school and, a former classmate recalled, "could read Hebrew well."[4] To his father, Azmat Begg, Moazzam was simply a "fun-loving man who enjoys cricket."[5]

Begg's family hired attorneys to file a habeas corpus petition in the Pakistani courts, which ordered the government to produce the prisoner. It was too late.[6] He already had been taken to Kandahar for interrogation, en route to Guantanamo.

An FBI agent said the aim was to persuade Begg that by cooperating and pleading guilty, they could move him to civilian custody and help him see his family again.[7]

REVIEWING BEGG'S FILE, Scott Lang had a question: "What's the crime?"

Figure it out, Lietzau said.

This was not an easy task, because no crimes yet had been defined for military commissions. Lang was confronted with the inverse of a regular criminal case. Police and prosecutors normally began with a crime report and then tried to find the likely suspects. At military commissions, however, "they gave you the criminals and said, 'Go find crimes that might fit these criminals,'" Lang said.

The Justice Department also had been investigating Begg, so Lietzau sent Lang to see an assistant US attorney in Manhattan, David Kelley, who specialized in terrorism cases.

"We can learn from those guys, they're the terrorism experts," Lietzau said. "Let's establish a good relationship."

"It was a suicide mission," Lang told Couch.

A FORMER COP AND FIREMAN, David Kelley was one of the Justice Department's top counterterrorism prosecutors. He was the deputy US attorney for the Southern District of New York, the most powerful and prestigious federal prosecution office and home to the grand jury that had indicted Osama bin Laden in 1998. Like many Justice Department officials, he considered military commissions an impediment to actual counterterrorism work. Unknown to Lang, Kelley already had experience outflanking the Pentagon, when he seized control of the so-called American Taliban, John Walker Lindh.

Lindh was the Pentagon's Detainee 001, the unlikely young American who became the first enemy taken prisoner by the United States military in Afghanistan.[8] The twenty-year-old from Northern California was a Muslim convert who, before 9/11, went to Afghanistan to join the Taliban. He was found in November 2001 among fighters held by a US-allied warlord in the fortress of Mazar-e-Sharif, after US forces put down a prisoner uprising that also claimed the war's first acknowledged American casualty, CIA officer Johnny Micheal Spann.[9]

The news of a white, middle-class American youth joining the enemy provoked confusion and outrage. Senator Hillary Rodham

Clinton called Lindh "a traitor to our country."[10] But to prove treason, the Constitution requires "the Testimony of two Witnesses to the same overt act."[11] Lindh had told interrogators about his activities with the Taliban, but his statements might not be admissible. Military and FBI agents had brushed off Lindh's requests for a lawyer, potentially violating his constitutional rights.

In any event, it was unclear whether Lindh broke any federal laws by affiliating with the Taliban before 9/11. As an enemy belligerent captured in battle, however, he seemed squarely bound by the laws of war—the traditional jurisdiction of military commissions. Colonel Larry Morris, then heading the Army tiger team, immediately proposed trying Lindh by commission. But there was an obstacle: the presidential military order Bush signed less than two weeks before Lindh's capture covered only aliens—a decision the administration made to avoid the political firestorm that would result if American citizens believed they could be stripped of constitutional rights and tried by commission.

Was Lindh classified "as an American citizen or as a Taliban enemy soldier being held captive?" a reporter asked Defense Secretary Rumsfeld.[12] Under Bush's military commissions order, "he cannot be tried if he is an American citizen; is that correct?"

Rumsfeld had not paid attention to such minutiae. In fact, he had little interest in military commissions at all, privately describing the legal experiment as something "the White House shoved up my ass." It was a distraction from the military's real job, which soldiers typically described as "killing people and breaking things."

"I do not recall exactly what the military order establishing the commissions said," Rumsfeld told the press conference. "But my impression from all the meetings that I've had is that it is not intended for Americans," he said. "Whether it's explicit in there or not, I've forgotten."

At internal meetings, Larry Morris argued that the loose standards of a military commission were tailor-made for battlefield captures where evidence couldn't be carefully collected, exclusionary rules didn't apply, and field officers, rather than civilians, sat in judgment. The only problem was that President Bush had explicitly denied commissions jurisdiction over US citizens—something the president could himself remedy with the stroke of a pen.

Morris gave Jim Haynes several options. The president could amend his November 13 military order to include US citizens; given the public outrage at Lindh, there should be little political resistance. Alternatively, Bush could leave the November 13 order intact and authorize a separate military commission for Lindh, an ad hoc trial such as the one Roosevelt convened for the Nazi saboteurs.

At congressional hearings and in media appearances, however, administration officials and proxies had emphasized that Bush's military order applied only to aliens, so the American public would have nothing to fear from commissions. A *New York Times* op-ed published under Alberto Gonzales's byline stressed that "the order covers only foreign enemy war criminals."[13]

Meanwhile, at the Justice Department, David Kelley moved aggressively to get Lindh into federal court.[14] Since 9/11, judges had been extraordinarily deferential to executive branch actions; the Justice Department assured the White House that courts were all but certain to find Lindh's interrogations justified by battlefield conditions. Besides, the department argued, Lindh could be convicted even without using his statements to the FBI. Before US forces had arrived, a war correspondent found Lindh in a prison infirmary and interviewed him for CNN about his Taliban activities. The interview could be admitted without worrying about the Fifth Amendment, because journalists have no duty to read anyone the *Miranda* warning.

Although Lindh's actions didn't quite fit any existing crime, prosecutors devised a novel way to use the federal offense of providing "material support" to terrorists. The material support statute originally was created to go after financial donors and others who offered passive assistance to terror groups; under the Justice Department theory, Lindh's own labor, shouldering a rifle for the Taliban, could be considered a form of material support. To further tilt the odds, the government could steer the trial into the Eastern District of Virginia, known for its prosecution-friendly judges, simply by repatriating Lindh through Dulles airport or one of the military bases within the district.[15]

Attorney General Ashcroft brought the Justice Department plan to Bush on December 19, 2001.[16] That night, Jim Haynes went to brief Rumsfeld on strategies to keep Lindh in Pentagon custody.[17] If a military commission was too problematic, Lindh could always be tried before a conventional court-martial, military lawyers advised. Although it hadn't been done in decades, courts-martial could try civilians in some circumstances.

Bush put off a decision. His initial reaction to Lindh's capture had been surprisingly mild, offhandedly puzzling over "this poor fellow."[18] After Bush's father called Lindh "despicable," the president's attitude hardened.[19] "This is a man who faces a grim future," Bush said two days after meeting with Ashcroft.[20] The Justice Department upped its offer to the president. By adding additional charges, including conspiracy to kill Americans, Lindh could get life. Prosecutors would continue to work the case and, with luck, might later be able to add a capital charge.

While Ashcroft fought to secure the Lindh case for his department, Rumsfeld made no corresponding effort for the JAGs. At the same time, after criticism from legal authorities, administration lawyers were loath to amend the presidential military order, concerned that doing so could open the door to additional revisions that might undermine its sweeping declaration of executive primacy.

Rumsfeld's abdication made it simple for Bush to award the prize to the Justice Department. Kelley began the prosecution in January 2002. Five months later, he obtained a twenty-year sentence, after Lindh copped a plea rather than risk life in prison.

ARRIVING AT THE US ATTORNEY'S office in Lower Manhattan, Scott Lang expected a get-acquainted meeting with Kelley and perhaps an FBI agent. Instead, he was confronted with a show of overwhelming force. Kelley had assembled thirty lawyers, investigators, and assistants, many of whom had spent years on al Qaeda's trail.

Kelley informed Lang that the US attorney's office was ready to handle Moazzam Begg. In Afghanistan, Begg had agreed to enter into a long-term cooperation agreement with the FBI. The Justice Department expected Begg to become an important asset to a counterterrorism task force that had resources, expertise, and a virtually unbroken record convicting al Qaeda operatives.

In contrast, Kelley asked, what did Lang have? He peppered the naval officer with questions about commissions and the resources the Pentagon was devoting to them. What theories underlay Lang's case against Moazzam Begg? How would it fit into the larger strategy against al Qaeda? How would Lang make sure that he and his Mickey Mouse system didn't screw up the real work the Southern District of New York had been doing for years?

Lang had no answers.

Kelley had one more question:

"When can we have our suspect back?"

THE JUSTICE DEPARTMENT SAW Begg and another Guantanamo inmate—Feroz Abbasi, a Ugandan-born British Muslim—as bricks in the case they were building against Abu Hamza al-Masri, the militant London imam whose Finsbury Park mosque was a center of al Qaeda recruiting and organizational activity.

Too bad, was the Pentagon's response. Jim Haynes and his staff were convinced that the British prisoners would make an excellent debut for military commissions.

Federal prosecutors had been building their own case against Moazzam Begg since his early 2002 arrest in Islamabad. Although Begg had been held without charge, denied counsel, and coerced into making statements, prosecutors believed that, as with the Lindh case, such treatment could be justified because Afghanistan was an active war zone. The Justice Department was ready to take charge as soon as Begg landed in the United States.

The Pentagon, however, neglected to advise the Justice Department before transferring Begg directly to Guantanamo Bay. Prosecutors were livid when they found out. The offshore prison was so far from the battlefield—and so obviously designed to evade the law's restraints on government misconduct—that a federal judge would surely scrutinize claims that military necessity justified Begg's treatment.

Justice Department prosecutors already felt the Pentagon nearly had sabotaged the cases of Lindh and Zacarias Moussaoui, an al Qaeda operative picked up before 9/11, by blocking access to Guantanamo detainees who were potential witnesses. The Defense Department would not acknowledge any summons from a federal court directed to Guantanamo.

Fortunately for prosecutors, Lindh and Moussaoui both pleaded guilty. But relations between the Defense and Justice Departments remained poor.

Communicating with the Justice Department was "a one-way street," Lang told Couch. "We tell them what we know, and they nod their heads. They've given us nothing." Even the FBI's witness interview summaries, known by their form number as 302s, were off limits. The Justice Department barred commissions officials from contacting FBI agents directly.

LANG DID HAVE A YEAR'S worth of Begg's military interrogation summaries. He told Couch that before filing charges, he went to Guantanamo to have Begg reaffirm those admissions in person.

While Lang waited nearby, two CITF agents presented Begg a six-page confession to sign. The alternative: prosecution before military commission.

"It's going to be one very short trial, they're going to look at the evidence *we* present, and they're going to take that on face value. That means you'll be imprisoned for life, or you could face execution, or both—execution after a very long time," the agents said.[21]

Begg laughed as he read the confession. "The English used here is terrible. Nobody could ever believe I could write such a document," he said.

But Begg figured he had nothing to lose. After editing the statement, he signed it.[22]

"His writing was much better than anything we had," Lang admitted.

The statement said that Begg sympathized with al Qaeda's cause, trained at terrorist camps in Afghanistan, Pakistan, and England, "associated with and assisted several prominent terrorists and supporters of terrorists and discussed potential terrorist acts with them."[23]

Back at commissions offices in Crystal City, Lang said, prosecutors kicked around the right sentence for Begg. Some suggested twelve to fifteen years. Others preferred twenty. All that remained was authorization from the defense secretary.

But Rumsfeld was busy with the impending attack on Iraq. Even officials responsible for Guantanamo policy were caught up in excitement over the invasion. On March 30, 2003, when Lang went to the Pentagon to seek approval for his casework, the aerial assault on Baghdad began. In Rumsfeld's office, the deputy who handled detainee matters was too giddy to worry about military commissions.

"Shock and awe, baby!" the deputy shouted as he ran through the corridors. "Shock and awe!"

THE JUSTICE DEPARTMENT WAS resigned to the fact that it wouldn't have access to Begg and the other Britons at Guantanamo until military commissions were done with them. It began pressuring the Pentagon to get things moving.

At a White House meeting, Ashcroft put Rumsfeld on the spot for a date when commissions would begin.

Rumsfeld turned to Jim Haynes.

"Thirty days," Haynes blurted out. Fred Borch, the chief prosecutor, had all but promised that Begg would plead guilty.

Secretary of State Powell telephoned the British foreign minister, Jack Straw, with news of the suddenly impending trials. But British legal authorities had condemned the commissions plan from the outset, and Tony Blair's decision to follow Bush into Iraq was deeply unpopular at home. Politically, London told the Americans, it could not publicly consent to stripping so many rights from British citizens. Discussions began to find a formula for the Begg trial that London could support.

The talks dragged past Haynes's thirty-day deadline, but eventually a deal seemed at hand. Capital punishment, which Britain had abolished, was ruled out for British defendants. Begg would be allowed a British attorney "consultant" to augment his legal team, amending commissions rules to allow a foreign attorney to participate in the defense.

Finally, the phone call came: Her Majesty's government would interpose no objection to commencing trial. Expecting a plea bargain, Haynes figured the case would wrap up in a week or two.

"I rolled around on the floor when I was told they really thought that's how it was going to work," Lang told Couch. "Do you really think, on the first military commission in history after fifty years, some defense counsel's going to roll over in one or two weeks and take the deal?" Lang said. "You've got to be kidding me." Defense lawyers have an array of standard motions they file in ordinary criminal cases to test the prosecution's evidence; at commissions, they were sure to file reams more, easily delaying proceedings for six months, if not a year.

TO ENSURE POLITICAL CONTROL of the Guantanamo trials, the military order provided that the president personally select prisoners whom he had "reason to believe" were eligible for prosecution before commissions. The process began when the Office of Military Commissions prepared an RTB—jargon for the packet prosecutors sent to the White House recommending a detainee for trial.

Mark Fallon, the CITF investigations chief, signed the first batch of Reason to Believe packets, for Begg and five other prisoners. Sensing history, he used a different pen for each RTB and kept them as mementos. The RTB forms received far less ceremony at the end of their journey, when Bush okayed them like any other routine memo-

randum crossing his desk. The White House made no announcement, issued no photographs. The only public notice came from the
Defense Department, which, shortly before closing down for the
Independence Day weekend, posted a release on its website: "President Determines Enemy Combatants Subject to His Military Order."

The release withheld the identities of the prisoners; briefing
reporters, a senior official said their names might never be released,
not even after trial and conviction.[24] "Have a great Fourth of July," he
added.

News released on the eve of a three-day holiday normally gets
little attention. American Independence Day, however, is not a holiday in London, where the Foreign Office disclosed that two Britons,
Begg and Abbasi, had been selected for commissions. The reaction
was immediate.

"No British court—or U.S. civilian court—would accept the case
prepared against the two, who were interrogated under duress and
without access to legal advice," said the *Observer* newspaper, in a
typical comment.[25] "British citizens fought and died alongside U.S.
troops in Iraq and in Afghanistan. British citizens deserve a fair trial."

Opposition Conservatives and even Blair's own Labourites one-
upped each other in outrage. Bush's decision was "wrong, potentially
unjust and gravely damaging to the Americans' reputation," said a
Tory leader.[26] Stop "this kangaroo court that could well end up with
the killing of my constituent," demanded the Labour member of
Parliament representing Abbasi's London borough.[27] A multiparty
group of more than two hundred members of Parliament demanded
the Britons' repatriation. In the course of a weekend, the *Guardian*
reported, the Begg-Abbasi issue had become Blair's "most serious
crisis [yet] in his relations with George Bush."[28]

It was disastrous timing for Blair, who was about to visit Washington to receive the Congressional Gold Medal and address a joint
session of Congress.[29] Frantic British diplomats warned Washington
that Blair needed a clear concession on Begg and Abbasi. One British
proposal: use the Lockerbie model to try the Britons in a third coun-

try, under American law, and send them home to serve their sentences.[30] The Bush administration refused.

In an address to Congress, Blair jokingly apologized for British troops' discourtesy in setting fire to the White House during the War of 1812. He made no reference to Guantanamo, but a British reporter raised it later, at Blair's press conference with Bush. The two leaders said they would be discussing the subject privately that very evening.

"Do you have concerns they're not getting justice, the people detained there?" a reporter asked.

"No, the only thing I know for certain is that these are bad people," Bush said.

The next day, the White House announced that Blair's attorney general, Lord Peter Goldsmith, would visit Washington to continue negotiations. Meanwhile, proceedings against the Britons at Guantanamo were suspended.

"The President and the Prime Minister are confident that their experts will be able to agree on a solution that satisfies the mutual interests of the U.S. and the U.K.," the statement said.

LORD GOLDSMITH ARRIVED IN Washington with his reputation under fire.[31] Taking office in 2001, he had said that sometimes a lawyer must provide his client "advice which will be wholly unwelcome."[32] If necessary, he promised, "I will not hesitate to say so and to do so firmly."

Goldsmith had been accused of shirking that pledge by providing Blair with a legal opinion blessing the invasion of Iraq, despite virtual unanimity among international law authorities that only the UN Security Council could authorize military action predicated on Saddam's purported violation of a UN resolution requiring him to forgo weapons of mass destruction. The commissions issue gave Goldsmith a second chance to demonstrate his professional integrity. He refused to back Blair, insisting that defendants be free to employ British counsel, challenge coerced statements, and appeal convictions to the regular courts.

Pentagon officials felt that they had been double-crossed. London "went wobbly on us, as Margaret Thatcher would say," one complained. "Many, many people in DoD were very upset about how it all played out with the British detainees."

With Jim Haynes as its principal negotiator, the Pentagon offered several minor concessions and floated others. The Americans considered putting a British military officer on the commission but decided it was too risky. It created a precedent that could bring demands to appoint Yemeni or Pakistani officers when their nationals were tried.[33]

Other proposals did get White House clearance, such as repatriating Begg and Abbasi after conviction to serve their sentences in Britain. Goldsmith said no.

Some in the administration were fed up and urged launching the trials anyway. But Paul Wolfowitz, then the commissions appointing authority, vetoed any proceedings without Blair's assent. He considered British participation in the Iraq war far too important to jeopardize by sparking a political crisis in London.

It came down to Bush's own priorities. The president had no desire to provide rights to commissions defendants. But Bush's cursory interest in the commissions project paled alongside his personal affection for Blair. Visiting England in September, Bush privately assured the prime minister that no British citizen would face a military commission.[34] There was no public announcement.

Soon afterward, the Pentagon quietly began releasing the Britons from Guantanamo.[35] The decision to prosecute Begg and the other Britons by military commission actually had made America less safe than if there never had been any such effort at all, Justice Department officials complained. Rather than remaining under US control as an intelligence source and witness against al Qaeda operatives and organizers, Begg returned home to Britain to rail against American counterterrorism policies, founding a nonprofit group to advocate for Guantanamo prisoners.

STU COUCH COULD SENSE THE pall cast by the British cases over the commissions office. Either men like Begg were dangerous international terrorists whom Bush set free for political reasons, or they were nobodies whom the Pentagon had intended to railroad through a jerry-rigged system of rough justice. Neither possibility reflected well on the United States.

Yet Bush had another option that was wholly disregarded: transferring Begg for trial in US district court, as David Kelley had urged from the start. British authorities, who had no love for Begg, would have cheered his prosecution. And given the Justice Department's track record on terrorism cases, Begg may well have chosen to cooperate with the FBI rather than face a legitimate trial. In any event, a trial in federal court would have resolved whether, in fact, there truly was proof beyond a reasonable doubt of Begg's criminal misconduct.

THE LOSS OF THE BRITISH defendants was significant for another reason: they were among the best cases commissions prosecutors had.

True, the United States had captured several top al Qaeda figures, including Khalid Sheikh Mohammed and Ramzi Binalshibh. But the White House considered them too valuable to prosecute, preferring to keep them in secret CIA prisons whose very existence it refused to confirm to the Office of Military Commissions.

Denied access to the most serious perpetrators, commissions prosecutors had to find other candidates for the new system.

"The ideal would have been a Goering kind of guy, a big fish, a really bad guy whose trial could be the story of al Qaeda," Lietzau said. "But we just didn't have those." Instead, "the new paradigm became, 'We'll use some of the smaller fish to test the system.' That perhaps would give people"—particularly the CIA, which held a near-pathological distrust of commissions—"more confidence so we can later do some of the bigger fish."

Of the Guantanamo detainees, Stu Couch had the most promising candidates for prosecution, suspects who could be tied to specific al Qaeda plots. Most of the other prosecutors, however, had detainees only tenuously linked to acts of terrorism. They despaired over the disconnect between commissions' presidential conception and the project's near irrelevance to the actual war on terrorism.

"The joke we used to have at commissions is, we'd call them the butcher, the baker and the candlestick maker," said one prosecutor, Air Force Major Rob Preston. "Because we had the cook, the bodyguard, the A/V guy," rather than the masterminds who planned, directed, and financed international terror.

Preston was brought on as the prosecution specialist in international law, having completed a one-year advanced degree in the subject. That training, however, seemed to contradict the administration's assumptions about commissions trials. When Preston raised legal questions in meetings with political officials, he was told to shut up and salute smartly. "What we want is rough justice," Whit Cobb said, slapping the table with his hand. That's all these prisoners deserved.

Lacking evidence tying individual detainees to wrongful acts, the commissions prosecution decided to charge every detainee with conspiracy. The conspiracy charge is among the most powerful in a federal prosecutor's arsenal, because it can impute the worst crimes of one defendant to his least culpable codefendant.

Commissions charge sheets would follow a template, listing Osama bin Laden, Ayman al-Zawahiri, and other notorious al Qaeda figures along with the unknown detainee actually slated for prosecution. It was "basically an aider and abettor theory" alleging that even the most minor figures were "responsible for 9/11," Preston said.

The problem, Preston told superiors, is that international law rejects conspiracy as a war crime. Because armed conflict involves organized and hierarchical forces, conspiracy could be used to make any soldier culpable for the war crimes of another.

Preston didn't know it, but the same argument had raged far above the commissions office at the political levels of the Bush administration, where some lawyers proposed an even more radical legal theory of criminalizing membership in al Qaeda itself. That way, convictions could be wrung from tangential evidence, such as a name on a training camp roster or a witness statement that the suspect pledged *bayat*, or allegiance, to bin Laden.[36] "This is a moment in time where international law can develop to account for a new situation," said one hopeful White House aide.

An October 2001 draft memo from Associate Deputy Attorney General Daniel P. Collins proposed "classify[ing] as war criminals any persons who can be shown to have joined or supported al-Qaida with knowledge that it was not a sovereign entity and that it would engage in armed attacks against the United States."[37] Criminalizing joiners or supporters "avoids entirely the evidentiary quagmire" of having to prove "that particular members of al-Qaida agreed to participate in particular *types* of unlawful violence (such as targeting civilians)," the memo observed.[38] It offered "a vehicle for trying nearly all of the membership of the al-Qaida organization, including those who cannot be shown to have personally participated in the September 11 attacks."

Legal precedent, however, disfavored prosecutions for ideological or group affiliations; defendants traditionally were punished for their wrongful acts rather than status or beliefs.[39] Collins acknowledged that his proposal "may be viewed by critics as too innovative." For support, he unearthed a July 1865 opinion by Attorney General James Speed, which justified President Andrew Johnson's choice of a military commission "to try and execute the assassins" of Abraham Lincoln.

"What I have in mind is an extension of what Attorney General Speed described long ago: 'To unite with banditti, jayhawkers, guerrillas, or any other unauthorized marauders is a high offense against the laws of war; the offense is complete when the band is organized or joined,'" he wrote. "Analogizing these principles into the modern context seems to me to make membership alone an offense," he continued. Speed had concluded that "these banditti . . . may be hunted down like wolves."

But even Jim Haynes was doubtful. He fretted that to legal authorities, criminalizing "mere membership" sounded like *thoughtcrime*, George Orwell's term from *1984*. Ultimately, the administration ducked controversy by avoiding the term *membership* but adopting its essence by creating a new war crime of conspiracy.

Although it required an "overt act" beyond mere membership, adding conspiracy to the list of war crimes accomplished much of the Collins memo's goal.

"Conspiracy is very close to what a status crime would be," a senior Justice Department lawyer explained. By the time Major Preston arrived at OMC-P, prosecution strategy hinged on charging every Guantanamo defendant with conspiracy.

The Ides of March

FIVE MONTHS AFTER President Bush signed the military order authorizing commissions, the CBS television show *JAG* imagined how they might work.

"This morning, the president authorized the convening of a military tribunal," the first in more than half a century, a senior Pentagon official, Admiral A. J. Chegwidden, announced.

The defendant, Mustafa Atef, had been captured by Special Forces in a cave in Afghanistan. Officials said Atef was al Qaeda's No. 3 leader, known as Mohandese—"the architect."[1] A former Saudi army officer, Atef was believed to have directed al Qaeda's training operations, producing some four thousand committed fighters. Trial began aboard an *Enterprise*-class aircraft carrier, the USS *Seahawk*.

On the stand, CIA agent Clayton Webb testified that, following a thirteen-day interrogation, Atef admitted he had trained the men behind the 9/11 attacks.

"And during this thirteen days, what was Mr. Atef's environment like?" asked one of Atef's military-appointed defense lawyers, Commander Sturgis Turner.

"Bright phosphorescent lights on all day," Webb said. "Loud, heavy metal music. And alternating extremes of cold and heat."

"And did being sleep-deprived, sore from restraints and rattled by noise, temperature and light get Mr. Atef to confess?" Turner asked.

"No," Webb said. "We introduced a pentothal agent"—truth serum.

The defense moved to strike Atef's statements. "Thirteen days of torture to obtain an involuntary confession shocks the conscience, violating both the spirit and the letter of the Fifth Amendment," said Admiral Chegwidden, who, reflecting his devotion to American ideals of justice, had assigned himself the distasteful mission of heading Atef's defense team.

The prosecutor, Commander Harmon Rabb Jr., strenuously objected to the word *torture*. "At no time was the accused beaten," he said. "Nor was there ever any intentional infliction of pain. Furthermore, we are at war. The Fifth Amendment doesn't apply to our enemies. The very idea is ridiculous."

The tribunal voted to sustain the defense objection nonetheless. While the Fifth Amendment didn't apply, "we're excluding Mr. Atef's involuntary confession as lacking probative value to a reasonable person under the circumstances," the presiding officer said. Fortunately for the prosecution, Atef himself was happy to take the stand—and boast of masterminding 9/11: "I picked the men. Trained them. Planned it. And I'd do it again."

"You'd do it again if ordered by Osama bin Laden, is that right?" Rabb asked.

"You will never catch him," Atef declared.

"We caught you, didn't we?" Rabb retorted.

Atef was convicted in rapid order, but he still managed to cheat the executioner's needle. In his cell at night, he slit his wrists. With a pen.

The reality of military commissions, however, was proving far less efficient. More than eighteen months after the TV version, Paul Wolfowitz, the commissions appointing authority, still was unsure how a real military commission would function. To clarify things, he asked prosecutors to conduct a mock trial for senior administration officials.[2] They had two weeks to put the show together.

The order caused immediate distress in an office demoralized by the British detainee debacle, bedeviled by hostility from other government agencies, concerned about the implications of prisoner abuse, and adrift without assertive leadership. Colonel Borch seemed oblivious to those issues; typically, he focused on the positive.

"This is our chance to shine," Borch told the staff. To minimize the risk of embarrassment, prosecutors selected the easiest case they could find.

The defendant would be Detainee 039, Ali Hamza Ahmad Suleiman al-Bahlul. As his serial number indicated, the dark-bearded, five-foot-three Yemeni, about thirty-five years old, was among the first prisoners shipped to Guantanamo, arriving at Camp X-Ray in January 2002.

Bahlul was an ideologue whose shrill harangues were so annoying, fellow inmates asked to be moved away from his cell.[3] In interviews with FBI and CITF agents, he declared his loyalty to Osama bin Laden and determination to kill Americans and Jews. "He believes this war is only the beginning. It is Armageddon," his FBI interviewer reported.[4]

Bin Laden had personally assigned Bahlul to "the al Qaida media office," as charge sheets put it, where he produced "instructional and motivational" videos. One such video included a crude montage of plaintive Muslims suffering at infidel hands, prompting al Qaeda's revenge through vicious acts of sensational terrorism. Bahlul proudly told interrogators he had spent six months assembling the video on his laptop from television clips and bin Laden speeches.[5] Its centerpiece was a segment titled "The Destruction of the American Destroyer USS *Cole*."[6]

"Everything I believe is in that tape," Bahlul said.[7]

Investigators believed Bahlul had roomed with two of the eventual 9/11 hijackers and had produced video "martyr's wills" for suicide pilots Mohammed Atta and Ziad Jarrah. On 9/11, in a hideout near Tora Bora, bin Laden had Bahlul set up a satellite receiver to follow coverage of the hijack attacks. In the following days, his job was collecting data on the attacks' damage to the US economy. Bin Laden wanted factoids for his "talking points."[8]

The case against Bahlul lacked only one desirable element: evidence of any act of terrorism that Bahlul himself committed. Indeed, there was no reason to believe that Bahlul had helped plan or even knew in advance about 9/11.

THE MOCK TRIAL WAS STAGED on November 6, 2003, in the Crystal City office's windowless conference room, before a gallery of senior officials assembled to review the performance. Prosecutors took most of the roles. An FBI agent made a guest appearance as a witness. No one would play the star of the show; it was assumed that Bahlul would boycott his own trial.

Rob Preston, the Air Force prosecutor handling international law questions, stood in as Bahlul's defense attorney. He tried to make an issue of detainee abuse, arguing that the prosecution case depended on Bahlul's statements to interrogators—and that those statements were inherently unreliable, since they had been coerced by abuse and threat of torture.

One of the senior officials present chided Preston.

"I appreciate your ardor and everything, but that's just too over the top," the official said. The United States government would never torture prisoners. The argument was offensive.

Colonel Borch jumped in. "One of the things we're doing is, right now, we're just taking clean cases, ones with no allegations of abuse whatsoever," he said.

No one contradicted Borch, but his statement was incorrect. Like Couch, other prosecutors had discovered that abuse allegations permeated the case files. "I anticipate that in every case the accused will say they were tortured," Scott Lang wrote in a November 2003 memo.

Borch seemed so intent on getting trials under way that nothing could be permitted to interfere—be it abuse allegations, insufficient resources, lack of cooperation from the CIA and other agencies, or inadequate preparation for the novel legal issues certain to arise in the courtroom.

Instead of confronting Jim Haynes and the political leadership regarding the project's present-day problems, Borch seemed transfixed by its future historical significance. He devoured works about past military tribunals and even invited one book's author to address the commissions staff. Joshua Greene, whose *Justice at Dachau* recounted Army lawyer William Denson's prosecution of concentration camp personnel, was Borch's special guest at the commissions office Christmas party, where prosecutors shared their Secret Santa gifts.[9]

When staffers worried that the cases weren't ready to launch, Borch brushed them off by paraphrasing a line from the baseball fantasy *Field of Dreams.*

"If we build it, they will come," he liked to say. Once it was clear that commissions were for real, the resources, cooperation, and White House support needed for success surely would follow, he said.

Such reassurances did little to prop up office morale, which sank further when word came that the two top lawyers in the Air Force, the judge advocate general and his deputy, both major generals, had requested a briefing on commissions. Stu Couch took it as bad sign, coming so soon after the mock trial and Borch's wildly optimistic promises to senior officials. Borch, however, saw another chance to assure top officers of the project's progress.

With his entire staff in attendance, Borch made a thoroughly upbeat presentation to the visiting Air Force generals. Everything was excellent. The cases were solid. Other government agencies were cooperating. Morale was tops.

In military units, such dog-and-pony shows are a familiar ritual when the brass drops by for a visit. This time was different.

A "happy face briefing," said Major General Tom Fiscus, the Air Force judge advocate general.[10] "Puffery," said the deputy, Major General Jack Rives.[11] They bored in with sharp questions, things only office insiders could know. Stu Couch guessed the source—the Air Force contingent within the prosecution staff, several of whom were vocal complainers about the way things were running.

"Look, what you're talking about is all smoke and mirrors here," Fiscus told Borch, in a private meeting after the presentation. "You don't have anything to go forward on in the cases that you're saying that you do."

Rives said it was obvious that Borch's office first drafted charges and then searched for evidence to back them up. "Absurd," he said.[12]

After the generals left, Borch began frantically reorganizing the office. Soon he handed new responsibilities to the Air Force officers on his staff. The moves irritated officers from the other services, particularly those who were pushed aside to give better opportunities to the airmen. Yet Borch's concessions seemed only to make the Air Force contingent bolder in its dissatisfaction. At home, Couch told Kim that something in the office was going to explode.

ONE MONDAY MORNING AFTER weeks of office turmoil, prosecutors received a surprising email from Colonel Borch.

There were "serious allegations against me as the Chief Prosecutor—charges that, if true, mandate that I be relieved of my duties," he wrote. "I am convinced to the depth of my soul that all of us on the prosecution team are truly dedicated to the mission of the Office of Military Commissions—and that no one on the team has anything but the highest ethical principles. I am also convinced that what we are doing is critical to the Nation's on-going war on terrorism, that what we have done in the past—and will continue to do in the future —is truly the 'right' thing, and that the allegations contained in these emails are monstrous lies."

Borch appended a sequence of emails he had received, beginning the previous Thursday. The first came from Major Preston.

"I sincerely believe that this process is wrongly managed, wrongly focused and a blight on the reputation of the armed forces," it said. "I don't think that anyone really understands what our mission is, but whatever we are doing here is not an appropriate mission. I consider the insistence on pressing ahead with cases that would be marginal even if properly prepared to be a severe threat to the reputation of the Military Justice System and even a fraud on the American people—surely they don't expect that this fairly half-assed effort is all that we have been able to put together after all this time.

"At the same time, my frank impression of my colleagues is that they are minimizing and/or concealing the problems we are facing and the potential embarrassment of the Armed Forces (and the people of the United States) either because they are afraid to admit mistakes, feel powerless to fix things, or because they are more concerned with their own reputations than they are with doing the right thing. Whether I am right or wrong, my utter contempt for most of them makes it impossible for me to work effectively.

"Frankly, I became disgusted with the lack of vision and in my view the lack of integrity long ago and I no longer want to be part of the process—my mindset is such that I don't believe that I can effectively participate—professionally, ethically, or morally.

"I lie awake worrying about this every night. I find it impossible to focus on my part of the mission—after all, writing a motion saying that the process will be full and fair when you don't really believe it will be is kind of hard—particularly when you want to call yourself an officer and a lawyer. This assignment is quite literally ruining my life."

Another Air Force officer, Captain John Carr, followed with a five-page email to Borch at 7:56 that very morning.

"An environment of secrecy, deceit and dishonesty exists within our office," he declared. "You have stated for months that we are ready to go immediately with the first four cases. At the same time, emails are being sent out admitting that we don't have the evidence to prove the general conspiracy, let alone the specific accused's culpability . . . Of course, it should also be noted that we have substantially changed course even since November and now acknowledge that the plan to prove principal liability for TANBOM, KENBOM, COLE and PENTBOM was misguided to say the least," Carr wrote, using code names for the

1998 embassy bombings in Tanzania and Kenya, the 2000 attack on the USS *Cole* and 9/11.

"In our meeting with OGA [Other Government Agency, code for the CIA], they told us that the exculpatory information, if it existed, would be in the 10% that we will not get with our agreed upon searches. I again brought up the problems that this presents to us in the car on the way back from the meeting, and you told me the rules were written in such a way as to not require that we conduct such thorough searches and that we weren't going to worry about it . . . You have repeatedly said to the office that the military panel [jury] will be handpicked and will not acquit these detainees."

When volunteering for commissions, "I expected there would at least be a minimal effort to establish a fair process and diligently prepare cases against significant accused," Carr wrote. "Instead, I find a half-hearted and disorganized effort by a skeleton group of relatively inexperienced attorneys to prosecute fairly low-level accused in a process that appears to be rigged."

There was silence in the office as staffers read the emails on their computer monitors. Difficult as the work environment had become, such accusations against a superior officer were stunning—as was Borch's decision to blast them to the entire staff. Office doors, typically left open, began slamming shut.

No one emailed a response in Borch's defense. But at 1:41 p.m., a third Air Force officer, Captain Carrie Wolf, joined the coup.

"Frankly—for my own sanity—I have made a point not to keep a running tally of the incidents" that disgusted her, Wolf wrote. But now that cards were on the table, she seconded Preston and Carr, complaining that the prosecution team was disorganized and inept, concerned only with personal agendas, blasé to allegations of detainee abuse, and operating with little interest in fairness or propriety.

Stu Couch wryly noted the date. March 15.

"Beware the Ides of March," Couch said to himself.

The next day, Colonel Borch addressed the staff.

"Yesterday was a bad day for me and the organization," he said.

Yet commissions would be stronger for it. "The best antidote for lies is the truth," he said.

"I think it is shameful the way you released that email to the office," said Preston.

■

The Ides of March crisis soon landed on Jim Haynes's desk. It was an unwelcome distraction.

After the frustrating negotiations with Lord Goldsmith over the British detainees, Haynes had been looking ahead to the day when military commissions would be someone else's problem. In September 2003, President Bush had nominated Haynes to a federal judgeship, on the Fourth Circuit Court of Appeals, in Richmond, Virginia. The Senate Judiciary Committee had scheduled a vote on the nomination for March 11.[13]

One senator, Ted Kennedy, long had been troubled by Haynes and the commissions, detentions, and other counterterrorism policies of the Bush Pentagon. Two weeks after Bush signed his presidential military order, the Massachusetts Democrat signaled his concern.

"We have stated that military tribunals in Sudan do not provide procedural safeguards. We've criticized Burma, China, Colombia, Malaysia, Nigeria, Russia, Turkey on similar grounds. Yet, now we're calling for the use of military tribunals," Kennedy said at a Senate hearing. "Aren't we doing exactly what we've criticized other nations for doing?"

Kennedy continued to monitor the project, and Jim Haynes's performance had caused him increasing distress. When Bush sought to reward Haynes with a seat on the Fourth Circuit, Kennedy responded with a 3,200-word indictment of Haynes as patently unqualified.

At his confirmation hearing, Haynes had refused to explain his role in the administration's detainee policies. Nevertheless, Kennedy said, "after a detailed review of the record we have, I do not believe that he has a sufficient commitment to the core constitutional values in our democracy" to merit a judicial appointment.

"As general counsel, Mr. Haynes bears major responsibility for the serious mistakes the Defense Department has made in developing its military tribunal plan," he continued. "Mr. Haynes's disregard for fundamental principles of domestic and international law has led to increased tensions with our closest ally"—Britain—"and violated our own basic principles."

Since joining the Senate in 1962, Kennedy had reviewed hundreds of judicial appointments. Now the old lion delivered his judgment of William J. Haynes II.

"Nominations," he thundered, "don't get much worse than this."

But Kennedy stood practically alone. Other Senate Democrats barely noticed Haynes, who had no clear record on litmus-test issues like abortion rights or affirmative action. The committee sent Haynes's nomination to the Senate floor on a ten-to-three vote, with just two Democrats joining Kennedy in opposition.[14]

Having survived Kennedy's fusillade, Haynes seemed assured of confirmation. Then he was notified about the Ides of March, the mutiny within the Office of Military Commissions that blew open four days after the committee voted. If made public, the crisis within the general counsel's signature project, with its allegations of incompetence, suppression of evidence, and fixed trials, could be devastating for Haynes. He moved quickly, keeping the scandal secret by ordering up a confidential "operational assessment" of the commissions office rather than a full-blown inquiry. The investigator, assigned to review "structure and process issues" but not "criminal allegations or ethical conduct," had less than a week to complete the assignment and report back privately to Haynes.[15]

Still, Stu Couch saw an opportunity to get higher-ups to realize the obstacles facing commissions. On March 18, he filed a five-page memorandum with the investigator. Problem No. 1 was the "significant tension" between intelligence agencies and prosecutors. "While in theory these two entities should be able to co-exist, the practical reality is that the intelligence initiatives . . . have complicated our prosecution efforts," he wrote. "I do not think that senior authorities truly appreciate the lack of inter-agency cooperation we have experienced." The second issue was detainee treatment. "The techniques employed by the intelligence community in obtaining information" would critically affect the prosecution effort, "yet we are powerless to influence such activities. Again, the lack of complete cooperation from the intelligence community is a major contributing factor to this issue."

Ultimately, Couch wrote, the problems stemmed from the political leadership's "misunderstanding . . . about the nature of the military justice system, and the capabilities of the uniformed attorneys who practice it." The Ides of March offered a chance to correct these problems before they doomed the commissions experiment, he wrote. In addition to increasing commissions staff and clarifying the CIA's obligation to share information with prosecutors, Couch proposed a key structural reform: Take the Office of Military Commissions away from Jim Haynes and place it under Southern Command, like other operations in the Caribbean. Left unstated was the effect of such a move—embedding commissions deep within the armed forces traditional hierarchy, protecting it from direct political interference.

It was unclear whether that advice made it to Haynes; he required the investigator present his report orally, behind closed doors. There would be nothing in writing that could leak out.

Someone in the commissions office wasn't satisfied with Haynes's response and filed a confidential complaint with the Pentagon inspector general alleging "potential criminal conduct," including "false statements, suppression or destruction/disappearance of evidence, dereliction of duty, and conduct unbecoming an officer."[16] The inspector general dismissed the complaint as "unfounded."

FRED BORCH AND HIS HISTORY books were packed off to the Army JAG School in Charlottesville. His Army career was over.

The rebellious Air Force officers, however, received prestigious new assignments from their superiors. General Rives, who had taken over as Air Force judge advocate general, believed his airmen were right about commissions—and that the project could only damage the military justice system. From then on, the Air Force distanced itself from commissions. When called on to supply staff for the project, JAG commanders sent their dregs.

■

Stu Couch tried to tune out the office turmoil and focus on his own cases, first among them the alleged al Qaeda operative Mohamedou Ould Slahi.

One allegation against Slahi had hit a dead end; no evidence turned up implicating him in the Millennium Plot. To the contrary, Ahmed Ressam, the failed bomber, insisted he didn't even know Slahi.

Couch was convinced, however, that Slahi had spent years organizing the al Qaeda network in Europe, culminating with recruitment of the Hamburg cell that supplied hijackers for 9/11.[17] If any detainee deserved the death penalty, it was Slahi.

Yet Couch hesitated.

As a prosecutor in courts-martial and the state courts of North Carolina, Couch pictured himself vindicating the moral principles American society expressed through its criminal codes. The sadistic way military intelligence treated Slahi undermined the moral superiority government asserts when it seeks to punish an offender. Yet without that abuse, Slahi might never have confessed, never provided the corroboration essential to convict him. In other words, Couch realized, *torture worked*.

He ruminated for weeks. Was the United States justified in beating Slahi, in subjecting him to isolation, sensory deprivation, temperature extremes, and sexual humiliation? Was it justified in constructing elaborate scenarios that literally put the fear of death in him, convincing him that he was about to be killed?

One threat, Couch believed, was the worst of all: To have his mother raped.

"Military guys are real big about their mommas," Couch said. And few more than Stu Couch. "Other than my wife, my mom is my best friend," he said. "That's just who I am."

Couch wondered if he could prosecute Slahi at all.

FIRST CAME A LEGAL QUESTION. Were Slahi's statements admissible before a military commission? The presidential military order allowed all probative evidence, which the statements certainly were. It also required a "full and fair" trial. This was much harder; would it be fair to use confessions obtained through such methods?

Obviously, American law would forbid admission of coerced statements in civilian court or court-martial. Yet President Bush's order set aside the rules applying to American courts. But the laws of war necessarily were international in character. What did they require? The Bush administration provided no guidance to frontline lawyers like Couch. He would have to research the question himself.

The Geneva Convention classified detainees either as prisoners-of-war—POWs—or as civilians. President Bush, in a confusing directive issued in February 2002, stated that while the Geneva Convention applied to the Afghanistan conflict, no one fighting the United States qualified for its protection. The declaration authorized American forces to ignore detention standards the treaty provided for POWs or civilian detainees.

Couch wasn't sure the president actually had the unilateral authority to set aside those provisions. But even if he did, there was another treaty section that came into play, known as Common Article 3 because it appeared in all four Geneva Conventions. It provided minimal protections for enemy prisoners during armed conflicts that didn't involve one state against another—something very much like the US campaign against nonstate forces such as the Taliban and al Qaeda.

The official *Commentary* on the Geneva Conventions, published in 1952, stated that the article "should be applied as widely as possible. . . . It merely demands respect for certain rules, which were already recognized as essential in all civilized countries . . . long before the convention was signed."[18]

Under Common Article 3, "cruel treatment," "torture," "taking of hostages," and "outrages upon personal dignity, in particular, humiliating and degrading treatment" were "prohibited at any time and in any place whatsoever." Moreover, such prisoners could only be tried and sentenced "by a regularly constituted court affording all the judicial guarantees which are recognized as indispensable by civilized peoples."

How did Slahi's treatment measure against the standards of Common Article 3?

Couch came upon another treaty, of more recent vintage, the Convention Against Torture and Other Cruel, Inhuman or Degrading Treatment or Punishment.

"The United States participated actively and effectively in the negotiation of the Convention. It marks a significant step in the development during this century of international measures against torture and other inhuman treatment or punishment," President Ronald Reagan said after signing the treaty in 1988.[19] It was ratified by the Senate six years later.

The convention defined torture as "any act by which severe pain or suffering, whether physical or mental, is intentionally inflicted on a person for such purposes as obtaining from him or a third person information or a confession . . . by or at the instigation of or with the consent or acquiescence of a public official or other person acting in an official capacity."

In contrast to the Geneva Conventions, which were drafted to put bounds on war, the Convention Against Torture was not limited to armed conflict. It allowed no exceptions "whatsoever," specifically rejecting those that governments routinely cited as necessitating the brutal mistreatment of prisoners: "a state of war or a threat of war, internal political instability or any other public emergency." Individual perpetrators could not assert the Nuremberg defense: "An order from a superior officer or a public authority may not be invoked as a justification of torture."

The Torture Convention, unlike many human rights instruments, had a provision to encourage compliance, one familiar to American law: an exclusionary rule. Any statement "made as a result of torture shall not be invoked as evidence in any proceedings, except against a person accused of torture as evidence that the statement was made," Article 15 of the convention said.

Still, in what seemed an intentional act of diplomatic ambiguity, while forbidding use of statements obtained through torture, the convention was silent on whether statements coerced through cruel, inhuman, or degrading treatment also were automatically excluded from evidence. If Couch could convince the military commission—and himself—that Slahi's treatment, no matter how cruel, inhuman, or degrading, fell short of torture, could he use the statements?

Couch consulted a specialist in international law.

"It's an open issue," the specialist said.[20]

But the law wasn't Couch's only guide.

COUCH HAD BEGUN FEELING unease about his October 2003 visit to Guantanamo, where he stumbled on the shackled detainee under torment by American interrogators. Couch's distress grew as he slowly realized that prisoner abuse pervaded America's war on terrorism.

He would lie awake for hours almost every night. During the ten-hour workdays at commissions, dark circles under Couch's eyes exaggerated his hangdog look. When he did manage to sleep, his dreams were haunted by failures past, including the families of Aviano he felt he had let down.

A prescription for sleeping pills provided some relief. Weekends, when he took his sons to baseball games, were a sanctuary. As each Monday approached, stress and melancholy would return. Because of secrecy restrictions, he could vent to his wife only in the most roundabout ways.

"I called it the Sunday Night Blues," Kim said. "It got worse and worse."

SOME OF COUCH'S CLOSEST friends were Kim's brothers, Bill and Briant. The three had been Eagle Scouts together, and they still shared good times, bringing along their own sons on hunting trips.

Bill Wilder was a Protestant theologian. After missionary work in Nigeria, he had joined a campus ministry in Charlottesville, near the University of Virginia. "He can really take a complex, complicated subject and break it down, *Barney*-style," Couch said, like the purple dinosaur popular with preschoolers.

Guardedly, Couch approached Bill with his dilemma.

"Stuart certainly wanted to do the right thing as an American and felt there were certain basic American values that should be respected," Bill recalled. "But he was most concerned to do the right thing as a Christian, and how to live out his vocation as a Christian man."

Bill Wilder could sense his brother-in-law's anxiety. "He didn't want in any way to undermine his country, to undermine the effort against terrorism," he said. "He wanted to be a good soldier and yet on the other hand felt his duty to his God to be the greatest duty."

But the Slahi case was classified, and Couch could discuss it only in the form of theological abstraction.

"Human beings are created in the image of God," Couch would say, almost as question, hoping to prompt Wilder into an exegesis that might be translatable into concrete instruction. "As a result," Couch continued, "we owe them a certain amount of dignity. Correct?"

That dignity neither could be earned nor denied a man, any man, even a deceitful, murderous adherent of a false faith, Couch reasoned. "Whether he knows it or not, he is created in the image of God, and it's your way of respecting the image of God in which he is created," Couch said, his voice trailing into uncertainty.

Wilder couldn't disagree.

"So," Couch continued, "I honor God when I observe certain boundaries with—uh, with this person. Is that right?"

"This is not simple. There are complex issues here and people of faith and people of integrity do differ on these things," Bill Wilder said. But at bottom, he did have some specific advice.

"Stuart," he said. "You need to pray about this."

IF BILL WILDER WAS THE angel on Stu Couch's shoulder, Briant Wilder played the devil.

These days, Briant Wilder sold industrial water treatments for a chemical company in Virginia. But when Couch attended Duke, Briant was down the road at NC State, and the two spent more than one weekend carousing. Briant could be a tad more fun than Bill.

Like Couch, Briant had joined the Marines intent on becoming a pilot. But a bad eye ended that dream, and he switched to the infantry, going on to command a platoon in the first Gulf War. He was familiar with Guantanamo; in 1991, he had helped put down a riot among migrants then held there.

"You know I'd be—*I am*—first in line to prosecute terrorists," Couch told Briant. "But I'm having some issues with some of these cases." He hinted at the reasons, and continued: "I'm not sure, based on the circumstances by which the information was obtained, that I can go forward with it."

JAGs were made of softer stuff than infantrymen, Briant thought.

"I don't know the particulars, and you're not at liberty to tell me," he said. "But I would suggest you think about what the definition of *torture* is." Briant didn't buy the ACLU line about prisoner mistreatment. "If some of the things that people say are torture really were torture, then I was tortured at Officer Candidate School at Quantico," he told Couch. "And so were you."

In the war against terrorism, obtaining intelligence was crucial to saving American lives, Briant said. "Stuart, let me give you an example from an infantry officer's perspective. There was a case at Tora Bora where a lieutenant colonel indicated to a prisoner that he'd shoot him if he didn't tell him where a gun emplacement was. And the guy told him where it was, and they subsequently were able to take out the gun emplacement. In that circumstance, the lieutenant colonel would rather traumatize the guy than lose his own people."

Briant said he had similar experiences in the Gulf War. "Our objective was to complete the mission in the most efficient way," he said. "So what I'm saying is this: The prosecution of a war is an inexact science. Sometimes, there are no good choices."

Think about the big picture, he added.

"We're in a situation not entirely of our making, Stuart." Should a terrorist walk just because the US military didn't treat him perfectly? Briant figured he canceled out Bill's advice. "I may come off as the bad cop and my brother may come off as the good cop," he said, chuckling.

ON SUNDAYS, COUCH DROVE HIS family to the Falls Church. George Washington and Francis Scott Key once belonged to the congregation; nowadays, its members included Alberto Gonzales and Jim Haynes. As on most Sundays, they were nowhere to be seen.

Couch was distracted as the service unfolded, possessed by the Slahi case. He mechanically obeyed when the minister called on worshippers to stand.

"Will you continue in the apostles' teaching and fellowship, in the breaking of bread, and in the prayers?" the minister said.

The congregation's response was simple and repetitive. Hearing the liturgy year after year, even the most faithful could allow its meaning to recede into reflex.

"I will, with God's help," the congregation repeated.

"Will you persevere in resisting evil, and, whenever you fall into sin, repent and return to the Lord?"

Again: "I will, with God's help."

"Will you proclaim by word and example the Good News of God in Christ?"

By rote: "I will, with God's help."

"Will you seek and serve Christ in all persons, loving your neighbor as yourself?"

"I will, with God's help," came the echo. *All persons.* That included Osama bin Laden. And Mohamedou Ould Slahi.

"Will you strive for justice and peace among all people, and respect the dignity of every human being?" *Every human being.*

He was surrounded by people, but suddenly Couch felt very, very small. It was as if he stood alone in a dark, cavernous hall, a bright, single shaft of light illuminating him, unseen persons, or powers, awaiting his answer.

"*I will,*" he said. "With God's help."

WHEN COUCH FIRST BEGAN voicing misgivings about prisoner treatment, his wife, Kim, wasn't sure what to make of them. Stu liked to talk everything out, airing every possible angle and contingency. This time, with so much classified material forcing Stu to keep things vague, she had little ground for her own judgments.

"Maybe it's not so bad," she had suggested early on. "Maybe you don't have the context for what you saw."

Yet the word *torture* had been creeping into their conversations, as Stu groped for a line of conduct that could not be crossed. Kim tried to imagine the roles of prisoner and prosecutor reversed—and what she would want for Stu were he captured by the enemy.

After the Falls Church service, he told her of the threat to rape the prisoner's mother. It was the linchpin to the prisoner's cooperation, the foundation of the entire case.

In 1939, Justice Felix Frankfurter wrote a Supreme Court opinion reversing a conviction because it relied on evidence from an unlawful wiretap.[21] Government misconduct could not produce a legitimate conviction, Frankfurter explained, for evidence so obtained was "fruit of the poisonous tree."

This metaphor was not new. "A corrupt tree bringeth forth evil fruit"—Matthew 7:17.

He told Kim he would have to drop a case. A 9/11 case.

Couch's career repeatedly had fallen short of distinction—Aviano, the Osprey scandal, and now 9/11. Still, Kim knew her duty was to support her husband. "He felt it was the right thing to do, and at that point, it is what it is," she later said. "I'd much prefer for him to feel good about himself as a man and as a Christian than to try to further his career."

However, the stress on Couch's face, the tension in his body, made clear that he didn't feel quite that good about himself. He wondered how he would tell the new chief prosecutor—Borch's replacement, an Army colonel named Bob Swann—that no case could be brought against the highest-value detainee at Guantanamo.

Stu said he would pray about it.

"You're not letting your country down, you know that," Kim said, unsolicited.

It didn't matter. "I hate to say it," he said, "but being a Christian is gonna trump being an American."

BOB SWANN, A MILITARY judge at Kentucky's Fort Campbell, initially had been rejected for the chief prosecutor job that went to Fred Borch. But Swann was a longtime friend of John Altenburg, a retired major general recently hired to relieve Paul Wolfowitz as commissions appointing authority.

Altenburg had reached the No. 2 slot in the Army JAG Corps before retiring to join the military contracts practice at a corporate law firm. As appointing authority, Altenburg put several of his Army buddies, both active duty and retired, on the commissions payroll. Staffers respected Altenburg, but word got around that he had a blind spot for cronyism. Commissions became his "full employment program for Army O-6s," went the joke, using the numerical grade for colonel, as high as a typical officer could hope to rise.

Stories about Swann soon circulated at commissions. One was endearing: Swann had been a child actor, and staffers pegged him for appearing in a 1964 Walt Disney movie, *Emil and the Detectives*. A contemporary *New York Times* review called it one of Disney's "best children's pictures," featuring "a band of children, scorned by skeptical adults, [who] use their ingenuity to track a gang of nefarious criminals."[22]

Colonel Swann no longer resembled a Disney character. He was "crusty" and "mean," the word was. "He's a yeller," one staffer heard. Another learned Swann's nickname was Mr. Sandman. Why? "Because he rubs everybody the wrong way," came the answer.

Swann was pot-bellied and double-chinned, his squarish head coated with an oily layer of thinning hair. He wore aviator-style eyeglasses that could have sat on an Army commissary's shelves since 1978.

"You're very dismissive with us," one unhappy prosecutor told Swann soon after the new chief took charge.

"Yes, I am," Swann confirmed. "That's my leadership style."

Stu Couch marveled at Swann's candid self-assessment. "It's one thing to be a jackass. It's another thing to admit you're a jackass," he said.

Swann had been at Crystal City for three days when Couch went to see him about Detainee 760, Mohamedou Ould Slahi.

Couch sketched out the Slahi case and its many problems. He had determined that Slahi's treatment was torture, and Article 15 of the Convention Against Torture prohibited using his statements. Couch said he had reflected deeply on this troubling situation before reaching the conclusion: He could not bring charges.

Swann's small eyes bore in on him, angry and impatient. He previously had taught legal ethics and considered himself an expert on the topic.

"What makes you think you're so much better than the rest of us around here?" he said.

"That's not the issue at all! That's not the point!" Couch said, slamming his hand on Swann's desk. "I am not trying to appoint myself as holier-than-thou around here. I'm not trying to speak for any of you guys. I'm just trying to tell you what I've got going on with me."

An argument followed. Swann said the only rules applying to commissions were those President Bush provided through his military order of November 13, 2001. The United Nations Torture Convention was not among them.

Couch said Bush's military order could not nullify the legal obligations of the United States.

"Sir, the U.N. Torture Convention is a treaty. It's a treaty," he said. The Constitution says that treaties made by the United States "shall be the supreme Law of the Land."[23] This treaty states that evidence derived by torture is barred from "*any* proceedings"—which must include trials before military commissions, Couch said.

Swann grunted, and made a dismissive gesture with his hand. Commissions staff would grow familiar with it; they called it "the wave." It indicated the discussion wasn't worth his time.

"Gimme the stuff and I'll give it to someone else," Swann said.

"Fine," Couch said. He turned to leave.

Later, Swann made his thinking clear.

"I don't want to hear anything else about international law," he told a staff meeting.

A WEEK LATER, COUCH sent Swann a memorandum.

"Due to legal, ethical, and moral issues arising from past interrogations of this detainee, I refuse to be associated with any further prosecution efforts against him," it said.

"As a legal matter, I am of the opinion these techniques violate provisions of the 1984 United Nations Convention Against Torture and Other Cruel, Inhuman, or Degrading Treatment or Punishment, and any statements produced by them should be excluded as evidence against this detainee pursuant to Article 15 of the Convention. If these techniques are deemed to be 'torture' under the Convention, then they would also constitute criminal violations of the War Crimes Act, 18 U.S.C. §2441."

In other words, the *interrogators* should be prosecuted. Couch continued:

"As an ethical matter, I opine that the interrogation techniques utilized with this detainee are discoverable by defense counsel, as they relate to the credibility of any statements given by him. As discoverable material, I have an ethical duty to disclose such material to the defense.

"As a practical matter, I am morally opposed to the interrogation techniques employed with this detainee and for that reason alone, refuse to participate in his prosecution in any manner.

"I respectfully request that you share this memorandum with the Appointing Authority, and our senior leadership in the Office of General Counsel."

The Nuremberg Defense

DAYS LATER, STU COUCH left for Afghanistan to gather information on his other cases.

Colonel Swann gave him an instruction. "You are not to ask questions about detainee treatment," he said.

That, however, was a major reason for going. Couch planned to interview detainees about their capture and custody.

His motivation wasn't protecting prisoners from mistreatment. It was to protect prosecution cases. By getting detainee accounts now, it would establish a baseline regarding their treatment—and make it harder to embellish their stories with additional claims of coercion after defense attorneys entered the picture.

"This stuff's gonna be key as to what I'm gonna face at trial," Couch told Swann. "We need to pin them down now."

"No, we're not going to go there," Swann said. "Stay in your lane."

"But it *is* my lane, sir," Couch said. "This is a trial issue. It touches and concerns every case, that must be our assumption."

"Nope," Swann said. News reports of prisoner abuse had, in fact, forced the Pentagon to open reviews of detainee treatment. "We want those investigations to run their course and we will get that information in due time."

"But you gotta understand, sir, we're not gonna find that out for a long time down the road, and we might be expending energy on a case that we can't prosecute," Couch said. "We need to know *now*."

"Stay in your lane," Swann repeated.

COUCH TRAVELED TO AFGHANISTAN via the US base in Qatar, where Major Rob Preston, the Air Force officer who set off the Ides of March mutiny, now was stationed. The two met up during the overnight layover, and Preston brought Couch to his office.

"I've got to show you something," Preston said quietly. He shut his office door. "You can't tell anybody where you saw this."

He pulled out some documents and handed them to Couch. They included the special interrogation plans for detainees Mohamedou Ould Slahi and Mohammed al-Qahtani, personally approved by Donald Rumsfeld. One document was a memorandum from Jim Haynes seeking Rumsfeld's authorization to use several categories of SERE "counter-resistance techniques" on Guantanamo detainees, including forced standing for up to four hours a day.

Couch's eyes fixed on a handwritten scrawl at the bottom of the memo—a rare human touch amid the laser-printed text.

"However, I stand for 8–10 hours a day. Why is standing limited to 4 hours?" It was initialed, "D.R."

"Holy smokes! That's frickin' Rumsfeld's signature," Couch said. "This stuff went all the way up to the head shed?"

"Man, if they find out I'm showing you this, I'll be in a helluva lot of trouble," Preston said.

They had to cut the discussion short. It was time to board the C-130 to Afghanistan.

THE STENCH WAS OVERWHELMING when Couch entered the prison at Bagram. "Smells like the monkey house at the zoo," he thought.

The prison was built inside a converted hangar at an old Soviet air base, some sixty miles north of Kabul. Prisoners were kept inside huge wire pens, perhaps thirty to a cage, under floodlights that blazed

twenty-four hours per day. They had buckets for defecation and uri-
nation. Cells were named after al Qaeda's targets: Lebanon. Somalia.
USS *Cole*. Pentagon. World Trade Center.[1]

It was known around the commissions office that soldiers liked to
humiliate inmates at Bagram. At least two detainees had been beaten to
death at the facility.[2] Speaking to inmates and guards, Couch learned
that body cavity searches were frequent. Detainees typically received
them before interrogations. Guards sometimes took souvenir photos of
each other performing rectal exams on prisoners. Inmates often were
subjected to enemas. The "intel guys" considered rectal penetration a
"mechanism to exert control," a CITF investigator explained.

Couch stayed alongside the hangar in a SEA—for South East
Asia—Hut, a prefab structure the military had been using since the
Vietnam War. With a bunk and a sleeping bag, the accommodations
were not comfortable, but he was spared the noise and odor of the
prison. He started drafting a memorandum. "Prosecution Standards," he wrote on the subject line.

DAYS AFTER HIS RETURN TO Washington, Couch filed the finished document with Colonel Swann.

"Over several conversations during the past month, we have
discussed serious concerns, issues, and reservations about our prosecution effort in the Office of Military Commissions," it began. The
memo was to memorialize "standards that I believe are necessary in
order to protect the Office of Military Commissions from collateral
attacks and allegations of legal ethics violations."

"We have discussed the issue of detainee treatment and allegations
of abuse, and I have raised this issue with your predecessor, Colonel
Borch," it continued. "My concerns with this issue have risen steadily
over the past ten months and are based upon the following factors:

    a. Incomplete information provided by agencies
       (namely DoD, DIA, JTF-GTMO, DIA Directorate of
       Humint [Human Intelligence] Services) regarding

the circumstances of detainee capture, interrogation, and internment.

b. Documents I have reviewed that pertain to "Special Projects" interrogations of selected detainees at GTMO.

c. Lack of access to legal memoranda held by DoD relating to the treatment and interrogation of detainees captured during Operation Enduring Freedom (OEF).

d. Documented statements made by detainees during law enforcement interviews that allege similar patterns of abuse.

e. Informal conversations with agents, security personnel, military personnel, and intelligence officers that describe similar examples of detainee abuse from disparate perspectives.

f. The CIA's failure to respond to my formal requests for information.

"Allegations of detainee abuse impact our prosecution efforts in three ways," Couch's memo continued. "First, they call into question the voluntary nature of any admission made by an accused. This is a critical issue because in the majority of our cases, the admissions of the accused comprise the bulk of what we can allege about the accused's culpability, and therefore the admission must be credible. I agree that under our admittedly controversial evidentiary standard for military commissions the voluntariness of a statement goes to its weight and not its admissibility. However, it remains that our cases will be judged not only by military officers as panel members, but in the 'court' of public opinion and more importantly, in the forum of international legal opinion as well. Thus, the credibility of these admissions by the accused will play an essential role in the credibility and acceptability of our military commission process as a whole.

"Second, all statements of other detainees offered against the accused will have the same voluntariness issue as it relates to their credibility . . . In the vast majority of our cases, these statements are the only evidence we have that either corroborate the accused's admissions, or prove the criminal conduct of the accused in the first place." Moreover, he reiterated, "statements obtained as a result of coercion could be excluded as evidence in military commissions if they are determined to be the product of torture, pursuant to Article 15 of the 1984 UN Convention Against Torture and Other Inhuman, Cruel and Degrading Treatment . . . and therefore constitute a criminal violation" of American domestic law.

Couch then expanded the issues he had raised with the Slahi case to the entire commissions project.

"In relation to our duties as prosecutors and officers of the court, the issue of alleged detainee abuse has three component parts: legal, ethical, and moral. *Legally*, a number of the classified statements we have used in the preparation of our cases could be the product of torture as defined by the UN torture convention. At this stage we are unable to determine exactly how many classified statements may be affected because we have not been provided enough information from the respective intelligence services, and it appears we never will be. The new policy of not inquiring about detainee abuse during detainee interviews, or with outside agencies until the myriad investigations pending within DoD are completed, will slow down our ability to prepare for trials. Even though I disagree with it, I respect your policy decision and I am following it. From a practical standpoint, I am still concerned whether any of these investigations will be completed in time for us to efficiently use any information they provide at trial, much less fulfill our discovery obligations to the defense.

"*Ethically*, we have a duty to disclose to the defense all known statements by the accused, both unclassified and classified. Undoubtedly the defense will seek to discover the attendant facts and circumstances under which these statements were given by his or her client, as well as those under which statements of other detainees were given that the government intends to use at trial. Additionally, our ethical duty extends to the point that we should disclose any information we may have that a statement was obtained by coercive means, in order that the defense may seek to have the statement excluded under the UN torture convention. The defense may be entitled to this information in order to test the credibility of the statements, if they can, as this would be 'evidence probative to a reasonable person' in order that the accused is afforded a 'full and fair trial,'" as President Bush's order stated.

"*Morally*, some of the interrogation techniques that have been used with some detainees resulting in statements they have provided are deplorable. In light of these moral misgivings, we cannot advocate the acceptability of such interrogation techniques and therefore cannot do so as a counsel of record.

"The reservations outlined above are deep issues, and clearly open to debate between reasonable minds and well-meaning people. The issue of detainee treatment and alleged abuse must be discussed within the office, and resolved in a manner that all prosecutors involved in this process can live with. Undoubtedly, this issue will significantly affect our mission. We must address it now before we get any further into the discovery process and our preparations for trial. For this reason, I suggest that we adopt 'prosecution standards' that we must adhere to given the circumstances, and for you to provide oversight."

The memo spelled those standards out:

a. We will not pursue any case involving a detainee who has been subject to a "Special Project" interrogation plan or program (even though such plan or program may have been approved by Commander, JTF-GTMO; Commander, U.S. Southern Command; the Secretary of Defense; or any of their designees) until we have been provided all documents related to that detainee, and assessed whether his case can be legally and ethically prosecuted.

b. We will provide defense counsel all statements of the accused, both unclassified and classified.

c. We will provide defense counsel all documentation in existence regarding approved interrogation plans and memoranda . . . that memorialize the conduct of the accused's interrogation in which he provides a statement.

d. We will provide notice to defense counsel of any information we have that a statement was obtained by coercive means.

e. We will pursue complete copies of all internal legal memoranda of the U.S. Government regarding interrogation techniques to be employed with detainees captured during Operation Enduring Freedom.

This, Couch wrote, represented "the minimum required for me to be satisfied that any participation in the military commission process is ethically and morally correct." Unless he and Swann could agree on prosecution standards, "I am willing to request reassignment by Judge Advocate Division, Headquarters U.S. Marine Corps," he wrote. "I appreciate your careful consideration of this request."

That wasn't the only step Couch took. He went to a pay phone in Crystal City and placed a call to Vice Admiral Tom Church, one of the senior officers the Pentagon had assigned to investigate detainee abuse allegations.

"This is Commander Smith," Couch told the receptionist, who put him through to the admiral's legal adviser.

"Look, the name I gave is a false name," Couch said. "I'm not telling you who I am, just that I'm involved in military commissions. When you guys go down to Gitmo, you need to look at 760." That was Mohamedou Ould Slahi's detainee number.

"Well, that's a number we've already been provided," the JAG on the other end of the line said. "We've already been told we need to look into that one."

"You do," Couch said. "You need to look into that case."

Church filed his report ten months later, in March 2005. The nearly four-hundred-page document was classified, except for a twenty-one page executive summary released to the public. It made no mention of Detainee 760.

■

Couch commiserated with his friend Mark Fallon, the CITF investigations chief who had taken career-risking moves himself in trying to stop prisoner abuse. In late 2002, Fallon had pushed the problem up his chain of command, where it ultimately reached Alberto Mora, general counsel of the Navy Department. Although a political appointee, Mora nevertheless was not part of the ideological vanguard epitomized by John Yoo. After obtaining a copy of the interrogation protocols, Mora told Jim Haynes that what Rumsfeld had authorized was "torture."[3]

"No it isn't," Haynes replied.[4]

Mora pointed to Rumsfeld's handwritten addendum to the list of approved interrogation techniques: *"However, I stand for 8–10 hours a day. Why is standing limited to 4 hours? D.R."*

Given Rumsfeld's characteristic sarcasm, Mora said he assumed "the comment was intended to be jocular."[5] But "defense attorneys for the detainees were sure to interpret it otherwise," he said he told Haynes. "Unless withdrawn rapidly, the memo was sure to be discovered and used at trial in the military commissions." Rumsfeld's "signature on the memo ensured that he would be called as a witness," Mora continued, for "a long interrogation" on whether he was sending "a coded message, a written nod-and-a-wink to interrogators." In sum, Mora said, "the memos, and the practices they authorized, threatened the entire military commission process."

Haynes "listened attentively," Mora remembered.

But when nothing changed, Mora threatened to put his objections in writing unless Haynes acted. That eventually led Rumsfeld to appoint a working group to review interrogation policy. Mora assumed the group would rein in the brutal regime at Guantanamo. Instead, the working group did the opposite, producing a document invalidating any limits on prisoner mistreatment.[6] The Pentagon had selected John Yoo to serve as the working group's legal adviser, and its report reflected the ideas he had been developing through reams of legal-sounding memorandums and opinion letters at the Office of Legal Counsel.[7] The *Wall Street Journal* obtained the draft report, and its front-page story on June 7, 2004, for the first time revealed the legal thinking behind the Bush administration's detainee policies.[8]

"Pentagon Report Set Framework for Use of Torture," read the headline.

"Bush administration lawyers contended last year that the president wasn't bound by laws prohibiting torture and that government agents who might torture prisoners at his direction couldn't be prosecuted by the Justice Department," the story began. The Pentagon document "outlined U.S. laws and international treaties forbidding torture, and why those restrictions might be overcome by national-security considerations or legal technicalities," the *Journal* said. The Pentagon report covered "a range of legal issues related to interrogations, offering definitions of the degree of pain or psychological manipulation that could be considered lawful. But at its core is an exceptional argument that because nothing is more important than 'obtaining intelligence vital to the protection of untold thousands of American citizens,' normal strictures on torture might not apply.

"The president, despite domestic and international laws constraining the use of torture, has the authority as commander in chief to approve almost any physical or psychological actions during interrogation, up to and including torture, the report argued. Civilian or military personnel accused of torture or other war crimes have several potential defenses, including the 'necessity' of using such methods to extract information to head off an attack, or 'superior orders,' sometimes known as the Nuremberg defense: namely that the accused was acting pursuant to an order and, as the Nuremberg tribunal put it, no 'moral choice was in fact possible.'"

Major General Tom Romig, the Army judge advocate general, had tried to stop Yoo's theories from supplanting established law. In a memorandum to Jim Haynes, Romig warned that Yoo's position would authorize "detainee interrogation techniques that may appear to violate international law, domestic law, or both."[9] Haynes ignored him.

Instead, the working group assembled its report by importing portions of earlier Office of Legal Counsel memorandums Yoo drafted in an effort to shield CIA agents from prosecution for criminal abuse of prisoners. Rather than stop mistreatment, Mora's complaints had prompted the Bush administration to expand impunity from a relatively small number of CIA operatives to the vast ranks of the armed forces.

"A military lawyer who helped prepare the report said that political appointees heading the working group sought to assign to the president virtually unlimited authority on matters of torture—to assert 'presidential power at its absolute apex,' the lawyer said," the *Journal* article continued. "Although career military lawyers were uncomfortable with that conclusion . . . they focused their efforts on reining in the more extreme interrogation methods, rather than challenging the constitutional powers that administration lawyers were saying President Bush could claim," the newspaper said.

"Methods now used at Guantanamo include limiting prisoners' food, denying them clothing, subjecting them to body-cavity searches, depriving them of sleep for as much as ninety-six hours and shackling them in so-called stress positions," a military intelligence official said.

A military official involved in drafting the report told the *Journal* that at Guantanamo, "'people were trying like hell to ratchet up the pressure,' and used techniques that ranged from drawing on prisoners' bodies and placing women's underwear on prisoners heads—a practice that later reappeared in the Abu Ghraib prison—to telling subjects, 'I'm on the line with somebody in Yemen and he's in a room with your family and a grenade that's going to pop unless you talk.'"

The interrogation report asserted as legal fact "the Bush administration's view that the president has virtually unlimited power to wage war as he sees fit, and neither Congress, the courts nor international law can interfere," the *Journal* said. Moreover, the document stated that "neither the president nor anyone following his instructions was bound by the federal Torture Statute, which makes it a crime for Americans working for the government overseas to commit or attempt torture."

The Pentagon report explained it this way: "In order to respect the president's inherent constitutional authority to manage a military campaign ... (the prohibition against torture) must be construed as inapplicable to interrogations undertaken pursuant to his commander-in chief authority."[10] The Justice Department could not prosecute "a defendant who had acted pursuant to an exercise of the president's constitutional power." Repeating, as it did throughout, Yoo's perfervid vocabulary when writing about the presidency, the document stated that the executive held "sweeping" powers to act as it believed appropriate because "national security decisions require the unity in purpose and energy in action that characterize the presidency rather than Congress."

Yoo knew, however, that he stood nearly alone in the belief that the president and his underlings could ignore federal law. So the report provided instructions for the day when the Bush administration's true policies were exposed and those who carried them out were tried for their crimes.

The interrogation report listed the charges administration officials and those who acted on their legal theories were likely to face: *Torture,* defined by Title 18, United States Code, Section 2340, was the first. Also *assault* (18 USC § 113), *conspiracy* (18 USC §§ 2, 371), *stalking* (18 USC § 2261A), *maiming* (18 USC § 114), *manslaughter* (18 USC § 1112), and Title 18, United States Code, Section 1111: *murder.*

To help administration officials beat the rap, the report included a section titled "Legal Doctrines under the Federal Criminal Law That Could Render Specific Conduct, Otherwise Criminal, not Unlawful."

First was "commander-in-chief authority." The report argued

that because military forces commanded by the president lawfully could kill enemy soldiers who were fighting them on the battlefield, they were equally entitled to kill them during interrogations, after they surrendered or had been captured, disarmed, and posed no physical threat. "Congress can no more interfere with the President's conduct of the interrogation of enemy combatants than it can dictate strategy or tactical decisions on the battlefield," the report said. However, since the right to assault, torture, maim, or kill captives "is inherent in the President, exercise of it by subordinates would be best if it can be shown to have derived from the President's authority through Presidential directive or other writing," the report suggested.

Next was "necessity," which the report noted was "often referred to as the 'choice of evils' defense." That is, the defendant had no choice but to commit the crime to avoid even greater harm. In law schools, a typical example might be committing trespass over private property to rescue a child from a burning building. When it came to torturing prisoners, "the necessity defense may prove especially relevant," the report asserted.

But if courts rejected the claim that "necessity" justified "violation of a criminal statute, a defendant could still appropriately raise a claim of self-defense," it said. Self-defense typically is invoked by people who pummel muggers or shoot burglars. To prevail, the defendant must show the court his action was reasonable and proportional in order to prevent imminent harm. For instance, once you throw a violent drunk out of a bar, you can't then chase him down the street and beat him to death.

The report extrapolated the individual defendant's self-defense argument to the scale of the entire nation. "If a government defendant were to harm an enemy combatant during an interrogation in a manner that might arguably violate a criminal prohibition, he would be doing so in order to prevent further attacks on the United States by the al Qaeda terrorist network," it said.

Another option, the report suggested, was to justify torture as a "law enforcement" activity. Military police were authorized to use force to prevent "theft or sabotage of assets vital to national security," stop escapes and apprehend fugitives, the report said. The same concept "could be argued to apply, at least by analogy, to the use of force against a detainee to extract intelligence to prevent a serious and imminent terrorist incident."

At the end of the list came the Nuremberg defense. Here, the report advised Bush administration officials to follow the example of Nazi war criminals prosecuted after World War II. They should say they were only following orders.

"An order requiring the performance of a military duty or act may be inferred to be lawful and it is disobeyed at the peril of the subordinate," the report observed. Only orders that were "obviously" and "patently unlawful" need be disobeyed. When prosecuted, administration officials should say that lawyers told them torture was lawful, the report advised: "Proof that the defendant relied in good faith on advice of counsel . . . may be a complete defense to such a charge." In other words, administration lawyers concluded that they could immunize Bush and his subordinates from prosecution simply by providing them erroneous advice that they were free to torture prisoners.

If a court rejected that circuitous argument, Bush officials might still escape punishment by claiming that there was no choice but to obey.

"The International Military Tribunal at Nuremberg declared in its judgment that the test of responsibility for superior orders 'is not the existence of the order, but whether moral choice was in fact possible,'" the report said. For instance, Nazis often insisted they would be executed if they disobeyed orders to commit atrocities. If US personnel could show that the Bush administration exerted similarly tyrannical discipline, the superior orders defense could work.

Even if convicted of war crimes, Bush officials could still invoke the Nuremberg defense to seek lighter sentences, the report said. It quoted the August 1945 Nuremberg Charter, in which the Allies laid out the rules for trying the Nazi leadership. "The fact that the Defendant acted pursuant to order of his Government or of a superior shall not free him from responsibility, but may be considered in mitigation of punishment if the Tribunal determines that justice so requires," the Charter said.

The image of American officials taking positions espoused by Nazi war criminals to escape punishment was not simply some fevered thought experiment concocted by John Yoo. It was approved by the White House when Yoo met there to discuss the matter with Alberto Gonzales and David Addington.

"Good," Addington said at the meeting. "I'm glad you're addressing these issues."[11]

ON JUNE 28, 2004, THE Supreme Court handed down its first ruling on Guantanamo Bay, in the case *Rasul v. Bush*.[12]

Suits had been filed on behalf of fourteen inmates demanding access to lawyers, freedom from interrogation, and release from prison. Their cases "present the narrow but important question whether United States Courts lack jurisdiction to consider challenges to the legality of the detention of foreign nationals captured abroad in connection with hostilities and incarcerated at the Guantanamo Bay Naval Base, Cuba," Justice John Paul Stevens wrote for the Court.

Specifically, Stevens said, the issue was whether the right of habeas corpus applied to "executive detention of aliens in a territory over which the United States exercises plenary and exclusive jurisdiction, but not 'ultimate sovereignty,'" under the perpetual lease first obtained in 1903 from the client government Washington established in Cuba.

Stevens declined to spell out the rights the prisoners had. Instead, he sought to clarify a principle: When "individuals who claim to be wholly innocent of wrongdoing" face "potentially indefinite detention," the judiciary retained authority to ensure the laws were followed.

The opinion drew on a line of American and English precedents stretching from 1619. "At common law, courts exercised habeas jurisdiction over the claims of aliens detained within sovereign territory of the realm," he wrote, "and all other dominions under the sovereign's control," such as the Cinque Ports and the Isle of Jersey.

In dissent, Justice Antonin Scalia wrote that affirming judicial review for unlawful detentions was "a monstrous scheme in time of war." The majority got the history all wrong, he said, because the English cases applied to "colonies, acquisitions, and conquests," rather than territory "merely leased for a particular use."

In addition to history books, however, "judges do read newspapers," Justice Ruth Bader Ginsburg liked to say.[13] In the days after 9/11, as they had in past emergencies, courts stood aside while the executive branch took whatever steps it considered appropriate. But as time passes, exigencies fade, and with them the justification for government encroachment on individual rights. The Bush administration, however, acted as though 9/11 had forever changed the constitutional order, creating a permanent state of emergency where legislative and judicial powers must yield to executive policy decisions. Even so, the administration insisted there was no risk to human rights, because its secret policies were consistent with legal obligations and American traditions.

An increasing stream of press reports suggested otherwise, however, and by the time the first detainee cases reached the Supreme Court, the administration had begun to lose the benefit of the doubt.

"May I ask just one other question?" Stevens had said at oral arguments on April 28, 2004.[14] "Do you think there is anything in the law that curtails the method of interrogation that may be employed?"

"Well, I think there is, Justice Stevens," replied Paul Clement, the administration's lawyer.

"And what is that?"

"Well, just to give one example, I think that the United States is signatory to conventions that prohibit torture and that sort of thing. And the United States is going to honor its treaty obligations."[15]

That night, the CBS News program *60 Minutes II* broadcast the first report on Abu Ghraib, soon followed by Seymour Hersh's exposé in the *New Yorker* magazine.

STU COUCH SHOOK HIS HEAD as he read Justice Scalia's *Rasul* dissent, with its full-throated endorsement of the administration's detainee policies. Because three months earlier, with no idea of its implications for Guantanamo, Scalia had written a majority opinion that Couch saw as a significant threat to the premise of the commissions experiment.

That case, *Crawford v. Washington,* was one of the Supreme Court's periodic clarifications of criminal procedure, this time addressing the Sixth Amendment's Confrontation Clause.[16] Police had taken a statement from a woman implicating her husband in a crime. But state law prohibited spouses from testifying against each other, meaning that the prosecutor couldn't put her on the witness stand. To bypass that obstacle, the prosecutor played for the jury a recording of the wife's statement to police. On appeal, the defendant argued that the tactic violated his constitutional right "to be confronted with the witnesses against him"—that is, to cross-examine prosecution witnesses.

Scalia strongly agreed. The Framers, he wrote, understood confrontation as fundamental to the very concept of justice, codifying in the Constitution a right "that dates back to Roman times." To make that point, his opinion recalled an infamous counterexample, the 1603 trial of Sir Walter Raleigh, convicted of treason based on hearsay—a letter from an alleged accomplice read before the court.

"Call my accuser before my face," Raleigh had demanded, but the judges refused. "Despite Raleigh's protestations that he was being tried 'by the Spanish Inquisition,'" Scalia wrote, "the jury convicted, and Raleigh was sentenced to death." The notorious trial prompted restrictions on hearsay testimony, something that could be seen even in the Constitution's requirement of two witnesses for any treason prosecution.

In the *Crawford* case, the state argued that fears over miscarriage of justice were misplaced. Judges could be trusted to ensure that only

"obviously reliable" hearsay statements, like the wife's recorded interview, would be admitted into evidence.

Scalia scoffed. "Dispensing with confrontation because testimony is obviously reliable is akin to dispensing with jury trial because
a defendant is obviously guilty," he wrote. "The only indicium of
reliability sufficient to satisfy constitutional demands is the one the
Constitution actually prescribes: confrontation."

When *Crawford* came down, Couch wondered how it might
apply at commissions, where virtually every case depended on hearsay statements taken from detainees. His superiors were less concerned; the presidential military order said commissions proceedings
were exempt from any body of law, including the Constitution of the
United States.

But in June, the *Rasul* decision vitiated administration assumptions that its actions at Guantanamo were immune from judicial
review. Courts could now examine, in some unspecified way, what
took place at the offshore prison. Couch wondered how federal judges
could square commissions' claim to "full and fair" trials with the
Supreme Court's latest paean to confrontation rights.

"If we can prosecute somebody without having to produce the
person who implicated him, how is that any different from the Star
Chamber?" Couch said, invoking the notorious secret court where
Raleigh was tried.

A Justice Department lawyer working with the commissions
office agreed.

"If the Supreme Court ever gets ahold of this thing, it's game
over," he told Couch.

■

Publicly, the Bush administration treated *Rasul* as a technical ruling
with little significance for detention policies.

In a statement, the Justice Department said it was "pleased that
the U.S. Supreme Court today upheld the authority of the President

as Commander-in-Chief of the armed forces to detain enemy combatants," something that never had seriously been questioned, burying the addendum that "the Court also held that individuals detained by the United States as enemy combatants have certain procedural rights to contest their detention."

The Defense Department acted as if *Rasul* was irrelevant to commissions. One day after the decision, the Pentagon announced that commissions would prosecute Ali al-Bahlul, the detainee whose case was used in the mock trial; David Hicks, the young Australian prisoner; and Ibrahim al-Qosi, a Sudanese who allegedly served as an al Qaeda financier. Two weeks later, a fourth and final detainee was added to this first slate of defendants: Salim Hamdan, the bin Laden driver captured near Kandahar.

Once again, the charging decisions were driven by the White House's political calculations. The key figure was Hicks, because his disposition was critical to the Australian prime minister, John Howard, Bush's most stalwart ally. Prosecutors were told to add the other defendants as cover.

Unlike Tony Blair, Howard had no objection to US military commissions trying his countrymen. Indefinite detention was another matter, however, and Howard wanted Hicks's fate adjudicated before it became a political liability.

Hicks's father, Terry, a likable everyman from suburban Adelaide, had begun a campaign to free his son, even traveling to Manhattan for a sidewalk protest where he donned an orange jumpsuit and climbed into a cage. Howard didn't want Hicks to evolve into a cause célèbre.

Howard's endorsement offered Washington something of a consolation prize following Britain's condemnation of commissions. In a press release, the Pentagon announced Australia's agreement that "the military commission process provides for a full and fair trial for any charged Australian detainees held at Guantanamo Bay."

Even so, the Pentagon would not provide a timeline for proceedings. National Security Adviser Condoleezza Rice, who was receiving regular complaints from Canberra, pushed Paul Wolfowitz to get Hicks tried.

Wolfowitz turned to Tom Hemingway, a retired Air Force brigadier general who had been recalled to active duty to manage the commissions project, with the title of legal adviser to the appointing authority.

"AS YOU ARE AWARE, DR. RICE has asked for a projected date by which we can begin conducting military commissions," Hemingway wrote in a memo explaining the plan. To get things rolling, he had assigned a defense lawyer to meet with Hicks "for the purpose of exploring the possibility of a guilty plea."

Jim Haynes and other senior officials assumed the defendant would play along. Hicks was a weak and not particularly bright ne'er-do-well who broke instantly when questioned by American and Australian interrogators.

"Frankly, he was viewed as kind of a pussy," said one prosecutor.

But Hicks never had spoken to an attorney or anyone else representing his interests. If interrogators found him pliable, so could a defense attorney. And several prosecutors doubted that any defense attorney would go along with the Pentagon's plan. It would be "malpractice" for a defense attorney to let Hicks plead guilty, one prosecutor told Hemingway, "unless the deal we're offering him is, he walks."

That was not the deal being contemplated. To prove commissions' efficacy, prosecutors felt pressure to match the benchmark set by the Justice Department when it persuaded John Walker Lindh to plead guilty and take a twenty-year sentence. Hicks, after meeting with his lawyer, rejected the offer.

Likewise, the Pentagon had appointed a Navy lawyer, Lieutenant Commander Charles Swift, to negotiate a guilty plea from Salim Hamdan. Swift discarded those instructions and instead advised his new client not to agree to anything.[17]

Back in Washington, Swift was working with Neal Katyal, the Georgetown law professor who had decided to go beyond an academic critique and build a legal challenge to the Bush military order. Katyal urged Swift to strike first and file a lawsuit against the commissions project rather than wait for the Pentagon to bring charges against Hamdan. That way, Katyal could frame the legal issues on his own terms.

■

At Crystal City, Stu Couch got the most concrete signal yet that commissions actually would occur: a presiding officer for the trials had been selected. Retired Army Colonel Pete Brownback, a former military judge, was returning to active duty for the assignment. Along with other prosecutors, defense attorneys, and support staff, Couch took a seat in the windowless conference room for the introduction.

"My name is Pete Brownback and on the eighteenth of May, 1999, they held a retirement ceremony for me in Heidelberg, Germany, at which time I took off this uniform. This is the first time I've put it on since," he said. That's why the decorations on his chest were "drab and dreary" instead of polished to a shine. "I will note that no one in the prosecution office had any Brasso," he added, attempting an icebreaker.

Couch thought of the Nuremberg tribunal, at which the American chief judge was FDR's former attorney general, Francis Biddle, a World War I veteran who also had been a federal circuit judge, chairman of the National Labor Relations Board, director of the Immigration and Naturalization Service, and personal secretary to Justice Oliver Wendell Holmes. Brownback had a narrower range of experience.

"I spent thirty years in the Army. I was an infantry officer for eight years, and a JAG for twenty-two years. I spent sixteen years at Fort Bragg. I was on jump status for sixteen years. My first, probably, thirty jumps were on propeller aircraft or jet-assisted propeller aircraft and I spent significant amounts of time in combat," Brownback continued. "The point of this is," he continued, "my hearing sucks! I can't hear things. So when you talk and I say, 'Huh?' it's not because I'm not paying attention, it's because I can't hear!"

Couch had done some research when Brownback's name first surfaced. Though only fifty-six, Brownback had chosen not to start a second career after leaving the military. He had instead retired to Florida, where he worked occasional odd jobs like census-taker and flagman at the beach. He gave up his law license rather than pay the annual registration fee.

Nevertheless, earlier that year, Brownback had unexpectedly made waves in the world of military justice: his most important decision as a military judge, a death sentence he imposed in 1996, was reversed by an Army appeals court. Brownback had run the murder trial at warp speed—more "a rodeo than a court of law," one defense lawyer said—taking all of three days to go from opening statements to death sentence.[18] Along the way, Brownback denied a defense request for a sentencing specialist to help make the case that the defendant did not deserve to die, a standard element in civilian capital trials. The appeals court called Brownback's ruling an "error of constitutional magnitude."[19]

Nevertheless, commissions' new appointing authority, John Altenburg, passed over thirty-three other candidates to give the job to Brownback, whom he had known since 1977. In a Pentagon memo, Altenburg explained that Brownback was "uniquely suited to fulfill this vital role in the Global War on Terrorism," which involved overseeing "trials in a unique legal regime that will influence the development of domestic and international law."[20]

Perhaps Altenburg knew something that justified such confidence, Couch thought. He listened closely as Brownback turned to his main message: weaning the JAGs from their loyalty to the Uniform Code of Military Justice. "I was a judge from '88 to '91 and from '92 to '99, so I have got a lot of experience judging cases, trying cases, and I have the same problem that each of you counsel have," he said. "You're stuck in the *RCM* mindset. And you can't help it—we're all brought up with the code." Brownback meant the *Rules for Courts-Martial,* setting out procedures to provide fair trials. They would have no place in the Guantanamo courtroom. "We're going to have to learn new terms," he said.

Brownback now introduced Keith Hodges, another retired Army colonel and former military judge, whom he had added to the commissions payroll. "My trusted assistant—and I sound like I'm being sarcastic, I'm not," he said. "Keith and I first met when he viciously prosecuted an innocent young child who just wanted to help her lover, a female, find a better life—"

"—in heaven," Hodges interjected. They laughed.

Brownback continued: Hodges would draft procedures that, after road-testing in the first four trials, could handle the remaining six hundred or so Guantanamo detainees when their turns came. In effect, Brownback said, he and Hodges should be considered a single entity.

"In the last two weeks, I've gotten 150 emails from Keith—"

"Actually, gotten more," Hodges corrected.

"I've gotten 260 emails from Keith," Brownback said, smiling. "Keith is an inveterate emailer. And we both believe in email and we both read our email all the time so we're always accessible by email," he said. "And cc Keith whenever you send me anything, because he's smarter than I am in some things." Defense counsel later nicknamed Hodges "Mini-Me," after Dr. Evil's dwarf-sized clone in the Austin Powers spy comedies.

Under the Bush military order, commissions would use procedures the Pentagon issued and could alter or withdraw at any time. Hodges explained that these directives would be called "commission law." They would range from directions on how to conduct attorney meetings to what defendants should wear at trial. Describing his plans, Hodges made just one slip—referring to a "Mr." Brownback.

"Ahem," Brownback interrupted.

"I'm sorry. *Colonel* Brownback," Hodges said.

"OKAY, HAVE ANY OF Y'ALL sat down and thought . . . about how this is going to work out?" Brownback said. "What do you think? How's this stuff going to work out?"

"You mean for today, sir?" someone asked.

"No! For these *trials*." Time was short. Proceedings would begin at Guantanamo in five weeks. "Give me a name. Okay, let's talk about Jones," Brownback said, misremembering the Australian defendant's name.

"Hicks," several corrected.

"Does Hicks have an attorney here?"

"No, sir," they replied. Hicks's attorney, Major Dan Mori, was traveling.

"Okay, good," Brownback said. "Let's talk about Hicks. Hicks has been referred to trial, right? There is no procedure that I have seen that requires an arraignment. Has anyone seen anything like that?" Before anyone could answer, Brownback continued: "There's no such thing as a speedy trial clock in this thing, right?"

Brownback's presumptions were coming so fast and stretching so far that even Bob Swann, the chief prosecutor, grew concerned. Hamdan's lawyers, Charlie Swift and Neal Katyal, had raised the speedy trial issue months earlier. They weren't present at Brownback's meeting, but other defense attorneys were, and all would surely seize on anything suggesting that the presiding officer had prejudged disputed issues.

"No, sir," said Swann, "I wouldn't even be commenting on that in light of the fact that Mr. Katyal and, I believe, Commander Swift believes that Article 10"—the military version of the Constitution's speedy trial requirement—"applies to these proceedings, so I think we ought to stay away from that issue."

The deputy chief defense counsel, Lieutenant Colonel Sharon Shaffer, agreed. "I don't think that is appropriate either, sir. These are the subject of motions that are going to be filed and your comments here—"

"I'm asking a *question*," Brownback said, defensively.

"Is there any problem with going to Guantanamo with all the commission members and advising [the defendants] seriatim in court of what the charges are and taking any other things there—"

"There is, sir," said Bahlul's defense attorney, Lieutenant Commander Phil Sundel. He was a studious, serious lawyer who had worked at the UN war crimes tribunal for Rwanda. "I haven't been able to speak to my client for three months."

"Why not?" said Brownback.

"I'm not prepared to go forward on any scheduling of any events at all until I have an interpreter so that my co-counsel and I can meet with our client," Sundel said. "Anything other than our being able to meet with our client and speak with him is premature."

Sundel said the government had rejected the interpreter he selected and that he hadn't been able to find an acceptable replacement.

"What does your guy speak?" Brownback asked.

"Arabic," Sundel said.

"Why is it that only this one person is—"

"I don't think this is something that is appropriately addressed in an informal conference like this," Sundel said.

"Okay, it's a *formal* conference now," Brownback snapped. "Why is this the only one?" he said. "How many Arabic speakers do you think there are in the United States?"

"Surprisingly few that are not only qualified but interested in participating in *this* process," Sundel replied.

THE PROSECUTION HAD NO objection to Brownback's trial plan. What about the defense?

"I'm not going to speak as a defense perspective, sir," Shaffer said. "The other three counsel are away and I'm just not going to speak on their behalf."

Sundel wouldn't respond, either. "Beyond getting an interpreter so I can speak with my client, I don't feel qualified to discuss anything," he said.

"You've never spoken to your client?" Brownback asked.

"I have spoken with my client for a two-day period in mid-April. That is the last time I was able to communicate with my client."

"Okay. I'm confused as to—I've seen a lot of interpreters before and I didn't know there was such a requirement for them," Brownback said. "But send us what you want—are you in email contact with the other counsel?"

"Not really, sir," Shaffer said.

"Why not?"

"Well, one is in Yemen, for one, sir."

"They don't have email in Yemen?"

"I don't know. I don't know if they do or not."

"Aaargh!" Brownback exclaimed. Throughout the meeting, the prosecutors were guarded, the defense attorneys verging on obstructionist.

Hodges tried to take charge. "Colonel Shaffer, we're not asking you to find—or to speak on behalf—"

"I'm not sure what the colonel's asking," Shaffer said.

"I'm asking where I can find the counsel. That's all I'm asking," Brownback said.

"And as I mentioned to you yesterday, sir, one is at Gitmo, Major Mori—"

"And he's going to be there next week, or she—?"

"I don't know where he's going to be next week," Shaffer said.

"Okay, who are the military counsel for Hicks?" Brownback asked.

"Major Mori," Shaffer said.

Swann tried to rescue Brownback. "We've got a document or something that has all that information on it," he said.

"Who's Hicks?" Brownback continued. "Morris?"

"*Mori. Major Mori,*" the prosecutors and defense lawyers said in unison.

"Mau?" Brownback said. He had poor hearing, remember.

"*M-O-R-I,*" the gathered officers all said.

Brownback struggled to grasp the names of the defendants and their lawyers, and what particular details were hampering each case.

"Ahhhrg!" he grunted, again.

Suddenly, Swann cut in. "What's this?" he said, accusatorily.

There was a small device on the conference table, immediately in front of Phil Sundel.

"It's a tape recorder," Sundel said. He had put it there, in full view, when he sat down.

Swann looked to Brownback. "Sir, did you give him permission to tape here?"

"No, I wasn't even asked permission," Brownback said. "You're not taping something without my permission are you?"

"I didn't realize I needed permission," Sundel said. "I walked in here and turned on the tape machine."

"Did you ask me my permission?"

"I did not ask your permission."

"Turn it off and blank the tape," Brownback ordered.

In his notebook, Stu Couch wrote: "Things are getting hot in here."

"I thought this was an official hearing, sir," Sundel said. He turned off the recorder. The room sat in silence. Seconds dragged as Brownback contemplated what to do.

"Okay, I now give you permission to turn it back on," Brownback said. "I don't want to get into a fight with people."

Keith Hodges turned to the issues on his own list: Would formal or everyday uniforms be required for commission hearings? Should documents be emailed in Microsoft Word or Adobe PDF format? At least one point had been decided: "No JPEGs, BMPs, databases, spreadsheets and all that," Hodges said.

Pete Brownback was ready to end the meeting. "Okay, anything else, from anyone?" he said. "Okay, have a nice day."

As the officers got up to leave, Brownback turned to Sundel. He wanted to make sure something else got on the tape.

"Leave that on for a second," Brownback said. "I do not give you permission to share that with anyone."

The Man from al Qaeda

A WEEK BEFORE PRETRIAL hearings were to begin at Guantanamo, the commissions appointing authority, John Altenburg, stepped to the Pentagon lectern to brief the press.

"First of all, there are several ways that the United States government could have proceeded to prosecute alleged war crimes," he said, including civilian courts, which were in fact being used to try some defendants. "They could have done courts-martial in the military. They could have sought out international ad hoc tribunals. And there are other ways. But the government chose, for many different reasons, to use a military commission process. It doesn't mean that the others were wrong; it just means that the government chose on balance, given the nature of the allegations that were being made and, I think, especially national security interests, they chose to use the commission process."

Responding to questions, he acknowledged that defense attorneys had "legitimate" complaints about getting interpreters. When a reporter asked about detainee statements obtained through "questionable techniques," Altenburg strayed from the administration line that abuse claims were canards spread by terrorists to discredit the United States.

"That's a very incisive question," Altenburg said. "I think that that will be an important issue in at least some of the trials."

Even without evidence that their own clients had been abused, defense attorneys could argue that the Guantanamo environment was so pervasively coercive that all statements implicitly were involuntary, Altenburg said. For instance, a defense attorney could argue that his client confessed solely "because he'd heard that other people [detainees] had had things happen to them that he didn't want to happen," he explained. "Not to do the defense counsels' work for them," he added.

But such disputes lay in the future, when the trials' main phase began. In contrast, Altenburg said, there should be few fireworks at the pretrial hearings.

"Next week may be interesting" for historical reasons, he said, "because it's the first time in sixty years" that the United States was convening a military commission. "But I expect that beyond that it'll be fairly pedestrian."

■

At Guantanamo, on a hot, humid August day, Stu Couch stood on an abandoned airstrip called McCalla Field. Looming on a hill above was a decommissioned control tower, the structure Whit Cobb and Bill Lietzau selected to house military commissions. With the naval base staff unwilling to share its own prime facilities for the legal experiment, commissions had few options.

The desert tan building was called the Pink Palace, Cobb heard, a vestige of its former color of institutional salmon. Under Lietzau's direction, a million dollars was spent to turn the musty structure into a courthouse. Despite the Bush administration's disdain for international legal institutions, the Pentagon sent a team to study UN courtrooms in The Hague designed for simultaneous translation of trials involving participants who spoke different languages.

Lietzau himself set up the Pink Palace's single courtroom. Instead of an elevated bench for a single judge, there was a long table to accommodate the commission members. He placed the military services' flags on poles behind the commission table and their circular seals on the wall, stage right.

The spectators' gallery consisted of several rows of black office chairs. Flat-screen monitors were affixed to pillars so that those with obstructed views could see the proceedings, which also would be transmitted by closed-circuit feed to an auditorium next to a make-shift press room in Bulkeley Hall, the base's headquarters building. Initially, the Pentagon planned to reserve sixteen of the sixty courtroom seats for the press but later cut that number in half to make room for more government officials.[1] Most journalists who made it to Guantanamo would have to watch on the auditorium screen, unable to see what military camera operators left out of the frame or to overhear an incidental comment.

A military escort showing the facility to reporters ahead of the hearings said no video feed would be transmitted outside Guantanamo. Nothing, she said, would be recorded. Half a century on, she said, smiling, "you won't be seeing this on the History Channel." The contrast, again, was Nuremberg. Newsreels of the proceedings against surviving Nazi leaders underscored the Allies' claim to represent the rule of law.

A reporter asked what purpose was served by prohibiting recordings. The escort had no answer.

Secrecy pervaded. A sketch artist was permitted in the courtroom, but drawings had to clear a military censor who required that all faces be obscured—except, if they consented, the defendant and his attorneys. Prosecutors and commission members would have no faces, just blank, oval, flesh-toned voids.

They would have no identities, either. Although previously included in public documents, the names suddenly were deleted from materials disseminated to journalists. Military spokesmen said that concealing the officials' identities would protect them from al Qaeda retaliation. The policy was based on speculation, as no terrorist threats had been detected against commissions participants. Moreover, officials including Chief Prosecutor Bob Swann and Presiding Officer Pete Brownback already had been identified in news reports, as had defense attorneys, and nothing suggested any danger to them. Reporters who had taken down the names before they were deleted published them anyway. They considered the identities of officials involved in historic proceedings to be newsworthy.

Even so, fears over what reporters might learn gripped the military. "Right now, the heightened state of tension on this island is tangible," a military spokesman told the press at a Bulkeley Hall briefing the night before the first hearing.[2]

Existing law already authorized the government to conceal information by marking it "classified." Commissions regulations allowed suppressing unclassified information as well by using a new designation, "protected." No definition was provided.

At John Altenburg's Pentagon briefing, a reporter had asked for clarification of the circular term.

"I haven't defined it any better than it is in the rules," Altenburg said, where it wasn't defined at all. "I try to draw a balance—Should I release this name? Should I allow this to be public? Should we put this up on the website? When I analyze and I see that there are national security interests or potential intelligence issues, I'm inclined to err on the side of being careful."

At Guantanamo, officials fretted that despite their precautions, the public still might learn something the government preferred to conceal. To prevent that, the video feed to journalists in Bulkeley Hall was placed on five-minute delay, giving security officers time to cut the transmission.[3]

For the eight reporters physically in the courtroom, Brownback had a more intrusive solution. If something "protected" slipped out, the spokesman said, soldiers would seize their notebooks, read them for proscribed information, and tear out the offending pages. Later, a photocopy of the seized pages, with the newly secret information blacked out, would be returned.

The announcement stunned the three dozen reporters the Pentagon had authorized to cover the events. One correspondent dared soldiers to seize her notebooks; she used old-fashioned shorthand, making her notes indecipherable to anyone else. Other reporters began contacting their editors to lodge formal protests. Two hours later, Brownback rescinded his order.

COUCH HAD WATCHED CONFLICTS intensify between Pete Brownback and defense attorneys since the first meeting in Crystal City. Like a military judge running a court-martial, Brownback had begun acting on legal motions, only to meet defense objections that he was powerless to do so. Bush's military order made "the military commission . . . the triers of both fact and law." Defense attorneys insisted that meant the entire five-member commission must consider arguments and vote on the outcome. As "presiding officer," Brownback's function was like that of a jury foreman or committee chairman, they said—not a judge.

The politicals had imagined that a commission made up of combat or logistics officers, unburdened by legal training, would hurry trials to conclusion rather than ponder every step with lawyerly caution. Instead, defense attorneys had seized on that very structure to gum up proceedings.

Brownback grew testy, complaining by email about defense lawyers' "misapprehension concerning my authority." Rather than fixate on the text of the presidential military order, "perhaps a better way of looking at the matter is to say I have authority to order those things which I order done," he wrote.[4] But he backed off his initial plan to preside alone over pretrial hearings. The full commission—four other officers and an alternate, also selected by Altenburg—would sit at Guantanamo.

In an orientation memo, Brownback told the commission members to keep an open mind, not discuss the case with anyone, and avoid news coverage. If approached by a reporter, "walk away and do not even listen to [any] question they may ask," he wrote. "The appearance and demeanor of all of us should reflect the seriousness with which we view the trial."[5] But don't get too serious, he added. "We have arranged a private boat cruise. Enjoy the NEX"—the Naval Exchange store, offering discounted liquor and souvenirs—"the sites, the varied eating establishments, and the broad variety of [recreational] activities," he wrote. "You will also note that each of your rooms has cable TV."

NEARLY THREE YEARS AFTER President Bush's order, Stu Couch took a seat in the Pink Palace courtroom when the military commission came into session on Tuesday, August 24, 2004. He felt excited, and anxious; although he would not be arguing in any of the four minor cases slated for pretrial hearings that week, the precedents set would shape the more serious cases—his cases—to follow. He would pay close attention.

Bill Lietzau had envisioned a solemn proceeding, with officers in tie and jacket, following the practice at Nuremberg. Brownback took a more casual approach, striding to his seat wearing no robe, no tie, just lime green Army short-sleeves. A side door opened and Salim Hamdan, wearing a blazer over his traditional white gown, a red-checked kaffiyeh over his shoulders, was brought in by two soldiers in battle dress. He had a thick mustache, but not the scraggled beard that many Islamists favored.

Hamdan had been in solitary confinement for the eight months since he was charged; the Pentagon did not want him telling other detainees that he had seen a lawyer or of the possibility of legal process. Charlie Swift said the seclusion had been hard. Hamdan lost his appetite and dropped fifty pounds. He was put on antidepressants but received no counseling. There was no doctor-patient privilege at Guantanamo, Swift said, so anything Hamdan told a therapist would be given to prosecutors.

If Hamdan was depressed, however, he showed no sign of it when led into court. Eyes twinkling, he grinned broadly as he took in the scene. It was obvious why the guards called him Smiley.

The defendant's demeanor seemed at odds with proceedings that could lead to life imprisonment. But for Hamdan, the hearing was a dramatic break after years of indefinite confinement under difficult, sometimes harsh, conditions. Now he was in an air-conditioned hearing room, in clean, respectable clothes instead of prison duds, unshackled and seated in an upholstered swivel chair, alongside Swift and his interpreter. Three guards stood behind Hamdan, should he try anything.

After some excited conversation with Swift, Hamdan donned the headphones provided for simultaneous translation, big, over-the-ear 1970s-style earmuffs, and settled in, as if to observe a long-anticipated concert or play.

Charlie Swift rose. Big and soft, he had a boyish face, bright eyes, and a mop of hair that vaguely suggested an overgrown, blondish Beatle. He was outgoing, talkative, exuberant, sometimes oppressively so. Enraptured by his own train of thought, Swift could lose track of a conversation's conventions of space and time. Stuffed into his Navy whites, gesturing in his awkward way, Swift reminded one callous observer of the Stay Puft Marshmallow Man, the sailor-suited confectionery mascot from the movie *Ghostbusters*. To Stu Couch, Swift seemed pitifully outclassed by Scott Lang, who would be prosecuting Hamdan.

Lang spoke with assurance, if not impatience. He shared many of Couch's frustrations about commissions, but none seeped through his polished courtroom persona. That he wore the same Navy whites as Swift only heightened the contrast between them.

Lang's mission was to set a trial date and end the proceedings as quickly as possible. For Swift, however, the hearing was a chance to attack the commissions project itself. His first target was Colonel Brownback.

Under the procedure called voir dire, attorneys can question prospective jurors—and in this instance, commission members, starting with Brownback—to smoke out potential bias, conflicts of interest, or other disqualifying factors.

"Are you eligible to practice law in Virginia currently?" Swift said.

"I am eligible to practice in Virginia if I change my status to active member," Brownback said, somewhat evasively. Because his bar membership had lapsed, he would have to take continuing education courses and pay fees to reinstate his law license.

"Sir, would you be eligible to serve as a civilian defense counsel for *this* commission proceeding?"

"I don't know. I haven't examined that," Brownback said. In fact, he could not; Pentagon regulations required that civilian attorneys, in addition to being US citizens with security clearances, be authorized to practice law.

Swift continued: When volunteering for commissions, had Brownback read Bush's military order or Rumsfeld's implementing instructions?

"I scanned them," Brownback said.

"After scanning them, did you believe that the [commissions] process was lawful?" Swift said.

"I choose not to answer that question at this time. Thank you," Brownback said. Among other verbal tics, Brownback seemed to express displeasure by appending "thank you" to his remarks. Pressed, he said he would keep an open mind, for now, on whether the commission he headed was unlawful.

Swift moved to disqualify Brownback. Added to everything else, Swift said, Brownback's long friendship with John Altenburg, the appointing authority, created "an appearance of unfairness."

NEXT CAME THE OTHER commission members. Silent until now, they seemed interchangeable, five middle-aged white men in soldier outfits.

Brownback recited a standard colloquy.

"Does any member know the accused?" he began.

No one raised a hand.

"Apparently not," Brownback said. "Does any member know any person named in the charges?"

Nobody moved.

"Apparently not," he said again. Among trial observers, Brownback's habitual use of "apparently not," and its converse, "apparently so," became a frequently mocked characteristic.

The prosecutor, Scott Lang, rose.

"Can all members set aside any feelings generated by the attacks of 9/11 and render a verdict in this case that's based solely on the evidence presented?" he said.

No one indicated otherwise.

"Apparently so," said Brownback. The prosecution was satisfied. Next was the defense's turn.

"Good morning, sirs. My name is Lieutenant Commander Charles Swift, and—I'm too far from the microphone"—he moved closer—"and I represent Salim Ahmed Hamdan in this case, and I also have some questions," he said. "Does every member understand what the term *jurisdiction* means in the context of judicial proceedings? Do you understand what that means?"

Negative. The members shook their heads.

"They're going to be doing that a lot," Swift said.

THE PANEL LEFT THE room, and Brownback called them back one at a time, in order of rank, for individual questioning.

The first up, Marine Colonel Jack Sparks, once commanded a battalion including reservists who were New York City cops and firefighters. One died on 9/11. Sparks attended his funeral.

Swift asked how that experience affected him.

"I have been in the Marine Corps twenty-eight years. It is not the first Marine that, unfortunately, that I have seen die," Sparks said flatly. "The death of every Marine I have known or served with has a deep effect on me."

Did he visit Ground Zero?

Yes, Sparks said, about two weeks after 9/11. "It is a sad sight. A lot of destruction there. Hard to fathom what was there and what was left."

"Were you angry, sir?"

"I imagine that everybody that saw it was angry," Sparks said.

The next member, Marine Colonel R. Thomas Bright, had even closer connections to the case. On 9/11 itself, he was ordered to begin planning the invasion of Afghanistan. After operations began, his job was "coordinating the logistics" for moving detainees to Guantanamo, he said. The name of every prisoner—including Salim Hamdan—crossed his desk.

"The list, when I would get it, would come with a series of names. My job was to ensure that it was in the proper format," Bright said, his careful, mechanical voice, like his crew-cut appearance and khaki uniform, almost indistinguishable from that of Colonel Sparks. Bright would send the list to his boss, who then sent it to his boss, "and ultimately that would go up through the joint staff to OSD [Office of the Secretary of Defense] for approval."

Swift drew out that Bright's assignments exposed him to the early decision-making process that set aside the Geneva Conventions, established rules for killing enemy forces, and gave criteria for sending prisoners to Guantanamo.

Air Force Colonel Christopher Bogdan came next. Bogdan ran the unit that supplied Predator unmanned drones bearing Hellfire missiles to "another government agency"—the alias for the CIA—for targeted strikes on enemy personnel. He had been cited for "fantastic results tracking and killing Taliban."[6]

Bogdan knew an Air Force colonel who had died on 9/11. He also had read *The Crisis of Islam,* an analysis of Islamist terrorism by the Middle East scholar Bernard Lewis. "We must stand tall," Bogdan had written earlier, in answers to the lawyers' written questionnaire about 9/11. "Freedom isn't free," he added.

Scott Lang asked Bogdan to explain.

"Terrorism, in my opinion, is much like many of the other threats throughout the course of history of our country," Bogdan

said. "That threat must be met with the same resolve as those previous threats to our country, and that was my intention when I said
we must stand tall."

An Air Force intelligence officer, Lieutenant Colonel Timothy
Toomey, was next. He helped plan missions to capture enemy prisoners in Afghanistan. In a thick, bureaucratic monotone, he said he
never came across Hamdan during that assignment.

"Is it possible that you would have seen intelligence on him and
simply not remember it?" Swift asked.

"Yes, it is possible," Toomey said.

Last to the stand was the alternate, Army Lieutenant Colonel
Curt Cooper. He seemed the most exercised about the threat of Islamist terrorism, mentioning *The Clash of Civilizations,* the 1996 book by
Harvard political scientist Samuel P. Huntington predicting that future global conflict would be defined by culture rather than ideology.

Cooper was fidgety. Being on the commission could make him
and his family a target for terrorists, he said. Since 9/11, he had been
watching television and searching the Internet to learn about the Taliban and related threats. The attacks made him "very angry," and he
wanted to serve on the commission to secure justice for the victims.

"Do you know what the Geneva Convention is?" Swift said.

"Not specifically, no. That's being honest," Cooper said. "I know
it is very specific and there are three different articles."

"Actually," Swift said, "there are four articles, sir."

Bright, Bogdan, and Toomey had refused to answer several
questions in open session, saying they involved classified materials.
Brownback ordered the hearing to continue in secret, with only the
lawyers present. Swift wanted Hamdan with him in the room.

Scott Lang objected. "The accused does not have the clearance
to be exposed to this information," he said. Brownback denied Swift's
motion.

RETURNING TO THE COURTROOM after 6:00 p.m., a tired Brownback stumbled into the Navy flag behind the commission table, knock-

ing it over. He picked it up and gaveled the proceeding back into open session.

Swift filed objections to Sparks, Bright, Toomey, and Cooper, as well as Brownback. If all were granted, only Colonel Bogdan would remain on the commission, forcing the Pentagon to round up a new set of members.

Now came time for Hamdan's plea.

"Accused and counsel, please rise," Brownback said. "Salim Ahmed Hamdan, how do you plead?"

The answer was anticlimactic. Swift said Hamdan would defer pleading until his various legal motions were resolved.

"Okay," Brownback said. "Does counsel for either side have anything further at this time?"

Apparently not. Brownback turned to the officers on the commission. "Members, anything further at this time?"

Sparks, Bright, Bogdan, Toomey, and Cooper said nothing.

"The court is in recess," Brownback said—but Swift, after some seemingly spontaneous commotion at the defense table, interrupted.

"Sir, actually—I'm sorry. Sorry," he said.

"Yes, Commander Swift?" said Brownback. He sounded tired, exasperated.

"I'm sorry," Swift continued. There was just one more thing, he said, an "administrative note" to get on the record. "It has to do with your voir dire of the presiding officer," he said.

"Yes, Commander?" Brownback said.

Earlier in the day, Swift had asked Brownback whether, at his July 15 Crystal City meeting with prosecution and defense attorneys, he had ventured an opinion regarding speedy trial rights at commissions. Brownback had replied that the issue was "mentioned," but he had not expressed any view on it. Stu Couch bit his lip at that answer; at the Crystal City meeting, Couch had heard Brownback blithely assume there was no speedy trial provision for commissions. Swift had been traveling when the meeting took place, so he had no direct knowledge of what Brownback actually had said.

"Yes, sir," Swift continued. "It came to my attention after the voir dire that there was a tape made regarding the 15 July meeting. I'd like permission to send that tape along with the other matters that I'm submitting on your voir dire regarding your qualifications."

Couch couldn't decide which was more unbelievable: Brownback's dissembling answer or that the stumbling, smiling, somewhat out of phase Charlie Swift had pulled a *Columbo* moment.

Brownback dropped his head to his hands, as if shutting out the world around him. It was another of his recurrent gestures. An entire minute lapsed.

"And the tape goes to show what?" Brownback said.

"Your opinion at the time, sir."

It was the tape Phil Sundel had recorded, the one Brownback had ordered him not to share with anybody. Swift said he had been told that it recorded Brownback saying there was no speedy trial right at commissions.

"Okay. I would be—let me think about this," Brownback haltingly responded. "I believe in the meeting—I don't remember speedy trial, I remember Article 10 being mentioned, and I believe I said something to the effect of, Article 10, how does that come into play? Or words to that effect," he said. Article 10 of the Uniform Code of Military Justice concerned pretrial confinement of criminal suspects. "I did not know that my words were being taped, and I must confess that when I walked into the room that day I had no idea that Article 10 would come into play because I hadn't had an occasion to review Article 10. It is not something that usually comes up in military justice-prudence. Jurisprudence."

The tape "was made without my permission, without the permission of anyone in the room," Brownback added, but "I do give you permission to send it to the appointing authority with the other matters."

He looked sharply at Swift. "Before I call—I put the court in recess, Commander Swift, do you have anything else?"

"No, sir, I don't," Swift said, smiling. "I really don't. We really don't, sir."

"Court in recess," Brownback said.

■

"David has been an adventurer all his life. He has always wanted to see what was over the next fence, and as he got older, the fence got taller," David Hicks's father, Terry Hicks, told reporters at Guantanamo. He had traveled from Adelaide after the Pentagon authorized him to attend the hearing.

As a lad, David loved *The Lord of the Rings* and played with a Ouija board.[7] Incorrigible after his parents divorced, David was sent to a reform school and worked as a jackaroo, or ranch hand, in the rustic Northern Territory, then returned home, where he got an eighteen-year-old girlfriend pregnant. They split up, and David went to work at a kangaroo slaughterhouse, pulling innards from marsupial carcasses. The ever-rising fences his father described led Hicks to Japan for a job training horses and then to Kosovo, inspired by photos of the fighting there between Serbs and ethnic Albanians.

Returning home, Hicks tried to join the Australian army but was rejected because he never finished high school. He joined a mosque, insisted on calling himself Dawood—the Arabic version of David— and made his way to a Taliban unit in Afghanistan.

Hicks, now twenty-nine, was easily led. First, he sought to ingratiate himself to US interrogators; now he was taking cues from his defense counsel, Major Dan Mori. That apparently included a mischievous jab at the officer who helped design the commissions structure.

"I request LtCol William K. Lietzau, USMC, be detailed to represent me as my Selected Detailed Defense Counsel under Military Commission Order No. 1," read a letter Hicks signed with his tiny, cramped scrawl. The regulations Lietzau drafted permitted defendants to select any "available" JAG as a defense attorney; he had not anticipated being called himself to represent a detainee. The request, filed two weeks before the hearing, was denied; Lietzau was "not available," the Pentagon said.

Hicks was taken to the courtroom in a charcoal gray suit Mori had brought for him, the first he had ever worn.[8] Unlike the childlike Hamdan, who gaped around with amazement, Hicks seemed determined to appear somber and serious. Lips pursed, he stared straight ahead, avoiding eye contact with his parents. The diminutive defendant sat in a padded leather chair, his feet barely touching the ground.

Hicks's lawyers moved to exclude the same commission members Swift had. The trial, in effect, would be "a referendum on their conduct and the conduct of their chain of command" in capturing, interrogating, and prosecuting Hicks, the defense said. How could they be impartial?

Prosecutor Kurt Brubaker objected. "The attacks of September 11, 2001, had a huge impact on the United States military. To try to find a panel that is not impacted by those attacks of September 11 is just not the appropriate standard," he said.

Brownback turned to Hicks, charged with conspiring with Osama bin Laden to commit murder, among other crimes.

"Mr. David Hicks, I now ask: How do you plead?"

"Sir," Hicks said. "To all charges, not guilty."

■

The routine broke on the third day. Ali Hamza al-Bahlul, unaware that he previously had been convicted in absentia at the mock trial, wore a too-big gray polo shirt and black slip-on sneakers, an outfit that the military bought for thirty dollars at the base exchange. Less defiant than indifferent, Bahlul remained seated when the bailiff, wearing combat fatigues, yelled, "All rise." The commission members entered from stage left.

In Yemen, Bahlul's father had told a reporter that his son was "cultured and peace-loving," a writer of poetry and devoted father of four.[9] "He has not committed any crimes and he hates no one."

Colonel Brownback recited the same script he had read to Hamdan and Hicks, informing Bahlul that he had been provided military defense counsel at no charge but also could engage a civilian attorney who met Defense Department requirements, provided there would be no expense to the government.

"Am I allowed to represent myself?" Bahlul said in Arabic, translated by a contract interpreter in the courtroom box.

Brownback stopped. He seemed stunned by the question.

REGARDLESS OF IDEOLOGICAL stripe, fanatics typically demand to act as their own attorneys. They reject the legitimacy of the system prosecuting them and deny that an officer of its courts could present the epic, even existential rationale behind their actions. Squeaky Fromme, Ted Kaczynski, and, more recently, Zacarias Moussaoui all had insisted on representing themselves. Confirming the conventional wisdom regarding "a fool for a client," each was sentenced to life in prison.

Still, in the 1975 case *Faretta v. California,* the Supreme Court had found a constitutional right to self-representation.[10] Only one tribunal in Anglo-American history "ever adopted a practice of forcing counsel upon an unwilling defendant," Justice Potter Stewart observed. "The tribunal was the Star Chamber."[11]

At commissions, however, Bush administration lawyers had insisted that defendants be represented by military counsel whether they wanted them or not. An enemy alien permitted to act for himself would be a loose cannon, a disruptive, unpredictable factor in a forum intended to demonstrate American power.

AS BAHLUL'S QUESTION HUNG in the silent courtroom, Pete Brownback rubbed his eyes and stared at the ceiling. He fashioned a response.

"I'm referring to Military Commission Order No. 1, Paragraph 4(c), sub (4)," Brownback said. "It states: 'The accused must be represented at all relevant times by detailed defense counsel.' So the answer is no, you're not allowed to represent yourself."

Why not? Bahlul asked.

Brownback listed the qualifications of his appointed defense lawyers, Lieutenant Commander Phil Sundel and Major Mark Bridges. They held law degrees and were trained in military law. They had security clearances, "so they can see all the information." Sundel had a Maryland bar license, Bridges one from Kentucky.

"And—I resist making a comment about Kentucky—they both are fluent in English, which is a necessity here," Brownback added, his untranslatable joke about Appalachia only further befuddling Bahlul.

"Perhaps even more importantly, they are not on trial here, which means they are not personally involved, which means they can remain objective in situations when a person about whom things are being said might become emotional or heated," Brownback said. "Given their background and training, they have the skill and knowledge to force the commission to apply the rules and the law on your behalf, and if they feel that the commission has not done so, they have instant access to computers to make and file motions. They can make objections. They can argue by analogy to federal, military and international law, and they have research resources, both computer and personal, which will help them ensure that your rights are represented or protected in these proceedings. Do you understand what I just said now?"

"Yes, I understand. I have a question based on what you said," Bahlul said. "Are you done?"

"Not yet," Brownback answered.

"When you're done," Bahlul said.

"No, I'm sorry," Brownback said. "You may ask your question now."

"I have some idea about practicing law in Yemen," Bahlul said.

A murmur went up among the Arabic speakers in the court-room—interpreters working for defense lawyers, observers from human rights groups, journalists from Arabic-language news channels.

Brownback squinted at the commissions interpreter.

"I have some idea about practicing law in Yemen," the interpreter repeated.

At the defendant's table, the defense linguist whispered something to Phil Sundel.

Sundel rose. "Excuse me, sir. I'm not sure that was exactly what Mr. al-Bahlul said. My understanding is he said that he knows *some people* who practice law."

The commissions interpreter was embarrassed. "I do apologize, sir," the interpreter said, trying again. "Correction: I have—"

Bahlul interjected: "Nobody represents me until this point. I wish nobody would interrupt while I'm talking. I have some people that do practice or are familiar with law in the country of Yemen," he said, according to the increasingly overwhelmed official interpreter. "Is it possible that I can be granted this, a Yemeni attorney? And as far as I know, if I'm right, that I cannot be represented by anybody other than an American. Is it possible that the Yemeni attorney, through the American attorney, can be involved in my case?"

"Now," said Brownback, "is what you are telling me is that you want to have a Yemeni attorney provided—at no expense to the government, meaning the United States government—present to assist your detailed counsel, Commander Sundel and Major Bridges, for this proceeding?"

"Yes," Bahlul said.

"Sir," Sundel again interjected, "I think perhaps what we may want to do is to clarify if his first preference is to represent himself; if that is not allowable, his second preference is to be represented exclusively by a Yemeni attorney; and if that is not allowable, his last preference is to be represented by military counsel, with a Yemeni attorney assistant."

Brownback addressed Bahlul: "As you're sitting there, please just tell me, right now, what do you want? Do you want a second to talk to someone? Honest, I mean, do you want to take a—"

Bahlul cut him short. "I have mentioned previously, and you answered it. I asked if I can represent myself. You said no. But what I meant—I do not want an attorney representing me. I'll attend the sessions if it's mandatory to attend. I'll be here," he said. "If I do have that choice, I'd rather not be here."

Brownback, however, didn't seem to realize what he himself just had said. "I do not recall directing or stating that you are not allowed to represent yourself. What I said and read was the provision of the military commission order. I am trying, honestly, to find out your desires and to find out something more about you and those desires. I have not ignored what you said, but I want to find out some more before I say anything in that regard, okay?"

"Good," said Bahlul.

Brownback turned to the prosecutor. "Commander Lang, did I say, on the record, did I say he couldn't represent himself, or did I read from the—I'm not trying to trick anyone. I don't remember saying he could not represent himself."

Lang had a better memory. "Sir, I believe that when you read the instruction, that's the reasonable interpretation," he said.

Brownback returned to the defendant. "Before I say anything on that subject, Mr. al-Bahlul, I'd like to know something more about you. If you wish, you can take a moment and talk with anyone and you can tell me whether or not you want to answer these questions."

"You can ask me anything," Bahlul said. "I don't need to go back to anybody."

"How old are you?"

"Thirty-six years."

"How many years of formal education do you have?"

"Sixteen years."

"Have you spent much time in American culture other than your time here at Guantanamo? I'm asking the question because the proceedings that you're in front of are derived from our culture, and different cultures have different ways of handling things. And I guess what I'm asking is this: Is your knowledge of our culture sufficient to make things that would appear strange if you had no knowledge, not appear so strange? That's all I'm asking."

"I have a large amount of knowledge," Bahlul said.

"Have you ever studied international law or the law of war? It's not something that most people pay much attention to."

"Yes, I did. I've read," Bahlul said.

"Do you realize that because—well, that in accordance with the president's Military Order and Military Commission Order No. 1, there may be evidence against you which you would not be allowed to see because of its protected nature?"

"I don't think it's fair," Bahlul said. "The accused cannot defend himself without seeing such evidence for himself."

"That wasn't my question," Brownback said. "My question was, whether you believe it's fair or not fair, do you understand right now that you will not be able to see certain evidence because it is either classified or protected. Right now, you can't see it. Do you understand that?"

"For the protected evidence [issue], let's put it aside," Bahlul said. He then launched an incoherent rant—at least as rendered by the official interpreters: "It's all well-known in all those—the civilian, or the local—the decision is the evidence, especially as the decision is under no pressure, and based on the person without any—without being placed under any pressure, and based on personal decision or preference."

Again, a low rumble spread through the courtroom as the Arabic speakers whispered their disagreement. In fact, they protested, Bahlul had said something else: "It's well known in both secular and religious law that a confession is [strong] evidence, particularly a confession given free of coercion and as a result of the person's own decision."

The reason for Bahlul's windup soon became clear, even as the government interpreters continued to mangle his words.

"One point that I would like the judge to understand and the members of the panel, and the people—the people that are the jurors, or the people that were sworn in—and the prosecutor, and the defense team that until this point does not represent me, and the visitors and detainees and if it's being, you know, viewed via media channels, people that are watching as well, people of the entire globe should know," he said.

The courtroom was spellbound. "I testify that the American government is under no pressure. Nobody has put the United States government under pressure," he said. (Actually, according to other linguists present, Bahlul said, "The American government has not coerced me to say this, nobody from the United States government has put me under pressure.")

Bahlul continued: "*I am from al Qaeda and the relationship between me and 9/11—*"

"Stop!" said Brownback.

Bahlul obeyed. Stu Couch looked first at Scott Lang, seated next to him, and then around the courtroom. No one else was exhaling, either.

"Members," Brownback said, turning to the commission. "You all understand that I am questioning Mr. al-Bahlul in order to determine his representation. Y'all understand that, right? Y'all understand that Mr. al-Bahlul has not been placed under oath?"

The commission members nodded.

"Apparently so," Brownback said. "You further understand that none of this is evidence in any way. Do y'all understand that?"

The members nodded.

"Apparently so," Brownback said. He turned to Bahlul. "I apologize for interrupting you," he said.

To lawyers in the courtroom, much less Bahlul, Brownback's action made no sense. In a normal courtroom functioning under standard rules of evidence, a judge might be expected to intervene to preserve a defendant's rights, such as the Fifth Amendment privilege against self-incrimination. But commissions were designed to dispense with such obstacles to conviction. All evidence "probative to a reasonable person" was to be admitted, and—as Bahlul himself observed—a voluntary confession in open court obviously qualified.

Scott Lang certainly thought so. "Sir, before we go on, we'd note our objection to [your] statement and ask for a recess," he said. "We don't think that's an accurate statement of commission law."

Brownback told Lang to file a brief on the question and turned to the defendant. "Go on," he said.

Bahlul resumed. But he did not pick up where Brownback had interrupted him. Couch felt he had been cheated.

"I know that this is like an arraignment, and the questions are limited," Bahlul said, displaying a surprising degree of legal sophistication. "In short, I would like to represent myself," he said, adding that he was familiar with "new laws" drafted "after the September 11 incident."

He promised to behave. "Nobody should be worried relating to me causing problems, or being loud, or basically saying things that might be inflammatory," he said. "I can give you my word."

Brownback called a recess.

ONE MORE CASE REMAINED, that of Ibrahim Ahmed Mahmoud al-Qosi, a forty-three-year-old Sudanese said to be one of bin Laden's longest-serving assistants. Intelligence reports indicated that Qosi had taken part in a failed plot to assassinate Egyptian President Hosni Mubarak during a 1995 trip to Ethiopia. As one of few commissions prosecutors with at Top Secret security clearance, Stu Couch pursued that tip and managed, in this rare case, to gain access to CIA files on Qosi. They showed that he had brought funds to an operative in Ethiopia before the attack, but not a connection to the Mubarak plot. Though good enough for an intelligence agency hypothesis, it wasn't sufficient to prove a crime beyond a reasonable doubt, and the charge was dropped from the case. Now, Couch wanted to see what Qosi would do when given his chance before the commission.

According to the charges that were filed, Qosi joined al Qaeda in

Sudan in 1989 and by 1991 was an accountant in the terror network's Peshawar office. He returned to Sudan to work as an "accountant and treasurer" for the Taba Investment Company, an al Qaeda front, and even signed "checks on behalf of Usama bin Laden," the charge sheet said.

Oddly, his more recent assignments seemed to carry less responsibility. "From about 1996 until his capture in December 2001, al Qosi served as one of Usama bin Laden's bodyguards and drivers," the charges said. "Additionally, al Qosi was responsible for the supplies and cooking for the detachment."

Still, of the four initial cases, Qosi's looked most likely to provide a picture of al Qaeda's operations. In addition to the boilerplate list of al Qaeda bigwigs like bin Laden and Zawahiri, Qosi's alleged co-conspirators included Salim Hamdan, who had told interrogators about Qosi's work in the bin Laden motor pool, and Jamal al-Fadl, an al Qaeda turncoat who had become the US government's star informer.[12]

But by the time Qosi's hearing came around on Friday morning, Pete Brownback was in no mood to conduct another courtroom disaster. Hearing defense attorney Sharon Shaffer's complaints about insufficient resources and uncertainty over a pending transfer to another assignment, he recessed the hearing for six weeks.

Habeas Corpus

AT WEEK'S END, THE PROCEEDINGS' exhausted participants—
defendants excepted—gathered at Guantanamo's Leeward air terminal for the return trip to Andrews Air Force Base. The commission
members, prosecutors, defense attorneys, interpreters, courtroom
staff, news media, and humanitarian observers had arrived at the base
on different days, were housed in separate quarters, and were kept
apart from one another by military guards. Their paths had been
permitted to intersect only at the Pink Palace, where each performed
his or her role in the ritualized setting of a military courtroom.

Now, with official minders off duty—and military personnel in
their civvies for the flight—the rigid castes of the Guantanamo system
relaxed. Dressed in polos or T-shirts, toting their own luggage, wearing
baseball caps or souvenir hats bought at the base's gift shop, military
officers and liberal activists alike stood in line grumbling about the
wait to get through the terminal's single metal detector. Like actors out
of costume, those who played antagonists in the courtroom now chit-
chatted like backstage pals. Nearly the entire commissions apparatus,
people and equipment, was packed onto the military transport, a show
on the road, a traveling circus.

The Defense Department had spent between three hundred thousand and five hundred thousand dollars to stage the week's events.[1] The

reviews, nonetheless, were not positive. Normally rivals for media attention and member donations, the ACLU, Amnesty International, Human Rights First, and Human Rights Watch issued a joint statement urging the Bush administration to scrap commissions. The American Bar Association's legal observer said the government should revert to the Uniform Code of Military Justice; his Australian counterpart, who attended to observe the David Hicks hearing, said a fair trial would be "impossible." *USA Today* reported that "the tribunal's performance raised concerns about whether the new system will work, or collapse in confusion."[2]

Democratic presidential nominee John Kerry, who had been arguing that George Bush's counterterrorism policies were ineffective, seized on the news from Guantanamo.

"In dealing with detainees, our first question should always be a simple one: 'What should we do to keep America safe?' The Bush administration unfortunately has asked a different question, 'How much power can we possibly exercise?' They tried to set up Guantanamo Bay as a legal black hole, subject to neither courts nor laws," the Kerry campaign said.[3]

A Democratic administration instead would base future detainee trials on courts-martial. "We will ensure that this process, from the quality of translators to the treatment of evidence to the selection of judges, is handled with the seriousness and competence that is essential for such sensitive national security cases."

The Bush campaign issued a scolding response. "John Kerry should not play politics with the system of justice in place to deal with terrorist suspects," a spokesman said.

Nonetheless, the Defense Department rushed to blunt the criticism. At a Pentagon press conference, Brigadier General Tom Hemingway, the commissions' legal adviser, pledged to clean up the translation problems. Bob Swann, pushed by senior officials to meet with reporters, surprisingly announced that the prosecution favored providing additional resources for defense lawyers.

"More than anyone in the courtroom, I want a full and fair

trial," Swann said, if only to diminish the chances of a successful appeal.

Swann made clear he was eager to get past the initial slate of obscure defendants he had inherited from his predecessor, Fred Borch. He promised that prosecutors soon would begin filing charges, possibly including murder, against the next batch of inmates. There were nine charge sheets on his desk, he said. In some cases, "the American people will recognize the names of the individuals."

Ramzi Binalshibh? Khalid Sheikh Mohammed? Swann wouldn't say.

UNDER THE COMMISSIONS rulebook, the secretary of defense was to appoint a review panel of military officers to approve convictions before they were finalized by the SecDef himself. Whatever he thought of the commissions project as a whole, Donald Rumsfeld made the most of this power.

Thousands of active-duty and retired JAGs had experience with military courts. But instead of turning to the military's own ranks, Rumsfeld used a loophole in federal law to appoint his friends to the review panel, in the process awarding them the rank of major general.

Normally, military officers are appointed through the same formal process as civilian federal officials; they are nominated by the president, confirmed by the Senate, and then receive a "commission" with the president's signature—a certificate much like a diploma. While the Senate holds confirmation hearings for a handful of senior military positions, it rubber-stamps thousands of routine officer commissions each year. But an obscure provision of federal law, apparently intended to apply when the capital was under enemy occupation or some other catastrophe disabled the Congress, allowed the president, "in time of war, or of national emergency declared by the Congress or the President," to "appoint any qualified person (whether or not already a member of the armed forces) to any officer grade in the Army, Navy, Air Force, or Marine Corps" up to the rank of major general or rear admiral, for a maximum of two years.[4]

The statute specified that the temporary assignments "shall be made by the President alone." That problem was solved by Executive Order 13221, which appeared on December 23, 2003, on page 74,465 of the *Federal Register*. "The emergency appointments authority at section 603 of title 10, United States Code, is invoked and made available to the Secretary of Defense in accordance with the terms of that statute and of Executive Order 12396 of December 9, 1982," the order read, with no further explanation.

A week later, Rumsfeld exercised that new authority to appoint four men to the review panel, instantly making them major generals.[5] Ranging in age from sixty-three to eighty-five, all were his friends or prominent supporters of commissions plan. Two were Rumsfeld Sages who had advised on the trial structure: Bill Coleman, Rumsfeld's colleague from the Ford cabinet, and Griffin Bell, the Carter attorney general and onetime Southern liberal who had become increasingly conservative in his ninth decade. Both agreed to serve on the condition that they could continue their private law practices.

Rumsfeld's third appointee was Edward "Pete" Biester, a Pennsylvania Republican with whom he had served in Congress during the 1960s.[6] In 1985, Rumsfeld had sold Biester some of his property outside Taos, New Mexico, and the two were still neighbors there.

The fourth appointee apparently had no prior Rumsfeld connection but compensated with his enthusiasm for military commissions. Frank Williams, the chief justice of Rhode Island, was an amateur historian of Abraham Lincoln and fascinated with Civil War–era commissions. Soon after reading news of Bush's military order, Williams wrote the Pentagon to offer his services in support of the project.[7]

"I thought I was uniquely qualified to assist if they could use me," Williams told the *Providence Journal*.[8] More than 4,200 military commissions were staged during the Civil War, he said. "Lincoln authorized them as commander in chief, just as President Bush has authorized them through the secretary of defense."[9]

In September 2004, a month after the first hearings at the Pink Palace, Rumsfeld conducted a ceremony to swear his instant generals into office. The oath was administered by a senior federal judge, Anthony Alaimo, himself a World War II hero whose exploits, Jim Haynes observed, helped inspire the Steve McQueen blockbuster *The Great Escape*. Williams interrupted the proceedings to hand out souvenir "chief justice" coins he had struck, bearing Lincoln's likeness.

After his appointment, Bill Coleman received a note from an old friend.

"Congratulations on becoming a major general," Colin Powell wrote. "If you lose some weight, you can use my uniform."

■

In the Pink Palace courtroom, Scott Lang and Kurt Brubaker had vigorously disputed defense claims that Pete Brownback and other commission members should be disqualified. Consider Brownback's "sterling reputation" and the five Bronze Stars he was awarded for "heroism" in Vietnam, Brubaker had argued.

In reality, the prosecutors were stunned that Altenburg had stacked the commission with officers who had no business being there. Back at Crystal City, they told Bob Swann that the defense was correct: every challenged commission member should go, including Pete Brownback.

The staff quickly divided into opposing camps over the issue. "There was a lot of blood on the floor," said prosecutor Tom Umberg, an Army Reserve colonel from California. Umberg himself had poked around, finding out that combat experience had been a criterion for appointment to the commission. "It was to make sure we didn't get a panel full of weenies," he said.

Colonel Bright and Lieutenant Colonel Toomey had been involved in planning the capture and managing the transport of enemy prisoners to Guantanamo—including all four defendants. A plausible argument perhaps could be made that experience with combat operations in Afghanistan was qualifying, rather than prejudicial, for service on a military commission. But most lawyers would agree that officials involved in capturing and jailing a defendant should not also be his judge and jury.

Colonel Sparks and Lieutenant Colonel Cooper were no better. One of Sparks's Marines had died at the World Trade Center, while Cooper had nursed a continuing outrage, if not obsession, with the 9/11 attacks. It was at least an open question whether they could separate their emotions from the legal and fact-finding role they were supposed to play on the commission.

Swann said the complaints didn't meet the narrow standards for disqualification. He wasn't going to make legal decisions based on bad press. But with most of his staff against him, he agreed not to contest defense motions against some of the commission members. The sticking point was Pete Brownback. To Lang and Brubaker, the presiding officer's decades-long friendship with the appointing authority, John Altenburg, was an automatic conflict of interest. But as Swann saw it, it was one thing to dismiss a couple of Marine officers; calling the boss's buddy unqualified was another matter.

Swann dumped the problem in Stu Couch's lap, telling him to research the legal issues and recommend a course of action. In the eight-page memo he filed, Couch went back to bedrock principles of legal procedure. Drawing on federal and military law, as well as the standards used at UN war crimes tribunals, he concluded that disqualification was required whenever "there is good cause to believe that the member cannot provide the accused a full and fair trial, or the member's impartiality might reasonably be questioned based upon articulable facts."

Swann could live with that. But reading through the memo, he grew furious. The first precedent Couch cited was *United States v. Quintanilla*. The ruling, by the US Court of Appeals for the Armed Forces, established the test for impartiality used in military trials. But it also happened to concern a trial conducted by Keith Hodges, Pete Brownback's Mini-Me.

Hodges had been a military judge at Fort Hood, Texas, in 1996. While presiding over a court-martial, Hodges had assailed a witness outside his courtroom, the appellate decision recounted. The witness later complained that Hodges called him a "motherfucker" and pushed him around, smacking him on the chest.[10] Hodges compounded matters by failing to fully disclose the incident, the appellate court indicated, and then attempting to sanitize the trial record by deleting references to himself.

"The trial judge should be the exemplar of dignity and impartiality," the appeals court said. "In this case, the military judge [Hodges] committed several acts that would reasonably put his impartiality into doubt." Hodges was extremely sensitive about the case, even scolding a reporter who mentioned it in a news story for taking a cheap shot.

Swann told Couch to delete citations to the case. "You're just poking your finger in Hodges's eye," he said.

Couch said the case was precisely on point, the precedent studied at the JAG School for impartiality standards. Any military lawyer would expect to see *Quintanilla* cited in a disqualification motion—or wonder why it had been omitted.

"Nope," said Swann. "Take it out."

Couch blew up. "It's the frickin' *benchmark case* under military law," he said. Delete it? "That's an example of how we're doing shit for how it looks, not for what it is in reality," he said.

Couch's draft cited eighteen precedents. After Swann edited it, there were seventeen. All references to *Quintanilla* had been deleted.

Moreover, Swann's version took a strangely equivocal position on Brownback. Instead of supporting—or opposing—his removal, it merely requested "that he closely evaluate his own suitability to serve as the Presiding Officer." Brownback should then "forward a recommendation to the Appointing Authority as to whether good cause exists for his [own] removal."

At a testy meeting with his senior prosecutors, Swann said he preferred to drop a hint rather than call outright for Brownback's disqualification. That way, Brownback and Altenburg could "do the right thing" and "take the credit" for it, he said.

Couch couldn't believe that the egos of superior officers were to take precedence over rules of legal ethics. Lang and Brubaker joined him in a joint memo to Swann. "We disagree ardently," it said.

The prosecution's legal position "should not be based upon who gets credit, but upon what is the right thing to do," they wrote. "As we have stated before, our concern is not the image of the Military Commissions in the immediate news cycle, but more with the credibility of the proceedings when seen in a historical sense years from now. We do not want there ever to be an avoidable appearance that any convictions we may obtain came from a 'rigged' system. Our position is that because Colonel Brownback's friendship and past associations with the Appointing Authority may reasonably create just such an appearance, we should speak up and put it on the record now." They refused to sign the motion Swann presented them.

Swann didn't talk to Couch, Lang, or Brubaker for three days. He filed the motion under his own name. The trial prosecutors crossed their fingers and hoped the defense motion would be granted—or that Brownback himself would get the message. Apart from his relationship with Altenburg, the prosecutors, like the defense attorneys, believed he was embarrassingly underqualified for the job.

"It's not Justice Jackson sitting there," Lang said. "Brownback was a horrendous selection. Everybody knew that, just from the mannerisms and the way he conducted himself. He still thought he was strong-arming first-tour O-3s [captains] in an Army court martial," rather than heading a historic proceeding at the center of America's war on terrorism, with "extremely experienced counsel and ninety media watching your every move." Commission staffers, in a scornful reference to one of Brownback's part-time jobs as a Florida retiree, nicknamed him the "crossing guard."

The message, however, didn't get through. Brownback refused to step down and Altenburg declined to remove him.

Likewise Altenburg rejected the motion to disqualify Sparks. Nothing suggested Sparks "is experiencing any ongoing emotions as a result of his 9/11 experiences," Altenburg said in his ruling.[11]

He dismissed only Bright, Toomey, and Cooper—the three the prosecution had agreed should go. The Hamdan and Hicks trials would proceed with the three remaining original members, Brownback, Sparks, and Bogdan.

On its face, the decision seemed like a partial victory for the defense. The Pentagon congratulated itself.

"We believe this decision validates the system," said a Defense Department spokesman.[12] "It shows the system is flexible and can respond to change."

Defense lawyers, however, saw the selective dismissals as a ploy that actually *helped* the prosecution. Commissions convictions required a two-thirds vote, so whether five members or three, the defense faced the same burden: persuading two members to vote for acquittal.

For prosecutors, however, the hurdle for conviction had just dropped by 50 percent. A five-member commission required four votes to convict; on a three-member panel, it took two.

"This is a clear win for the government, disguised as being fair to the defendant," said Hamdan's lawyer, Lieutenant Commander Charlie Swift. Proceedings at Guantanamo were scheduled to resume on November 1—one day before the 2004 presidential election.

■

For months, Guantanamo defense attorneys had been pressing their case in the news media, which found the image of uniformed officers challenging the president's policy irresistible. Lieutenant Commander Swift had been profiled on page 1 of the *Wall Street Journal* and later featured in *Vanity Fair* and on *60 Minutes*.[13] David Hicks's lawyer, Major Dan Mori, had become a media sensation in Australia, where he sought to whip up public pressure on the Howard government to get his client out of Guantanamo.

The Pentagon felt it had no choice but to permit the defense attorneys free rein. Because the adversary system demands "zealous advocacy," muzzling defense attorneys would further undermine administration claims of "full and fair" justice at Guantanamo.

Commissions prosecutors, however, reported through a chain of command that led to the president. Aside from a handful of formal press briefings, the Bush administration refused to permit prosecutors to speak with reporters.

For prosecution staffers, officers who considered themselves the good guys, the gag order was painful. "It was crushing morale and we had to sit there," Scott Lang said. "We couldn't say anything back."

When Tom Umberg, the Army Reserve colonel, joined the staff, Couch urged Bob Swann to make him the prosecution spokesman. Umberg was a media-savvy corporate lawyer who had spent time as a federal prosecutor, in elective office, and on the White House staff.

But Umberg brought some handicaps. For one, he had been recruited by the prior chief prosecutor, Fred Borch. Worse yet, Umberg was a Democrat. He had served in the California legislature before an unsuccessful 1994 run for state attorney general. After that, he worked on Bill Clinton's reelection campaign and followed him to the White House as deputy drug czar. Bob Swann couldn't stand him.

"People from large law firms think they're so smart," Swann said. "These hotshots think they can come in here and tell me what to do." Swann said he personally had tried three hundred cases and was proud of them. Sure, he got his degree at the University of Memphis, which "some people would regard as a second-rate law school." But now he was a full colonel in the United States Army and "just as smart as anyone."[14] With his trademark wave, Swann rejected proposals that Umberg become the public face of the prosecution.

"You're a politician and you're worried about the press," he sneered at Umberg.[15] Besides, Swann said, "if we had known you were a Clinton guy, we never would have asked you to come back here." As it was, Swann treated Umberg as if he were a spy for the current Democratic presidential nominee, Senator John Kerry of Massachusetts.

Kerry had first gained fame as a Vietnam veteran who turned against that war. In 1971 testimony before the Senate Foreign Relations Committee, Kerry appeared in olive drabs to complain that America was sending men "to die for the biggest nothing in history."[16] Swann considered Kerry little better than a traitor. He repeatedly complained about Kerry and Bill Clinton, yelling down the hallways of Crystal City that Kerry was a liar, quizzing people about their political views, and bragging about the votes he had rounded up for Bush.

Soldiers typically avoid blatantly partisan talk, but anti-Kerry sentiments were not unusual in the heavily Republican military, and Swann's diatribes hardly registered with most commissions staffers. To Tom Umberg, however, Swann treated Bush's election as a patriotic mission akin to defeating Saddam.

And it was clear that higher-ups believed that getting commissions running before the election would help the president's chances.

"The implication was that we were all on the Bush-Cheney team, and we had to be focused on the politics of this," Umberg said. "I'd been around the military and government for many years, and never seen anything like that. *Ever.*"

■

Two months after Salim Hamdan had been brought to the Pink Palace for the first commissions hearing, his lawyers showed up at the federal courthouse in Washington, DC, to argue that the Guantanamo proceedings against their client were illegal. The Bush administration considered it little more than a nuisance suit.

The case had begun in April 2004, when Lieutenant Commander Charlie Swift filed a habeas corpus petition in the federal district court in Seattle. Swift had lived in Washington State before being assigned to commissions, and it remained his official residence, allowing him to file suit there as, in legal parlance, Hamdan's "next friend." Neal Katyal had seized on that opportunity to turn the tables on the Bush administration, which routinely steered its important cases into the most conservative judicial circuits. Washington State was part of the liberal

Ninth Circuit, and Katyal expected to prevail in its courts, providing a leg up for an eventual Supreme Court review.

Katyal's strategy was immediately validated in the Seattle federal courthouse. Judge Robert Lasnik, a Clinton appointee, observed at the outset that in the American legal system, even "the most vulnerable and most powerless can still get into federal court and have their cases heard"—contradicting the entire premise behind the Guantanamo military commissions.[17]

The government persuaded Lasnik to delay proceedings until the Supreme Court decided the *Rasul* case; if the administration won, Guantanamo detainees would have no right to habeas petitions and Hamdan's lawsuit would have to be dismissed. Lasnik resumed proceedings after the Supreme Court ruled in June 2004 that habeas claims could go forward, but the government moved to dismiss Hamdan's case anyway, or at least transfer it to the District of Columbia—one of the conservative judicial circuits that already had backed the administration's most extreme theories of unilateral executive power.

Lasnik refused to dismiss the case but reluctantly agreed to the transfer; following *Rasul,* the federal judiciary had decided that it was more efficient to consolidate Guantanamo claims in the DC courts.[18] There, the case was assigned to US District Judge James Robertson, another Clinton appointee but also a Navy veteran who had spent most of his career practicing corporate law. At the commissions office, Stu Couch and Scott Lang sensed that the administration did not take the hearing, scheduled for October 25, 2004, particularly seriously. They were little consulted as administration lawyers prepared their arguments and received a courtesy copy of the government's brief only a few days before the hearing. It was riddled with errors.

Lang decided to attend the hearing. Looking at the government table, and then the Hamdan counsel, he was not reassured.

The administration had sent a youngish lawyer named Jonathan Marcus to argue its case. Hamdan had three attorneys: Katyal, Joseph McMillan, part of a pro bono team provided by the Seattle firm Perkins Coie, and Charlie Swift, in his Navy whites. The uniform immediately registered with the judge; at the outset, Robertson said he would address him as *Mr.* Swift, "in Navy fashion."

Marcus, arguing first, said Hamdan's fears of being tried unfairly were "totally speculative." Let the Guantanamo commission go forward. If convicted, Hamdan could raise challenges under Pentagon procedures. Federal court shouldn't consider Hamdan's complaints until those procedures were exhausted.

Robertson asked which source of law controlled commissions legal decisions. "You say it's not the Uniform Code of Military Justice," he told Marcus. "Would it be, by any chance, the Geneva Conventions?"

The Bush administration had never stated a position on this bedrock question, perhaps because acknowledging *any* source of law could provide defendants with rights the government could not ignore. By default, the issue had landed on John Altenburg's desk, where he first confronted it a few days earlier, when ruling on the motion to disqualify Colonel Brownback and the other commission members. Altenburg's twenty-eight-page decision, citing a grab bag of legal sources, was the only reference Marcus had.

"Judging from the decision that was issued last week, I would imagine they would look to all sources. They would look to federal law. They might look to international law standards." But anyway, it didn't matter if the Geneva Convention applied, Marcus said, because Geneva "contemplated only diplomatic means of enforcement"—apparently meaning, in Hamdan's case, the improbable spectacle of negotiations involving the Bush administration, the Yemeni government, the Taliban, and al Qaeda. In other words, no enforcement at all.

"It's basically the government's position, isn't it, that the president's findings here are not reviewable?" Robertson said.

"Historically, courts have always deferred to the president's war powers, as exercised against alien enemy combatants outside the United States," replied Marcus.

Robertson turned to Common Article 3. "That basically says that you've got to have the same sort of trial that everybody else gets.

You have to have a court-martial," he said. "You're not basically quarreling with the proposition that Common Article 3 is passed into customary international law or that it is a minimum yardstick and gives voice to elementary considerations of humanity. You buy all that?" Robertson said.

Actually, no. "We don't necessarily agree with that with respect to conflict with terrorist organizations," Marcus said. Even if Common Article 3 was customary international law, "the president's executive act [to ignore it] would trump that standard."

In the courtroom gallery, Scott Lang took notes.

"Judge asked how do you know who are AQ and who are Taliban," Lang wrote. "DOJ blew this at oral argument and we need to make sure we have this down."

Neal Katyal stood next. Where Marcus had portrayed the Guantanamo prosecutions as heir to a hoary American tradition, the Georgetown professor called them a radical departure from past practice, military commissions "in name only." Unlike prior commissions established by armed forces in the field, he said, this tribunal was a political entity in which "the president is acting as a prosecutor, lawmaker, jury, judge, jailer and sentencer." How, Katyal asked, can the government claim that it created the commission "to enforce the laws of war" and then "turn around and say they are not bound by those very laws of war, like the Geneva Conventions"?

Katyal argued that Bush's creation held even less legitimacy than the 1942 Nazi saboteur trial. "President Roosevelt's order applied to eight individuals by name. This applies to four billion individuals, everyone who is not a U.S. citizen," he said. Moreover, during World War II, the Eastern Seaboard, where the Nazis were captured and tried, had been designated as the "Eastern Defense Command." That meant "that military trials of enemies could happen there," Katyal said.

In contrast, "Guantanamo is not even conceivably a theater of war." And "without that basic geographical limitation, military commissions look a lot more like creatures not of necessity, but creatures of convenience," he said.

In his notes, Lang summarized these points under the heading, "Katyal Posturing."

Charlie Swift rose last.

"The civilian architects of Mr. Hamdan's commission have ignored history, and they've selectively read the Uniform Code of Military Justice and the Geneva Convention with an eye to escaping their mandates rather than following them," Swift said.

"Swift grandstanding on why commissions are unfair," Lang wrote.

The arguments went back and forth for nearly three hours. "I think we've come to, if not the end of everybody's time, we've come to the end of everybody's rope," said Judge Robertson. "The matter is submitted, and I will rule as quickly as I can."

Back at commissions, Lang told Couch what had happened.

"Katyal cleaned our clock," he said. "DOJ got their ass kicked."

WHILE MARCUS EXTOLLED THE Guantanamo commissions to Judge Robertson, Stu Couch and a few others urged Bob Swann to respond to the serious flaws exposed during the experiment's first week of Pink Palace proceedings. Press coverage would intensify, they warned, human rights and legal groups would pile on criticism, and defense lawyers were filing dozens of substantial legal attacks, any one of which could catch the attention of a federal judge.

Swann responded with The Wave. "Blah, blah, blah, blah, blah," he said. "Nobody's gonna care."

Getting nowhere with their immediate superior, Couch and his allies drafted a memorandum for Jim Haynes, the Pentagon general counsel.

"During the past two months, the first four trials of Military Commissions have begun and with that, recognition by us that the system—in its current state—is insufficient to accomplish the long-term mission of bringing alleged terrorists to justice," they wrote.

"Despite the earnest efforts of all trial participants, these systemic problems have now paralyzed the process." Without significant changes, they wrote, "the outlook for moving along just these first four cases looks grim."

Such a letter from midlevel officers to a senior political official of uncertain sympathies was nearly unknown within the military hierarchy. It could result in career suicide.

They never sent it.

ELECTION DAY CAME AND went without a ruling on Hamdan's case from Judge Robertson, but after President Bush's November 2004 victory, the future of commissions seemed assured. At Guantanamo, things began to settle into a routine. Military minders relaxed some off-hours restrictions on the news media. Reporters sunbathed and snorkeled, held cookouts and fed the tame iguanas that ambled from the brush.

Most base personnel exuded worshipful regard for George W. Bush. With their stylized *W*, caps for the new baseball team in Washington, DC, the Nationals, were seen as markers of support for the commander in chief. In the mess hall, the soft-serve dispenser offered "Freedom Vanilla," a flavor that had been called French vanilla before Paris opposed the Iraq invasion. Dissidents were accommodated, however; the freezer offered Ben and Jerry's Peace Pops, which the hippie-themed Vermont creamery introduced to promote nuclear disarmament.

Like other military bases, the official workday began and ended with bugle calls, provided by recording, due to the shortage of trained buglers. Third-tier acts came through to entertain the troops, including Cyndi Lauper, Hootie and the Blowfish, and the Denver Broncos Cheerleaders, who jiggled through dance numbers to riotous applause from the disproportionately male population of service members.

Real life sometimes crashed into this artificial society. Lengthy separations strained relationships, and more than one marriage broke up under Guantanamo's weight. But isolation, close quarters, and shared experiences also sparked romance, among journalists, attorneys, and military personnel.

The commissions office generated volumes of paperwork as it

geared up to resume proceedings. Pete Brownback set a symbolic date to commence the first trial: December 7, Pearl Harbor Day. Before those proceedings could begin, however, several pretrial motions remained to address, so Brownback reconvened the commission for a hearing on November 7. The entire assemblage—the commission members, lawyers, courtroom staff, press, human rights observers— returned to the Pink Palace, where few expected that anything could now derail the trial.

Resuming open court, Charlie Swift asked for clarification of yet another procedural unknown: Once the "burden of persuasion" was assigned to prosecution or defense—that is, which side had the higher hurdle to overcome in order to prevail on a legal point—Swift asked, what "standard of review," or degree of scrutiny into the argument, would the commission apply? As with most procedural questions, the answers would have been long established in federal court or courts-martial, but they had never been clarified for military commissions.

"Thank you for springing that on me," Brownback said. He asked for a written submission.

"Yes, sir," Swift said brightly. He then moved to undo his apparent accomplishment in getting commission members Bright and Toomey disqualified. Swift now asked that they be *reappointed* to the commission because the reduction to three members from five made it mathematically more difficult for the defense to win an acquittal.

"It seems incredibly ironic that a member would be removed because they were likely or perceived as likely to vote for the government, but once removed, the government did not need their vote at all," Swift said.

As Swift spoke, a Marine bailiff in battle dress strode over to Brownback and handed him a slip of paper. Brownback looked at the note and went pale.

"Court in recess," he barked, and abruptly left the courtroom, followed by the two remaining members of the commission, Sparks and Bogdan.

Bailiffs told spectators to remain seated. Some catastrophe must have taken place, the whispers went. People in the courtroom flashed on the Madrid train bombing of the previous March, an al Qaeda-linked terror strike against the conservative Spanish government that backed George Bush. It was now less than a week since Bush's own electoral victory, and many locked in the windowless courtroom assumed that al Qaeda had struck America again.

Five minutes later, spectators rose as a somber Brownback returned to the courtroom, flanked by the two silent commission members.

"Be seated," Brownback said. "We are going to have an indefinite recess, and that is all the business I am taking care of. Commission is in recess." He quickly exited, followed by the two members.

Neal Katyal repressed a sly smile.

"We won," he mouthed.

A FORTY-FIVE-PAGE OPINION had arrived from the US District Court in Washington. In it, Judge Robertson revisited questions that the administration's lawyers thought they put to rest when President Bush signed the military order and later issued a directive nullifying the Geneva Conventions.

To be sure, there had been some dissenting views within the administration, not only the senior military leadership but also the State Department. They were easily disregarded. But Judge Robertson stood outside the presidential chain of command. His opinion rejected the sweeping inferences from skeletal precedents that administration lawyers imagined would undergird a new age of executive power.

The administration's claim that al Qaeda fighters in Afghanistan fell beyond Geneva's framework "finds no support in the structure of the Conventions themselves, which are triggered by the place of the conflict, and not by what particular faction a fighter is associated with," Robertson wrote.[19] The only question was whether Hamdan was entitled to "the full panoply of Convention protections" afforded POWs or the smaller subset of rights provided by Common Article 3.

Robertson described administration policy as "starkly different from the positions and behavior of the United States in previous conflicts." In 1993, for instance, the United States had demanded that a Somali warlord treat a captured American pilot according to Geneva. Under the Bush administration's theory, the judge wrote, the warlord could have ignored the treaty's protections because he was not a "state."

Robertson dismissed Bush's claim that courts were powerless to stop the president from mistreating prisoners. The Geneva Conventions were "written to protect individuals," Robertson observed. While some provisions might require implementing legislation, America had enforced its key guarantees for decades—until the Bush administration. No "diplomatic channels" existed to ensure enforcement, Robertson added; the Pentagon had barred Yemeni diplomats even from visiting Hamdan at Guantanamo.

The question, then, was what did Geneva require? The treaty provided for a "competent tribunal" when there was doubt regarding the status of a prisoner such as Hamdan. If he was a POW, the treaty required that he be tried by the same procedures as a US soldier—in effect, by court-martial. If Hamdan was something other than a POW, Common Article 3 still required that he be tried only "by a regularly constituted court, affording all the judicial guarantees which are recognized as indispensable by civilized peoples." That might not encompass the entire Uniform Code of Military Justice, but it certainly included the right to see prosecution evidence and attend the proceedings against him—something already denied Hamdan during voir dire.

Unless the government corrected those violations, Robertson concluded, "Hamdan's trial before the Military Commission would be unlawful."

FROM THE PENTAGON TO Crystal City to the Pink Palace, officials were in shock. They had expected at most a judicial scolding that urged the administration to treat detainees fairly before deferring to the president and dismissing the case.

Instead, accompanying Robertson's opinion was a two-page order barring Hamdan's trial until the violations were corrected. But Bush's military order stated that no federal court had jurisdiction over commissions. Was Robertson's order anything more than a piece of paper?

At the Pink Palace, prosecutors retreated to their cramped second-floor offices.

A Navy prosecutor suggested they should ignore the court order and proceed anyway. Several others agreed.

Someone said that Colonel Brownback, whatever his shortcomings as a lawyer, still might have reservations about defying a federal judge.

"There are two of them"—nonlawyers Sparks and Bogdan—"and one of him," one prosecutor responded. If the prosecution pushed hard, it might persuade the lay members to outvote Brownback and proceed with trial, he said. "We could get the panel to go with us."

Tom Umberg, the most senior officer present, after Swann, thought the others were kidding.

"Yeah, those federal marshals are all fat asses," he joked. "I'd like to see them try to wade ashore when we've got the Marines on the high ground here."

No one laughed.

"Well, how *would* they enforce it?" one prosecutor said.

"They wouldn't be able to enforce it," said another.

Umberg realized they were serious. "Guys, this is huge," he said. "If we're going to go forward, we have to call Haynes or somebody in the White House. This is *Marbury v. Madison.*" The 1803 Supreme Court case was the foundation of American constitutional law, establishing the judiciary's role as final arbiter of legal questions.[20]

No one responded. The attitude, Umberg felt, was clear: "Fuck this Clinton-appointed judge, we don't have to listen to him." He raised a more recent precedent.

"It would be the equivalent of Nixon not turning over the tapes," he said. In 1974, even Richard Nixon dared not defy the federal courts.

Similar discussions were taking place in Washington. Several officials questioned the necessity of obeying Robertson's order. Administration lawyers had cited prior examples of the executive branch ignoring court orders, although none more recent than the Civil War.[21]

But John Altenburg, shocked as he was by Robertson's decision, was in no mood to instigate a constitutional crisis. "You don't screw around with a federal district judge," he said. "End of discussion."

A somewhat more debatable question was whether military commissions cases other than Hamdan's could proceed. Every detainee had an identical legal claim, but in fighting each separate case in federal court the government might draw judges more sympathetic to its position and win at least some of the time.

Several administration lawyers pushed for that course, resisting adverse court rulings with everything short of outright defiance. But Altenburg did not see his mission as reworking the constitutional order. Besides, a multitude of conflicting court rulings on commissions would only complicate matters, he argued. "I don't need a pissing contest among federal judges. So let's just stop. Let's take a pause. Time out."

AT THE PINK PALACE, a message arrived from the Pentagon: Recess the proceedings.

Once again, the entire commissions production—prosecutors and defense attorneys, interpreters and paralegals, reporters and human rights activists—was packed up and hauled to the air terminal for a flight back to Andrews.

Commission members Jack Sparks and Dan Bogdan seemed confused by the rapid turn of events. In the terminal's VIP lounge, reserved for colonels and above, Sparks pulled Tom Umberg aside.

"I don't understand why we couldn't go forward," Sparks said. Umberg apologized, but said it would be improper to speak with a member of the commission panel.

Sparks next approached Pete Brownback.

"You're not coming back," Brownback said. "From your perspective, this is over."

Listening to Sparks and Bogdan, Umberg realized that his colleagues were probably right. Had the prosecution moved to disregard Judge Robertson's order and proceed with trial, he said, "I think they would have gone with us."

Mr. Bean

THE BUSH ADMINISTRATION WASTED no time appealing Judge Robertson's order. By holding the United States to its treaty obligations, Robertson had interfered with "important military determinations of the commander-in-chief during a time of active armed conflict," the Justice Department said in a brief filed with the US Court of Appeals for the District of Columbia Circuit.[1]

Although the administration considered eventual legal victory certain, the appeal would take months. In the meantime, prosecutors were to work up new cases that would be ready to launch the moment the stay of proceedings was lifted.

Stu Couch was assigned the White House's highest priority: satisfying John Howard, the Australian prime minister who had taken a political risk by approving the military prosecution of his citizens. Proceedings against David Hicks had begun, but nothing yet had transpired for the other Australian at Guantanamo, Mamdouh Habib. Canberra wanted him tried immediately after David Hicks, lest it be accused of favoring a young, Adelaide-born white Australian over an awkward, overweight, and often unpleasant forty-eight-year-old Egyptian immigrant.

But Habib, Couch realized, would be far more complicated to prosecute. Hicks was little more than Taliban cannon fodder, and his

case involved nothing of national security significance. Habib, the
files said, was in on the 9/11 plot. He had not only confessed to
training the suicide terrorists in martial arts but also admitted planning to hijack a plane himself.

The proof was incontrovertible, Couch was told: The United
States had intercepted a telephone call in which Habib described the
attacks before they took place.

BY MANY MEASURES, MAMDOUH Habib was a misfit, "a bit of a
blunderer," his attorney said, "an Arab version of Mr. Bean," the
hapless character played by English comedian Rowan Atkinson.[2] An
assessment by British intelligence reached a similar conclusion, describing him as "a frigging idiot, a mope," an official said.

Habib left Egypt about age twenty, after three years as an army
conscript.[3] He recounted journeys through Bulgaria, Iraq, and Yugoslavia, among other places, and such jobs as delivering gas cylinders,
selling Scotch whisky, and tending elephants for a circus.[4] Eventually,
he reached Australia, where his brother and sister lived.

There, he met and married Maha, the Lebanese-born sister of
his brother's wife, and they had four children. "It was love at first
sight, or something like this," Maha recalled. In 1984, two years after
he arrived, Habib obtained Australian citizenship.

But Australia proved no promised land. Habib learned a few
random skills, such as tai chi and massage, but failed at several ventures over the years, including a cleaning business, a security service,
and a café.[5] Living in sketchy neighborhoods, neither fully accepted
by other Muslims nor trusted by his adopted country, Habib grew
frustrated and depressed. The government provided him a disability
pension and a prescription for Prozac, but it wasn't enough.[6] He
began finding solace in radical Islamic causes.

Visiting New York, where his sisters lived, Habib reconnected
with school chums from Egypt who had relocated to the city. He
visited the Statue of Liberty but spent more time attending the trial of
El Sayyid Nosair, accused of assassinating Rabbi Meir Kahane, a right-

wing Israeli politician.[7] After returning to Australia, Habib's Egyptian friends in New York asked him to raise funds for Omar Abdel Rahman, the terrorist leader known as the Blind Sheikh, who ultimately received life imprisonment for conspiring to blow up the United Nations headquarters, the Lincoln Tunnel, and other landmarks. Habib enthusiastically agreed, even organizing rallies for the cause. "My husband is the type of person who, if you ask him for help, he doesn't hesitate," Maha said.

Such activities led Australian authorities to begin monitoring Habib as a potential threat, something he angrily resented. At the same time, many in Sydney's Muslim community considered Habib's behavior too outlandish to be authentic and concluded that he was spying on them for the police. Feeling unwelcome on both sides, Habib began planning to leave Australia, even soliciting foreign patrons for his move.

He approached the Lebanon-based terrorist organization Hezbollah and, in early 2001, reached out in separate letters to the rulers of Iraq and Libya, Saddam Hussein and Moammar Gadhafi.[8] Habib told them that he had been living in a "country of infidelity for more than twenty-one years." Australia contained "many Jews" and "advocates homosexuality and the marriage of one man to another," he wrote. "I pray to God to help me to get out of this place with my family as soon as possible." He invited Saddam and Gadhafi to facilitate this by underwriting his relocation and financing his new business ventures. The dictators, apparently, failed to respond.

Dejected, Habib turned to his fallback option, Pakistan. Returning from a visit there, he boasted about meeting Osama bin Laden, one former friend said, and brought back a bin Laden T-shirt he sometimes wore to prayer.[9] Even this display fell flat, however, as serious Islamists considered such attire inappropriate.

"You don't wear a shirt like that, this is for the children," Sheikh Abu Ayman, leader of a radical Sydney mosque, said he told Habib.[10]

In July 2001, Habib headed again to Pakistan, intending, his wife would tell reporters, to scout Islamic schools for his children and business opportunities for himself. In fact, Habib soon crossed the border to his true destination, Afghanistan. He stayed there through the 9/11 attacks and didn't try to leave the country until weeks later, when he boarded a bus for Karachi, Pakistan.

At a roadblock, Pakistani police, pressed by Washington to find terrorists, grabbed two passengers whom Habib had met at the bus terminal, young Muslims with German passports.[11] Habib couldn't contain his temper. He interceded and was arrested, too.[12] The two German nationals admitted attending al Qaeda camps in Afghanistan but nonetheless were quickly repatriated at Berlin's request.[13] Habib, however, was taken for questioning by American intelligence agents who, with Canberra's acquiescence, directed his rendition to Egypt.[14] After six months of interrogation there, Habib arrived in Guantanamo.

"People who muck about with organizations like al Qaeda are bound to get themselves into a great deal of trouble," the Australian foreign minister, Alexander Downer, said in May 2002, after Habib's capture was disclosed.[15]

GOING THROUGH THE FILES, Couch saw that at Guantanamo Habib had been interrogated by an alphabet soup of agencies: CITF, FBI, NCIS, Army CID, Air Force OSI, INS, NYPD, and CIA. In their reports, interrogators described an irritable, self-righteous prisoner whose complaints of mistreatment remained constant while his substantive story repeatedly changed. Habib claimed he had "fled Australia because a radical Islamic fundamentalist group . . . was trying to murder him because of his moderate views regarding Islam," according to a May 21, 2002, interrogation summary. Yet Habib also maintained that "the Australian government will not assist him because it is racist."

Habib said he "previously lied to interrogators when he stated that he [had] not been in Afghanistan," the summary continued. "He actually had been in Afghanistan and was now ready to truthfully tell his entire story." But that, Habib insisted, simply was that he visited Kabul "in search of a place for his family to live" where he could "raise his children in a true Islamic lifestyle as opposed to the Western lifestyle they were exposed to in Australia." At other times, however, "Habib stated that he wanted to find a wealthy Saudi sheik that would loan him money to open a restaurant in Singapore."

Habib's story changed again when interrogators confronted him with emails he had sent to an Islamist online chat room offering to join the struggle. "Habib admits that . . . he wanted to go to Afghanistan for jihad and jihad training," an agent wrote. "Habib stated that when he emailed Hezbollah, he was interested in traveling to Palestine to defend the Muslims against the infidels." In another session, Habib admitted that he also had visited Afghanistan earlier, in 1999, and went to a training base run by al Qaeda commander Mohammed Atef. He said Atef told him "he could stay in Afghanistan, but it would be one to two years before he could be trusted."

When it came to his 2001 trip, however, Habib was hazy. He said he stayed at a Kandahar guesthouse where he was prohibited from asking about other guests, "going outside by himself or talking to the Afghani people." In this version, Habib said he did "part-time work in the guesthouse as a holistic masseuse." As in Sydney, however, Habib made a poor impression. "The other men seemed not to trust him and believed that he might be a spy."

One such acquaintance was a fellow Australian called Abu Muslim; in photographs, Habib identified him as David Hicks. The two were sent on "surveillance training" missions, Habib said. "Abu Muslim would go to a building [and] take notes about the building," and "then give a report." But Hicks shared little, "because Habib was rumored to be a CIA spy." Even at Guantanamo, "Hicks continues to tell Camp Delta detainees that Habib is a spy," the report said.

Asked to identify people he met in Afghanistan from a sequence of mug shots, Habib selected the British detainees Feroz Abbasi and Moazzam Begg, as well as the shoe bomber Richard Reid. These identifications were undercut, however, when Habib also picked out Zacarias Moussaoui and told agents he "may have seen this individual in Afghanistan in September 2001." That was impossible; Moussaoui had been arrested in August 2001 and held in American jails ever since.

At an October 2002 interrogation, Habib hinted "that he might be suicidal" and "depressed about having been detained for a year." Later, "he stated that he had a history of depression," observing that he had continued receiving Prozac from the Guantanamo dispensary. According to yet another report, Habib said that he previously lied about his activities in Afghanistan "to please his interrogators, both Egyptian and American." The Egyptians, he said, "had offered him $10 million to be split with them, six for them and four for him, if he would admit to being part of a conspiracy to commit attacks against Americans." The Egyptians had methods beyond bribery, however; Habib "said that he had been shocked, beaten and nearly drowned in a room full of water," and was kept blindfolded for much of his detention.

Asked why he kept making contradictory statements, Habib said "it was the Americans who had put him in this position and that it was their problem to sort out his story."

OF THIS MORASS OF repetitive, inconsistent, and incoherent detail, one incident stood out: the phone call. When handed the Habib case, Couch was told that the suspect had telephoned his wife hours before the 9/11 attacks to warn her that they were coming and to prepare for the clampdown that would follow. Anyone with advance knowledge of the plot must have been a confidant of Osama bin Laden. A recording of that call would virtually guarantee Habib's conviction.

Unfortunately, Couch had been provided no direct information about the call, much less a recording or transcript. The intelligence community considered such information far too valuable to share. Instead, CITF and FBI investigators laid into Habib, hoping he would himself confirm what the call was rumored to prove.

A few days before 9/11, "all the Europeans, Americans and Australians staying at the Kabul [guesthouse] were ordered to leave,"

Habib told the FBI. But he stuck around, and on the day of the attacks was in the mosque when he overheard one man tell another "that America had been bombed that day, or something to that effect," the interrogation report said. "Habib went to a telephone and called his wife in Sydney, Australia. He asked her what had happened in America. She told him that there had been no news of any bombing in America. Habib stated that his wife checked the television news and there was still no news of any bombing attack in America."[16]

The call took place at approximately 10:00 p.m. Sydney time— or "about 7:00 a.m. in New York City, prior to the attacks." "Official word" of the operation came two hours later, and things moved quickly.

"Habib related [that] immediately after the attacks on America, all of the remaining men at the Hamza Guesthouse were dispersed to other locations," the FBI report said. "Habib stated that he was moved to the Malik Guesthouse about a 1½ hour drive (at 60 kph) outside of Kabul. Habib stated that they left Kabul during the night and was not sure of the direction that they drove."

Passing a road littered with "blown up tanks," they arrived at the Malik compound, which Habib described "as being 4,000–5,000 square meters," surrounded by mines and "a two meter-high mud brick wall with a 2½ meter-high gate in its center. The property also had two guard towers that each had one man with an AK-47 rifle that watched the front and rear of the property." The facility had no telephones; it relied on walkie-talkies for communication.

Malik's arsenal included "an antiaircraft weapon that was mounted in the back of a truck," the report continued. "Habib and the other men received training on the weapon and learned how to fire it." He also saw "a silver 'missile' that was about two meters long and about 10 inches in diameter." Two wires, one red and the other blue, extended from the tail. He was told "not to touch the missile." Instead, Habib was sent to unload a truck containing chemical weapons to be used "against American soldiers if they invaded Afghanistan" in response to 9/11.

"Habib described the weapons as being cylinder-shaped items, a little over a foot long and about six inches in diameter. He stated that the cylinders were cream colored with metal caps on each end and had plastic bodies while others had a fiber cardboard type body. There was no writing or inscription on the cylinders," the report said. "Habib stated that there were about 1,000 of these items and they made a swishing sound when they picked them up. Habib did not know if the cylinders contained a liquid or powdered substance but stated that he and the other men were instructed not to shake the cylinders or they might explode."

After staying two or three days at Malik, Habib said he returned to Kabul for ten days, then went on to Kandahar, across the Pakistani border to Quetta, and onto the bus that eventually led him to Guantanamo.

WITHOUT ACCESS TO HABIB'S pre-9/11 phone call, Stu Couch realized he had a typical commissions case. He had a defendant. Now he needed a crime.

Despite countless hours sifting through the dossier, he couldn't find one. Habib came across as obnoxious and untruthful, but his contradictory and uncorroborated statements added up to nothing approaching a war crime. He needed to see what the intelligence community had on Habib.

Couch sent a request marked "high priority" to the CIA. Two weeks later, the agency invited him to its Langley, Virginia, headquarters to review the Habib files. Couch was thrilled; there were 150 entries. When he got to Langley, however, he received only fifteen inconsequential and duplicative documents. Senior officials had stepped in at the last minute to withhold 90 percent of the CIA's files, Couch later heard.

But there was no letup in the pressure to move the case. Couch got a whiff of it when he ran into Tom Hemingway at the commissions office talking with a staffer about getting Habib RTB'd. Barely a day later, while changing planes during an investigative trip, he saw a newspaper report on Vice President Cheney's plans to meet with Prime

Detainees await processing after their arrival at Guantanamo Bay, February 2002. (US Marine Corps photo by Sgt. Diana Ruiz)

Interrogation buildings at Guantanamo Bay, March 2002. (Photo by Jess Bravin)

Guantanamo Bay, occupied by the United States since 1898, shown in a 1985 CIA map. Detainees and others arrive on the leeward shore, then are ferried to the windward shore, where the prison, courthouse, and other facilities stand. (Courtesy of the University of Texas Libraries, The University of Texas at Austin)

The Bush administration selected Lt. Col. William Lietzau to set up military commissions in 2002, and he served as acting chief prosecutor. In 2009, as a National Security Council aide, he urged the Obama administration to scrap the experiment. (US Marine Corps photo by Sgt. Alvin Williams)

Pentagon General Counsel William J. (Jim) Haynes II oversaw the commissions experiment for its first six years. While military commissions historically operated under the Army chain of command, the Bush administration put them directly under the control of political appointees. (Department of Defense photo by R. D. Ward)

Mark Fallon, deputy director of the Guantanamo Criminal Investigation Task Force, at Fort Belvoir, Virginia. A career naval criminal investigator, Fallon warned that abusive interrogation methods could destroy efforts to prosecute suspected terrorists. (Courtesy of Mark Fallon)

Marine Lt. Col. V. Stuart Couch, a lawyer and pilot, signed up to prosecute terrorists after one of his squadron buddies, a United pilot, was killed on 9/11. (Photo by Patrice Gilbert)

Stuart Couch (in hat), accompanied by military commissions criminal investigators, on assignment in Afghanistan. (Courtesy of V. Stuart Couch)

Journalists head toward the Pink Palace, the Guantanamo air control building converted into a courthouse. (Photo by Jess Bravin)

Defendant Salim Hamdan, flanked by an interpreter and his military defense counsel, Lt. Cmdr. Charles Swift, appears at the first commission hearings in August 2004. The military censor required the sketch artist to blank out faces of military officials and fill in the bald spot on chief prosecutor Bob Swann's (center, foreground) head. (Sketch by Arthur Lien)

Chief prosecutor Col. Bob Swann, right, and (from left) trial prosecutors Lt. Col. Kurt Brubaker and Cmdr. Scott Lang, await their luggage at Andrews Air Force Base after a return flight from Guantanamo. (Photo by Jess Bravin)

Defense Secretary Donald Rumsfeld (right) watches as the men he selected to review commissions convictions are sworn in. From left, they are former Attorney General Griffin Bell, former Transportation Secretary William Coleman, Rhode Island Chief Justice Frank Williams, and former U.S. Rep. Edward (Pete) Biester, all of whom received temporary appointments as major generals. (Department of Defense photo by Helene C. Stikkel)

Salim Hamdan's attorneys, Georgetown law professor Neal Katyal and Lt. Cmdr. Charles Swift, speak to reporters following arguments at the US Court of Appeals for the District of Columbia Circuit. (Photo by Jess Bravin)

Col. Lawrence Morris was tapped by the Army to run military commissions in 2001, before being sidelined by the Bush administration the next year. In 2008, the Pentagon reconsidered, appointing Morris chief prosecutor as proceedings against "high-value" detainees including Khalid Sheikh Mohammed ramped up. Here, he discusses prosecution exhibits with reporters at Guantanamo. (Photo by Jess Bravin)

When the Obama administration took office, Pentagon General Counsel Jeh Johnson helped persuade the new president to retain the military commissions structure established under Bush. (Department of Defense photo by R. D. Ward)

Brig. Gen. Mark Martins was appointed chief prosecutor, the sixth in less than a decade, after Pentagon General Counsel Jeh Johnson found out the military commissions' 9/11 prosecution case prepared by the holdover staff was in shambles. (Photo by Dina Temple-Raston/NPR)

Minister Howard in Australia. Couch surmised that the administration intended to assure Canberra the case was making rapid progress—
regardless of the reality. He called a commissions colleague and begged
him to stop Hemingway from sending Habib's RTB up the chain.

Too late. The cumbersome process to formally authorize Habib's prosecution had begun. It would take six months for the Reason-
to-Believe file to reach the White House, and Couch had to hope that
by the time the president signed the papers the critical intelligence
material would have shaken loose. In the meantime, however, the
Habib RTB largely was speculation; most allegations, the document
carefully noted, were uncorroborated.

Frustrated by his own government, Couch once again moved to
outflank it. He approached the Australian delegation in Washington
for their Habib dossier. While the CIA might not trust him, Couch
figured it would have shared its Habib files with Australian intelligence. The Australians agreed to show Couch some of their material,
on condition that nothing in their files be disclosed to the public or the
defendant. That condition would render it useless as evidence at trial.

AT GUANTANAMO, HABIB FACED increasing pressure to confess a
role in 9/11. According to an FBI agent who sat in, military interrogations sometimes lasted fifteen hours straight.[17] In April 2004, Habib
"repeatedly vomited during the course of a lengthy interrogation,"
one report said.[18] A military medical doctor present, a lieutenant
colonel, did nothing.

Tarek Dergoul, a British detainee held in an opposite cell, said
he saw Habib maced, beaten, and dragged from his cell by his feet in
chains.[19] He was "screaming in agony," Dergoul said.[20] Interrogators
told Habib he would never see his family again. On at least one
occasion, he allegedly was told they had been killed.

Military intelligence plastered an interrogation room with
photos showing his wife lying naked with bin Laden, Habib later
said.[21] A female interrogator threw what he thought was menstrual
blood in his face.

Still, Habib admitted nothing useful. Couch told Bob Swann that without the CIA files, he was at a dead end. "We discussed the fact that the case had always been diplomatically driven and not based on evidence," meeting notes say. "We further discussed the fact that the case had always been 'thin' on corroboration evidence."

Swann said that because of Australian pressure, there were but two options: "RTB Habib or release him." President Bush chose the former option, signing a document formally asserting there was "reason to believe" Habib was a war criminal.

Along with several others Bush also approved for trial, Habib "may have attended terrorist training camps and may have been involved in such activities as financing al-Qaida, building explosives, planning or facilitating maritime operations, and providing protection for Osama bin Laden," the Pentagon announced.[22] Commissions prosecutors heard that Bush told Prime Minister Howard that Habib would be charged by Christmas.

With his RTB signed, Habib's conditions actually improved somewhat. He was permitted a thirty-minute phone conversation with Maha—in English, so military monitors could follow along.[23] The line briefly was disconnected after Habib told her his life in custody resembled *Lock Up,* a 1989 prison movie in which sadistic warden Donald Sutherland inflicts brutal mistreatment on heroic inmate Sylvester Stallone.

CANBERRA PROTESTED WHEN THE Bush administration broke its promise to charge Habib by Christmas. Reminded by the Howard government, the White House pushed the Pentagon, which in turn pressed downward on Tom Hemingway, the appointing authority legal adviser. With Bob Swann on vacation, Hemingway called the deputy chief prosecutor, Carol Joyce, on Friday, December 31. She then called Stu Couch.

"We're being ordered to get charges on Habib," she said. Deliver them tomorrow—New Year's Day.

Couch was incredulous. "Not gonna happen," he said. He still had no access to the intelligence files on Habib.

Joyce said she would tell Hemingway. She called back later that day with an update.

"Stu, you will have access on Monday, you will have access to everything you want," she said.

STU COUCH FINALLY COULD see the CIA's prized secrets. Some of them, anyway. Missing was the case's Rosetta stone, the transcript of the intercepted call Habib placed to his wife on 9/11. Still, together with the leads he had developed through other sources, Couch had the fullest picture yet of the case's strengths and weaknesses.

The best evidence was Habib's own statement, admitting not only to advance knowledge of 9/11 but to training the suicide terrorists in martial arts and plotting to hijack a plane himself. The confession, however, had been obtained during Habib's detention in Egypt—and almost certainly was produced by torture.

"The list of tortures is long, but it includes, to give only the general flavour, the removal of fingernails, the use of electric prods, threatened sexual assault with a dog, forcible injection with drugs, extinguishment of cigarettes on flesh, the insertion of unspecified objects and gases into his anus and the electrocution of his genitals," according to allegations summarized by an Australian court.[24]

Thus, he signed "whatever they wanted me to sign," Habib later said.[25] "I signed to survive."

Egypt operated a notoriously brutal security apparatus, something the US State Department regularly noted in annual human rights reports.[26] Even within the CIA, at least one agent had misgivings about transferring Habib to Egyptian intelligence.

Couch read internal CIA documents discussing Habib's capture in Pakistan and debating what should be done with him. Repatriating him to Australia was ruled out because, CIA officials wrote, the country would not use sufficiently aggressive interrogation methods. They sent him to his native Egypt instead.

One CIA official, apparently the station chief in Canberra, vigorously dissented. "Would we be talking about doing this if he was an

American citizen?" she asked in a cable to the CIA's chief lawyer, John Rizzo.

"That's it," Couch said to himself. He dropped his head to his hands.

Another case infected by torture.

COUCH RETURNED TO THE prosecution offices at Crystal City.

"Sir, I've seen the best the government has to offer. I can't make a case against this guy," Couch told General Hemingway. Given the "rendition issue," he added, Habib "is not somebody we want to charge."

Noted, Hemingway said. "Now, where are the charges?" he repeated.

Desperate to stop the case, Couch took another gamble, circumventing the chain of command to see John Altenburg, Hemingway's boss. As commissions appointing authority, Altenburg's signature was required before the prosecution could proceed.

Couch said the case should be dropped. Even Bob Swann, now back from vacation, agreed.

Altenburg had been galled when President Bush plucked British terrorism suspects from the commissions system and, as a favor to Tony Blair, set them free. Now, the Bush administration's political needs again were interfering with a supposedly judicial process. But this time, instead of freeing men suspected of deep connections to Islamist terror networks, the Bush administration was pressuring prosecutors to manufacture a case the evidence did not support.

Altenburg had other factors to weigh, however. Tom Hemingway, effectively his No. 2, was a hardworking, decent man in a difficult position. Moreover, Hemingway was a brigadier general; it would be humiliating for him—and disruptive to the military hierarchy—to let a lieutenant colonel pull an end run.

Altenburg told Couch to follow Hemingway's orders. File the Habib charges as soon as possible, Altenburg said.

Couch was incredulous. Before he could speak, Altenburg interjected:

"And I'll refuse to approve them."

THE THREE-PAGE CHARGE SHEET, sent to Altenburg on January 3, 2005, accused Habib of "conspiracy to commit murder by an unprivileged belligerent."

Altenburg issued his ruling the next day: Charges dismissed. Prosecutors had presented insufficient evidence "to warrant trial by military commission," he wrote.

The decision shocked the Bush administration. To date, the White House had ignored complaints from commissions prosecutors that the intelligence community's refusal to cooperate was jeopardizing the project. White House officials saw no reason to intervene; if any particular trial was derailed because the CIA withheld evidence, the defendant could simply be held indefinitely without charge as an enemy combatant.

But indefinite detention wasn't an option for Habib; George Bush had promised John Howard that the Australian citizen would be either tried or released. Altenburg's surprise decision forced the administration into a corner. Paul Wolfowitz decided it was essential to provide the intelligence to Altenburg.

Within three hours, Altenburg had the intercept, in a color-coded file marked with the highest levels of classification. Now he knew the US government's most damning intelligence against Mamdouh Habib, evidence the CIA believed proved Habib's complicity in the 9/11 conspiracy.

"Interesting," Altenburg said after reading it. "Doesn't change my mind."

If the White House wanted Habib tried, it would have to replace Altenburg with a more compliant appointing authority. But the administration concluded that the political risks of firing Altenburg exceeded any threat to national security in freeing a suspected 9/11 conspirator. The decision to release Habib was disclosed by a terse press release on January 11, 2005.

Donald Rumsfeld refused to supply a plane or even to permit Habib to travel over US airspace. That forced Canberra to charter a special flight traversing Mexico instead, costing Australian taxpayers half a million dollars to bring Mamdouh Habib home.[27]

■

Disgusted by the Habib episode, Stu Couch wanted to get as far away as he could from commissions. A military judge position had opened at the Marine base in Okinawa. That seemed about far enough. Better still, the chief military judge there was one of Couch's closest buddies, Lieutenant Colonel Daniel "Doc" Daugherty, another veteran of the Aviano prosecution team.

Couch had shared many of his frustrations at commissions with Daugherty, who was determined to help his friend get out of Crystal City. In a recommendation to Marine superiors, Daugherty stressed Couch's "ethics and professionalism." At commissions, "daily, he demonstrates the emotional, intellectual and leadership capacity required for service on the bench," Daugherty wrote. It wasn't enough; Couch was passed over.

The Marine detachment in Bogotá, where US forces were advising the Colombian military on counternarcotics operations, needed a Spanish-speaking legal officer for a two-month assignment. Couch, who knew Spanish and had worked counternarcotics as a KC-130 pilot, volunteered. Denied. With no alternative to commissions lined up, Couch was ready to hand in his resignation anyway, consequences be damned.

Daugherty pulled him back. Rather than swallow the problems at commissions, make the chain of command acknowledge them, he urged.

"Put the ethical and moral issues in their laps and let them tell you how they want it handled," Daugherty wrote by email from

Okinawa. "Then put the ethical and moral objections in writing, give it to them and then do as you are told to do. You know the 'good [soldier] routine.'" But if "you firmly believe you must pull the eject handle consider the following: A) You are looking at an unsat [unsatisfactory] or poor fitrep [fitness report] that will take you OUT of the running for Colonel. B) There are shittier assignments—yes—there are!"

If Couch decided to quit commissions outright, Daugherty told him to take responsibility.

"Put up or shut up: You are a Lieutenant Colonel of U.S. Marines," he wrote in a later email. "If the place is so screwed up, it needs fixing or forgetting. No one, including a fellow Marine, should be forced to follow into your billet, when you know they are going to be faced with the same legal issues and ethical problems. If the problems cannot be fixed at your level, they must be pushed up to the level that can fix them. It must be done in big bold print so there is no mistake on the part of high HQ as to the problems below."

It was Daugherty who, early in 2001, had recommended bringing Couch back into the Corps to clean up the Osprey scandal. The squadron had falsified safety records rather than inform higher-ups the aircraft was unreliable. What if the squadron's commanding officer had found the guts to tell the Marine brass the truth about their precious weapons program?

"If the Osprey CO had done that, there would have been a problem in the MV-22 Squadron," Daugherty wrote.

Yet Couch still hesitated. As before, he turned to Colonel Kevin Winters. They agreed to meet for beers.

Winters arrived at the pub with a surprise guest: Bill Lietzau, now a newly minted full colonel. Winters had conducted the promotion ceremony.

The ambitious, politically dexterous Lietzau made Couch uncomfortable. But there was no losing him, and the chance to see Winters was too precious to squander. Couch laid out the situation at commissions and his fervent wish to escape.

Winters unwittingly echoed Daugherty. He told Couch a patriot would stay put. "Continue to write memos and call fouls," he said. "The United States government needs to get this commissions mess figured out, and they need your help to do it." He added that he knew that Couch wanted to be a military judge. See it through at commissions, Winters said, and "I'll take care of you."

Lietzau wanted to make clear his own inside knowledge of the commissions project, bemoaning the selection of Fred Borch and confiding that Bob Swann initially was passed over for chief prosecutor. Recent events—the calamitous hearings at Guantanamo, Judge Robertson's jaw-dropping order, the Habib disaster—had been noticed by senior levels of the administration. Recently, Lietzau said, people at the White House had been calling him for advice on the way forward with commissions.

"Everything's on the table, from changing the Military Order to pulling the plug altogether," he said. Still, he hadn't realized that things were as bad as Couch relayed. "Does Swann need to go?"

"Yes," said Couch.

Lietzau said that the following Tuesday, the new White House counsel, Harriet Miers, was scheduled to be briefed on commissions.

"I want to paint a realistic picture," Lietzau said. "Give me whatever paper you have."

It was Friday evening. Couch would have a busy weekend.

ON MONDAY AFTERNOON, COUCH sent Lietzau a seven-page memo titled *OMC—Prosecution Big Picture.*

Of some 550 military detainees then at Guantanamo, perhaps 30, or less than 6 percent, had "real prosecutorial value"—including the 12 President Bush already had RTB'd and the 4 formally charged, the memo said.

Prosecution staff numbered fourteen attorneys, three paralegals, and four analysts, but with scheduled retirements and transfers, the office faced "significant loss of experienced litigators within the next four months."

The memo listed several "liabilities" prosecutors faced.

"None of the cases currently identified involve more than low-level, 'worker bee' type operatives," and even so, each depends "on confessions of the accused, with little corroboration evidence other than the admissions of other detainees," it said. "Issues of detainee abuse and interrogation techniques directly affect the credibility of most detainee statements we intend to use as evidence," a significant concern after the Supreme Court's recent *Crawford* decision, which suggested that "the right of confrontation is fundamental to a fair trial," Couch wrote.

At the same time, "systemic and pervasive problems with inter-agency cooperation" remained, despite more than two years of protest from the Office of Military Commissions. "The lack of response by some intelligence agencies could be considered obstructionist," he wrote.

More broadly, "the current process has grown incrementally, on an ad hoc basis, with no real concerted strategic planning involved," the memo observed. "The President's Military Order of November 13, 2001, does not sufficiently address the realities of military justice practice," and its provision for "non-lawyers deciding what the law is" was "inefficient, and prone to appellate attack."

Unsurprisingly, "office morale is extremely low." The memo outlined why:

- inadequate staffing for assigned mission
- upcoming turnover of personnel with institutional knowledge
- recent release of [British detainees] Abbasi and Begg, who were serious offenders and initially intended as the first two cases to go to trial
- pervasive lack of cooperation among agencies and within DoD
- lack of respect within DoD and legal community for military commissions
- history of office turmoil

- lack of adequate office facilities (must see it to believe it)
- systemic failure of leadership

Couch proposed five policy options. The best, he suggested, was a "congressional fix" that would provide statutory authorization for reconstituted commissions to proceed "with procedures similar to courts-martial." Doing so would undermine "constitutional challenges based on unilateral Executive action" while providing the "best chance of acceptability from legal community" and the "most defensible system" on appeal. On the negative side, at least from the administration's perspective, it meant abandoning the "legal theory of unilateral Executive authority."

A second choice would be revising the presidential military order to follow the "Nuremberg model," using "certified military judges" on the commission rather than nonlawyers. That would better resemble both the Nuremberg tribunal and current United Nations courts, "thereby garnering some degree of legitimacy in international law." Alternatively, commissions could be restructured as "courts-martial light," with a military judge to rule on law and a lay panel to decide fact. But that, the memo noted, would expose commissions to "the 'why not use courts-martial' argument."

"The most radical change of policy," the memo said, would be to "abandon military commissions." Doing so, he acknowledged, would constitute a "major policy reversal that compromises acceptability of military commissions in future" and "significantly [damages] government's ability to prosecute high-value detainees in the future." Couch ranked only one option as worse than scrapping commissions altogether: "Stay the course."

Among other drawbacks, he wrote, the "current system is full of issues, and likely to be struck down."

IF COUCH'S MEMO MADE IT to Harriet Miers, it wasn't evident on March 15, 2005, at the National Security Council meeting on detainee and commissions policy. She barely said a word.

Jim Haynes laid out the legal situation. Commissions had been halted after Judge Robertson's order, but the government's appeal would be heard by the DC Circuit Court of Appeals on April 7, 2005.

"I'm confident we'll win, but I've been wrong before," Haynes said.

The Justice Department was represented by Paul Clement, recently promoted to solicitor general. "Things seem to be lining up in our favor," Clement said. The three judges selected to hear the government's appeal were reliable conservatives.

"Is there a Plan B if the case doesn't go well?" asked the new deputy secretary of state, Bob Zoellick. He was a newcomer to the quarterly meetings on detainee policy, having spent Bush's first term as US trade representative.

No one responded.

Clement broke the silence. "We'll defer to DoD on the operational side, but we're confident on the legal side," he said.

"Without commissions, we really don't have any options," Haynes interjected. The administration had prepared no alternatives should the courts find the project unlawful.

"We think we'll get a decision soon," said Stephen Hadley, the national security adviser. Once the DC Circuit reversed Judge Robertson, "I want to make sure we can accelerate things, to make sure that things can move," he said. "We want to be sure the procedural rules have been cleared up."

Hadley's predecessor, Condoleezza Rice, initially had accepted administration lawyers' assertions regarding executive power as fact; she, in fact, had personally conveyed authority for waterboarding to the CIA.[28] Now, however, Rice was secretary of state, heading a department whose professional staff was appalled by administration policies and demoralized by the difficult task of defending them diplomatically. Her legal adviser, John Bellinger, was deeply loyal to Rice. He believed that repairing America's reputation abroad was crucial to her legacy.

Rice accepted Bellinger's advice to reaffirm American commitments to international law, but such claims lacked credibility as long as the administration operated military commissions that defied Geneva Convention requirements.

To bring commissions closer to international legal standards, the State Department wanted to strengthen appellate review of convictions and adopt a blanket rule excluding statements obtained through torture. They were backed by John Altenburg, who had used the time-out ordered by Judge Robertson to draft a 232-page proposed rulebook that, if adopted, would more resemble court-martial procedure.[29]

Hadley agreed to assign a committee of lower-level staffers to examine changes to commissions procedures.

But Vice President Cheney's counsel, David Addington, told them it was a waste of time. "We're fine with what we've got," he said.

A Twentieth Hijacker

TO ARGUE ITS APPEAL IN *Hamdan v. Rumsfeld,* the Bush administration sent one of its most trusted litigators, Peter Keisler, a cofounder
of the Federalist Society. He entered the DC Circuit courtroom confident of a sympathetic panel. All three judges were Republican appointees.

In 2003, two of them, Stephen Williams and A. Raymond Randolph, sat on the panel that held that Guantanamo prisoners had no
legal rights, a ruling the Supreme Court reversed in *Rasul v. Bush.*
Both had been on the court for more than a decade.

The third judge would have had nearly as long a tenure on the
DC Circuit had Senate Democrats not blocked his nomination in
1992 and, again, in 2001. Only after Republicans took control of the
Senate in 2003 did John G. Roberts Jr. finally ascend to the bench.[1]

Whatever their leanings, however, at oral argument the judges
aggressively challenged the government's positions. When Keisler said
that prisoners captured in Afghanistan didn't merit Geneva Convention protections because they didn't wear uniforms, Randolph shot
back with a Vietnam analogy.

"The Viet Cong were given protection under the convention," he
said.

"Excuse me, Your Honor?" Keisler said.

"The Viet Cong—weren't they?"

"That we gave them protection under Geneva? If that's so, it was—"

"They weren't wearing insignia."

"It may have been a discretionary act that we were not required to do," Keisler said.

HARD AS THE PANEL WAS on Keisler, it was harder still on Hamdan's lawyers.

"The government wants to make this case about judicial interference with executive functions, but what this case is really about is executive interference with the judicial function," Neal Katyal said. "Simply put, the essence of our challenge today is that this"—military commissions—"is not a system of law."

"You're making it sound as if the particular individual prosecutor . . . will just freely change the rules," scoffed one judge.

Charlie Swift argued that by excluding Hamdan from portions of the voir dire, the commission had violated international law.

Other countries had "legal systems where the accused is not present during all proceedings," retorted one judge.

"Yes," said Swift. But "we are enforcing not the law of Rwanda, not the law of Saudi Arabia."

"There are legal systems in the world that—from *civilized* countries—that don't allow cross-examination," countered Judge Roberts, with a trace of sarcasm.

As a young man, Roberts had worked in the Reagan White House and Justice Department, where he was quickly recognized as perhaps the brightest of a new generation of conservative lawyers. Many considered the DC Circuit just a way station on Roberts's ascent to the Supreme Court. In fact, the previous Friday, he had interviewed privately for just such a vacancy with Bush's new attorney general, Alberto Gonzales.

ON JULY 15, 2005, THE DC Circuit issued its decision. The administration won, three to zero.

Judge Roberts joined Judge Randolph's opinion, which found that the lower court erred on nearly every point. The Geneva Convention was irrelevant because al Qaeda was not a state, Randolph wrote. "Even if al Qaeda could be considered a Power, which we doubt, no one claims that al Qaeda has accepted and applied the provisions of the Convention."

Yet that question itself was pointless, Randolph said, because courts were powerless to stop the president from flouting America's international obligations. "If a treaty is violated, this 'becomes the subject of international negotiations and reclamation,' not the subject of a lawsuit," he wrote, quoting from a legal digest published in 1906, when international law was almost exclusively considered a form of relations between governments. The century-old handbook, of course, did not reflect legal developments after World War I, and especially following World War II, when international law was expanded to protect individual human rights from officially perpetrated atrocities.

What of the Supreme Court's *Rasul* decision, which the previous year reversed Randolph's own DC Circuit opinion denying Guantanamo detainees access to the courts? Randolph dismissed it as a technical clarification of procedural rules, a jurisprudential abstraction with no practical impact.

Rasul, he wrote, meant only that courts have "jurisdiction," or the formal ability to hear a claim, when Guantanamo detainees challenged their detention. "But *Rasul* did not render the Geneva Convention judicially enforceable," he wrote. "That a court has jurisdiction over a claim does not mean the claim is valid." In other words, Randolph interpreted Justice Stevens's opinion as merely forcing the lower court to hear Hamdan's complaint before automatically rejecting it, rather than blocking Hamdan from complaining at all.

The day the ruling came out, John Roberts went to the White

House to speak with President Bush. Four days later, Bush nominated him for the Supreme Court.

■

The administration decided that commissions would resume immediately. Bob Swann was ready.

While proceedings were dormant, the chief prosecutor had been working on commissions' biggest roadblock, the CIA. His visits to Langley had paid off, he told Stu Couch.

"They trust us," Swann said. "We're gonna start getting the help we need."

Swann let on that he had been briefed on the top-secret program for "high-value" detainees—the ones shuttled through the CIA's secret overseas prisons. The agency, he sensed, was getting comfortable with the prospect of transferring the big fish to Guantanamo.

Couch had his own contacts in the intelligence community. Swann, he thought, was naive about the CIA.

"I've heard rumors that they're tired of being in the jail business and, anyway, the big fish are at the end of their intelligence value," Couch said. Before the CIA could shut down the prisons, it had to unload its detainees.

"They want someone to take out their trash, and we're the only people who can do it for them," Couch said. "I'm a prosecutor, not a trashman."

Swann glared at Couch. "I have had it up to here with your bad attitude and pessimism," he yelled. "I have tried to work with you, but your attitude must change."

"You don't think I'm doing my job?' said Couch.

"You have till Monday to tell me whether you will quit, and I'll send you back to the Marine Corps to figure out what to do with you," Swann replied.

It was Thursday.

Couch spent another uneasy weekend in prayer and ruminations, in talks with Kim and emails to Doc Daugherty, in imagined dialogues with his heroes, the Bonhoeffers and Shackletons.

On Monday, he marched into Swann's office.

"Here it is: I ain't leaving till you fire me or my time is up," Couch declared. "But you have to understand, I am not gonna shut up. You will continue to get my emails and you will continue to get my memorandums, but I am not gonna shut up, 'cause if I shut up, I am not doing my job. I have a duty—"

Swann interrupted. "Okay, got it," he said. "Get back to work."

■

For all their conflicts, Swann relied on Couch for the prosecution's most significant cases. The day after the Supreme Court's *Rasul* decision, Swann handed Couch a memo on Khalid Sheikh Mohammed, the self-declared architect of 9/11. The Office of the Secretary of Defense wanted an update on the case, including "the viability of a prosecution of KSM at a DOD military tribunal."

Included was a report on the Criminal Investigation Task Force inquiry. "Several of the top 60 DOD detainees identified by CITF and OMC as potential commission candidates have provided information about KSM," it said. A number of terrorists in federal prison, including Zacarias Moussaoui, also were potential witnesses.

However, because the CIA still refused to share its files with CITF, "open source material" such as newspaper articles made up the "vast majority" of evidence. "KSM has been held and interviewed by CIA for a long period of time. CITF will need access to the results of those interviews, both to generate investigative leads and to aid in law enforcement interrogations in the event that KSM is released to DOD custody," the report said. "With proper access to evidence, CITF and OMC can build a solid case to ensure KSM is held accountable for the atrocities he allegedly committed."

Swann assigned Couch to analyze the prosecution case based on the CITF report.

"KSM IS THE MOST SIGNIFICANT potential military commission case of any detainee held by the United States Government, and is arguably the most serious offender of any al Qaida operative other than Usama bin Laden," Couch wrote in a July 2004 memo. "The first assumption is that the Prosecution would seek the death penalty if KSM is convicted."

He then turned to an issue the file omitted.

"The nature of KSM's detention and the techniques employed during his interrogations . . . are the most important factors related to any prosecution of KSM," he wrote. Couch's analysis addressed only the legal implications of torture, with no moral gloss. "The only information I have reviewed regarding detainee treatment of KSM . . . are open source news articles, which indicate KSM was subjected to the most severe interrogation techniques authorized by the USG [US Government]," including waterboarding.

"Absent evidence to the contrary, these techniques may violate provisions of the 1984 United Nations Convention Against Torture and Cruel, Inhuman or Degrading Treatment or Punishment, and therefore any statements produced by them could be excluded as evidence against this detainee pursuant to Article 15 of the convention. It is impossible to assess whether KSM's prior statements to intelligence agents were the product of torture without more information," Couch wrote. Thus, "the second assumption" was that prosecutors must avoid "statements made by him to any USG interrogator unless the Prosecution can show they were not the result of torture."

While other detainees had implicated KSM and corroborated much of what he told interrogators, "these statements conceivably have the same issue . . . as to whether they were obtained as a result of torture," Couch wrote.

One problem, he explained, was that the CIA would not identify its interrogators, much less permit them to testify regarding the way confessions were obtained. If "KSM were to assert that his statements and those of other detainees were the product of torture or some lesser form of coercion, then the Prosecution would be unable to rebut the charge that the statements lack credibility," Couch wrote.

Physical evidence, such as documents and computer drives seized from al Qaeda safe houses, presumably would be far easier to introduce. Unfortunately, Couch wrote, "I cannot properly evaluate the quality of this evidence" because neither the CIA nor the FBI would let commissions staff near it. In one critical example, "OMC and CITF have made numerous requests to both FBI and CIA for access to physical evidence seized in the Abu Zubaydah raid in Faisalabad, Pakistan, on 28 March 2002. After several rounds of correspondence and meetings with both of these agencies, we still do not have access to this evidence."

Moreover, despite months-old news reports citing unidentified "Bush administration officials" saying that they believed KSM had murdered Daniel Pearl, the *Wall Street Journal* correspondent kidnapped in Pakistan, commissions had received no information on the case, Couch added.[2]

The remaining evidence included statements from Guantanamo detainees whose interrogations were sufficiently documented to stand up to defense challenges, plus informants and convicted terrorists in federal prison who could be called as witnesses, Couch said. In addition, prosecutors could introduce *Masterminds of Terror*, a 2003 book based on two days of interviews al Jazeera reporter Yosri Fouda conducted with KSM and Ramzi Binalshibh in 2002.[3] The book quoted Mohammed and Binalshibh boasting about the operation they called "Holy Tuesday," Couch wrote, but no tapes of the actual interviews were available.

The message to Rumsfeld was clear: Military commissions were incapable of trying the 9/11 case unless the president provided them the authority, independence, and resources commensurate with the task.

"The prosecution of KSM will be the most significant undertaking in the history of American criminal justice," Couch wrote. "I recommend that the decision to prosecute KSM be made by the National Command Authority to the extent that *all U.S. Government agencies* be directed to assist fully, and provide all information they may possess to the Prosecution upon request."

He advised creating a separate trial team to prosecute Mohammed, including military and Justice Department attorneys, CITF and FBI agents, and CIA and DIA analysts. It must be "a joint effort with the full participation of all these representatives to ensure success."

After receiving the memo, the administration concluded that holding Mohammed accountable for 9/11 was less important than concealing the circumstances of his CIA interrogation. Couch was informed that KSM would not be available for prosecution.

■

With the most serious al Qaeda terrorists withheld from commissions, Couch turned to suspects the military already held at Guantanamo. Top of the list was a Saudi named Mohammed al-Qahtani—the Twentieth Hijacker.

At CITF, Mark Fallon recounted the case for Couch. Three years earlier, Fallon said, he had hoped to open military commissions by putting Qahtani on trial.

While nineteen hijackers had died on 9/11, Fallon said he wanted the public to learn quickly that No. 20 had been captured. Qahtani's trial would demonstrate that America responded to terror not with force alone but with justice. Fallon had recommended that charges be filed just ahead of 9/11's first anniversary.

The administration, however, had other plans for Qahtani.

THE THREE SUCCESSFUL 9/11 hijack teams each had five members. The remaining team, which commandeered United Airlines Flight 93, had only four—and was overpowered by passengers. The plane crashed into a Pennsylvania field, averting further destruction in the presumed target of Washington, DC.

From the outset, investigators assumed there was a missing man from the United 93 team, a Twentieth Hijacker who somehow failed to show up. It wasn't until months later, when they processed a report from an immigration officer in Orlando, Florida, that the likely suspect's identity came into focus.

The immigration officer, Jose Melendez-Perez, was familiar with Saudi tourists, who often traveled to Disney World through Orlando International Airport. The Saudi who arrived on August 4, 2001, was something different. "He gave me the creeps," Melendez-Perez said.[4]

Dressed in black from head to toe, Mohammed al-Qahtani had flown from Dubai via London, arriving on Virgin Atlantic Flight 15. He spoke no English and couldn't fill out the entry forms, so customs agents pulled him aside for questioning and called for an interpreter. Qahtani, fingerprinted and photographed, became "arrogant and threatening," Melendez-Perez said.

Qahtani carried $2,800 in cash but had no hotel reservation, credit cards—or return ticket. His story was incoherent.[5] First, he said someone was coming to pick him up, then that a friend would arrive at a later date with information about his accommodations. Next, he said someone was waiting for him "upstairs," but when asked who that was, denied that anyone was there. He said he was supposed to call someone local to pick him up but refused to say who that was.

Melendez-Perez suspected Qahtani was a contract killer. "A hit man doesn't know where he is going because if he is caught, that way he doesn't have any information to bargain with," he said.

The officer refused to let Qahtani enter the United States. Forced onto a plane back to London, Qahtani offered these parting words: "I'll be back."

Barely a month later, it was 9/11. Melendez-Perez immediately thought of Qahtani. The officer sent his August 4 incident report to the FBI, where the fingerprints eventually were matched with a prisoner captured in the battle for Tora Bora in December 2001, the selfsame Qahtani.

Investigators later concluded that while Qahtani was arguing with Orlando customs, he indeed did have a friend waiting at the airport to pick him up: Mohammed Atta, the 9/11 operation's ringleader. Surveillance cameras recorded Atta's rented Mitsubishi Galant entering the parking lot just before Qahtani's flight landed, and payphone records indicated that Atta had placed calls from the airport to Mustafa al-Hawsawi, an al Qaeda paymaster in the United Arab Emirates who funneled money to the 9/11 hijackers.[6] Qahtani, whom Melendez-Perez described as having a "military appearance" and being "in impeccable shape, with large shoulders and a thin waist," seemed obviously to be the twentieth man. Questioned at Guantanamo, Qahtani admitted he had come to the United States for a "martyrdom operation," an interrogation summary said.[7]

"An absolute simpleton" is how Couch described him. "Pure muscle" for the hijackings. That view was corroborated by a knowledgeable source: Khalid Sheikh Mohammed.

KSM identified Qahtani as an "operative who came into the operation very late," according to a summary of CIA interrogations.[8] He sent Qahtani "to round out the number of hijackers for the 9/11 attacks." Qahtani, however, had been given no details other than that he had been selected for a suicide operation. Apparently, he had been truthful when telling the customs officer that he didn't have the names of any contacts in the United States and didn't even know who exactly was supposed to meet him at the airport.

Qahtani was "an extremely simple man," KSM said, "an unsophisticated 'bedouin'" unequipped "to function with ease in a modern, Western society." Nonetheless, given weak security screening at US airports and the crush of tourist season, KSM figured that Qahtani would be able to slip through customs.

In retrospect, KSM told interrogators, Qahtani should have been better trained and supplied with a round-trip ticket that would look less suspicious. After his deportation, "Sheikh Mohammed decided that he had no further use or patience with Al-Qahtani," the summary said.

Hawsawi, the 9/11 operation's paymaster, had been captured with KSM in Rawalpindi, Pakistan. Interrogated separately, he confirmed KSM's account. Mohammed Atta "needed Qahtani to 'complete the group,'" an interrogation summary said.[9] After 9/11, KSM "told Hawsawi that Qahtani's job was to control the passengers," clearly a skill that would have been useful on United 93.

The CIA, however, refused to provide those summaries—or any information—to Stu Couch. He got them from the US attorney's office in Alexandria, where the documents would be filed in the Zacarias Moussaoui trial.

Similarly, Couch tracked down FBI agents and prosecutors who had investigated Qahtani's failed effort to pass customs at the Orlando airport. They had telephone records, travel itineraries, and other evidence linking Qahtani to the 9/11 hijackers. The material was unclassified, meaning that it could be introduced in open court. Along with the CITF investigation file, Couch was sure he had enough evidence to convict Qahtani in the 9/11 conspiracy.

The hitch, however, might be what happened to Qahtani at Guantanamo.

AFTER HIS CAPTURE IN December 2001, Qahtani initially told interrogators that he came to Afghanistan to buy and sell falcons. He was "obtuse and confrontational," an interrogator said, and his implausible story was suspicious enough to get Qahtani sent to Guantanamo in February 2002, even though no evidence linked him to any specific crime.

Then the fingerprint match came through.

President Bush was briefed on the discovery, and another struggle began over how to handle a detainee. The Justice Department's criminal division wanted to prosecute Qahtani in federal district court. The White House, however, decided that talk of trial was premature. Qahtani seemed too valuable an intelligence resource.

Still, the FBI, claiming priority because it had made the identification, managed to hold on to the interrogation. Qahtani remained uncooperative, first denying that he ever sought to enter the United States, then claiming his Florida trip was part of a business venture involving used cars. FBI agent Ali Soufan, a twenty-nine-year-old Lebanese American and one of the bureau's few Arabic speakers, was called in to work the case. Soufan had proved his worth on the *Cole* bombing investigation in Yemen, along the way becoming friends with Mark Fallon. Since 9/11, Soufan had been working nearly nonstop, interviewing Arab informants and prisoners.[10]

At Guantanamo, Soufan cranked up the pressure on Qahtani well beyond what would be permissible in the United States. On August 8, 2002, Qahtani was taken by force to another cell, where the windows were blocked and harsh industrial lighting stayed on continuously. The only human faces he would see were his interrogators'. Soufan warned Qahtani that until he cooperated, this was his home.

UNDER SOUFAN'S INTERROGATION, Qahtani admitted that he had been assigned to join the 9/11 operation and supplied important details, such as attending a January 2000 meeting in Malaysia with two of the hijackers. Qahtani also acknowledged knowing Ali al-Marri, a Qatari man arrested in Peoria, Illinois, on suspicion of being an al Qaeda "sleeper agent."[11]

That was enough, Mark Fallon told Couch, to prosecute Qahtani for the 9/11 conspiracy.

But confirming Qahtani's links to 9/11 wasn't enough for the Pentagon. Had Qahtani been identified in Afghanistan, the CIA would have snatched him from military custody for transfer to the black sites. Now that Qahtani had been linked to 9/11, the CIA was pushing to take charge.[12]

Donald Rumsfeld could not abide that. "The secretary was very jealous of other agencies," Richard Shiffrin, the Pentagon's deputy general counsel for intelligence, later testified.[13] Rumsfeld "was quite upset that the CIA was more effective in Afghanistan than we were," and he was determined to build "a capability that mirrored the CIA," Shiffrin said.

Rumsfeld wanted "actionable intelligence"—details about future terrorist plots, identities of operatives, locations of safe houses. Jim Haynes, the general counsel, worried that Qahtani might have had a companion who got through customs. Perhaps Qahtani knew of other "people roaming around the country," Haynes said, waiting for the right moment to strike.[14]

At Guantanamo, the military warned FBI and CITF investigators that they weren't producing enough from the prize detainee. Soufan explained the urgency to Qahtani.

"You will find yourself in a difficult situation if you don't talk to me," he said.[15] By early September, the military's patience ran out. "Step aside," they told the FBI.[16]

Qahtani was the first prisoner subjected to a special interrogation plan approved by Rumsfeld. Couch knew what that meant; it was the reason he had to scrap prosecution of Mohamedou Ould Slahi, the second detainee put through the Varsity plan.

As with other detainees, the program focused on sexual and excretory humiliations, including forced enemas. In Jim Haynes's office, lawyers jokingly referred to Qahtani as an "enema combatant."

MONTHS OF PHYSICAL AND psychological abuse failed to extract any useful intelligence from Qahtani, and even if it had, Stu Couch refused to touch anything produced through it.

But it had happened, and its implications for the case were enormous. At minimum, defense lawyers were certain to argue that any Qahtani prosecution had been infected by torture. Before he could begin the prosecution, Couch said he needed to know everything about Qahtani's case.

He sent Bob Swann an email recalling their 2004 discussion after Couch discovered that Slahi had been tortured. "We agreed that our office would not pursue any case involving a detainee who has been subject to a 'Special Project' interrogation plan or program until we have been provided all documents related to that detainee, and assessed whether his case can be legally and ethically prosecuted," Couch wrote.

"Accordingly, as lead counsel for the case against al Qahtani, I renew my prior requests for a complete copy of Vice Admiral Church's [detainee abuse] investigation (including the classified portion), access to all documents related to this detainee held by the Department of Defense (including Office of General Counsel), and to attend any formal briefings related to this detainee that may occur in the future."

Swann poked his head into Couch's office and told him to get what information he could on Qahtani's treatment.

About a month later, Couch was in Swann's deputy's office and saw a binder marked "63"—Qahtani's detainee number. "What the heck is that doing here?" Couch asked.

"Oh, that's a bunch of information that Swann had gotten together on al Qahtani," the deputy said. "He told me not to share it with you."

"Oh, really?" Couch picked up the binder. Tucked into the front cover was a printout of Couch's email, including a reply from Swann that said, "Okay. Get what you can." With a green Sharpie, Swann had scrawled "Put in 63 file" across the top.

Couch was puzzled; he didn't recall getting a reply from Swann. He double-checked his email account and found nothing. Couch had a hunch: Swann had drafted an email reply and then printed it out—but never actually sent it. It was a bureaucratic trick to have it both ways, doing nothing to back Couch but, should the winds later blow in another direction, creating evidence to show that he had been responsive to detainee abuse concerns. Just to be sure, Couch checked with the office's computer technician: he confirmed that no response to Couch's email had been sent from Swann's account on the server or received by Couch's.

"Swann was willing to lie to cover his own ass," Couch said. Furious, he reiterated his concerns about the Qahtani case in a formal memorandum that he printed and personally delivered to Swann.

Swann acted dumbfounded that Couch had not received his email reply.

"The IT guy couldn't find any record of you sending it," Couch said.

Swann shut up. Realizing he had been caught in a lie, he quietly accepted Couch's memo and indicated he would send it up the chain.

Once again, the Bush administration had to choose between prosecuting a 9/11 suspect and risking disclosure of its detainee practices. Weeks later, Swann returned the memo to Couch.

"This case is on hold," he had scribbled on it.

■

Couch turned to another candidate for prosecution: Juma al-Dossari, the Guantanamo detainee who allegedly recruited the Lackawanna Six. Statements taken from Dossari helped crack a suspected al Qaeda cell in upstate New York. In his 2003 State of the Union address, President Bush cited the bust as a major victory against terrorism.

The Lackawanna Six themselves proved faint-hearted jihadists. They quickly made plea bargains, promising cooperation in exchange for prison terms capped at ten years. Couch interviewed all six in prison.

THE LACKAWANNA INVESTIGATION had begun in June 2001, when an anonymous letter, handwritten in broken English, warned the FBI's Buffalo office that "two terrorist came to Lackawanna . . . for recruiting the Yemenite youth."[17] The case crystallized a year later at Guantanamo, after Dossari, a Saudi Bahraini captured in Afghanistan, told interrogators about his visit to the rusting steel town on Lake Erie.[18]

Dossari had left fingerprints across the jihadist world, from an Afghanistan training camp in 1989 through Bosnia and Azerbaijan. In 1999, he came to Terre Haute, Indiana, where he had been invited to preach at a mosque. He reached out to young Muslims at Purdue and Indiana Universities and, in fall 2000, settled at the Islamic Center of Bloomington.[19] In April 2001, Kamal Derwish, a Lackawanna

Muslim who knew Dossari from Bosnia, invited him to help evangel-
ize the local Yemenis.[20]

Sahim Alwan, one of the Six, told Couch that Derwish introduced Dossari as a distinguished imam from Indiana. Dossari had a
certain touch with the youth, able to make radical ideology approach-
able. He could give an incendiary sermon calling for jihad to avenge
the repression of Muslims, then have lunch at Fuddruckers and go
sightseeing at Niagara Falls.[21]

Dossari hosted a cookout for potential recruits and soon was
escorting them to a sporting goods store to equip them for their
adventure. By month's end, Derwish had left for Yemen and seven
recruits, divided into two groups, began crossing the nearby Canadian border, the first leg of the journey to Afghanistan.

Once in the Taliban state, however, the reality of terrorist training shook them up. Some flunked, others dropped out. They later
told authorities that they expected to fight in Chechnya and were
horrified to learn that their target would be the United States. When
Ali al-Bahlul's crude recruiting video was shown at their guesthouse,
other jihadists cheered. Not Yassein Taher of Lackawanna.[22] "I was
surprised, shocked," he later testified. "And I was afraid."

The six made excuses about needing to go home to make ar-
rangements for their wives. Alwan told Couch that he had an exit
interview with bin Laden, whose main interest seemed to be recruiting more Muslims with US passports. "What do the brothers"—
American Muslims—"think of America?" bin Laden asked. "Are they
willing to do martyrdom missions?"

Once back in Lackawanna, unaware that the FBI long had been
on to them, the six dissembled about their travels to Afghanistan.
After 9/11, such deception only intensified official assumptions about
them being a sleeper cell. The six transfixed the highest levels of the
Bush administration; the president himself received regular briefings
on the investigation.[23]

Vice President Cheney and his counsel, David Addington, urged
Bush to order the Army into Buffalo to capture the men and had a

John Yoo legal opinion to justify the operation. Attorney General John Ashcroft, FBI Director Robert Mueller, and criminal division chief Michael Chertoff objected. Bush ultimately rejected Cheney's plan, and in September 2002 the six were arrested without incident—five in the Buffalo area, another in Bahrain.[24] A seventh Lackawannian, Jaber Elbaneh, remained at large, and later was placed on the FBI's Most Wanted Terrorists list.

Derwish did not last long in Yemen. In November 2002, he and several suspected al Qaeda figures were incinerated when their car was hit by a Hellfire missile fired by a CIA Predator drone.

Dossari was another matter. He had a flight booked to Saudi Arabia on the notable date of September 10, 2001. Somehow, he missed his plane and returned to Lackawanna, "as nervous as a snake in a belt factory," Couch said. Three weeks later, Dossari slipped out of the country and made his way to Afghanistan, where he was captured near Tora Bora.

This time, Couch ran into obstruction from the FBI, which had handled the Lackawanna case and refused to share its files on Dossari. Working with a CITF analyst, Couch retraced Dossari's path himself, searching for evidence to prove that the traveling imam was an al Qaeda talent scout. He caught a break in Indianapolis, where, in contrast to headquarters, the FBI field office was willing to help.[25]

Since late 2002, the Indianapolis office had been investigating possible terrorist activity by a group of Muslim students at Indiana University. A witness had reported the students to the FBI, noting that they regularly met at a particular apartment after 9 p.m., removing their shoes before entering. Peering through a window, the witness had seen maps marked with Xs and arrows but no furniture. By counting the pairs of shoes left outside, she provided an exact number of participants.

The agents found some of the students' activities suspicious. One had enrolled in a microbiology lab section—without the corresponding lecture course. Two were seen in a boat in a nearby reservoir, taking photographs. Such clues didn't prove anything, but after

9/11, FBI agents weren't taking chances. The Indianapolis office launched an operation to figure out what was going on in Bloomington. It did not go well.

The bureau sent a Cessna 182 to conduct aerial surveillance of the college town. Residents soon began complaining to local authorities about the noisy plane flying from noon to midnight; when both the police and the FBI office denied knowledge of the aircraft, fears of terrorism swept Bloomington.[26]

Local press coverage intensified, and the FBI office was forced to acknowledge the plane was its own.[27] With the Iraq invasion looming, Bloomington peace activists complained that the FBI was spying on their demonstrations.[28] "Heavens, no," a bureau spokesman told the *Indianapolis Star*. To the contrary, the FBI said, the plane was part of a counterterrorism investigation that focused on foreign students.[29]

When Couch got to Indianapolis, he learned what happened next.

"We got into a shitload of trouble," an agent told him. With the operation exposed, the targets vanished. Headquarters, furious, cut the field office out of the loop, leaving Indianapolis agents in the dark about counterterrorism operations. They offered Couch a look at their files. "We're really not supposed to be showing you this," an agent added.

Couch and his CITF analyst spent two days examining the surveillance records. The centerpiece was a huge chart, a spiderweb of lines linking names, calls, and telephone numbers, spiking in April 2001—the period that Dossari visited Lackawanna. Couch and the analyst thought they had stumbled on a miniature *shura* council, with a religious leader at the center: Juma al-Dossari.

Back at Crystal City, Couch briefed Swann on what he had turned up.

"This guy Dossari is dirty," Couch said. "But I can't get anything on him past the rah-rah-sis-boom-bah speech he gives in Lackawanna." Thanks to the First Amendment, Dossari couldn't be prosecuted for his anti-American sermon. To prove Dossari's role in the al

Qaeda network, Couch needed the intelligence files, including the FBI's full dossier.

As with other Guantanamo prosecutions, Couch did not want to pin his case on statements obtained by military intelligence. Dossari had not been on the Varsity plan, but nonetheless his treatment would be an obstacle if interrogation statements were introduced. Dossari claimed he had been beaten, tormented with light, sound, and temperature manipulation, deprived of sleep and food, and threatened with death or the death of his daughter.[30]

This time, however, Couch thought he could leverage what he learned in Indianapolis to get cooperation from FBI headquarters. He asked the bureau for the "FISA stuff"—the telecommunications records he assumed had been collected under the Foreign Intelligence Surveillance Act. The 1978 law made it easy for federal investigators to tap communications of suspected foreign agents in the United States, creating a secret court to issue surveillance warrants for intelligence purposes without meeting the Fourth Amendment's stricter requirements for criminal prosecutions.

Instead, the FBI reacted with alarm when Couch described what he had seen. It refused to turn over any files for a military commissions prosecution.

Later, Couch had a hunch as to why. In December 2005, the *New York Times* reported that the Bush administration had been conducting electronic surveillance inside the United States without warrants of any kind—even from the secret FISA court.[31] While a secret memorandum written by John Yoo apparently approved the warrantless wiretapping program, it later came out that several senior lawyers within the administration disagreed—among them Deputy Attorney General James Comey and FBI Director Robert Mueller, who threatened to resign unless changes were made.[32]

Maybe the FBI didn't have warrants for the Bloomington phone surveillance, Couch later thought. That would explain the FBI's determination to bury the episode.

DOSSARI, MEANWHILE DISPUTED the government's allegations,
giving harmless explanations for his travels to such battle zones as
Afghanistan and Bosnia. At a Guantanamo detention hearing, the
military introduced a *Buffalo News* story describing his April 2001
Lackawanna sermon as "full of rage and politics."[33]

"I have a right to free speech," Dossari responded, denying that
he incited attacks on the United States. "If I was al Qaeda, would I go
to New York and say these things? I am not that crazy." During his
Guantanamo incarceration, however, he did make several suicide at-
tempts using a razor or a noose.

Abruptly, in July 2007, he was released.

"A colonel told me that I was going home. He did not explain why
I was suddenly no longer too dangerous to live in freedom," Dossari
said.[34] Back in Saudi Arabia, he was sent to a "de-radicalization" institution, where in 2008 he was among half a dozen model inmates
selected to meet a distinguished visitor, British prime minister Gordon
Brown.[35]

Dossari told Brown he simply had been "in the wrong place at
the wrong time." Now, Dossari said, he was looking forward to a new
career in computing.

■

Couch turned to another prospect: Ahmed al-Darbi, the Saudi implicated in a plot to attack an oil tanker in the Persian Gulf. Darbi had
a family connection to 9/11—hijacker Khalid al-Mihdhar was his
brother-in-law.

Darbi was arrested in June 2002 after taking a flight from Dubai
to Baku, Azerbaijan, to visit his mistress.[36] Azerbaijani customs agents
claimed they jailed him for carrying $150 in counterfeit American
currency, but more likely they had acted on instructions from US
intelligence, which apparently had been intercepting Darbi's telephone calls. The Azerbaijanis held Darbi for two months before telling

him he was being sent home. Instead, he was taken to Bagram and, in March 2003, Guantanamo.

Darbi was a veteran of jihad in Bosnia and Afghanistan. Investigators believed that in early 2001, he was selected for more important projects by Abdelrahim al-Nashiri, the suspected organizer of the *Cole* bombing. Nashiri specialized in maritime operations; before the *Cole*, he had orchestrated the failed January 2000 attack on the Navy destroyer USS *The Sullivans*. Darbi was to organize a similar suicide attack on an oil tanker. With any luck, blowing up a supertanker would interrupt the global petroleum supply and send the world economy into a tailspin.

While others worked on the 9/11 plot, Darbi went about his mission. He bought GPS units, satellite telephones, and, with a wire transfer from Nashiri, a thirty-foot wooden dhow in Dubai for $130,000. Darbi paid $2,700 to register it under the São Tomé flag, hired a seven-man Indian crew, and recruited three Yemenis as ship hands—or possibly suicide pilots for smaller boats the dhow would launch against its target. After planning to sail to Yemen, he docked instead at Bosaso, Somalia, on the Gulf of Aden's opposite shore. Darbi was not a single-minded fanatic, however. He had a pregnant girlfriend on the side and, as Couch put it, blew much of the $250,000 budgeted for the tanker operation on "wine, women and song."

Unlike most Guantanamo cases, prosecutors could rely on substantial extrinsic evidence against Darbi. US Special Forces had located Darbi's dhow and interviewed its Indian crew, meaning that Couch could introduce statements, photos, and boat registration documents. But Darbi's voluminous confessions, prompted by FBI agents using the classic good cop–bad cop routine, provided the heart of the case. Darbi not only recounted his own activities in detail, he had fingered other al Qaeda operatives who were quickly rounded up.

The case also had some weaknesses. For instance, Darbi's original confession, including his handwritten corrections, somehow had been lost.

Other issues were more serious. The two detainees whose statements corroborated Darbi were held at CIA black sites; one was Nashiri himself. The agency long had made clear that its prisoners were off limits to commissions.

Then there was Darbi's own treatment. The period he spent at Bagram—late 2002—was marked by extraordinary abuse of prisoners. There were rumors, later proved true, that some detainees had been killed during sadistic interrogations. To put the issue to rest, in February 2004, Couch had sent his CITF investigator to find out more. As with other cases, Couch wanted to stake out Darbi's treatment claims now, before he had a chance to embellish them under the guidance of a defense attorney.

"Get in the interrogation box with al Darbi and ask him flat out: Have you ever been abused? Tell me everything you can about it."

The investigator reported that Darbi described being slapped around and shoved—harsh treatment but nothing sufficiently shocking to derail the case. Nevertheless, in a March 2004 memo, Couch recommended a thorough review of detainee treatment at Bagram and CID, the Army's criminal investigation command, opened a file. Couch heard nothing more. He assumed that CID had found things in order.

DARBI LOOKED LIKE A possible plea bargain. He had cooperated extensively. Investigators considered him sincere and credible. So did Couch; on his first visit to Guantanamo, in 2003, Darbi was the detainee military intelligence had rolled out to demonstrate a model interrogation. Two years later, Couch decided to meet Darbi face to face.

Normally, it would be considered improper for a prosecutor to talk to a suspect jailed without access to an attorney. But such rules were not enforced at Guantanamo, and Couch wanted to open his own direct line to Darbi while he could.

"My hope is to plant the seed that he's not being totally screwed by the system," Couch said. "I want to get to him before a defense attorney pollutes his mind with the idea that he's just being railroaded."

Couch took along a junior prosecutor and an investigator. They brought Darbi a sandwich from the base's Subway outlet, and Couch insisted that the prisoner be unshackled. He wanted to shake hands with his suspect.

"I represent the United States government. In fact, I'm prosecuting you," Couch told Darbi. "I do not represent you. But I'm down here to tell you in advance that I value the information you've given up. You have assisted the government greatly. I recognize that. I honor that. And I will give you my word that if I've got anything to do with it, you're gonna be treated fairly."

Darbi listened.

"Look, there's gonna come a time when you're represented by a defense attorney, and when that happens, I can't talk to you any more," Couch said. In fact, Couch added, Darbi didn't even have to talk to him now. But if he chose to, there were some things to discuss.

The meeting lasted an hour or two, and by the end, the defendant and his prosecutor were almost joking together. One evidence photo showed Darbi in the 1990s, when foreign fighters were expelled from Bosnia after the Dayton Peace Accords. Couch teased Darbi for the trendy Air Jordan footwear he sported in the snapshot.

"Man, look at you in your Air Jihads," Couch said.

"Yeah, yeah," Darbi laughed. "It was a long time ago," he added, after a pause.

"You know, for an al Qaeda guy, he's all right," Couch said.

They shook hands, and Couch and the junior prosecutor went to get some food. The CITF investigator stayed behind, saying she had a few more things to clear up.

The prosecutors were having dinner at the officers club when Couch's cell phone rang. It was the investigator.

"You're not going to believe this," she said.

WHILE GOING OVER THINGS with Darbi, their February 2004 meeting, when the investigator had first asked about his treatment, came up. Darbi mentioned that at that meeting, he had been too afraid of retaliation to give her the full story, but when agents came later in 2004 to follow up, he trusted them enough to describe what really happened.

"What are you talking about?" the investigator said. CITF had sent no one to follow up.

It turned out that after Couch's request, Army CID investigators came to interview Darbi. He gave them a nightmarish account of his time at Bagram and picked out his alleged tormentor from a photo lineup. The CID agents filed a report in June 2004, but no one at commissions knew anything about it. Couch told the investigator to track down the CID report and go back to Darbi to take his complete statement.

Two CITF agents interviewed Darbi over two days. The Bagram he described was a chamber of horrors, and he personally had witnessed soldiers torturing an Afghan man named Dilawar, a taxi driver mistakenly held as a terrorist. From his own cage, Darbi had watched a screaming Dilawar suspended from his arms for two days, his feet dangling above the ground, as soldiers beat him. Darbi said he heard —correctly, it turned out—that Dilawar died soon thereafter.

Darbi's own experience involved continuous pain, degradation, and fear. "His hands were cuffed above his head, his face was sprayed with water and pepper was blown onto his face. He was dragged and thrown against walls. The dragging and being thrown were considered normal things that occurred [every] day," the agents wrote. "He was punched in the chest and stomach," while a military police sergeant who called him "sex boy" "pressed his finger so deeply under Al Darbi's jawbone into the soft flesh" as to make him gag.

Soldiers put diapers on Darbi's head, and made him urinate and defecate in the street. For two weeks he was kept chained with his hands above his head and was unshackled only to scrub the floor with a toothbrush and perform other humiliating chores.

Much of the abuse had sexual themes. Hooded during questioning, Darbi recalled an episode in which a female interrogator said she was going kiss him and began rubbing his thigh. A male interrogator on his other side then told Darbi, "I'm going to fuck you," the report said. "That male pushed Al Darbi onto his knees, positioned himself behind Al Darbi and mimicked anally sodomizing (i.e., 'humped') Al Darbi," moaning as he did so. After they left, new interrogators arrived playing what Darbi called "very loud 'devil worshipping music'" on a cassette player, throwing him against the wall, kicking him in the groin, ripping hairs from his chest, and dragging him around the room.

One interrogator, described as tattooed and muscle-bound, "pulled his pants down and showed Al Darbi his buttocks. He wiped the area between his buttocks as well as his anus with toilet paper and then threw the toilet paper onto Al Darbi," the report said.

The other, "(described as the fat guy) pulled out his (interrogator's) penis, put it near Al Darbi's face and said, 'This is your God.'"

The CITF agents asked Darbi if the interrogator's penis had any distinguishing marks.

"Al Darbi jokingly laughed and said he tried not to really look at it," the report said. But Darbi said the interrogator, who he later learned was of Italian descent, had a Virgin Mary tattooed inside his forearm and wore a cross around his neck. "The 'fat' Italian interrogator," he told the agents, was the "'head' of torture."

Darbi said the pair interrogated him ten to fifteen times, frequently kicking and punching him, while varying other forms of abuse, such as throwing trash on him or hurling him into walls. "The fat Italian interrogator also once showed Al Darbi a condom and stated, 'This is special for you. I'm going to fuck you.'"

Darbi promised investigators that if released he would keep quiet. "He will not tell the press if he is released," the report said. "Al Darbi then sighed and said he still sometimes has nightmares about the fat Italian interrogator and his muscular tattooed partner."

Asked if there were any witnesses, Darbi mentioned fellow prisoners Omar Khadr, a teenage Canadian citizen, and Moazzam Begg, the British detainee freed from Guantanamo at Tony Blair's request.

After several weeks at Bagram, Darbi said, FBI agents took over and the abuse subsided. It was only then that Darbi developed into a valuable source.

COUCH HAD BEEN ON THE brink of filing charges against Darbi. Now he had to tell Bob Swann things had changed.

"As we have discussed previously, this case is arguably the strongest one on its facts of any other case now being investigated by CITF," he wrote in a July 2005 memo. But "in light of recently discovered information, I must inform you that certain confessions by al Darbi may be tainted by allegations he was abused by military interrogators." Because his confessions to the FBI followed alleged abuse by US interrogators, "the strongest evidence against al Darbi is now subject to doubt." Under the Convention Against Torture, the statements might not even be admissible, he warned.

Darbi's claims were credible, Couch wrote, and such treatment was indefensible. Nevertheless, "I still believe that al Darbi needs to be prosecuted." In contrast to cases like Slahi, the allegations against Darbi were corroborated by extrinsic evidence.

Couch advised entering all the facts into evidence and allowing the military commission to decide whether Darbi's statements could be admitted. Before proceeding, however, he recommended warning superiors that inevitable disclosures about the interrogation could "overshadow the more important issue of Darbi's alleged misconduct."

AS THE COMMISSIONS OFFICE weighed how to proceed, Couch looked into Darbi's interrogator, a soldier named Damien Corsetti.[37] He had several nicknames, including Monster, which was tattooed on his torso in Italian, and "King of Torture." After Bagram, Corsetti's unit went to the Abu Ghraib prison in Iraq, where reportedly he had been demoted after forcing a female prisoner to strip during questioning.

Now, Couch discovered, as a result of the CID investigation, the Army was planning to prosecute Corsetti for abusing Darbi and two other Bagram detainees.[38]

Once again, Couch realized, government misconduct had damaged, if not destroyed, the prosecution of a terror suspect at Guantanamo Bay.

"I hate to do this, but we need to put the brakes on," Couch told Swann. "My advice is that we let the Corsetti investigation and court-martial run its course, and then decide what to do about al Darbi." Swann agreed.

Dejected, Couch turned to the last plausible case remaining in his portfolio. It was a handover from Scott Lang, who had retired from the Navy after being denied promotion.

The defendant was Salim Hamdan.

The Marble Palace

THE HAMDAN AND HICKS TRIALS could resume within four to six weeks, Brigadier General Tom Hemingway, the military commissions legal adviser, announced after the appeals court reinstated the program.[1]

But Neal Katyal, the Georgetown professor directing Hamdan's legal challenge, never considered the DC Circuit anything other than a bump on the road to the Supreme Court, where he immediately filed an appeal.

As Katyal's petition framed the issue, Hamdan "asks simply for a trial that comports with this nation's traditions, Constitution, and commitment to the laws of war, such as a court-martial."

While the Hamdan team pursued its Supreme Court appeal, Stu Couch was developing his case against Hamdan. He scheduled a meeting with Katyal to lay things out.

Couch expected the Georgetown professor to be a snob as well as a law geek. Instead, Katyal proved surprisingly candid when confronted with Couch's evidence, including photos of surface-to-air missiles recovered from Hamdan's car and CNN video of Hamdan, wearing camouflage and slinging an AK-47, happily taking his position in bin Laden's entourage.

"Well, that doesn't look too good for our guy, does it?" Katyal said.

ADMINISTRATION LEGAL THEORISTS considered Hamdan's appeal frivolous. But government lawyers charged with actually defending the commissions project in court or with foreign allies took it more seriously. At their urging, the administration announced changes it said would provide detainees fairer treatment and, therefore, make commissions more defensible before the Supreme Court.

Henceforth, the commissions presiding officer would function more like a military judge than a jury foreman. To underscore the change, presiding officers would start wearing black robes, while the regular commission members effectively became a jury, deciding guilt and punishment. Senior JAG officers had urged such a structure from the outset of the commissions project, only to be overruled by administration lawyers opposed to anything that resembled a real court.

But the presidential military order Bush had signed seemed to preclude that change, as it directed the full commission, not the presiding officer, to decide questions of both fact and law. Only Bush could revise his own order—and David Addington, the vice president's counsel, refused to contemplate such a move. The contradiction between the new structure and the text of the Presidential Military Order handed yet another issue to defense lawyers hunting for procedural flaws.

Moreover, the White House had turned down the most significant reforms on the table.

One rejected proposal would have allowed defendants to appeal if convicted—something Bush's military order prohibited. State Department officials suggested sending appeals to the US Court of Appeals for the Armed Forces, whose five civilian judges heard appeals from the uniformed services' internal criminal justice systems.

Addington and Haynes refused; the Court of Appeals for the Armed Forces was known to occasionally overturn convictions from courts-martial. The only concession they made was allowing the commissions review panel—the instant generals selected by Rumsfeld —seventy-five days, rather than thirty, to confirm convictions before sending them up to Rumsfeld for final approval.

More problematic was the torture question.

President Bush's public disavowal of torture had been discredited by news reports documenting detainee treatment. John Bellinger, now the State Department's top lawyer, pushed for a blanket ban on evidence obtained through torture. Such an exclusionary rule simply codified America's existing obligations under the Convention Against Torture, he argued.

Gordon England, the new deputy secretary of defense, agreed. Addington and Haynes vetoed the proposal.[2]

Nevertheless, Solicitor General Paul Clement seized on the few revisions that were approved when he urged the Supreme Court to reject Hamdan's appeal. The changes mitigated some of Hamdan's objections, Clement wrote, while his others were pure speculation.

Clement, of course, was pleased that the DC Circuit had adopted the administration's claim that Hamdan had no rights. Unlike Addington and Haynes, however, Clement was a shrewd litigator with a sense of how far he could push a particular court. And unlike Bellinger, he was close to the lawyers who had conceived the administration's legal framework.

Clement had come to the Bush administration after pitching in on the legal battle to stop the 2000 Florida recount. Ted Olson, the new solicitor general, had asked conservative elders, including Justice Scalia and Judge Silberman, to help him find a deputy "made from the mold of John Roberts." All fingers pointed to Clement, who like Roberts was charming as well as clever, sharing a Midwestern upbringing that smoothed the edge of a painfully sharp mind. And even more than Roberts, he could slip easily between the redoubts of the ideological right and the crossroads of the cultural mainstream, dazzling conservatives while leaving liberals disarmed.[3]

Despite his ideological purity, Clement had a clear-eyed view of the legal battlefield and knew that blustery declarations of executive supremacy would not win him the necessary five votes at the Supreme Court. He tried to chart a more modest path to victory, writing that the DC Circuit, despite ruling for the government, never should have reached the merits of the case. Instead, he suggested, the court of appeals should simply have dismissed Hamdan's claim as premature. Let the military commission trial proceed. Hamdan might be acquitted, Clement asserted, leaving nothing to appeal. Were he convicted, the trial record would lay out actual issues to consider, rather than the nightmare scenario Neal Katyal dreamed up.

HAMDAN V. RUMSFELD WAS calendared for the conference, as the Supreme Court calls the private meeting at which the nine justices decide which cases to hear, of September 26. It takes four votes to get a case before the court.

In their elegant conference room, seated around the table in order of seniority, the justices voted to hear Anna Nicole Smith's claim to the fortune left by J. Howard Marshall II, the ninety-year-old oilman who died fourteen months into their marriage. The centerfold's lawyers had identified a conflict between state probate law and federal bankruptcy jurisdiction.

The justices found it tougher to decide whether Hamdan's case was worth their time. September, then October, passed without word. Finally, on November 7, the case appeared on a list of petitions granted.

Defiance marked the administration's reaction. Because only Hamdan's case, technically, was stayed by court action, the Pentagon vowed to resume proceedings against David Hicks within two weeks. Next, it announced new charges against five additional Guantanamo prisoners. One new defendant, Omar Khadr, age fifteen when captured, was charged with killing an American soldier, a capital offense.

"We're aware of the Supreme Court decision," a Pentagon spokesman said.[4] But "we don't expect any changes to our current commissions procedure or schedule."

Because of pressure from Canberra, disposing of Hicks remained a top priority. Hopes for a rapid trial vanished, however, after Hicks's lawyers obtained a court order halting proceedings until the justices ruled on Hamdan's case.

Stu Couch secretly felt relieved that the Court had accepted the appeal, postponing the Hamdan trial indefinitely. It took the pressure off preparing the prosecution, allowing Couch to accompany his eldest son on a weeklong church mission to Bolivia.

FOLLOWING THE TORRENT OF detainee abuse disclosures that began with publication of photographs from Abu Ghraib, congressional Democrats and a few Republicans began pushing for legislation to protect prisoners from mistreatment by American forces.

The White House objected, but support from Senator John McCain, who drew moral stature from his ordeal as a POW in Vietnam, ensured passage. The administration regrouped to hollow out the proposed Detainee Treatment Act by amendment. And when Bush reluctantly signed the bill on December 30, he issued a signing statement indicating that he would disregard provisions he viewed as interfering with his own powers. As a result, a statute that originated as an effort to restrain the Bush administration from abusing prisoners became, in final form, a license for further excess.

That was clear when the administration immediately invoked the new Detainee Treatment Act to nullify the one Supreme Court ruling protecting Guantanamo detainees from mistreatment, *Rasul v. Bush,* which held that federal law permitted Guantanamo inmates to seek court review of their detentions.

The Detainee Treatment Act stated that "no court, justice, or judge shall have jurisdiction to hear or consider" claims "relating to any aspect of the detention by the Department of Defense of an alien at Guantanamo Bay, Cuba."

In a new brief, Paul Clement told the justices that Congress had revoked their authority to hear Hamdan's case and must therefore dismiss it.

The Supreme Court agreed this was a serious question. It told the parties to address it, along with the other issues under review, at the scheduled oral argument. Each side got an extra fifteen minutes to make its points.

SUPREME COURT ARGUMENTS WERE scheduled for March 28. As they approached, the Bush administration announced an apparent softening of its detainee policies. Jim Haynes had decided that torture was not an appropriate method of obtaining evidence.

Haynes changed his mind sometime after March 1, when, at a Guantanamo hearing for Ali al-Bahlul, a defense attorney asked presiding officer Brownback to exclude evidence obtained by torture.

The question prompted one of Brownback's uncomfortable courtroom cogitations. After a long silence, he answered.

"What you and I mean by torture could be different," Brownback said.[5] While "my personal belief is that torture is not good," as a legal matter it wasn't so clear.

After the hearing, reporters asked a commissions spokeswoman, Major Jane Boomer, to clarify whether a defendant could be convicted based on statements obtained through torture.

"'Hypothetically, is it possible?" she said. "Do the rules allow for it? Yes."[6]

With the Supreme Court scrutinizing commissions, Boomer's admission was unhelpful. Moreover, Haynes's own Fourth Circuit nomination remained stalled at the Senate Judiciary Committee. Senior officials confidentially passed word to a reporter ahead of the rule change. That prompted the reporter to contact Haynes's office, where a spokeswoman was ready to assert Haynes's fealty to the Convention Against Torture.

The Pentagon "had believed that a specific commission rule was unnecessary and would erroneously suggest that torture had actually occurred," she said. "Nevertheless, to eliminate any doubt that CAT Article 15, as understood by the United States, is applicable to these prosecutions, the general counsel has issued a formal instruction that bars prosecutors from offering as evidence any statement obtained as a result of torture, and bars commissions from admitting such evidence against an accused."[7]

Stu Couch learned about the new policy through the newspaper. It wasn't circulated within the Office of Military Commissions.

PAUL CLEMENT KNEW THAT arguing *Hamdan* would be difficult. The administration's theories were overwhelmingly rejected by the legal community, and aggressive news coverage had undermined official claims of humane detainee treatment.

Clement also recognized a factual handicap: the defendant. Salim Hamdan was accused of no violent acts, no leadership role, nothing, really, beyond proximity to his sinister employer, Osama bin Laden. As Charlie Swift never tired of remarking, the Allies didn't prosecute Hitler's driver.

Still, Clement now had the Detainee Treatment Act on his side, which seemed proof that Congress had joined the president in telling the Court to butt out. In moot courts leading up to the argument, Clement focused on deflecting any doubts that the new statute blocked the justices from considering Hamdan's claims at all.

As a pragmatic matter, Clement's fallback position—that the justices should let Hamdan's trial proceed before considering whether there was a claim to review—made sense. *Rasul*, after all, did not question the position that those who truly were enemy fighters could be detained without charge. Whether Hamdan stood trial or not, he wasn't going anywhere.

NEAL KATYAL COULD NOT match Paul Clement's litigation experience. Moreover, where Clement's easygoing style could make the most outrageous claims sound reasonable, Katyal sometimes came across as a bloodless technocrat whose thin voice hinted at impatience.

Charlie Swift long had worried over how the professor's aloof manner would come across before the justices.

In the courtroom, "I can communicate with somebody imme-diately, I know how to do this," Swift said. "Neal doesn't."

Back in fall 2004, with the district court hearing before Judge Robertson approaching, Swift had persuaded Katyal to meet with a litigation coach, a former actor who taught lawyers ways to sharpen their courtroom manner. Katyal agreed to try some exercises, learn-ing to make eye contact, improve his posture, and work the room.

In contrast to the early days after 9/11, by 2006 mainstream firms were clamoring for a chance to challenge Guantanamo policies. Katyal parceled out issues to dozens of interested parties—scholars, foreign parliamentarians, former officials, nonprofit organizations, retired generals and admirals—to present in friend of the court briefs. Bouncing ideas off a wide circle of experienced lawyers and enthusi-astic students, Katyal framed an argument portraying the Bush com-missions as a radical departure from legal norms, defining a vote for Hamdan as a vote to restore traditional American practice.

As argument day approached, Katyal rehearsed in more than a dozen private moot courts, at Georgetown and other law schools, with the help of friends like Laurence Tribe at Harvard and Akhil Amar, Katyal's mentor at Yale. Some moots went disastrously, others less so. Far from certain he would win, Katyal made a last-minute gambit. On the Friday before the argument, he contacted Jim Haynes to suggest that they sit down to negotiate a plea bargain that would end the Hamdan case.

Haynes said he would think about it. On Sunday, he told Katyal no dice.

Now there was no escaping the Supreme Court argument. And as the hours ticked down, Katyal could not shake one fear.

"Scalia was the terror," Swift said. "Scalia was this viper in the room."

Justice Antonin Scalia, the lion of the right whose outsize per-sonality and stinging pen had invigorated conservative legal thought, haunted Katyal. He knew he had no chance of winning Scalia's vote.

As a law clerk for Justice Stephen Breyer, Scalia's would-be foil, Katyal had watched polished litigators melt into puddles under Scalia's blistering tongue. Katyal feared falling into one of Scalia's rhetorical traps, losing his own way as the justice led him down a path of self-contradiction. Beyond looking a fool in the nation's greatest legal arena, a weak performance could cost him the vote of a wavering justice—such as Anthony Kennedy, the maverick conservative who, after Justice Sandra Day O'Connor's retirement, typically cast the deciding vote on the most controversial cases.

The litigation coach, called in days before the argument, tried every trick to deflate Katyal's fixation. How about picturing Scalia in a bunny suit? Didn't help. Maybe all nine justices as a row of stuffed animals? Nope.

Okay, the coach suggested, figure Scalia not in a bunny suit or naked or being hit with a cream pie but as merely a provocative student—the smart aleck who always tries to trip up the professor. Another dead end.

Finally, the coach turned to something simple. Instead of being standoffish or clinical, "imagine you're holding the justice's hand," he said, leading him to wisdom. Katyal found this approach comfortable; it was, he realized the hallmark of his adversary, Paul Clement. Indeed, it was the very style perfected by one of the Supreme Court's most successful litigators: John Roberts.

"I went back and played all of the chief justice's oral arguments, when he was in private practice," Katyal said. "They were very conversational, like Paul's. I tried to emulate them."

AT 3:00 A.M. ON MARCH 28, Charlie Swift brought his wife to the Supreme Court, arriving so early to ensure she would be at the head of the line for seats at the argument. Others had had the same idea, including four Wisconsin high school students who were studying the case. Swift, always garrulous, chatted with them to discover they also were going to meet with Paul Clement—the solicitor general, himself a Badger State native, had invited them to his office.

Six hours later, Swift was back at the court, this time in his uniform, among the senators, officers, scholars, and legal eminences coming to witness the contest.

"Well, Neal's going to have a real hard time of it today," a smiling Tom Hemingway, the commissions legal adviser, said to Eric Freedman, a Hofstra law professor on the Hamdan team.

"Yes," Freedman muttered. They waited while the court wrapped up the day's first argument, a dispute over contractual reimbursement obligations under the Employee Retirement Income Security Act of 1974.

Waiting for his turn, Katyal looked nervous. Swift tried to soften him up with a joke.

"What's the difference between God and the Supreme Court?" Swift asked.

Katyal pondered.

"God doesn't always think He's right!" Swift said.

A few feet away, Stu Couch walked over to the government table to give Paul Clement his best wishes. He brought a present—a glossy blow-up of a smiling Hamdan, taken from an al Qaeda video shown on CNN. Clement smiled, but not enough to hide his own anxiety.

ORAL ARGUMENT OVER THE retirement act dispute ended shortly after 11:00 a.m. John Roberts, now chief justice of the United States, stood up and left the courtroom. Because he had voted on Hamdan's case as a circuit judge, Roberts was disqualified from considering the appeal. Next, Justice Scalia stood up, eliciting gasps in the courtroom.

Three weeks earlier, during a visit to Switzerland, Scalia had chided critics of Guantanamo, calling it "crazy" to speak of civilian trials for enemy combatants. "Foreigners, in foreign countries, have no rights under the American Constitution," he said.[8] A group of retired admirals and generals opposed to military commissions asked Scalia to recuse himself from the case; had he agreed that his impartiality had been clouded?

Scalia looked down as if to gather his papers, then straightened his books, smiled, and sat back down.

"It's like he's saying, 'Up yours, paisano,'" Couch thought.

A court of eight would hear the case. The senior associate justice, John Paul Stevens, would preside.

Supreme Court arguments typically are fast and sometimes furious. Justices hurl questions at the arguing attorney without regard to his or her prepared presentation. Knowing that he quickly would be cut off, Katyal wanted to frame the issue swiftly and simply.

"Justice Stevens, and may it please the Court," he began. "We ask this Court to preserve the status quo to require that the president respect time-honored limitations on military commissions."

Justice Scalia was the first to interrupt. He was skeptical, repeatedly pushing back against Katyal's claims. But with Chief Justice Roberts absent, Scalia carried the government's ball virtually alone. Samuel Alito, barely a month in the seat once filled by Justice O'Connor, said little. Justice Clarence Thomas, as usual, sat in silence, occasionally leaning back in his leather chair to stare at the ceiling.

In contrast to the conservatives, the court's more liberal members, along with Justice Kennedy, seemed more curious than critical when questioning Katyal, as if seeking clarifications for opinions they already had begun to sketch.

When Solicitor General Clement rose to defend the government, he, too, tried to claim the status quo.

"The executive branch has long exercised the authority to try enemy combatants by military commissions. That authority was part and parcel of George Washington's authority as commander in chief of the Revolutionary Forces," Clement said, "That authority was incorporated into the Constitution," where it remained for President Bush to use against Hamdan.

The Constitution's text makes no reference to military commissons. It does state, however, that Congress may suspend habeas corpus only "when in Cases of Rebellion or Invasion the public Safety may require it." Justice Stevens asked if Congress asserted such power when it passed the Detainee Treatment Act provisions abolishing habeas for Guantanamo inmates.

"If the question is, 'Am I taking the position that Congress consciously thought that it was suspending the writ?,' then I would say no," Clement replied. But if "Congress sort of stumbles upon a suspension of the writ" by adopting legislation that eliminates it, the Court must defer, he said.

Justice David Souter erupted. Isn't suspending habeas corpus—a bedrock of constitutional liberty—"just about the most stupendously significant act that the Congress of the United States can take?" he said. "And, therefore, we ought to be at least a little slow to accept your argument that it can be done from pure inadvertence?"

Stu Couch gulped. He had helped Clement prepare for the arguments, attending moot courts and serving as a reference on military law. Unlike most political appointees the JAGs encountered, Clement treated them with courtesy and respect. The top people in Jim Haynes's office pulled rank to get themselves seats for the *Hamdan* arguments but didn't bother inviting the career Marine officer actually assigned to prosecute Hamdan at Guantanamo. Clement made sure Couch got a ticket.

Couch didn't consider himself a constitutional genius the way John Yoo and other political appointees in the Bush administration imagined themselves. Nonetheless, he sensed where the arguments were heading.

"It's gonna be close, but there's a probability we're gonna take a bath on this," Couch said.

Bob Swann dismissed such pessimism with his customary wave. He thought the government would win, six to two.

Couch found that Katyal, too, had a gut feeling things had gone the government's way. Talking with Katyal after the argument, Couch predicted the government would lose on most of the fifteen or so legal issues that arose in the case.

"Nah," Katyal replied. He figured on winning three—and those might not be significant enough to stop the Guantanamo trial from going forward under the Bush military order.

"You did better than you think," Couch said. "I'm betting you a beer that you won eight."

Katyal made the bet. For although he spoke modestly to Couch, in fact Katyal felt confident he had won the argument. He asked his colleagues on the Hamdan team if they should press their apparent advantage with the Defense Department and again seek a plea deal to resolve the case.

The others vetoed the proposal. They were sure they would get more from the Supreme Court's eventual ruling than the Bush administration ever would voluntarily surrender.

The Vampire Killers

OVER THE MONTHS LEADING TO the Supreme Court argument, the Pentagon continued rolling out charges against additional detainees, brought on additional staff, and resumed hearings at Guantanamo.

Bob Swann decided to retire from the Army but not from commissions. By switching to civilian status, he could collect his military pension atop a regular salary. But the Pentagon needed an active duty officer in the chief prosecutor slot, so a personnel shuffle was orchestrated, putting a new face in the front office while Swann continued his work.

Formally, Swann became deputy chief prosecutor, with broad supervisory responsibilities and a portfolio of high-value cases. His successor as chief prosecutor, Air Force Colonel Morris Davis, a tall North Carolinian who went by Moe, brought a change in style.

Years earlier, when commissions first staffed up, Davis had applied to serve as chief defense counsel. He received no response. So Davis was surprised when Major General Jack Rives, recently promoted to Air Force judge advocate general, asked him to take the chief prosecutor job.[1] The Air Force had pulled its people back from commissions after the Ides of March incident and now was under pressure to supply more personnel to the project.

Unlike his tight-lipped predecessors, Moe Davis was folksy and casual, the rare colonel who played electric guitar and blasted the Red Hot Chili Peppers on his car stereo. He worked his way through college in Boone, North Carolina, as a bail bondsman; the town was dry, and he found a clientele among students busted for DUI when driving back from drinking sprees across the county line.

After receiving a law degree from North Carolina Central University in Durham, Davis joined the Air Force, planning on picking up a few years of trial experience before moving to a civilian prosecutor's office. Like many JAGs, he ended up a lifer. Still, Davis had a reputation for sometimes bucking the hierarchy, once even filing a complaint against a superior officer he believed had abused his authority.

Davis had studied media relations and believed the military should aggressively seek to mold public opinion rather than retreat behind bureaucratic walls. After a sexual assault scandal at the Air Force Academy, Davis had written an analysis of the service's media response. "We totally screwed up the message and created the impression that there was nothing but sex offenders at the Air Force Academy," Davis said.

Davis held a similarly caustic view of how the Pentagon handled commissions. The initial plan, to strictly control what the public learned about the project, fell apart when defense attorneys unexpectedly began taking their clients' plight to the press. Defense attorneys like Charlie Swift and Dan Mori, uniformed officers standing up against their commander in chief, became celebrities of sorts, principled Davids facing a Bush administration Goliath intent on railroading their clients. Prosecutors, gagged by higher-ups, grew demoralized.

"The government side is having the crap kicked out of them in the press," Davis said when interviewing for the job with Jim Haynes. The defense was lobbing allegations of misconduct and unfairness, and "the prosecution side pretty much says, 'No comment.'"

Davis said the commissions had "a good story to tell" and should be out there telling it. Haynes agreed.

For Davis, that meant painting pictures in big, broad strokes.

"Remember if you dragged Dracula out into the sunlight, he melted? Well, that's kind of the way it is trying to drag a detainee into the courtroom," Davis told reporters at Guantanamo.[2] "But their day is coming."

Stu Couch wanted the new boss to have an accurate picture of the commissions project. He prepared a binder detailing the office's true history—the failed and frozen cases, the endemic problem of detainee mistreatment—and gave it to Davis. Davis returned it three days later but refused to discuss it with Couch. Its contents did not contribute to the good story he was hired to tell.

Omar Khadr, for instance, had been portrayed by his attorneys as a child victimized by war rather than a war criminal. They stressed Khadr's age—fifteen—when pulled from the rubble after a battle in Afghanistan.

"Nauseating," Davis retorted at a press briefing.[3] "You'll see evidence when we get into the courtroom of the smiling face of Omar Khadr as he builds bombs to kill Americans."

Born in Toronto, Khadr was a Canadian citizen. But his father, Ahmed Said Khadr, was a confidant of Osama bin Laden, and Omar spent much of his youth in Pakistan and Afghanistan, where he and his brothers attended al Qaeda camps and played with bin Laden's children. After 9/11, Ahmed left Omar for training with an al Qaeda unit and fled to Pakistan, where in October 2003 he was killed in a shootout.

Omar, meanwhile, had been captured at an Afghan village called Ab Khail. In July 2002, American forces surrounded an al Qaeda unit holed up in a mud brick compound. The enemy answered surrender demands with gunfire, beginning an hours-long firefight until F-18s dropped two five-hundred-pound bombs on the position. Assuming no one could have survived, US soldiers were advancing on the ruins when a grenade flew over a wall and exploded, killing Sergeant First Class Christopher Speer. Of the hundreds of US soldiers killed in Afghanistan, Speer was the only one whose combat death was charged as a war crime.

Forces entering the ruined compound found Khadr alive and shot him. Other soldiers, stifling the instinct to finish him off, called in medical treatment that saved his life, although he had lost most vision in his left eye. Prosecutors implied that Khadr must have thrown the grenade because everyone else in the compound was dead. Besides, under interrogation, he admitted it.

Khadr's lawyers raised numerous objections: A juvenile lacked the maturity to knowingly join a terrorist organization and by definition was a "child soldier"—a victim, not a war criminal. The allegations amounted simply to taking part in a battle, not a war *crime* like perfidy, sabotage, or targeting civilians. Khadr's confession, they said, had been coerced through abuse, including an interrogator's threat to send him to an American prison where "big black guys" would rape him.[4]

The importance of Khadr's confession would become clear two years later, with the disclosure that, contrary to the government's initial account, a second man was found alive by the first American commando to enter the compound. The commando instantly shot him dead before shooting Khadr.

Nevertheless, Khadr was no bystander. American soldiers later recovered a keepsake videotape that the al Qaeda team had made, depicting Khadr and his comrades joshing around as they assembled roadside bombs.

"When these guys went to camp, they weren't making s'mores and learning how to tie knots," Moe Davis told reporters.

His bravado extended even to the Supreme Court. After the *Hamdan v. Rumsfeld* arguments, Davis began a Guantanamo press conference by upbraiding Justice Stephen Breyer.

"Towards the end of the argument, Justice Breyer said, in talking about the current conflict, 'This is not a war, at least not an ordinary war,'" Davis said. "The dictionary defines war as being in a state of hostility or a state of armed conflict." Well, "a few hours after Justice Breyer said, 'This is not a war,' enemy combatants launched a major attack on coalition forces in southern Afghanistan," killing American soldiers. "The day after Justice Breyer said, 'This is not a war,' headlines read 'Afghanistan Fighting Deadliest in Months.'" Actually, it was obvious at the argument—and in the transcript and audio recording the Court released the same day—that Breyer was not stating an opinion but, in his typically discursive way, asking a question of Solicitor General Paul Clement.

"I take their [Hamdan's attorneys] argument as saying, 'Look, you want to try a war crime. You want to say this is a war crimes tribunal,'" Breyer said. "But, 'One, this is not a war, at least not an ordinary war. Two, it's not a war crime, because that [conspiracy charge] doesn't fall under international law. And, three, it's not a [legitimate] war crime tribunal or commission, because [there is] no emergency, [the trial is] not on the battlefield, civil courts are open, there is no military commander asking for it, it's not in any of those in other respects, like past history,'" Breyer said. "Now, I've tried to summarize a whole bunch of points for you to get at, as you wish."

"I think the events of 9/11 speak to the fact that this is a war where the laws of war are involved," Clement said.

After a reporter provided Davis the transcript, he apologized, sort of. He said he had jumped to conclusions after hearing "snippets on the news."

"I didn't rate a seat at the oral argument, so I wasn't there to watch it," Davis said.

■

Hundreds of lawyers, professors, consultants, and students attracted by a historic cause had joined Salim Hamdan's defense team, taking small roles and large, as the case evolved into a constitutional showdown between executive power and individual rights.

At the Office of Military Commissions, meanwhile, Stu Couch found himself practically flying solo.

"Here I am prosecuting allegedly the most important damn thing we've done in military justice since World War II, and I'm a frickin' Army of One," he grumbled, mocking the recruiting slogan.

Still, compared to other potential cases, Hamdan looked clean. The soldiers had done a relatively good job of documenting Hamdan's capture in November 2001. Couch obtained their real-time text messages and after-action reports. He also had heard that a CIA operative accompanying the Army unit had videotaped Hamdan's field interrogation.

The CIA, as usual, refused to cooperate. When Couch sought a copy of the recording, the agency informed him that it "neither confirms nor denies" the tape's existence. After further pressure, the CIA grudgingly relented.

Battlefield interrogations inherently are coercive; the prisoner knows his life rests in enemy hands. Hamdan—nervous, ingratiating, shifty—obviously did. But nothing on the tape suggested the intentional infliction of pain or terror.

"They played that thing by the book," Couch said. "The medic checked him out. The dang Afghani guards gave him a prayer rug and prayer beads and a Koran."

They held Hamdan in a mud hut, shackled at first with tire chains because they had no handcuffs. An Arabic linguist was flown in to interpret.

Hamdan soon dropped his cover story. Taken to Kandahar, he began responding to FBI interrogators. They drove him around the city, and he pointed out significant places—houses bin Laden used, the grave of Mohammed Atef, the al Qaeda military commander known as Abu Hafs al Masri.

Hamdan remained compliant once transferred to Guantanamo, yet investigators believed he was still holding back.

The FBI's native Arabic speaker, agent Ali Soufan, went to work on Hamdan. Soufan had learned of Hamdan months earlier from Hamdan's brother-in-law, whom he had interviewed in Yemen. When Soufan entered the interrogation room, Hamdan was defiant.

"All of you are liars," Hamdan said. Interrogators had broken their promise to let him call his wife, back home in Yemen. The next day, Soufan brought a satellite phone. Hamdan made the call—it lasted only a few minutes—then fell to his knees, weeping, thanking God for the chance to speak to his wife. After regaining his composure, he turned to Soufan.[5]

"Okay, I'll give you everything you need."

Hamdan's memory was encyclopedic. He seemingly recalled every person bin Laden met and every place he went during their years together. Hamdan sketched out al Qaeda's structure and personnel, from operational commanders to members of the farming committee. He still insisted he had been a simple functionary with no knowledge of terrorist operations. But he had been present while they unfolded and in retrospect could describe the activity surrounding them.[6]

Of immediate benefit, Hamdan identified dozens of fellow Guantanamo detainees when agents showed him mug shots, helping his jailers sort through a blizzard of aliases, translation errors, and cover stories to figure out who exactly they were holding.

Among them was Abdullah Tabarak, a Moroccan whom Hamdan fingered as bin Laden's chief bodyguard. Tabarak oversaw bin Laden's movements, physical security, and logistical needs. At Guantanamo, other detainees viewed Tabarak as a leader.

ACCORDING TO INTELLIGENCE FILES, Tabarak sacrificed himself to ensure bin Laden's escape after 9/11. When bin Laden fled during the battle of Tora Bora, Tabarak took his leader's satellite phone and led a contingent of thirty men, including Ali al-Bahlul and Mohammed al-Qahtani, in the opposite direction. Assuming that US intelligence was tracking the phone, Tabarak lured the Americans away from bin Laden and was captured in his stead.[7]

Tabarak was nearly fifty, an al Qaeda veteran who had followed bin Laden for more than a decade. He didn't break, giving US and visiting Moroccan interrogators inconsistent and probably deceptive statements. Nonetheless, other evidence implicated both Tabarak and Hamdan, including a 2000 Qaeda video, aired on CNN, in which both men, armed and alert, appeared prominently in bin Laden's entourage.

CITF agents, building the case against Hamdan, went to interview Tabarak. But military guards told them he was not available, and CITF investigators could not get a straight answer on his whereabouts. Mark Fallon took to calling Tabarak "the milk carton guy," after the missing children once featured on dairy containers.

Some clues suggested that Tabarak had been moved elsewhere on the island, perhaps to CIA custody. In August 2004, just before Hamdan's first commissions hearing at Guantanamo, the Moroccan state news agency reported that Tabarak was home in Casablanca.[8]

Stu Couch, now running the Hamdan case, pressed for an explanation. Moe Davis said the Moroccans had asked for Tabarak's return. At Guantanamo, the CIA had been unable to get much from him, and Morocco had earned some favors by hosting a CIA black site and interrogating prisoners sent via extraordinary rendition.

Couch frowned. "What kind of pull does that guy have in Morocco for them to get him back?" he wondered.

The Tabarak incident undermined the case. Defense attorneys were sure to ask how the government could justify punishing Hamdan when it had set free his far more culpable superior.

Then, as in every Guantanamo case, there was the mistreatment issue.

In an affidavit, Hamdan claimed to have been "physically abused" by soldiers in Afghanistan, transported in ways that exacerbated a back condition, "made to sit motionless on benches with other prisoners for days," and punched or kicked when he did not provide desired answers.

Couch wasn't much concerned. Compared to the brutal physical and psychological torture alleged in other cases and splashed across the headlines since Abu Ghraib, Hamdan's complaints sounded insignificant.

TO TEST HOW THE HAMDAN case might play out, Couch organized a focus group of officers attending the National War College at Fort McNair in Washington.

Acting as a mock jury, the focus group convicted Hamdan. But it was close. They were uncomfortable with the conspiracy charge, which suggested a far greater role in terrorist operations than the prosecution could prove.

As expected, the abuse claims didn't much trouble the panel. But they rejected Couch's argument that anyone with Hamdan's access to bin Laden qualified as a significant figure in the al Qaeda hierarchy. To American military officers, the job of driver-bodyguard seemed menial.

Tabarak compounded the problem. The panel could not understand why a compliant, cooperating underling like Hamdan deserved severe punishment for war crimes while his superior, a veteran al Qaeda leader who rescued bin Laden, resisted interrogation, and stoked detainee unrest, had been sent home, where he now was living with his mother.

The charges carried a potential life sentence. The mock jury delivered far less. A Marine lieutenant colonel was toughest, recommending fifteen years; an Air Force lieutenant colonel took the opposite view, voting for three years. The others settled on seven to eight years.

Couch reported the focus group results to Bob Swann.

"What's a focus group?" Swann said.

■

Moe Davis had brought play-hard, fight-hard swagger to the job. He slammed the civil liberties attorneys who attacked the indefinite detention of detainees even as they tried to block commissions from proceeding. "I hate to quote Bart Simpson as an authority, but damned if you do, damned if you don't," he said.[9] Highlighting the sound bites he dished out to the press, Davis had shirts drawn up depicting Bart Simpson with fangs and a cape, above the legend "Vampire Slayers: Office of Military Commissions—Prosecution." General Hemingway was not amused, and at the last minute the reference to the Office of Military Commissions was scratched.

Under Davis, the once-somber prosecution team developed a fun-loving reputation on rotations through Guantanamo. Davis himself took some buddies scuba diving before one hearing, and the highly pressured staff quickly followed his example. Tales of carousing, drinking, and flirting among commissions lawyers, staffers, and analysts circulated.

Nonetheless, commissions seemed to have established momentum, with proceedings attaining a kind of semi-regularity at Guantanamo. In June 2006, hearings in four separate cases were scheduled, keeping the Pink Palace courtroom operating for three weeks out of the month.

First would be Binyam Mohamed, a native Ethiopian who had grown up mostly in the United States and England, where he held legal residency. Mohamed had a largely secular youth, his brother said, untutored in the Koran but committing to memory *Police Academy*, the 1984 Steve Guttenberg comedy whose dialogue he repeatedly recited. "It was annoying," his brother said.[10]

But in his twenties, Mohamed fell into radical Islam and followed the path to Afghanistan. From there, in 2002 he accompanied Jose Padilla to the Karachi airport, where both were stopped by passport control. Padilla, a US citizen, was permitted to continue to Chicago, where he was arrested and jailed as a "material witness"—a category used often after 9/11 when authorities lacked enough evidence to bring criminal charges. On the eve of a court hearing over his continued detention, Bush declared Padilla an enemy combatant, whereupon he was taken to a military brig. Attorney General John Ashcroft interrupted his visit to Russia to make a televised announcement revealing Padilla's capture, declaring that the Brooklyn-born prisoner had been on a mission to explode a radiological "dirty bomb" in an American city.

Ashcroft gave no hint that Padilla had an accomplice, for the fact of Binyam Mohamed's existence was classified. According to Mohamed, however, he was arrested and held for fourteen weeks of interrogation by Pakistani and American agents, then shipped to Morocco for what his attorneys later described as "unspeakable torture."

Interrogators pressed Mohamed to admit the dirty bomb plot and pledge to testify against Padilla and other "big people," Mohamed later claimed. When he refused, the torture got worse.

"They took the scalpel to my right chest. It was only a small cut. Maybe an inch. . . . Then they cut my left chest. This time I didn't want to scream because I knew it was coming," Mohamed said. "One of them took my penis in his hand and began to make cuts. He did it once, and they stood still for maybe a minute, watching my reaction. One of them said it would be better just to cut it off, as I could only breed terrorists."

Mohamed said he signed the confessions put in front of him, and then endured SERE-style "brainwashing."

"They played Meat Loaf and Aerosmith over and over. I hated that," he said. After transfer to Afghanistan, where he suffered more abuse, including repeated exposure to Eminem's quadruple-platinum *Slim Shady LP,* Mohamed signed additional confessions and was shipped to Guantanamo. In November 2005, a military commissions charge sheet accused him of conspiring with Padilla, bin Laden, and a host of al Qaeda figures to commit a series of terrorist attacks.

The Pentagon charges discounted the dirty bomb Ashcroft had described, saying that Abu Zubaydah considered it unfeasible. In Karachi, Khalid Sheikh Mohammed allegedly explained that Mohamed and Padilla were to target gas stations and apartment buildings heated with natural gas, which could easily be blown up.

Mohamed's civilian attorney, Clive Stafford Smith, was a flamboyant Englishman, able to appear before commissions because he held dual American citizenship. He had spent much of his career fighting the death penalty in the American South, helping block hundreds of executions and receiving royal honors in 2000 for "humanitarian services." At Guantanamo, Stafford Smith brought a radical style wholly alien to military lawyers. In the British and American press, he repeatedly flagged Mohamed's horrifying account of mutilation in an effort to build public sympathy.

Commissions prosecutors ridiculed such claims. "If we examine Binny's dick," one joked while relaxing at a bar, "it'll be to look for Clive's teeth marks."

A weekend before Mohamed's June 12 hearings, Jim Haynes invited his staff, including commissions personnel, to his Arlington home for a morale-building cookout. At the last minute, the festivities were canceled. At Guantanamo, three detainees had hanged themselves.

THE PENTAGON SUSPENDED commissions proceedings indefinitely. None of the three suicides had been selected for trial, but Guantanamo commanders clamped down hard, expelling reporters and defense attorneys from the base to prevent independent coverage of the story and seal detainees off from the outside world.

On the mainland, however, one proceeding remained in progress: *Hamdan v. Rumsfeld.* As usual with Supreme Court cases, it had disappeared from public view after oral argument, as the justices hashed out their views within the quiet chambers at One First Street, NE.

The Court does not announce when a particular case will be decided. The opinions are revealed only when the justices take their seats and the chief justice calls on the author to read a summary.

Two rulings came on June 12, the Monday after the suicides, both death penalty cases, both delivered by Justice Anthony Kennedy. He stopped one execution and approved the other.

Four more opinions came the following Thursday, but not the commissions case. The justices sat four more times over the next two weeks, delivering another seventeen opinions in their annual rush to clear the docket before summer recess began in July. The suspense heightened when the justices let June 28 pass without announcing *Hamdan.* The decision would arrive the next day, the last sitting of the term.

On Thursday, June 29, key players in the case gathered in the courtroom. The advocates Paul Clement and Neal Katyal were present, along with lawmakers, administration officials, and military brass.

At 10:00 a.m. the Court's opening formalities began. They were simple: A buzzer sounded and the marshal cried, "All rise!" The crimson curtains behind the bench parted and the robed justices stepped forward. "The Honorable, the Chief Justice and the Associate Justices of the Supreme Court of the United States. Oyez! Oyez! Oyez! All persons having business before the Honorable, the Supreme Court of the United States, are admonished to draw near and give their attention, for the Court is now sitting. God save the United States and this Honorable Court!"

The justices, like everyone in the courtroom, stand during this brief ritual, something so familiar to them that they pose by reflex. Some stare straight ahead or glance at the audience, others bow their heads as if in prayer. As a rule, their mechanical expressions bear no relation to the cases at hand. But not this time.

"Breyer is smiling. Hamdan won," Pete Williams, the NBC News correspondent, whispered to a colleague in the press gallery. Any doubt vanished after Justice John Paul Stevens cleared his throat with a slight cough.

"I have the disposition to announce in No. 05-184, Hamdan"— the eighty-six-year-old Chicagoan pronounced it *HAM-dan,* like the luncheon meat—"against Rumsfeld.

"Petitioner, a foreign national held in custody in an American prison at Guantanamo, has been charged with one count of conspiracy to commit offenses triable by military commission," Stevens continued. "He concedes that a court-martial convened in accordance with the Uniform Code of Military Justice or, of course, a civilian court would have jurisdiction to try him; but he contends that the military commission convened by the president lacks such authority, because the charge does not allege a violation of the law of war, and the commission's procedures violate both the UCMJ and the Geneva Conventions.

"The district court granted him relief, the court of appeals reversed, and we now reverse the court of appeals."

Stevens laid out the Court's divisions. His opinion was joined in part or full by Justices Anthony Kennedy, David Souter, Ruth Bader Ginsburg, and Stephen Breyer. Kennedy had written a concurrence that Souter, Ginsburg, and Breyer joined, while Breyer had filed his own concurring opinion joined by Kennedy, Souter, and Ginsburg.

In dissent, Justices Antonin Scalia, Clarence Thomas, and Samuel Alito each filed separate opinions, joined in part or full by the other two.

"Our opinions are quite long—mine has seventy-three pages," Stevens said. "But I will try to be brief in this summary." He read for nearly fifteen minutes.

"I have a dissenting opinion, which is a mere twenty-four pages," said Scalia, typically sarcastic. He agreed completely with his former law clerk, Paul Clement, that the Detainee Treatment Act had eliminated the Court's power to hear the claim at all.

Hamdan, Scalia recalled, allegedly had "joined and actively abetted the murderous conspiracy that slaughtered thousands of American civilians without warning on September 11, 2001." By limiting President Bush's power to try and punish Hamdan as he saw fit, the Court had assumed a "new role as active manager of the details of military conflicts," Scalia said.

The most dramatic moment came next, when Justice Clarence Thomas, famously silent during oral argument, began to speak. "In fifteen terms on this Court, I have never read a dissent from the bench; but today's [decision] requires that I do so," Thomas said. He misremembered; six years earlier, he had read aloud his dissent from an abortion rights opinion.

But Thomas displayed no confusion regarding the heart of the case. George Bush, he observed, was commander in chief. "Yet today, far from affording the president the deference he is due, the plurality and the Court second-guess his judgments at every step."

THE DAY, HOWEVER, BELONGED to Justice Stevens. It was a long time coming.[11]

On December 6, 1941, a day before the Pearl Harbor attack, twenty-one-year-old John Stevens had enlisted in the Navy. He spent World War II as an intelligence officer and was awarded the Bronze Star for helping break Japanese codes. Returning to Chicago after the war, he enrolled in Northwestern University's law school and won a Supreme Court clerkship with Justice Wiley Rutledge.

Rutledge was a Midwestern academic appointed by FDR in 1943. He deferred to Roosevelt in the early wartime cases but broke with the executive when a case titled *In re Yamashita* reached the Court in 1946.

A US military commission, none of whose five members was a lawyer, had sentenced the Japanese general Tomoyuki Yamashita to death for atrocities committed while he was military governor of the Philippines. Yamashita's lawyers brought a habeas petition contending that his trial was unfair.

The Supreme Court held that it could not consider Yamashita's claim. "The commission's rulings on evidence and on the mode of conducting these proceedings against petitioner are not reviewable by the courts, but only by the reviewing military authorities," Chief Justice Harlan Fiske Stone wrote. Yamashita was hanged days later.

The Bush administration's legal cadre revered *Yamashita* as a constitutional landmark, a case that exemplified their vision of America's core principles. They cited it again and again as authority for executive primacy under George W. Bush.

Justice Rutledge, however, had a different view. "I think the decision was the worst in the Court's history, not even barring Dred Scott," he wrote to a colleague. That was evident from his ringing dissent.

"More is at stake than General Yamashita's fate," Rutledge wrote. "There could be no possible sympathy for him if he is guilty of the atrocities for which his death is sought. But there can be and should be justice administered according to law. In this stage of war's aftermath, it is too early for Lincoln's great spirit, best lighted in the

Second Inaugural, to have wide hold for the treatment of foes. It is not too early—it is never too early—for the nation steadfastly to follow its great constitutional traditions, none older or more universally protective against unbridled power than due process of law in the trial and punishment of men—that is, of all men, whether citizens, aliens, alien enemies, or enemy belligerents. It can become too late."

When John Stevens arrived to clerk for Rutledge the following year, another wartime case was pending, *Ahrens v. Clark*. The government had issued removal orders for 120 Germans it was holding at Ellis Island as alien enemies. Lawyers for the Germans challenged the attorney general's authority to deport them, filing a habeas petition in a Washington, DC, federal court. The government moved to dismiss the case, arguing that because the Germans were held in New York harbor, any habeas petition belonged in the federal district court in Manhattan. The Supreme Court agreed, by a six-to-three vote over Rutledge's dissent. Rutledge assigned Stevens to draft a memo on the case, then expanded it for the published opinion.

The Germans "are alien enemies interned during the war as dangerous to the nation's safety. They now seek to avoid deportation from a country which takes care for personal liberties, even when its hospitality may be abused, to one which denied its own citizens such rights until its structure of tyranny fell in ruins," Rutledge's dissent began. But the Court had ducked these "important questions" by hiding behind a "capricious" technicality.

The statute limiting a district court's habeas jurisdiction to its own geographic region was intended to promote judicial efficiency, not to interpose obstacles before prisoners with legitimate claims. "It is one thing to lay down a rule of discretion adequate to prevent flooding the courts of the District of Columbia with applications for habeas corpus from the country at large. It is entirely another to tie their hands, and those of all other inferior federal courts, with a strict jurisdictional limitation which can only defeat the writ's efficacy in many cases where it may be most needed," Rutledge wrote.

The next year, at age fifty-five, Rutledge suffered a fatal stroke.

His six-year tenure was too short to leave a deep imprint on the Court. But Rutledge made a formative impression on John Stevens, who in 1975 succeeded the justice who wrote the *Ahrens* majority opinion, William O. Douglas.

Over the decades that followed *Yamashita* and *Ahrens,* Stevens believed, law and history had vindicated Rutledge's constitutional vision.[12] When war powers cases returned to the Supreme Court after a half-century slumber, Stevens had attained the stature and experience to redeem his mentor's teachings. First in *Rasul* and now in *Hamdan,* he painstakingly dismantled the legal construct the Bush legal cadre had devised to create a new century of executive authority.

The administration had invoked the periodic phenomenon of military commissions during wars of earlier centuries as proof that dispatching enemy prisoners through abbreviated, unreviewable military trials was a bedrock American tradition. George W. Bush, the administration contended, honored a legacy that began in 1780 when General George Washington hanged the British spy Major John André following a brief proceeding before a military board, and continued through the electrocution of the *Quirin* saboteurs in 1942.

The administration misread history, Stevens wrote. "The military commission, a tribunal neither mentioned in the Constitution nor created by statute, was born of military necessity," he explained. Only three types of situations could justify them.

"First, they have substituted for civilian courts at times and in places where martial law has been declared. Their use in these circumstances has raised constitutional questions," he wrote. Hawaii was under martial law during World War II, but the Supreme Court overturned the convictions of civilians who were tried there by military tribunal.

Commissions also had been used during military occupations of enemy territory to plug the gap after local court systems collapsed. One such commission was established in occupied Germany after World War II, he wrote, and it applied the German criminal code in prosecutions of the local population for routine offenses.

The third type, Stevens wrote, was "convened as an 'incident to the conduct of war,'" as the *Quirin* court put it, to punish enemy prisoners for violating "the law of war" while resisting American forces. Such a commission was "utterly different" from the other varieties, he wrote. "Not only is its jurisdiction limited to offenses cognizable during time of war, but its role is primarily a factfinding one—to determine, typically on the battlefield itself, whether the defendant has violated the law of war."

That was the only category that could cover the Bush commissions, "since Guantanamo Bay is neither enemy-occupied territory nor under martial law," Stevens wrote. "At the same time, no more robust model of executive power exists; *Quirin* represents the highwater mark of military power to try enemy combatants for war crimes." Such commissions had to meet several preconditions that limited their jurisdiction to discrete war crimes committed in a time and place of armed conflict, he explained.

"The question is whether the preconditions designed to ensure that a military necessity exists to justify the use of this extraordinary tribunal have been satisfied here," Stevens wrote. He went on to dissect the conspiracy case against Hamdan, reducing it to dust at every juncture.

International law disfavored conspiracy as a war crime, he wrote. The Nuremberg tribunal after World War II had rejected the charge, and it is not listed in any "of the major treaties governing the law of war."

"The charge's shortcomings are not merely formal, but are indicative of a broader inability on the Executive's part here to satisfy the most basic precondition—at least in the absence of specific congressional authorization—for establishment of military commissions: military necessity," Stevens wrote. "Hamdan's tribunal was appointed not by a military commander in the field of battle, but by a retired major general"—John Altenburg, the appointing authority—"stationed away from any active hostilities."

Moreover, "Hamdan is charged not with an overt act for which he was caught redhanded in a theater of war and which military efficiency demands be tried expeditiously," but with entering bin Laden's employ years before 9/11. "That may well be a crime, but it is not an offense that 'by the law of war may be tried by military commission,'" as the UCMJ put it.

In its charge sheet, the government recited much about al Qaeda in general but said little about this particular defendant. "There is no allegation that Hamdan had any command responsibilities, played a leadership role or participated in the planning of any activity," Stevens wrote. The four "overt acts" alleged included being bin Laden's "bodyguard and personal driver," transporting weapons, accompanying bin Laden when he "encouraged attacks against Americans," and receiving "weapons training at al Qaeda-sponsored camps."

None of those allegations "is itself a war crime, or even necessarily occurred during time of, or in a theater of, war. Any urgent need for imposition or execution of judgment is utterly belied by the record; Hamdan was arrested in November 2001 and he was not charged until mid-2004. These simply are not the circumstances in which, by any stretch of the historical evidence or this Court's precedents, a military commission . . . may lawfully try a person and subject him to punishment."

But even if they were, Stevens wrote, military commissions must themselves comply with the law of war, including the Geneva Conventions. Bush's commissions, he wrote, failed the lowest Geneva standard, Common Article 3, which required trial "by a regularly constituted court affording all the judicial guarantees which are recognized as indispensable by civilized peoples."

Stevens noted the commission's wide discretion to exclude the defendant from his own trial—and even broader power to use any evidence it wished to justify a conviction. "Not only is testimonial hearsay and evidence obtained through coercion fully admissible, but neither live testimony nor witnesses' written statements need be sworn," Stevens wrote.

The principal difference between courts-martial and military commissions, he continued, was not procedural but in jurisdiction;

the statute that created courts-martial didn't cover the types of un-foreseen situations that might arise in the war zone.

"There is a glaring historical exception to this general rule. The procedures and evidentiary rules used to try General Yamashita near the end of World War II deviated in significant respects from those then governing courts-martial," Stevens wrote. "The force of that precedent, however, has been seriously undermined by post–World War II developments."

Wide criticism of the Yamashita case had helped shape both the 1949 Geneva Conventions and the Uniform Code of Military Justice, Stevens wrote. "The most notorious exception to the principle of uniformity, then, has been stripped of its precedential value."

Three times, the opinion cited Justice Rutledge by name.

THROUGHOUT ITS FIRST seventy-two pages, the Stevens opinion point by point refuted the legal and historical theories that defined the Bush administration's imagined constitutional universe. At the end, a single paragraph pulled it all together.

"We have assumed, as we must, that the allegations made in the Government's charge against Hamdan are true. We have assumed, moreover, the truth of the message implicit in that charge—viz., that Hamdan is a dangerous individual whose beliefs, if acted upon, would cause great harm and even death to innocent civilians, and who would act upon those beliefs if given the opportunity. It bears emphasizing that Hamdan does not challenge, and we do not today address, the Government's power to detain him for the duration of active hostilities in order to prevent such harm," Stevens wrote. "But in undertaking to try Hamdan and subject him to criminal punishment, the Executive is bound to comply with the Rule of Law that prevails in this jurisdiction."[13]

At the White House, President Bush was meeting with the Japanese prime minister, Junichiro Koizumi, when word came of the Court's ruling. An hour later, the two leaders made a brief press appearance, where they mainly joked about Koizumi's fascination with Elvis Presley. The first reporter's question, however, concerned the *Hamdan* decision.

"Thank you for the question on a court ruling that literally came out in the midst of my meeting with the prime minister," Bush said, with evident annoyance. "The American people need to know that this ruling, as I understand it, won't cause killers to be put out on the street. In other words, there's not a—it was a drive-by briefing on the way here—I was told that this was not going to be the case," he said. "And one thing I'm not going to do, though, is I'm not going to jeopardize the safety of the American people. People have got to understand that. I understand we're in a war on terror; that these people were picked up off of a battlefield; and I will protect the people and, at the same time, conform with the findings of the Supreme Court."

■

For months, Bob Swann's mantra had been "6–2." That was the margin by which the Supreme Court would uphold commissions, and the new era of military justice would finally commence. Arriving at the Crystal City offices the morning of June 29, Swann couldn't contain his anticipation. Even in the men's room, he could be overheard telling a urinal neighbor about the six-to-two victory that the Court would deliver within the hour.

At 10:00 a.m., practically every computer in the prosecution office was set to Scotusblog.com, a website providing granular coverage of the Supreme Court. As Justice Stevens delivered the *Hamdan* opinion, Scotusblog began sending incremental updates, trying to instantly decipher the decision's meaning as it was being read.

"We're gonna win, 6–2. We're gonna win, 6–2," Swann said.

But each time he hit the computer's refresh button, the Web browser brought more details of the Court's decision and Swann's face grew paler. By the end of the announcement, the office had fallen silent. Swann seemed stunned as he left for a planned trip home to his family in Tennessee. "He walked out like he was walking away from a car wreck," Moe Davis said.

Davis, like most in the office, also had expected to win. His expectations, though, were somewhat more modest, relying on Stevens's military record or Kennedy's conservative instincts to pull a vote to the government's side, for a four-to-four split that would leave the DC Circuit's decision intact without establishing new precedent.

The next day, Davis called a staff meeting.

"Start working on your résumés," he told his team.

Then they got some beers.

■

The same day, Secretary Rumsfeld also held a staff meeting to discuss the case. He turned to Jim Haynes, the Pentagon general counsel.

"So, Jim, *Hamdan v. Rumsfeld:* Who won?"

"I haven't read the whole case yet," Haynes said, "but—"

"You haven't read the whole case yet? Didn't it come out yesterday?" Incredulity replaced Rumsfeld's habitual sarcasm.

"I haven't read the whole case yet, but of course I've talked to people in DOJ about it," Haynes said. It turned out that Common Article 3 of the Geneva Conventions, which the Bush legal cadre had dismissed as irrelevant, applied, after all.

"So I'm going to go down in history as the only secretary of defense to have lost a case against a terrorist?" Rumsfeld said.

"I wouldn't look at it as a loss," Haynes said.

"Really?" said Rumsfeld.

The Supreme Court had identified another defect in Bush's commissions—that he had created a permanent offshore system of summary justice by extrapolating his constitutional function as "commander in chief of the Army and Navy" into the power to do whatever he wished in the name of national security. The Constitution contemplated no such thing, the Court said, directing Bush to seek congressional authorization before deviating from existing military justice statutes.

Finally, the very fact of the Court's ruling implicitly discarded another pillar of the November 2001 presidential military order—the provision denying prisoners recourse to any court.

As a statement of constitutional law, then, *Hamdan* repudiated Bush's claim that the executive could establish tribunals answerable only to him, that Congress had no authority to regulate his conduct as commander in chief of the armed forces, and that the judiciary was powerless to review anything he did in the name of national security.

For some in the government, including the judge advocates general of each service and even some political appointees, the Court's decision presented a chance to realign the war crimes trials with historical precedent. It was impossible to miss the path Stevens had laid out: Follow existing provisions of the Uniform Code, which stipulated that commissions employ court-martial procedures except when found "not practicable."

Justice Stevens, like the JAGs, understood this to mean that every deviation from normal process must have a specific, reasonable justification—perhaps, for example, amending the speedy trial rule because of difficulties in ensuring that prosecutions of prisoners captured in battle could follow a rigid timeline.

But the Bush lawyers had seized on that exception to swallow the whole, claiming that the president could set aside the entirety of established domestic, constitutional, and statutory law by declaring it "not practicable." Stevens returned this fantastical interpretation to earth, explaining that under the Uniform Code, "the rules applied to military commissions must be the same as those applied to courts-martial unless such uniformity *proves* impracticable."[14]

The government, Stevens wrote, "ignores the plain meaning" of the statute's text "and misunderstands the purpose and the history of military commissions. The military commission was not born of a desire to dispense a more summary form of justice than is afforded by courts-martial; it developed, rather, as a tribunal of necessity to be employed when courts-martial lacked jurisdiction over either the accused or the subject matter," Stevens wrote. "Exigency lent the commission its legitimacy, but did not further justify the wholesale jettisoning of procedural protections." The Uniform Code of Military Justice, he observed, "strikes a careful balance between uniform procedure and the need to accommodate exigencies that may sometimes arise in a theater of war."

The administration had offered no explanation for the president's determination of "impracticability." "There is no suggestion, for example, of any logistical difficulty in securing properly sworn and authenticated evidence or in applying the usual principles of relevance and admissibility," Stevens wrote. In the presidential military order itself, "the only reason offered in support of that determination is the danger posed by international terrorism. Without for one moment underestimating that danger, it is not evident to us why it should require, in the case of Hamdan's trial, any variance from the rules that govern courts-martial."

Still, from one perspective the Court's ruling could be framed as modest. Because the Bush military order violated acts of Congress, Stevens found no need to go further and address whether the commissions Bush envisioned would be constitutional even with congressional authorization. The simplest course would be to ask Congress, both houses in Republican control, to provide its blessing.

That's what Addington wanted.

The Kangaroo Skinner

ON CAPITOL HILL, COMMISSIONS' future rested with Senator Lindsey Graham. The South Carolina Republican sat on both the Judiciary and Armed Services Committees, where colleagues considered him an authority on military law. Graham also was a JAG in the Air Force Reserve, giving him an inside line on Jim Haynes's stewardship of the military justice system. Haynes's dismal reputation among rank-and-file JAGs led Graham to block his Fourth Circuit nomination. The torture policies Haynes approved disgusted Graham, whose best friend in the Senate was John McCain, the former POW. Likewise, the JAGs' long-standing antipathy toward David Addington left Graham loath simply to bless the commission system the Supreme Court had just condemned.

But Graham was no civil libertarian, and he believed that the nation's war posture justified curtailing rights that enemy defendants could invoke to avoid conviction. After the *Hamdan* ruling, Graham met with JAG contacts to develop his own version of commissions.

As defense attorney at a 1984 court-martial, then-Captain Graham got his client acquitted of drug charges. He bested a newly minted prosecutor trying his first case: Captain Moe Davis. In off hours, hanging around the pool at the San Antonio hotel where both were staying, the two young JAGs talked about their future plans.

Graham declared he would finish his Air Force commitment, head home to South Carolina, and run for Congress. The two remained acquaintances over the following decades, so when the time came to revise commissions, Graham had one main question for Davis.

"What do you need to get the job done right?" he said.

Davis asked Couch and several other senior prosecutors to put together a wish list. His own priority was insulating the prosecution office from outside interference, obtaining a degree of autonomy similar to that of defense counsel.

PROSECUTING THE HIGH-VALUE detainees—the alleged al Qaeda commanders who orchestrated the embassy bombings, the *Cole* attack, 9/11—never had been a priority for the Bush administration. At best, a trial would be superfluous; the defendants already were serving de facto life sentences. And for many reasons, a trial, no matter how secretive, could prove damaging to the president. Inevitably, the public would learn more details of the CIA's clandestine prison system and the brutal treatment of detainees Bush secretly authorized while publicly affirming America's commitments against torture. For years, the administration had preferred to warehouse Khalid Sheikh Mohammed and company in overseas cells than to invite such political and diplomatic risks. The *Hamdan* decision changed this calculus.

After refusing consultation with Congress for years, Vice President Cheney now demanded that legislation authorizing commissions be passed immediately. Midterm elections were approaching, and problems from Iraq to New Orleans had left Republican prospects bleak. If Democrats won control of Congress, his commissions legislation might never pass. Moreover, since fear of terrorism had proven Bush's best issue in the 2004 campaign, reviving it could help Republican candidates in November. Yet there was a stalemate with the Lindsey Graham faction over issues like torture-procured evidence.

Reluctantly, Bush played his trump card: the CIA prisoners. Pass the commissions bill or, he implied, KSM might walk free. Before a

White House audience seeded with 9/11 families, Bush suggested that it was the Supreme Court—rather than his own administration—that had blocked bringing them to trial.

"We're now approaching the five-year anniversary of the 9/11 attacks—and the families of those murdered that day have waited patiently for justice. Some of the families are with us today—they should have to wait no longer. So I'm announcing today that Khalid Sheikh Mohammed, Abu Zubaydah, Ramzi Binalshibh and eleven other terrorists in CIA custody have been transferred to the United States Naval Base at Guantanamo Bay," Bush said. "As soon as Congress acts to authorize the military commissions I have proposed, the men our intelligence officials believe orchestrated the deaths of nearly 3,000 Americans on September the 11th, 2001, can face justice."

The US attorney's office in New York had been building the 9/11 case for years and was ready to try the men in federal district court, but Bush implied that such a course was impossible. Like the secret memos issued by the Office of Legal Counsel, a principal aim of Bush's gambit was immunizing administration officials from prosecution for torture and other crimes—something that could not be guaranteed without special legislation.

Likewise, Senator Graham had no interest in holding officials accountable for abusing prisoners, but he took issue with other provisions in the Bush legislation, such as authorizing convictions based on evidence the defendant would never see.

"I do not think we can afford to again cut legal corners that will result in federal court rejection," Graham said. The legislation included a conclusory pronouncement that a military commission "is a regularly constituted court, affording all the necessary 'judicial guarantees which are recognized as indispensable by civilized peoples' for purposes of common Article 3 of the Geneva Conventions"—the standard the Supreme Court held the government must meet. Then the bill declared that no defendant actually tried by military commission "may invoke the Geneva Conventions as a source of rights."

But as the October congressional recess approached, Republican leaders pressed Graham to wrap up his objections and get the bill to the Senate floor.[1] Graham relented, allowing Bush to sign the Military Commissions Act of 2006 at a White House ceremony on October 17.

Thirty-five senators voted against the bill. One was a freshman from Illinois, Barack Obama.

■

When commissions resumed in February 2007, the first defendant was not 9/11 mastermind Khalid Sheikh Mohammed but the hapless kangaroo skinner, David Hicks of Adelaide.

Criticism of Hicks's detention had grown as the years without trial stretched on. Even the rock star Bono—who earlier had lent his credibility to Bush in a White House visit to discuss global poverty—chimed in.

"We're calling for David Hicks to be brought back to Australia to face fair trial here," Bono declared, midway through the song "Sunday Bloody Sunday" during a U2 concert in Brisbane.[2]

"High-grade Irish entertainers" had no business making Australian policy, retorted Prime Minister John Howard.

But with Australian elections coming and the Military Commissions Act now on the books, Howard wanted Hicks's case over and done.

OVER THE YEARS, PROSECUTORS periodically had discussed plea bargains with lawyers representing David Hicks. The sticking point was John Walker Lindh.

Charged with similar acts in federal court, Lindh had agreed to plead guilty and serve twenty years in prison. Military prosecutors would be humiliated with a sentence significantly below the Lindh benchmark. Ten years was as low as they would go.

For Hicks, spending a decade at Guantanamo was unthinkable. Moreover, the political momentum seemed in Hicks's favor, and his attorneys believed their bargaining position could only improve.

With so much distance between the two sides, the case rattled toward the trial, scheduled to begin Monday, March 26.

Moe Davis and the prosecution team already were at Guantanamo when Major Dan Mori, a Hicks attorney, telephoned Tom Hemingway. He asked for a meeting at 4:00 p.m., Friday, March 23.

Hemingway, typically, was punctual. Mori was not. He kept the general waiting for half an hour before showing up, dressed in sweats rather than his Marine uniform. That irritated Hemingway, who had no patience for sloppy young officers. Nonetheless, when Mori said he wanted "closure," Hemingway was ready. The Bush administration wanted the case over, too.

Their conversation lasted ninety minutes. Mori wanted Hicks home within a year. Hemingway wanted Hicks to admit wrongdoing, withdraw his mistreatment allegations, and accept the legal stigma of a war criminal. There was room here to deal.

The agreement they hashed out had Hicks pleading guilty to providing material support for terrorism, renouncing abuse claims, and agreeing to cooperate with US investigators. Hemingway insisted on a "Son of Sam" clause, waiving profits from selling his Guantanamo story to a publisher. Moreover, Hicks would promise to make no public statements for a year. That would ensure Hicks's silence through the Australian election, while John Howard campaigned for a fourth term. Hemingway denied any political considerations.

"This guy needs to spend some time incarcerated, thinking about what he did and not putting some kind of spin on it," Hemingway said.

In exchange, Hicks would be sent to an Australian prison for nine months, then released. The formal sentence was seven years, but the balance was suspended.

Mori flew to Guantanamo to present the deal to Hicks, while Hemingway sent the proposal to Susan Crawford, a former judge on the Court of Appeals for the Armed Forces who had succeeded John Altenburg as the commissions administrator, a position now called convening authority.

Crawford, who had served as Pentagon inspector general when Dick Cheney was defense secretary, approved the deal with no reservations, as did Jim Haynes, who later asked Hemingway what he made of the Hicks case.

"Of all the triable cases that have come across my desk, this guy was the least culpable," Hemingway said.

Why, then, were commissions prosecutors bent on a far harsher sentence?

"These guys had essentially four years of their military careers invested in the case," Hemingway explained. "When you put that much effort in there, the blood gets flowing."

CHIEF PROSECUTOR MOE DAVIS had not been informed of these developments. He and his staff were in court ready to fight when proceedings began on Monday. Later that day, when the military judge—another name change, from presiding officer, under the Military Commissions Act—called a recess, Davis learned that a deal had been struck.

The Pentagon's script required certain formalities before the deal could take effect. One was a sentencing hearing, even though the outcome secretly had been predetermined.

"Today, in court we are on the front line of the global war on terror. You are face to face with the enemy. The enemy is sitting at the defense table," the trial prosecutor told the jury panel.

The officers on the jury unwittingly went to work as if their deliberations mattered. Two hours later, they returned the maximum sentence, seven years. The military judge thanked the officers and dismissed them from the courtroom. Then he revealed that Hicks would be freed within a year.

In Canberra, there was relief. "The bottom line will always be that he pleaded guilty to knowingly assisting a terrorist organization," John Howard said.

■

The first casualty after Democrats retook Congress in November 2006 was Donald Rumsfeld, whom Bush discarded as the symbol of a losing war in Iraq. Jim Haynes paid a price, too, seeing his dreams of a judicial appointment finally extinguished. He began scouring for private sector employment before being forced from the general counsel's office at the end of the Bush administration.

First, however, Haynes wanted commissions to get busy.

Tom Hemingway, having finally secured a commissions conviction, stepped down as legal adviser. Despite Haynes's intimations that Hemingway's service would be rewarded with a second star, no promotion was recommended.

Haynes wanted a different type of personality as commissions legal adviser. He found it in Tom Hartmann, an Air Force Reserve brigadier general activated from his job as general counsel for an energy utility.

Hartmann saw his mission as whipping into shape an operation that repeatedly had failed its superiors. Arriving at commissions in July 2007, when Moe Davis was on leave recovering from surgery, Hartmann was appalled at what he found. He announced that the "can't-do" attitude pervading the office no longer would be tolerated.

Davis, with an eye toward media exposure, had focused on cases that could be presented at open trials with unclassified evidence. Since those cases involved the least significant charges, Hartmann considered Davis's direction a mistake. To justify commissions, Hartmann believed, the Pentagon had to present exciting cases with clearly villainous defendants.

With evident disdain for the staff he had inherited, Hartmann began inserting himself into case details and internal prosecution decisions. At the same time, he made himself the new face of military commissions, calling news conferences to personally announce new batches of charges. Prosecution staffers viewed him as not only a megalomaniac but a threat to the project's legitimacy. They believed that the legal adviser to the commissions convening authority, Hartmann's official title, should maintain an appearance of impartiality, because he would be acting on issues raised by both prosecution and defense. By aligning himself so obviously with the prosecution, they complained, Hartmann was handing defense attorneys grounds for objection when cases reached trial.

No one was unhappier with Hartmann than Moe Davis, who saw himself being sidelined from the office he nominally headed. Davis began pushing back, and the power struggle exacerbated the prosecution office's typical disarray.

"Moe, don't ever get in a pissing contest with a guy on a balcony," Hemingway advised Davis. "That's what happens when a colonel goes after a brigadier general."

But Davis had no intention of backing down. Instead, he filed a complaint with the Pentagon inspector general accusing Hartmann of violating the Military Commissions Act—specifically, a section Davis had helped Lindsey Graham write with the aim of protecting the chief prosecutor from outside pressure.

Among other sore points, Davis said that Hartmann had overruled Davis's policy of excluding statements taken by waterboarding prisoners. Hartmann, Davis said, had told him "there were opinions out there that there was nothing unlawful about waterboarding these guys, and these decisions are made at a much higher level."

To Davis's shock, the inspector general referred the matter to Jim Haynes—not only Hartmann's patron but the very official who instigated the "reverse engineering" of SERE training protocols to create interrogation methods the Justice Department recognized as potential war crimes. Haynes appointed a brigadier general to lead an investigation, which quickly cleared his fellow brigadier general, Tom Hartmann.

Moe Davis's irreverent swagger had disappeared. The Hicks plea bargain had shaken him, and now he saw his authority usurped by higher-ups for apparently political reasons. Hartmann's demeaning attitude and controlling style pushed Davis over the line. As rumors of the conflict began to circulate, Davis offered a solution.

"For the good of the process," Davis said, both he and Hartmann should resign. "If he believes in military commissions as strongly as I do then let's do the right thing and both of us walk away before we do more harm."

Hartmann felt that Davis was half right; Davis was forced out as chief prosecutor.

GENERAL HARTMANN WANTED commissions to feel as if they were at the front lines of the war on terror. He built a ten-million-dollar trial compound on the abandoned airfield by the Pink Palace, a *MASH* set of sixty eight-person tents and mobile latrine and shower units called "Camp Justice."[3] Journalists and other low-ranking trial participants would be sequestered there, making it easy to control their movements while bathing them in the atmosphere of a battle-field operation.

The Military Commissions Act, however, required the Pentagon to draft new manuals and procedures, sift the detainee population for new defendants, and revise old cases to fit the modified structure. Moreover, the arrival of the big fish presented particular problems, because even if a military commission admitted torture-produced evidence, there was no guarantee that a conviction relying on it would be upheld. The Military Commissions Act, in perhaps the most sig-nificant departure from Bush's military order, provided for an appeal structure echoing that for courts-martial: a new Court of Military Commission Review, consisting of military officers, would hear ap-peals first. Its decisions could then be appealed to the DC Circuit and, ultimately, the Supreme Court.

The Justice Department had been building cases against al Qaeda terrorists for years, and it supplied attorneys, FBI agents, and analysts to work with Bob Swann, who remained in charge of high-value prosecutions. The goal was to assemble a case apart from any-thing that the CIA had done to the defendants. By insisting there was no connection between the commissions prosecution and the CIA, the government hoped to avoid having to justify the agency's bru-tality or expose its perpetrators to possible liability.

The 9/11 trial of Khalid Sheikh Mohammed and his alleged co-conspirators would be a joint prosecution, like Nuremberg. There was no one in the JAG ranks, however, experienced in anything remotely comparable to such a case. The closest match was Colonel Larry Morris—the Army officer first assigned to set up commissions six years earlier, only to be sidelined in favor of the more politically savvy Bill Lietzau. Now he was recalled to take over as chief prosecutor.

Morris's vision of commissions always had tracked the Nuremberg model—a public trial to prove for all time the depravity of the Nazi state. Likewise, he wrote in a 2002 memo, commissions should open with the prosecution of the most culpable 9/11 defendants, a blockbuster trial brimming with "evidence of shocking criminality." The public, at home and abroad, must "viscerally realize" the momentous threat al Qaeda posed—and the legitimacy of resurrecting military commissions in response. In demonstrating the "fundamental justice" of America's cause, he wrote, prosecutors must present "the best historical case in a forum as open to press and public scrutiny as national security permits."

Moreover, Morris wrote, the first case would establish precedents for future trials. By showcasing those directly responsible for the core crimes—the "mass murder of innocent civilians"—the government bettered its odds for favorable evidentiary and procedural decisions, shaping commissions rules to the prosecution's liking before less significant defendants went on trial.

As at Nuremberg, "an ideal first case would feature a range of defendants that includes one or more top tier actors, as well as representative other defendants (e.g., a financial functionary, a bodyguard, etc.)," he wrote. Prosecutors would "establish a rough order of criminality, explicitly stacking them from No. 1 to No. X." The commission could impose a range of corresponding sentences, establishing "benchmarks for future trials."

A joint trial also would reduce the government's embarrassment should a defendant be found not guilty. If "three of twenty-two accused were acquitted, as happened at Nuremberg," he wrote, the

United States could point to the outcome as evidence of its "funda-mental fairness."

Morris reminded his superiors of the near-universal criticism the commissions project faced within the legal community and inter-nationally, even from such close allies as Britain.

"We must be prepared to explain how commissions serve as more than a semi-secret forum in which to dispose of some mid-lower level actors," he wrote. "If only small fry are taken to trial, then the question again will arise of why commissions at all."

Unfortunately, he added, after issuing the presidential military order, the Bush administration simply failed to respond to the JAG Corps's requests for guidance on commissions. The political leader-ship, he wrote, consistently refused to clarify "the level of criminality they envision taking before commissions."

LARRY MORRIS RETURNED TO commissions on November 13, 2007, the sixth anniversary of Bush's presidential military order. As usual, the office was in turmoil, with suspicions high and morale low following Moe Davis's ouster. The staff, now including some two dozen attorneys from the Defense and Justice Departments, had yet to resolve many of the legal questions that were vexing the project when Morris had departed years earlier.

"What constitutes a conspiracy? When did the war with al Qaeda start? What constitutes combatancy?" The issues were certain to arise at trial, and the prosecution had no clear answers. Despite passage of the Military Commissions Act and Tom Hartmann's rush to trial, the Bush administration continued its practice of withholding legal guid-ance from line attorneys, unwilling to disclose the secret Office of Legal Counsel memos containing its true views.

The prosecution staff had argued these questions in circles for years. Morris pushed for consistent positions that could be asserted if they arose in any trial. Debate was fine, but "that debate can't go on endlessly," he said.

LOOKING AT THE MESS of legal issues the 9/11 defendants presented, Morris was typically understated.

"We are in many ways not helped by the passage of time," he said. "There's nobody who would not rather have done this years earlier"—at least nobody on the prosecution staff.

Morris resurrected his original plan for the 9/11 trial. The case would expose the vast reach of the al Qaeda network and demonstrate the gravity of its threat to civilization. If any skeptics thought 9/11 was "just a really lucky day by a group of bad guys, they will recognize anew that it is the product of a sophisticated, coordinated, criminal enterprise," Morris pledged.

Morris knew the defense would try to turn the tables, making the case about government treatment of detainees rather than the defendants' crimes. "I'm very confident that any statements we would present from any of these detainees will have been obtained in a way that can withstand any scrutiny for the methods that were used to obtain them," he said.

The Bush administration considered the infliction of physical pain and psychological terror effective intelligence methods. Human rights activists, as well as some outspoken retired generals and admirals, insisted that apart from ethical and legal obligations, the techniques produced inherently unreliable information.

"Both extremes are unhelpful," Morris said. One side says, "'People will never tell the truth under torture.' That's untrue. People like Stockdale say, 'You will talk and you will tell the truth under torture,'" Morris said, recalling the American POW who spent years in North Vietnamese prisons. Uncharacteristically philosophical for a soldier, Morris believed that the torture question implicated "the great complexity of human personality, and trying to decide consistent with our identity as Americans . . . and what we know about Arab/Muslim culture" what boundaries might exist. Within the government, he said, "much of the debate centered around matrices where various interrogation techniques were evaluated in combination with one another to see what's permissible." The answer, he said, lay somewhere within "a chart of all these interlocking boxes."

Was waterboarding torture? Morris declined to say.

IT WAS LARRY MORRIS who prepared the 9/11 charges, but Tom Hartmann decided to announce them himself, calling a press conference in the Pentagon briefing room. Hartmann said the chief prosecutor, whom he did not mention by name, planned to seek the death penalty for all six defendants.

"The charges allege that Khalid Sheikh Mohammed was the mastermind of the 9/11 attacks by proposing the operational concept to Osama bin Laden as early as 1996, obtaining approval and funding from Osama bin Laden for the attacks, overseeing the entire operation and training the hijackers in all aspects of the operation in Afghanistan and Pakistan," Hartmann said.

Walid bin Attash, also known as Khallad, was accused of running "an al Qaeda training camp in Logar, Afghanistan, where two of the September 11th hijackers were trained. He is also alleged to have traveled to Malaysia in 1999 to observe airport security by US air carriers to assist in formulating the hijacking plan.

"Ramzi Binalshibh is alleged to have lived in the Hamburg, Germany, al Qaeda cell where three of the 9/11 hijackers resided." Bin Laden allegedly selected Binalshibh to be one of the 9/11 hijackers, and he made "a martyr video in preparation for the operation," Hartmann said. Denied a US visa, "it is alleged that Binalshibh assisted in finding flight schools for the hijackers in the United States and continued to assist the conspiracy by engaging in numerous financial transactions in support of the 9/11 operation."

KSM's nephew, Ali Abdul Aziz Ali, also known as Amar al-Baluchi, allegedly sent "approximately $127,000 to the hijackers for their expenses and flight training and facilitating the travel to the United States for nine of the hijackers.

"Mustafa Ahmed Adam al-Hawsawi is alleged to have assisted

and prepared the hijackers with money, Western clothing, traveler's checks and credit cards. He is also alleged to have facilitated the transfer of thousands of dollars between the 9/11 hijackers and himself on September the 11th, 2001."

All five had been held at CIA black sites until Bush sent them to Guantanamo to pressure Congress to pass the Military Commissions Act. The sixth and final defendant had been at Guantanamo all along —the Twentieth Hijacker who previously had been assigned to Stu Couch.

"Mohammed al-Qahtani is alleged to have attempted to enter the United States on August the Fourth, 2001, through the Orlando International Airport," Hartmann said, "where he was denied entry. It is also alleged that al-Qahtani carried $2,800 in cash and had an itinerary listing a phone number associated with al-Hawsawi."

The announcement, however, was only one step in determining the charges. Hartmann's recommendations would go to the convening authority, Susan Crawford, who would have the final word. And on second thought, Hartmann recognized that Qahtani's interrogation, which a Pentagon investigation concluded was "degrading and abusive," had damaged the case. In mitigation, he advised that Qahtani, alone of the six defendants, face life imprisonment instead of the death penalty.

In May, Crawford approved the five capital cases Hartmann had recommended. She dismissed all charges against Qahtani.

SUSAN CRAWFORD PROVIDED NO public explanation for quashing the Qahtani prosecution. But the reason was torture.

The prosecution files persuaded her that Qahtani readily would have joined the 9/11 hijack team if he had the chance.[4] But she was shocked by his treatment at Guantanamo, an interrogation regime that nearly killed him. "We tortured Qahtani. His treatment met the legal definition of torture," she later told investigative journalist Bob Woodward. It "has tainted everything going forward."

Under Hartmann's direction, an Indiana Air National Guard

unit had built a twelve-million-dollar high-security courthouse in Camp Justice for the 9/11 trial.[5] The courtroom had been designed specifically for the joint trial of the 9/11 conspirators, with six separate rows of desks, one for each of the defendants and his lawyers.

Now one row would be empty.

The remaining five defendants had been held by the CIA, under conditions that could hardly have been less onerous than Qahtani's. Why had Crawford approved the charges against them?

She said that she had no official records of their treatment by the CIA, and therefore could make no formal findings. But she wasn't blind.

"I assume torture," she said.

■

Hartmann wanted to clear the deadwood in the commissions docket. Plead out the weak cases, he told prosecutors. Like Hamdan.

Plea bargains always had been part of the commissions concept, but the gulf between prosecutors and defense attorneys over sentencing had stymied most negotiations. Hicks's deal demonstrated which side really held the cards when it came to trial. Hamdan's attorneys, celebrated in the legal press for their Supreme Court victory and convinced the case against their client amounted to nothing, were driving a hard bargain. Any deal acceptable to the defense would have to look a lot like Hicks's. Prosecutors balked.

"Think of our only other 'success' in this—David Hicks," said one prosecutor. "How is that a success for the United States government? How does that justify Guantanamo?"

Instead, the prosecution decided to proceed to trial.

The Hamdan team filed a motion claiming that General Hartmann had exercised unlawful command influence over the case—a prime violation of military justice principles. Among the first witnesses Hamdan's lawyers called was Moe Davis.

LIEUTENANT COMMANDER BRIAN MIZER, who had succeeded Charlie Swift as Hamdan's military defense counsel, had taken a gamble. He asked Davis to testify on behalf of Hamdan—even though Davis previously had supervised Hamdan's prosecution.

"It certainly was awkward," Mizer said. "This is our former foe in the courtroom."

But Davis, after reminding Mizer that he still considered Hamdan guilty, accepted. He was eager to even the score against Tom Hartmann.

Taking the stand as a defense witness, Davis presented a very different picture of commissions than the one of his press conferences as chief prosecutor. Even more than implementing the Bush administration's political agenda, the commissions office's top priority seemed to be self-preservation, he said.

"There was that consistent theme that if we didn't get this thing rolling before the election, it was going to implode," he testified. But "once you got the [9/11] victim families energized and the cases rolling, whoever won the White House would have difficulty stopping the proceeding."

Hartmann wanted cases that could make the news, Davis said. "If a guy had blood on his hands, that was a case that the public would understand and get excited about," Davis testified. "Moving money and forging documents wasn't that exciting. So he wanted to put the sexy cases out front."

The military judge who had taken over the Hamdan case, Navy Captain Keith Allred, watched carefully as Colonel Morris cross-examined his predecessor about conditions under their mutual superior, General Hartmann.

Allred, to the Pentagon's shock, granted the defense motion. He ruled that Hartmann had exercised unlawful command influence and barred him from any role in the Hamdan case.

Mizer drafted an identical motion against Hartmann on behalf of the other client he represented, 9/11 defendant Amar al-Baluchi.

REMARKABLE AS WAS HIS ruling against Hartmann, Captain Allred had denied defense motions to dismiss charges. In an effort to
stop the trial altogether, Hamdan's team returned to the site of their
first victory, the Washington courtroom of Judge James Robertson,
contending that the procedures at Guantanamo remained intrin-
sically unfair.

When he issued his ruling, Judge Robertson observed that many
of the trial procedures prescribed by the Military Commissions Act
resembled those of the Bush military order he previously had found
invalid. The prosecution could enter hearsay evidence, for instance,
unless the *defendant* proved it was unreliable. In courts-martial, as
well as civilian trials, hearsay generally is prohibited; there are exceptions to the rule against hearsay, but it's the *prosecution* that must
prove such evidence is reliable before it can be admitted. The result
was a significant tilt of the odds for conviction.

"Another departure, and a startling one, is that . . . evidence
obtained by 'coercion' may be used against the defendant so long as
the military judge decides that its admission is in the interest of
justice and that it has 'sufficient' probative value," Robertson wrote.

"That said, one of the most substantial improvements under the
MCA is in the structure for review of convictions," Robertson wrote.
Appeals now would reach the federal courts, rather than end with the
president. The new system, moreover, had been approved by Congress, requiring greater deference than did a unilateral presidential
order.

Robertson evidently had been following Hamdan's pretrial proceedings, where defense lawyers sometimes had prevailed in motions
before Captain Allred.

"The eyes of the world are on Guantanamo Bay. Justice must be
done there, and must be seen to be done there, fairly and impartially,"
Robertson continued. Federal judges, however, "do not have a mo-
nopoly on justice, or on constitutional learning. A real judge is presiding over the pretrial proceedings in Hamdan's case and will preside

over the trial. He will have difficult decisions to make, as judges do in nearly all trials," he wrote.

"If the Military Commission judge gets it wrong, his error may be corrected" by the Court of Military Commission Review created by the legislation. "If the CMCR gets it wrong, it may be corrected by the D.C. Circuit. And if the D.C. Circuit gets it wrong, the Supreme Court may grant a writ of certiorari" to consider Hamdan's appeal.

This time, Robertson let Hamdan's trial proceed.

Material Supporter

HAMDAN'S JURY—THE PANEL, in military parlance—was drawn from a pool of thirteen officers. Allred had issued a blanket order holding their names confidential, and the sketch artist covering the proceeding was required to blur their faces. They could be described only by superficial characteristics.

The foreman, called a president, was determined by seniority. He had attended the University of Virginia through ROTC and had remained in the Navy since his 1981 graduation. Now a captain, he was the only African American on the panel.

There was a white woman, an Army colonel. The others were white men: an Air Force colonel, two Army lieutenant colonels, and a Marine lieutenant colonel.

The Hamdan legal team had remained largely intact since its Supreme Court victory. While Charlie Swift had left the Navy after being passed over for promotion, he had stuck with Hamdan as a civilian lawyer. Neal Katyal and the Perkins Coie lawyers from Seattle were still there, along with a support contingent including paralegals, a psychiatrist, and an Arabic interpreter.

Not so the prosecution side. After three years at commissions, Stu Couch finally was appointed a military judge, receiving a seat on the Navy–Marine Corps Court of Criminal Appeals at the Washington Navy Yard. For parting gifts, his colleagues presented him a memento of his favorite supervisor; it was a photo of a swan with the red circle/backslash; it came with a plastic container of Kool-Aid labeled, "Do Not Drink."

In March 2007, the *Wall Street Journal* published a front-page report on the Slahi case—and Couch's reluctant conclusion that government misconduct had made prosecution impossible.[1] The story confirmed the long-whispered fear that abuse of detainees could destroy the chance of bringing them to trial, prompting the House Judiciary Committee to seek Couch's testimony. After receiving permission from his immediate superiors, Couch agreed to appear. Then Jim Haynes heard about it. The day before the November 2007 hearing, the Pentagon general counsel put Couch under a gag order.

"It is improper for you to testify about matters still pending in the military court system, and you are not to appear before the Committee to testify tomorrow," the general counsel's office told him by email. The committee chairman, Representative John Conyers Jr. of Michigan, said he was "outraged" that Haynes blocked Couch from testifying "in his personal capacity and not on behalf of the government, concerning what he saw and heard relating to interrogation practices at Guantanamo." New York's Jerrold Nadler, the subcommittee chairman who called the hearing, said he would consider a subpoena for Couch's testimony if the Pentagon didn't relent.[2] But the Democratic lawmakers' interest proved short-lived, and the issue soon was forgotten.

Couch remained, however, an informal resource for the frequently changing cast of commissions prosecutors.

His immediate successor as Hamdan prosecutor, an Army lieutenant colonel, already had come and gone before the case went to trial. The current prosecutor was Tim Stone, a Navy lieutenant commander, but he lacked full responsibility for the case. The reorganization that followed the Military Commissions Act brought a stronger role for the Justice Department, which had its own prosecutor on the case, an assistant US attorney named John Murphy.

Although present in his civilian capacity, Murphy was a captain in the naval reserve, putting him one rank above Couch and two over Stone. At the US attorney's office in New Orleans, which he joined in 1992, Murphy supervised a staff of a hundred, greater than the entire commissions prosecution office.[3] He and Stone did not always agree.

THE FACTS IN *UNITED STATES v. Hamdan* were little disputed. But at opening arguments, the prosecution and defense presented wholly incompatible theories of what those facts meant.

Prosecutor Tim Stone went first. Hamdan was so close to bin Laden, he said, that he heard the al Qaeda leader say that the target of United Airlines Flight 93, had it not crashed in a Pennsylvania field, was "the dome"—apparently, the United States Capitol.

Harry Schneider, a corporate litigator with Perkins Coie, presented the defense's opening. Hamdan was a simple laborer grateful to have a job that provided for his family, Schneider said, an apolitical servant who had nothing to do with terrorist acts.

The government's first major witness was Ali Soufan, who had since left the FBI, first working for Rudolph Giuliani's consulting firm, then setting up a security outfit of his own.

Soufan said he found Hamdan a "friendly, forthcoming" prisoner. His statements, when they could be verified, proved "right on the money." Moreover, Hamdan was no fanatic. Life in the bin Laden circle came with a constant soundtrack of extremist rhetoric that glorified suicide terrorists and condemned the United States. Hamdan got "bored with these statements, because he heard them again and again," Soufan said.

John Murphy cited al Qaeda videotapes showing Hamdan in bin Laden's entourage, toting a rifle or walkie-talkie. What did that signify?

Anyone permitted to carry such devices so close to bin Laden was considered a true loyalist, Soufan said. Bin Laden would trust such a person "with his life."

On 9/11, Hamdan had taken bin Laden to meetings in Kabul at which Khalid Sheikh Mohammed briefed al Qaeda leaders on the operation. Overhearing KSM's remarks, Hamdan learned that the hijacked planes were intended to strike their targets within ten or fifteen minutes of each other. Bin Laden prayed that heaven accept the hijackers as martyrs.

After the attacks, while driving bin Laden and KSM, Hamdan "heard bin Laden say he didn't expect the operation to be that successful," Soufan continued. "He only thought 1,000 to 1,500 would perish."

That was shocking information, Murphy noted. Did Hamdan quit in protest or disgust or even fear once he learned bin Laden was behind such an atrocity?

"No, he stayed," Soufan said.

AT ONE INTERROGATION, HAMDAN "said he pledged *bayat* to Osama bin Laden," said another government witness, NCIS agent Bob McFadden. Still, Hamdan added a slight reservation, specifying that rather than global war, his jihad extended only to killing Jews and Christians and "expelling them from the Arabian Peninsula."

The defense had fought to exclude McFadden's testimony, arguing that the interrogation was unreliable because it took place after Hamdan endured a period of severe treatment. Overruled.

"Being detained in Guantanamo Bay is undoubtedly an unpleasant, highly regimented experience, with instant rewards or loss of privileges for infractions," Allred found. Nevertheless, Hamdan's treatment fell short of "coercive measures" that would require exclusion of evidence. Allred's reasoning remained a mystery. Military censors blacked out most of the five-page ruling.

TESTIMONY BY ANOTHER CITF investigator, NCIS agent Michael St. Ours, suggested that Hamdan held intimate knowledge of the al Qaeda organization. Hamdan had identified thirty Guantanamo detainees from photographs investigators showed him. These included Abdullah Tabarak, "the head bodyguard of all the bodyguards," St. Ours said.

"Would it surprise you to learn he was released without ever being charged?" asked defense attorney Harry Schneider.

St. Ours looked startled. "Yeah," he said.

THE GOVERNMENT'S CONSPIRACY theory imputed al Qaeda's crimes to Hamdan. For support, prosecutors turned to Evan Kohlmann, a consultant the government often hired for terrorism cases. Kohlmann charged twenty-five thousand dollars to take the stand at Guantanamo, in addition to the twenty thousand dollars he previously billed to produce a ninety-minute film on al Qaeda's history. Kohlmann said that he modeled the picture, filled with horrifying images of terror attacks, on *The Nazi Plan,* a four-hour documentary Allied prosecutors screened at Nuremberg to demonstrate the sweep of the German conspiracy that plunged the world into war.

Larry Morris still wanted to follow Justice Jackson's template. He envisioned the film becoming a routine part of future conspiracy trials at Guantanamo.[4] To emphasize the Nuremberg connection, Kohlmann was told to change the film's title from *The Rise of al Qaeda* to *The al Qaeda Plan.*

Prosecutors cited Nuremberg as precedent for screening the movie. "There are substantial similarities between *The Nazi Plan* and *The al Qaeda Plan.* The differences between the two are minimal," they said in legal papers.

Still, even the prosecutors' own motion suggested some distinctions between the two films. For instance, "*The Nazi Plan* was assembled by Budd Schulberg, an Army soldier and writer who would later go on to win an Oscar for *On the Waterfront,*" the prosecution motion said.

"Between June 1945 and the opening of the Trial Against the Major War Criminals on November 21, Mr. Schulberg and his team went through more than ten million feet of film, and would fly regularly from Berlin, where they set up a studio, to Nuremberg, where they coordinated their material with the prosecutors preparing the U.S. part of the Allied legal case. Justice Jackson, the Chief Prosecutor for the United States at the IMT, was involved in approving the final script," prosecutors wrote.

The newsreels, propaganda footage, and official materials compiled in *The Nazi Plan* showed Goering, Hess, and other Nuremberg defendants as they built and led the Third Reich. Nothing in *The al Qaeda Plan* suggested any corresponding role for Salim Hamdan.

For that matter, comparing the two films was not especially helpful for a legal paradigm seeking to equate al Qaeda to Nazi Germany, bin Laden to Hitler, and, ultimately, George W. Bush to FDR. *The Nazi Plan* depicted an industrialized nation-state of ninety million people that committed its power and wealth to subdue a continent, enslave its enemies, and systematically murder millions of people deemed racially unfit to share the earth.

The al Qaeda Plan naturally showcased bin Laden's vicious rhetoric and his sirenlike appeal to Muslim fanatics. Measured against the Wehrmacht, the Luftwaffe, and the SS, however, the motley cadre produced by al Qaeda training camps looked pathetically insignificant. Al Qaeda had accomplished several spectacular terrorist attacks, but these primitive operations, even 9/11 itself, could hardly be compared to the Third Reich.

After World War II, Washington viewed the Nuremberg Tribunal not simply as a method to dispose of the surviving Nazi leadership but as a tool to discredit the Hitler era and legitimize the Allied cause. Unlike the secretive Guantanamo commissions, the Nuremberg trial was recorded, including hours of courtroom proceedings captured on film. The military assigned Stuart Schulberg, Budd's younger brother who had worked on *The Nazi Plan*, to produce a companion film, *Nuremberg: Its Lesson for Today*, to show the German public the evidence that convicted its leaders. Early on, the documentary cuts to Justice Jackson as he addresses the tribunal.

"The privilege of opening the first trial in history for crimes against the peace of the world imposes a grave responsibility," Jackson intones. "The wrongs which we seek to condemn and punish have been so calculated, so malignant, and so devastating, that civilization cannot tolerate their being ignored because it cannot survive their being repeated. That four great nations, flushed with victory and stung with injury, stay the hand of vengeance and voluntarily submit their captive enemies to the judgment of law is one of the most significant tributes that Power has ever paid to Reason."

Other than those present in the tiny Pink Palace courtroom, no one ever would see Commander Stone's opening statement in *United States of America v. Salim Ahmed Hamdan.* Nor would they witness Charlie Swift's cross-examination of Evan Kohlmann.

"Now, at Nuremberg, they charged the Nazi leadership. Is that correct?" Swift asked.

"I believe so," Kohlmann said. "But I hope you're not going to ask me detailed questions about the Nuremberg war crimes case. I mean, I studied it in terms of *The Nazi Plan,* but that's not my area of expertise."

"So you don't know whether Hitler's driver was one of the people sitting at the bench at Nuremberg?"

"Actually, I don't, to be honest," Kohlmann said.

THE PROSECUTION RESTED ITS case after calling fourteen witnesses, including ten federal agents and two Special Forces soldiers, some of whose names were declared secret. The defense's star witness was Khalid Sheikh Mohammed.

Over the government's strenuous objection, Captain Allred had ruled that Hamdan was entitled to the testimony even of the high-value detainees. Who would better know Hamdan's actual role in al Qaeda?

Given KSM's apparent megalomania, his first appearance at a quasi-public forum promised dramatic moments, even with government censors at the hair-trigger, ready to cut the transmission to journalists watching via closed-circuit feed. But when the day to testify came, the self-declared 9/11 mastermind balked, forcing the defense to use his written statements instead. Read into the record, KSM's egocentric personality still came through.

"I personally was the executive director of 9/11, and Hamdan had no previous knowledge of the operation, or any other one," KSM declared. "He was not a soldier, he was a driver." Hamdan "was not fit to plan or execute. But he is fit to change trucks' tires, change oil filters, wash and clean cars and fasten cargo in pickup trucks."

After closing statements, the panel began its deliberations. Hamdan marked the time with his annual telephone call to his wife, speaking to her for a full hour. After three days, the panel returned with a verdict.

Guilty of material support for terrorism.

There was a lag for Hamdan, wearing a headset that carried simultaneous translation of the proceedings, to grasp the verdict. He was shocked to be convicted, and it physically shook him. He bowed his head and wept softly, distracted as the next count, conspiracy, was read.

Not guilty.

CONSPIRACY WAS BY FAR THE more serious charge, one effectively implicating Hamdan in 9/11. In contrast, material support for terrorism was a catchall charge the Justice Department used when it couldn't tie a suspect to any actual terrorist act.

That didn't guarantee Hamdan any leniency, however. The commission panel could impose a sentence of any length. Hamdan potentially faced a life term.

Still, Hamdan's lawyers were confident. The defense team had conducted focus groups before trial, and sample jurors found Hamdan's crimes relatively insignificant—worth maybe five years.

Stu Couch had gotten a similar outcome from his prosecution focus group. He shared the results with Tim Stone, who saw them confirmed by the conspiracy acquittal. The panel's six officers did not equate Hamdan's menial work for bin Laden to specific al Qaeda attacks that killed thousands.

Stone brought Couch's focus group data to John Murphy and urged him not to go for broke in sentencing arguments. To be credible, Stone said, a sentencing proposal had to respect the panel's findings.

Murphy saw it differently. Even if the government failed to demonstrate every element required for a conspiracy conviction, it had proved Hamdan's material support for *terrorism*—and 9/11 was terrorism. Material support made 9/11 possible, Murphy reasoned, thus Hamdan's crime was no less reprehensible than conspiracy.

At sentencing, Murphy sought to make that point by calling an FBI agent who had pulled bodies from the World Trade Center's debris on 9/11.

The military judge refused to let the agent testify. Had Hamdan been "convicted of the conspiracy, he would be responsible for the acts of his co-conspirators," Allred said. But Hamdan's link to 9/11 was so tenuous that such testimony was prejudicial. It was far more likely to improperly "hold him responsible for the 9/11 attacks than be probative of what he actually knew. Or did. Or supported," Allred found. The agent was put on a plane home from Guantanamo.

Hamdan's lawyers had an easier time with their witnesses. Emily Keram, a psychiatrist working for the defense team, had spent more than a hundred hours with Hamdan since 2005, all at government expense. She testified that Hamdan wept when shown a video of the 9/11 attacks.

"He told me it was like watching a mouse hitting an elephant," she said. "He had no idea that skyscrapers had that kind of scale. When people started crying he felt . . . his head was going to explode."

Hamdan's wife, wearing a black *niqab* that exposed only her eyes, appeared in a four-minute videotaped statement.

"He's my husband. He's a friend. He's my brother. He's my mother. My sister. All the things in my life," she said.

Finally, the accused himself spoke.

"I would like to first thank the [panel] members for taking my trial. I would like to thank the judge himself, and all the present people," Hamdan said, through an interpreter. It was an unsworn statement, and the prosecution had no opportunity to question him.

"First of all, as regards to my having worked with bin Laden, it was a work relationship only. It wasn't a normal relationship at all. It was a relationship of respect, one of give and take between an employee and the director or the boss of the company. I respected him, and he respected me. I give him regard or I regard him, and he regarded me. I was treating him the way I would, keeping into account my position, my profession. And he, in turn, treated me the same way. So a very normal relationship had evolved. And this is a very normal or natural thing among us Arabs," he said.

Hamdan detailed the various family obligations that drove him to seek a steady income in bin Laden's employ. From his perspective, it seemed, al Qaeda's terror campaign was little more than background noise in a life crowded with domestic concerns.

What Hamdan said next was declared classified, and reporters were cleared from the proceedings. When the open session resumed, Hamdan discussed his interrogators.

"Of course, they were always asking me—talking to me about this subject," he said. "So I told them that [bin Laden] was causing a lot of problems and a lot of people killed in the US. It was a . . . sad thing to see innocent people killed. I don't know what could be given—presented to these innocent people who were killed in the US. All I can tell them is—is patience. I personally represent my apologies to them if any think what I did has caused them any pain.

"I also like to apologize to the members again. There was also the Australian, David Hicks, who was in the cell next to me, and he was presented for a trial at the commission here—military commission, and they had accused him of material support to terrorism, and they have sentenced him to nine months. His term of his prison is over with in his home country, and he's free with his family right now, with his children. And again, my apologies one more time. Thank you."

JOHN MURPHY MADE THE prosecution's closing argument. Hamdan's sentencing, he observed, came on the tenth anniversary of the African embassy bombings. He showed slides of those attacks along with the *Cole* and 9/11.

"You found between the time of February 1996 through and

including November 24, 2001, the accused provided material support for terrorism, all during a period in which the United States was in the armed conflict with al Qaeda," he told the panel. "You found that he became an actual member of the al Qaeda organization. You found he received training at the al Qaeda training camps. You found he served as a driver for Osama bin Laden, the most wanted and dangerous terrorist in the world today. You found he served as an armed bodyguard of bin Laden. You found he transported weapons and weapon systems and other supplies for the purpose of delivering these weapons to al Qaeda members and associates. You found he provided the services of transportation directly facilitating communication and planning used for an act of terrorism. You found he protected the leader of al Qaeda and facilitated communication and planning for terrorist acts, plural, *acts* of terrorism. You found that by providing armed bodyguard services for bin Laden, he was protecting the leader of al Qaeda and facilitating communication and planning used for acts, plural, *acts* of terrorism," Murphy said. "Anyone, *anyone* who provides material support for terrorism is a serious war criminal and a continuing threat to our society."

Murphy laced his argument with the full name of the offense, emphasizing the word *terrorism* over material *support.*

Hamdan "stands today as a convicted war criminal," he continued. "His material support of terrorism has changed our world as we knew it. They changed it dramatically in our lifetime and perhaps changed it forever," Murphy said. "Think of the victims of his material support of terrorism and their families, living each day without loved ones, and their photographs that are forever changed."

Hamdan "provided material support for terrorism not once but again and again. And now he's praying for victims? Are you hearing fake prayer and fake tears and a strained effort to manipulate you? We know one thing, Salim Hamdan, you see today, is a convicted provider of material support of terrorists," Murphy said.

"We need to have confidence as a society that he will never provide material support for terrorism again," he said. "Your sentence should send a message to all others that, if anyone thinks of providing material support to the sword of terrorism, directed at our citizens and the citizens of the world, there will be painful consequences." Hamdan's "social condition, life difficulties, and life in Yemen, and his need for a job cannot be seen as acceptable excuses for providing material support for terrorism," he continued. "When you think of his family and the photos you saw, you should remember that he abandoned them when he provided material support for terrorism."

The bottom line, Murphy said, was simple.

"Once you see your boss killing people, you leave. You get another job, period."

MURPHY TURNED TO THE sentencing deliberations the panel soon would begin.

"Take one second, just one second, and think about the victims of Hamdan's material support of terrorism," he said. "Please, do justice for all the victims of material support of terrorism in this case."

Murphy gave them a number.

"The government comes to you with an earnest and important sentencing recommendation. The government asks you to return a sentence in this case of not less than thirty years imprisonment."

Not less, but conceivably more, Murphy added, urging the panel to "consider the real possibility that a life sentence may be the most appropriate sentence." But were they inclined toward mercy, Hamdan "should get not one day less than thirty years."

"MY NAME IS CHARLIE SWIFT, and I've been on this case the longest. I was assigned to represent Mr. Hamdan all the way back in December of 2003." Five years later, Swift had returned to Guantanamo to present the closing argument for his client.

The prosecution had shown slides of terror attacks, Swift said. "Ask yourself a question: But for Mr. Hamdan being born, do you honestly believe that we would've been spared one attack? One? That one less person would be dead?"

Hamdan had been a pauper in Yemen, Swift said. "In the Arab world, if you don't have the money to pay for a wife, then you cannot have a wife. You don't have a family." Once on bin Laden's payroll, "suddenly, things that he didn't ever think were possible were made possible." Having stumbled upon such fortune, Swift conceded, Hamdan "looked the other way" when it came to bin Laden's business.

"Yes, he looked the other way because they were giving him something he wanted so very badly. Not to attack America, not to attack the world, but to have a family, to have a chance, to have a dream," Swift said. "In 1998, he got a family. Something he'd never thought he'd have. The problem was, it came with a price tag"—that is, faithfully serving the al Qaeda leader. "So he made a series of bad decisions." In retrospect, "they are terrible decisions, and he knows that."

Swift challenged Murphy's argument that a life sentence would deter future material supporters of terrorism. To the contrary, Swift said, it would harm American security efforts. Hamdan had been an extraordinarily compliant prisoner, sharing al Qaeda's secrets with American interrogators.

But "who will cooperate, when they're told that's the end of the road? At the end of the road, the reward for cooperation is life?"

Swift turned to 9/11.

"At some point, we will bring [to justice] the people who planned, the people who conspired, the people who brought those buildings down, but that's going to be a great day. That's going to be a great day," he repeated, his voice swelling with hope. "The victims of 9/11 and other places will receive their justice, and it will be all the more meaningful because we got the guys who did it. Not their driver."

DAVID HICKS ALSO HAD BEEN convicted of material support for terrorism, Swift said. He was sentenced to nine months beyond time served. Hamdan had been far more cooperative than Hicks, providing the United States with valuable intelligence. True, Hamdan had worked for bin Laden since 1996, far longer than Hicks's time in

Afghanistan, and contributing commensurately more material support. But no way, Swift said, was Hamdan's culpability more than five times worse than that of Hicks, particularly "when you subtract out his cooperation."

But assume, Swift said, that Hamdan *was* five times more culpable than Hicks.

"That would equal a maximum sentence of forty-five months."

CAPTAIN ALLRED GAVE THE panel its instructions.

"The prosecution showed you photographs of various terrorist attacks that have occurred over the years, and asked you to consider the victims of those attacks in reaching your sentence," Allred said.

Hamdan, however, "has not been convicted of those attacks or participating in them directly. A defendant who is convicted of material support for an international terrorist organization is punished solely for the criminal act of *material support* and not for the illegal conduct of the international terrorist organization," he said. "Does each of you understand this instruction?"

Each of the members nodded affirmatively.

Allred also commented on Swift's invocation of David Hicks. "The disposition of other cases is irrelevant for your consideration in adjudging an appropriate sentence for this accused," he said. "You did not know all the facts and circumstances of that case nor anything about the accused in that case, and it is not your function to consider that case at this trial."

The members indicated that they understood this, too.

"Our society recognizes five principal reasons for imposing sentences on those who violate the law," Allred continued, reciting instructions lifted from court-martial procedures. "Protection of society from the wrongdoer; punishment of the wrongdoer; rehabilitation of the wrongdoer; preservation of good order and discipline in society"— this puzzling assertion came from substituting *society* for the term in court-martial instructions, *military*—"and deterrence of the wrongdoer, and those who know of his crime and his sentence, from committing the same or a similar offense."

Allred instructed the panel on which factors to weigh in its deliberations. But the decision belonged to the members.

You "may sentence the accused to confinement for life," Allred said. Or "you may sentence the accused to receive no punishment. Anything between those two bookends is within your discretion."

The six-hour sentencing hearing over, the panel retired to deliberate.

Soon, two members sent notes asking if Hamdan would be credited for his pretrial confinement. Allred called the panel back to answer.

Hamdan would receive no credit for the period from his capture, in November 2001, to the filing of charges in July 2003. During that time, Allred said, Hamdan was a captured enemy combatant who could be detained indefinitely. His status changed, however, when charged, thus becoming a criminal defendant the law presumed innocent until proven guilty. Each day thereafter would be deducted from the sentence the panel imposed. Allred did the math:

"Sixty-one months, maybe it is, and eight days," he said.

LITTLE MORE THAN AN HOUR had passed before the commission reconvened. There was a verdict.

Allred told Hamdan and his lawyers to stand. The military judge then addressed the panel.

"Mr. President, you may announce the sentence of the court," Allred said, reflexively saying *court* rather than *commission*.

"Thank you, Your Honor," said the Navy captain who headed the panel. "Salim Ahmed Hamdan, it is my duty as president to inform you that this military commission sentences you: To be confined for sixty-six"—he seemed to pause momentarily—"months."

Spectators and participants looked to each other for confirmation: Not years? *Months?* 66 − 61 = 5. Five months, eight days. Hamdan would complete his sentence just before George W. Bush's presidency ended on January 20, 2009. A soldier in the pressroom passed a note to a comrade: "He goes home three months before we do! That's not fair."[5]

The punishment was more lenient than the most optimistic defense projection, a third shorter than David Hicks's sentence. Put another way, the commission imposed 1.6 percent of the thirty years prosecutor John Murphy called the absolute minimum Hamdan deserved.

As the significance of the sentence began to sink in, Allred moved to the trial's closing formalities.

"I thank you for your service in this most significant and historic case, and I discharge you," he told the panel. "You're free to withdraw from the courtroom and go about your duties."

"All rise!" called the bailiff, but Allred interrupted. "Oh, wait just a moment," he said. "Mr. Hamdan is acting like he might want to say something."

Hamdan, too, realized what just had happened. He was choked up.

"I would like to apologize one more time to all the members," he said through the interpreter. "And I would like to thank you for what you have done for me. And I would like also to say—to thank the judge, and I would like to thank everybody. And I apologize once again."

Swift, hulking over Hamdan, embraced his client.

Apart from those at the prosecution table, smiles filled the courtroom. Everyone else, it seemed, had been rooting for Hamdan.

"Thank you, Mr. Hamdan, that was very gracious," Allred said. "Members of the court, thank you very much. You're excused."

Allred then described Hamdan's post-trial procedures, including his right to appeal the conviction. But this being the first-ever trial of a new legal system, some matters remained unclear.

Hamdan would serve his sentence, but "after that, I don't know what happens," Allred said. Hamdan could not assume he would walk free. "Apparently, you'll become eligible for administrative review of your threat to the United States or to its allies, perhaps; I don't know," Allred said. "And at some point, you'll become eligible for release to return to your country. That's what I understand. You probably know better than I how that part works." Any questions?

None.

"Well, this has been a long journey for Mr. Hamdan, who began in 2001; for Mr. Swift, who began in 2004; for Mr. McMillan and Schneider, who began, I guess, in 2004; and for others who have joined the case along the way," Allred said. He sounded almost senti-mental, as if delivering a graduation day speech. "It's been a pleasure for me to work with you. I commend you all for your professionalism and your courtesy to each other and the tremendous investment of hard work and your professional skills that have gone into the trial of this case. I wish you all Godspeed in your future journeys and other cases you may try."

"And Mr. Hamdan: I hope that the day comes that you return to your wife and your daughters and your country. And that you're able to be a provider, and a father, and a husband in the best sense of all those terms," Allred said warmly, with obvious sympathy and concern.

"Insh'allah," Hamdan said.

"Insh'allah," Allred repeated.

The proceedings continued for several more minutes, as Swift and Stone wrangled over Hamdan's confinement conditions, but soon it seemed there was nothing left to say.

"Okay. I'm reluctant to end this, but I guess it's that time," Allred said. "I wish you well. This court is closed."

Guards began to lead Hamdan away, but as he was about to exit, he turned back toward the few journalists, lawyers, and officials re-maining in the courtroom.

"Bye-bye, everybody!" he said, in English, smiling as he waved farewell.

■

Prosecutor John Murphy called his stunning humiliation a "victory for the system."

"What happened—despite the system—is justice," retorted Charlie Swift.[6]

The members of the commission panel, however, said they gave no thought to "the system" at all.

"Salim Hamdan was working for a bad organization and he knew that," one of the panel members said.[7] "The defense would say the accused made the mistake of being in the wrong place at the wrong time," the panel knew, while "the prosecutors would give the image of him being a hardened terrorist."

For the panel, "it came down to the evidence that we were allowed to see." Nothing the government produced suggested Hamdan had any role planning or organizing terror attacks. The defense case, however, suggested that Hamdan was a lot like naive young people who get mixed up with drug gangs or organized crime anywhere—lacking other opportunities, they take what's available to them, the member said.

The panel had two weeks to observe Hamdan at the defense table. His demeanor made an impression. Wearing a blazer over traditional Yemeni garb, Hamdan was respectful and engaged—not a defiant fanatic. "He looked very mild mannered," the member said.

Despite the prosecution's repeated invocation of 9/11, the panel had no difficulty declining to punish Hamdan for the terrorist attacks. Before proceedings began, the six officers had resolved to put aside their personal feelings about 9/11. "We all had to reconcile that before we got on the plane" to Guantanamo, he said.

The two major presidential candidates offered their assessments.

"This process demonstrated that military commissions can effectively bring very dangerous terrorists to justice," said Republican John McCain, who helped craft the Military Commissions Act. "The fact that the jury did not find Hamdan guilty of all of the charges brought against him demonstrates that the jury weighed the evidence carefully."

While the "process of bringing terrorists to justice has been too long delayed," the Arizona senator said he was "encouraged that it is finally moving forward." The United States "cannot treat dangerous terrorists captured on the battlefield as we would common criminals."

"I commend the military officers who presided over this trial and served on the hearing panel under difficult and unprecedented circumstances," said Democrat Barack Obama, who had voted against the Military Commissions Act. Nonetheless, "that the Hamdan trial—the first military commission trial with a guilty verdict since 9/11—took several years of legal challenges to secure a conviction for material support for terrorism underscores the dangerous flaws in the administration's legal framework."

Bush's legal experiment should be scrapped, the Illinois senator said. "It's time to better protect the American people and our values by bringing swift and sure justice to terrorists through our courts and our Uniform Code of Military Justice."

■

Pressing to get the 9/11 trial under way ahead of the election, commissions officials scheduled the arraignment of Khalid Sheikh Mohammed and his four codefendants for June 5, 2008—even before some defense attorneys had a chance to meet their clients.

The five alleged conspirators had not seen each other during their years of captivity. But guards brought them to the courtroom ahead of the arraignment, and seated together with no lawyers present, the five had a chance to confer. According to defense lawyers, Ramzi Binalshibh preached defiance, intimidating two others who had been open to working with defense attorneys. KSM, who had been mulling whether to scorn the system entirely or work with lawyers to undermine it, wouldn't stand being out-fanaticized by Binalshibh. He decided the group would refuse representation by American lawyers and use the courtroom as a stage for martyrdom.[8]

KSM no longer resembled the pudgy, disheveled figure shown in the mug shot taken after his 2003 capture. Dressed in a white turban with a bushy salt-and-pepper beard, he looked far older than his forty-three years. He wore glasses in thick black plastic frames and spoke in a clipped, high-pitched voice.

Seated in the first of the five defense rows, KSM was accorded the respect due an enemy leader. He recited Koranic verses, lectured the military judge about American policies, and complained about being tortured by the United States.

His vanity showed through as well. Under commissions rules, courtroom sketches had to be cleared by military censors. During a break in proceedings, a security official reviewing sketches showed them to Mohammed, who was incensed at the rendering of his nose.[9] For guidance, KSM instructed, the illustrator should use the 2003 capture photo.

"I'll concede that the nose wasn't flattering," said the sketch artist, Janet Hamlin. She pulled out her pastels and reworked KSM's proboscis to his satisfaction. "I shortened it and slimmed it down."

During proceedings, KSM followed the pattern of fanatics on trial. When the military judge warned that "this is a death penalty case," Mohammed corrected him: "*Martyr* case," he said. "This is what I wish. I've been looking to be martyred for a long time."

Binalshibh chimed in. "I've been seeking martyrdom for five years. I tried for 9/11 to get a visa [to enter the United States] and I could not," he said, apparently confessing that, as the government alleged, he, too, had aspired to be a Twentieth Hijacker.

Mohammed's nephew, Amar al-Baluchi, seemed the most Westernized and coherent of the group, at least in terms of sarcasm. When told he could receive a military defense attorney free of charge, he scoffed, "the government tortured me free of charge for five years." Had the Americans "given me an attorney the *first* day I was arrested, I would have appreciated it," he said, before military censors cut the audio feed to the press gallery.

BOB SWANN, NOW IN A business suit, would prosecute the 9/11 defendants. FBI and Justice Department officials had assembled a "clean team" they said would build the 9/11 case with no reference whatever to anything the defendants told the CIA.

Military defense attorneys, aided by experienced death-penalty lawyers recruited by the American Civil Liberties Union and the National Association of Criminal Defense Lawyers, filed volumes of motions in the 9/11 case, seeking to dismiss charges, unearth records of CIA treatment, and obtain additional resources, among other matters. Such motions were part of the zealous defense the American justice system requires every lawyer to mount for a client.

The 9/11 defendants themselves experimented with various approaches to their trial, questioning the military judge at voir dire, dismissing or accepting, for limited purposes, the American defense lawyers.

But after a meeting on November 4, 2008—Election Day in the United States—the five defendants sent a letter to the military judge asking to withdraw their legal motions.[10] They requested a hearing "in order to announce our confessions."

The military judge, Colonel Stephen Henley, didn't see their letter until he returned to Guantanamo a month later for the next hearing in the 9/11 case, on December 8, 2008.

"Is the commission using a carrier pigeon?" KSM scoffed when Henley said he first read the letter the day before the hearing. On the mainland, Henley said, he lacked the secure facility military rules required to read a communication from the defendants.

Nevertheless, now that they all were gathered in the courtroom, Mohammed made clear he was tired of the legalistic procedures the United States expected them to follow on the route to trial, conviction, and, inevitably, execution.

"We don't want to waste time," he said. "We want to enter a plea."

The courtroom was floored.

For the first time, the government had brought relatives of 9/11 victims to observe Guantanamo proceedings. They had been told that the hearing would cover defense motions to dismiss charges or otherwise obstruct the government's case. Instead, they saw the defendants proudly claim responsibility for the attacks.

Hamilton Peterson, whose parents Donald and Jean were passengers on United 93, was dumbfounded. The defendants "are explicitly asking the court to hurry up, because they are bored with the due process they are receiving," he said.

In federal or state court, a judge could have accepted Mohammed's guilty plea to a capital charge.

Not that doing so would be a casual affair. "A guilty plea is a grave and solemn act to be accepted only with care and discernment," the Supreme Court observed in 1970.[11] "Waivers of constitutional rights not only must be voluntary, but must be knowing, intelligent acts done with sufficient awareness of the relevant circumstances and likely consequences."

Judges must examine defendants closely to ensure that those requirements are met. Nevertheless, if satisfied, a judge can accept a guilty plea—even to a capital crime.

Colonel Henley was ready to let Khalid Sheikh Mohammed, Amar al-Baluchi, and Walid bin Attash withdraw defense motions and enter pleas. Were this federal district court, 9/11's confessed mastermind and two of his henchmen would stand convicted by their own words. When the judge formally accepted their pleas, a sentencing hearing would follow. Whatever their other disagreements, both prosecutors and defendants wanted the death penalty.

But Henley was a military judge, heading a military commission.

Administration officials had drafted the Military Commissions Act to deny defendants the legal rights that could impede convictions. The statute favored hearsay, prohibited defendants from invoking the Geneva Conventions, and authorized admission of statements coerced through cruel, inhuman, and degrading treatment.

But the drafters gave little thought to the way fanatics typically behave at trial; ideologically motivated defendants often see the courtroom as a stage to justify their acts, rather than a chance to evade punishment. Federal and state courts occasionally run across terrorists, political protesters, religious zealots, and others who view their trials as a platform for their message. The justice system has developed procedures to protect the rights of such defendants without impeding the legal process.

Bush administration lawyers, little experienced either with trial courts or with uniformed service, envisioned the military system as a mechanism to deliver rough justice to prisoners who deserved no better. The actual military justice system had a different function, that of maintaining good order and discipline in the ranks of American service members, by fairly adjudicating their infractions.

Unlike federal or state courts, military justice operates in a rigid, rank-based, hierarchical society that all its participants—from judge to defendant—chose to join. By training, lifestyle, and disposition, the players share far more in common than their counterparts in civilian court. The procedures of military justice, internalized by its uniformed bar, reflect the values and characteristics of military service. For instance, soldiers are trained to subordinate their personal interests to that of the organization and to obey superiors without question—features of military life at odds with the adversarial structure of a criminal trial.

Court-martial rules, therefore, seek to insulate accused soldiers from institutional values and command influence that could undermine their rights in an adversarial legal system. Defendants convicted in federal or state court are entitled to appeal but not required to. In contrast, court-martial convictions automatically are reviewed by a military appellate court. As a result, military defendants need not worry that asserting their rights might further antagonize the commanders who authorized their trials to begin with.

Similarly, courts-martial cannot accept guilty pleas to a capital charge. A death sentence can be imposed only after trial in which the government has proved its case beyond a reasonable doubt and a court-martial panel, considering aggravating and mitigating evidence, unanimously votes for execution. That provision, like other aspects of military justice, migrated silently into the Military Commissions Act, leaving Colonel Henley uncertain whether President Bush and Congress had authorized him to let Khalid Sheikh Mohammed plead guilty.

He asked Bob Swann to file a brief addressing the question.

Turning the Page

ON JANUARY 20, 2009, A naval petty officer at Guantanamo Bay removed an eight-by-ten-inch headshot of George W. Bush from the display at base headquarters and replaced it with the official portrait of Barack Obama, newly inaugurated as forty-fourth president of the United States and commander in chief of its Army and Navy. Many other changes at Guantanamo were expected to follow.

As candidates, both Obama and his Republican opponent, Senator John McCain, had promised to close the offshore prison. They took different positions on military commissions, however, as McCain endorsed the existing apparatus while Obama called it a failure. His praise for the federal court system and courts-martial suggested little enthusiasm for George W. Bush's legal experiment.

In *The Audacity of Hope,* the collection of musings that amounted to Obama's manifesto, he had sharply criticized his predecessor for treating constitutional principles and fundamental rights as "niceties that only got in the way."[1] And as he began his campaign for president, Obama, an outstanding student at Harvard Law School who later taught constitutional law at the University of Chicago, had considered making the rule of law a defining issue. In 2007, he had called upon mentors from each stage of his legal career—his former professors at Harvard, Laurence Tribe and Martha Minow, his colleagues at Chi-

cago, Geoffrey Stone and Cass Sunstein, and more recent policy advisers including Eric Holder and Neal Katyal, now celebrated for his
victory in *Hamdan v. Rumsfeld*—to draft an address laying out a constitutional vision. He would deliver it on Law Day—an annual civic
observance on May 1, created in 1958 by President Eisenhower as an
alternative to the labor movement's May Day.

After the group hashed out drafts over email, Obama called
them to Washington to discuss the address. Some, like Tribe, flew in
for the day. Others dialed in by telephone. They waited at the campaign office near the Capitol until Obama dashed in. He apologized
for not having had time to study their draft in detail but made clear
he had been thinking deeply about the underlying questions. Virtually every member of the group viewed the Bush administration as
a lawless aberration from American constitutional tradition. And
when Obama spoke, they heard what they had dreamed an American
president might someday say.

"I'll never forget it. It was incredible," said Minow. "He proceeded to give in great detail illustrations from five different periods
in American history where the country had strayed from the principles of the Constitution. He had it all at its fingertips, and it was so
much better than our speech. It knocked us all back on our feet."
Minow's father, Newton Minow, the eminent Chicago lawyer, had
advised Rumsfeld on the initial rules for military commissions; he
also had helped groom Obama for legal and political leadership.

Obama, Martha Minow recalled, envisioned the Law Day address as a way to explain the constitutional dynamic to a broad audience. "He had this thesis already in his head that there are exigent
pressures that understandably impel political actors and the nation as
a whole to steer away from our fundamental commitments, but what's
brilliant about the Constitution is that it also sets in motion the process
for self-correction"—a process Obama intended to embody.

Yet after once again impressing his teachers, Obama later dropped
plans for the speech. Stone, who as dean at Chicago recruited Obama
to the faculty, was disappointed, although not entirely surprised. "It's a

very tricky theme to play out politically," he said, to argue for restraint when dealing with enemies or criminals. "You are asking people to be better than they have to be."

Echoes of the never-finished speech, however, could be heard in an August 1, 2007, address on national security Obama delivered at the Woodrow Wilson Center in Washington. He called out the Bush administration for squandering America's power and reputation in pursuit of phony threats in Iraq, promising to end the war there and redouble the campaign against al Qaeda in Afghanistan. "What's more, in the dark halls of Abu Ghraib and the detention cells of Guantanamo, we have compromised our most precious values," he said. "What could have been a call to a generation has become an excuse for unchecked presidential power." As president, "I will make clear that the days of compromising our values are over."

Obama, speaking a year before the Hamdan trial, turned to military commissions. "There has been only one conviction at Guantanamo. It was for a guilty plea on material support for terrorism," he said, referring to David Hicks. "The sentence was nine months. There has not been one conviction of a terrorist act. I have faith in America's courts, and I have faith in our JAGs. As president, I will close Guantanamo, reject the Military Commissions Act, and adhere to the Geneva Conventions. Our Constitution and our Uniform Code of Military Justice provide a framework for dealing with the terrorists," he said. "Our Constitution works. We will again set an example for the world that the law is not subject to the whims of stubborn rulers, and that justice is not arbitrary."

Yet Obama did not precisely say he would reject *military commissions* themselves—just the 2006 statute authorizing them. That implicit reservation, invisible to the casual listener, reflected the views of Jeh Johnson, a New York lawyer and Obama fundraiser who had been general counsel of the Department of the Air Force in the Clinton administration. Johnson's view of military tribunals had been forged less by the Bush experiment than *Judgment at Nuremberg*, the 1961 film starring Spencer Tracy and Burt Lancaster in a dramatization of the postwar trials. Whatever Obama's reservations, Johnson urged the candidate not to rule commissions out entirely. Once Obama was in power, they might prove useful, he argued, and Obama agreed to leave the door open a tiny crack. Even some of Obama's speechwriters missed the punctilious distinction in the Wilson Center speech, so Johnson made it a point to police drafts of future campaign speeches to excise passages explicitly repudiating military commissions.

For Johnson, it wasn't purely a disinterested question of legal policy. He was in line for the job once held by David Addington and Jim Haynes, Pentagon general counsel, which oversaw military commissions. Johnson was an active Democrat and no fan of the Addington ideology, but he had been a federal prosecutor in Manhattan and felt qualified to supervise tough terrorism prosecutions. Working on the Defense Department transition after the 2008 election, Johnson found his views of commissions validated. The officers running the commissions project, Brigadier General Tom Hartmann and Colonel Larry Morris, the chief prosecutor, had prepared extensive briefings to persuade the incoming team that their work was essential not only to the larger goal of defeating terrorism but to Obama's campaign pledge to close Guantanamo itself. Because of evidentiary rules in federal court, they argued, commissions were the only way to try some of the really bad guys held at Gitmo, taking them out of a legal no-man's-land and allowing the new administration to clear out the offshore prison. Johnson was their conduit to the White House.

A day after taking office, Obama signed a set of executive orders intended to wind down the Bush detainee structure. It put the attorney general, Eric Holder, rather than the Department of Defense, in charge of the process. One order established a cabinet-level task force to review options for detention and trial of prisoners captured "in connection with armed conflicts and counterterrorism operations." A second order repudiated the brutal interrogation methods Bush had authorized, while another provided for a searching review of the 241 detainees still held at Guantanamo, aiming to sift the culpable and set them for trial while confirming that those cleared by Bush officials should in fact be released.[2] To no one's surprise, another presidential directive suspended commissions proceedings indefinitely.

Holder and the White House counsel, Gregory Craig, viewed that as an interim step before permanently closing the tribunals. But Obama's deliberative nature disinclined him from snap decisions. Moreover, like any president, he was reluctant to surrender executive powers that his predecessor had claimed. And as the Justice Department began the difficult work of assessing the situation at Guantanamo, Obama was surprised to find himself under fire from Republicans for softness on terrorism. Congressional Republicans, now in the minority, were trying any available tactic to undermine Obama, while veterans of the Bush administration, some of whom were facing private lawsuits and calls for investigations into their roles in prisoner abuse, were determined to justify what they had done.

Greg Craig advised the president to make a clean break with Bush's legal experiments. As Obama knew, military commissions had been plagued with problems due both to internal mismanagement and to legal uncertainty. Justice Department prosecutors, meanwhile, had won dozens of terrorism convictions since 9/11, regularly sending defendants to life imprisonment without a single intelligence leak. Bush refused to transfer the 9/11 suspects to federal court—and agreed only reluctantly to military commissions—from fear that trial could disclose even more facts regarding his administration's actions. No such considerations colored Obama's decision, Craig argued, and by sending KSM and his cohorts to certain conviction in federal court, Obama could rapidly achieve a public victory over terrorism that had eluded Bush. Consign commissions to the list of ideologically driven policy failures that future historians would use to define the Bush era, the White House counsel said.

Craig had support from a particularly authoritative source: Bill Lietzau. The Marine colonel who had designed the commissions apparatus for the Bush Pentagon was now on the National Security Council staff, and he said it was time to pull the plug. In a memo for the White House counsel, Lietzau wrote that nearly a decade after 9/11, whatever "exigent circumstances" may once have justified establishing a parallel system of rough justice for enemy aliens long had passed. Conviction in federal court was the gold standard in criminal justice; neither the appellate courts, nor the legal profession, nor the international community would doubt the outcome. In contrast, a military commission conviction would be clouded for years by appeals through the federal court system, which would still have to resolve such basic questions as which, if any, constitutional provisions applied to commissions.

The White House political operation, headed by Rahm Emanuel, the chief of staff, saw things differently. Its priorities were domestic policies, such as priming the recessionary economy and launching a health-care overhaul. Detainee matters were becoming a distraction. While John McCain and even Bush himself once had said they wanted Guantanamo closed, almost immediately after Obama took office, Republicans had begun declaring the offshore prison essential to American security. Senator Lindsey Graham remained a rare Republican willing to shut Guantanamo—but he also was a principal advocate for military commissions, which he considered a necessary symbol of America's war footing against terrorism. Maintaining commissions, at least as an option, was necessary for Graham's support on Guantanamo and would dilute the Republican effort to paint Obama as soft on terrorism, the White House political shop argued.

Moreover, the Pentagon, headed by a Bush holdover, Defense Secretary Robert Gates, was unwilling to surrender its power to try prisoners to the Justice Department. Obama was reluctant to overrule a cabinet officer who contributed so much to his own credibility on national security. With a few reforms, such as an explicit ban on defendants' statements obtained through cruel, inhuman, or degrading methods, Obama technically could keep his campaign promise to reject the 2006 Military Commissions *Act* that authorized such evidence while maintaining commissions themselves as a presidential prerogative.

As in many other areas, Obama decided to split the difference, laying out his thinking in a May 2009 address, delivered at the National Archives. Standing before original copies of the Declaration of Independence, the United States Constitution, and the Bill of Rights, Obama said his policies would at once keep Americans safe while honoring "the sacred principles enshrined in this building."

In contrast, he said, the Bush administration "went off course." After 9/11, "all too often our government trimmed facts and evidence to fit ideological predispositions," he said. "Instead of strategically applying our power and our principles, too often we set those principles aside as luxuries that we could no longer afford."

Not only did Bush's legal framework reject "our legal traditions and time-tested institutions" and fail "to use our values as a compass," it also proved "neither effective nor sustainable." He recalled that until the Bush administration, "from Europe to the Pacific, we've been the nation that has shut down the torture chambers," letting hang the implication that his predecessor had opened them. In contrast, Obama said he had categorically banned "brutal methods like waterboarding" because they were unnecessary and counterproductive—not, apparently, because they were illegal. "We must leave these methods where they belong—in the past. They are not who we are, and they are not America," he said.

"There is also no question that Guantanamo set back the moral authority that is America's strongest currency in the world. Instead of building a durable framework for the struggle against al Qaeda that drew upon our deeply held values and traditions, our government was defending positions that undermined the rule of law," Obama said. "In fact, part of the rationale for establishing Guantanamo in the first place was the misplaced notion that a prison there would be beyond the law—a proposition that the Supreme Court soundly rejected."

Bush's military commissions represented that lawless excess, the president said. "Instead of bringing terrorists to justice, efforts at prosecution met setback after setback, cases lingered on, and in 2006 the Supreme Court invalidated the entire system." In the future, "whenever feasible, we will try those who have violated American criminal laws in federal courts—courts provided for by the United States Constitution." Obama said. Others, however, would face military commissions.

Not "the flawed commissions of the last seven years," he added, but ones that would operate "in line with the rule of law." His commissions "will no longer permit the use as evidence statements that have been obtained using cruel, inhuman, or degrading interrogation methods," nor presumptively admit hearsay. "These reforms, among others, will make our military commissions a more credible and effective means of administering justice."

Obama had another announcement: Despite his scathing critique of the Bush administration's bizarre legal claims and the institutionalized cruelty they enabled, Obama said that no one would be held accountable. "I have no interest in spending all of our time relitigating the policies of the last eight years," he said. Rather than "pointing fingers at one another . . . we need to focus on the future."

Politically, Obama tried to have it all ways. He sought to keep faith with his followers by condemning the inhuman practices of his predecessor and legal theories that, as John Yoo put it, could transmogrify "otherwise criminal" misconduct into policy choices that were "not unlawful." But he extended his hand to those he said had so transgressed America's moral standing and legal traditions, ruling out any accountability or even an independent inquiry, like the 9/11 Commission, that could authoritatively establish what had taken place. In exchange, Obama apparently expected his policies would receive the deference Republicans once had declared the courts and Congress owed to President Bush.

"We will be ill served by some of the fear mongering that emerges whenever we discuss this issue," Obama said, leaving Dick Cheney's name unmentioned. "Listening to the recent debate, I've heard words that, frankly, are calculated to scare people rather than educate them; words that have more to do with politics than protecting our country."

Cheney had scheduled his own speech the same day, at the American Enterprise Institute, barely a mile away. Offering no thanks for the de facto pardons Obama had granted, Cheney sought to seize history's verdict as well. He quickly dismissed the intricate set of policy and legal compromises that the young president had spent months attempting to perfect.

The Obama administration seemed to "take comfort in hearing disagreement from opposite ends of the spectrum," Cheney said. "If liberals are unhappy about some decisions and conservatives are unhappy about other decisions, then it may seem to them that the president is on the path of sensible compromise. But in the fight against terrorism, there is no middle ground, and half-measures keep you half-exposed."

Under Obama, Cheney said, "the terrorists see just what they were hoping for: our unity gone, our resolve shaken, our leaders distracted. In short, they see weakness and opportunity." Throughout the Obama administration, Congress largely would heed Cheney's call, not the president's, by obstructing Obama's campaign promise to close Guantanamo and even barring the government from transferring detainees to the mainland for trial.

OBAMA'S TASK FORCES SPENT months in secret meetings to discuss future policies, while senior officials wrangled over the political implications of the most significant case before them: the 9/11 trial.

The president had assigned the final word to his attorney general, Eric Holder, himself a former United States attorney and District of Columbia judge. As it had years earlier under John Ashcroft, the Justice Department's criminal division and, in particular, the US attorney's office in Manhattan, insisted it had the expertise and the mandate to handle the case. In October 2009, Holder met with Jeh Johnson to hash things out.

Johnson, professing his respect for the US attorney's office where he once worked, nevertheless stressed the problems in prosecuting the 9/11 case in federal court. The principal obstacle, he said, would be objections to the introduction of the defendants' statements, on grounds of hearsay or coercion. But commissions rules, Johnson insisted, still gave military judges enough leeway to let those statements in.

Holder, however, had reasons to doubt the competence of the commissions prosecution team. While conducting the detainee case review ordered by President Obama, Justice Department attorneys had been stunned to discover that commissions prosecutors had failed to interview key witnesses, dissect computer files recovered from al Qaeda safe houses, or even dust seized documents for fingerprints.[3]

Holder made no immediate decision, but he would have to resolve things soon. A military judge's order suspending the 9/11 case was to expire the next month, putting the administration in the awkward position of seeing charges dismissed or having to seek another continuance unless it launched a prosecution.

Holder waited until the last day—Friday the thirteenth—to announce his decision. The numbers reflected a bureaucratic compromise. Five detainees would be tried by military commission, including Abdelrahim al-Nashiri, the suspected planner of the *Cole* attack. But Khalid Sheikh Mohammed and his four codefendants would be tried for the 9/11 attacks, as the Constitution directs, in "the State and district wherein the crime shall have been committed."[4]

"After eight years of delay, those allegedly responsible for the attacks of September the Eleventh will finally face justice. They will be brought to New York to answer for their alleged crimes in a courthouse just blocks from where the Twin Towers once stood," Holder said. The Department of Justice would seek the maximum penalty, he indicated, death. "I am confident in the ability of our courts to provide these defendants a fair trial, just as they have for over two hundred years." That confidence was not mere bluster; among other things, the Justice Department's detainee team had discovered what it considered conclusive—and untainted—evidence of KSM's guilt. The military secretly had been recording KSM since he arrived at Guantanamo—recordings in which he discussed his 9/11 role with other detainees.

Recording detainees in recreation yards and other common areas was routine practice at the prison, but years earlier military prosecutors had decided against using such recordings at trial, for fear of alerting prisoners to the surveillance, along with doubts regarding their admissibility. Justice Department prosecutors, however, had no qualms about introducing the recordings in federal court.[5]

There was, however a practical obstacle. At Republican instigation, Congress had required the Obama administration to provide forty-five days' notice before bringing detainees to the US mainland. The rule may have been valid regarding detainees held without charge, but if applied to prisoners facing trial, it was a remarkable intrusion into the executive branch's prosecutorial discretion, as well as judicial authority over criminal proceedings.

A more aggressive attorney general might have ignored the notice requirement in the case of detainees under indictment in federal court. The Bush administration had preferred to undertake legally questionable or politically controversial actions first and disclose them later, if at all. It was easier to defend a status quo than to change it. Such an approach would have seen Khalid Sheikh Mohammed and his codefendants secretly haled before a New York federal magistrate for their initial appearance, followed by a public announcement that the 9/11 trial would take place in federal district court and a declaration that the forty-five-day notice requirement was inapplicable to active criminal proceedings. For that matter, Obama could have ordered Guantanamo closed in January 2009—before Congress imposed the notice requirement—and its inmates immediately transferred to a maximum security prison on the mainland.

The Obama administration instead announced its plans far in advance, giving the president's adversaries plenty of time to foment opposition. The plan to close Guantanamo was first delayed, then indefinitely postponed, after Republicans framed the decision as tantamount to loosing terrorists on the American public. Likewise, they argued that federal courts, where questions of guilt or innocence rested with ordinary Americans selected at random, couldn't be trusted to do justice.

"You've got juries in this country," said Senator Charles Grassley of Iowa.[6] He worried that a New York jury might sympathize with KSM, like Los Angeles jurors had done with another famous defendant. "I think a lot of Americans thought O. J. Simpson ought to be convicted of murder," Grassley said. New York Mayor Michael Bloomberg and other politicians who initially backed Holder's decision soon began to reverse their positions. Some suggested another venue within the Southern District of New York—perhaps even holding the trial at West Point, the fortresslike US Military Academy alongside the Hudson River.[7] House Majority Leader Steny Hoyer, a Maryland Democrat, went one further, proposing a federal court be set up at Guantanamo itself, thereby blunting arguments that the 9/11 trial site would become a target for an al Qaeda attack.

But that wouldn't do for Lindsey Graham. While KSM probably could be convicted in any venue, the South Carolina senator worried that the commissions system he had championed might not survive the loss of its marquee defendant.

"It's a vote of no confidence in military commissions," Graham fumed. "It makes it seem like second-class justice."

"Khalid Sheikh Mohammed is not John Hinckley," Graham told Bob Bauer, who had just replaced Greg Craig as White House counsel. KSM was no deranged loner but "the functional equivalent of a field general." If he didn't belong in a military commission, who did? Obama could forget about Graham's help in closing Guantanamo unless KSM were tried by military commission. Although it was unclear whether Graham could bring along enough—or any—additional Republicans to close the prison, it would be impossible without him.

Obama did not want to overrule Holder directly, so Bauer and Rahm Emanuel went to work on the attorney general, arguing that it would be politically impossible to proceed with a federal court trial. Clearly, the president was unwilling to spend any political capital of his own to bring the public behind Holder's decision. The message finally got through. In April 2011, the day Obama announced his reelection bid, Holder reluctantly told reporters that the 9/11 defendants would be tried by military commission.

Because few understood military commission procedures— much less the way the project actually had operated through the years—the public debate boiled down to the implicit presumption that like soldiers, *military* commissions were tough, and *civilian* courts, like defenseless noncombatants, weak. Given those options for dealing with terrorists, military commissions seemed the obvious choice.

In fact, while commissions retained many of the structural flaws that had hobbled them since 2001, subsequent Supreme Court rulings and congressional actions had erased the principal attributes that first inspired them: providing convictions based on coerced statements, concealing government misconduct in obtaining evidence, and speeding executions by prohibiting appeals.

The disparate political and legal realities crystallized in the 2010 prosecution of Ahmed Khalfan Ghailani, the only detainee taken from Guantanamo for trial in federal district court. Ghailani was a Tanzanian implicated in the 1998 al Qaeda bombing of the American Embassy in Dar es Salaam. He was captured in Pakistan after a 2004 shootout and spent two years in CIA custody until 2006, when President Bush cleared out the secret prisons following the Supreme Court's *Hamdan v. Rumsfeld* opinion.

A federal grand jury had indicted Ghailani for the embassy bombings in 1998, but he had evaded capture while four of his co-conspirators were taken to New York for trial and, in 2001, sentenced to life imprisonment without possibility of parole by a federal district court.

When Ghailani was brought to the same court to face 285 counts of murder and other crimes, he was acquitted on all but one charge of conspiracy. The outcome "demonstrates the absolute insanity of the Obama administration's decision to try al Qaeda terrorists in civilian courts," said Congressman Peter King, a Long Island Republican, expressing a typical view following the verdict.[8]

At trial, federal prosecutors had ruled out using any statements obtained by the CIA. Rather than litigate whether Ghailani was abused, the government conceded that for legal purposes, everything he told the CIA could be considered coerced in violation of the Fifth Amendment. The judge, Lewis Kaplan, went further still, excluding a key prosecution witness, a Tanzanian taxicab driver who sold explosives to Ghailani. The government had obtained the man's identity from Ghailani himself during the two-year period of CIA interrogation. Kaplan explained that under the Fifth Amendment, "fruits of a coerced statement" are as prohibited as the coerced statement itself.

Yet a military commission almost certainly would have reached the same result, because Obama's reforms, contained in the Military Commissions Act of 2009, prohibited evidence obtained through cruel, inhuman, or degrading treatment, as well as torture. Judge Kaplan himself, in footnote 182 to his sixty-page opinion, suggested there was little reason to believe the statute's standard was "any more forgiving" than the Fifth Amendment—and that, in any event, the Fifth Amendment itself could be held to apply to military commissions.

At sentencing in January 2011, Kaplan described Ghailani's crime as "a cold-blooded killing and maiming of innocent people on an enormous scale."[9] It was intended "to create terror by causing death and destruction on a scale hard to imagine in 1998 when it occurred." Without condoning "any illegal and improper actions by our government," Kaplan sentenced Ghailani, thirty-six years old, to the maximum term, life in prison.

ALTHOUGH ERIC HOLDER HAD relinquished the 9/11 case, the Pentagon still had not obtained the internal approvals necessary to restart commissions trials. The principal obstacle was Harold Hongju Koh, the State Department's chief lawyer. As professor and dean of Yale Law School, Koh had been perhaps the most influential international law scholar in the American academy. He had been among the most outspoken critics of the Bush legal regime, something that incensed him all the more because its chief architect, John Yoo, had been one of his students.

Koh considered military commissions an affront to the rule of law, but he was not confirmed to his position until June 2009, well after Obama had decided to continue the Bush legal experiment. Once in the administration, however, Koh did all he could to derail it, persuading his boss, Secretary of State Hillary Rodham Clinton, that resuming commissions trials would undermine international cooperation on counterterrorism efforts. At an August 2011 meeting with senior national security officials, Clinton was adamant. Restarting trials at Guantanamo would signal that the United States was going to keep the prison there forever, she said.

"We are throwing the president's commitment to close Gitmo in the trash bin," she said. "We should fight to close Gitmo. We should fight to have the trials in the United States." The White House, however, already had given up. The State Department would have to make do with a couple of consolation prizes; to mollify Koh, the administration agreed to ask the Senate to ratify agreements expanding protections under the Geneva Conventions, including one that had been collecting dust since President Reagan signed it in 1987. "Joining the treaty would not only assist us in continuing to exercise leadership in the international community in developing the law of armed conflict, but would also allow us to reaffirm our commitment to humane treatment in, and compliance with legal standards for, the conduct of armed conflict," a White House fact sheet said.

EACH YEAR AS PENTAGON general counsel, Jeh Johnson would hold a private dinner for about twenty authorities on national security law, a bipartisan affair that kept him connected to the thinking outside the government. At the April 28, 2011, dinner, guests ranged from the liberal Harvard professor David Barron, who recently had completed two years running the Office of Legal Counsel under Eric Holder, to Bush administration stalwarts such as Michael Mukasey, the former attorney general whose counterterrorism views some-times fell to the right even of John Ashcroft.

Johnson was in a particularly ebullient mood that evening, knowing, as few others did, that the raid to assassinate Osama bin Laden would soon commence. But his obvious cause for celebration was the reactivation of military commissions. Thanks to rule changes in legislation Obama signed, the Military Commissions Act of 2009, Johnson was confident his shop would run things right. The consensus around the room was decidedly different. The guests, some of whom had had significant exposure to the Office of Military Commissions over the years, warned him that the operation might not be up to the task.

The key voice came from Mukasey. Despite their partisan differences, the two were longtime friends from the Southern District of New York, where Johnson practiced law and Mukasey, appointed by Ronald Reagan, had been a federal judge. Publicly, Mukasey had been among the loudest Republican voices blasting the Obama administration for assigning the 9/11 case to his old courthouse in Lower Manhattan.[10] But from his own time running the Justice Department, Mukasey knew that the commissions project had been poorly run and that many of its cases were a mess. Privately, Mukasey told Johnson, "you've got to shape up commissions."

Despite more than two years as Pentagon general counsel, Johnson had never closely examined what transpired in the Office of Military Commissions during the Bush administration, nor had he looked closely at the people running the project. To the contrary, he had retained the staff virtually intact, including Bob Swann and John Murphy, the Hamdan trial prosecutor, whom Johnson promoted to chief prosecutor after Larry Morris retired from the Army. Braced by Mukasey's warning, Johnson asked Murphy, Swann, and other commissions staff for a briefing on the case and the overall prosecution structure.

Johnson was stunned at what he discovered. The team that had fought so hard to preserve its own jobs was unable to answer even basic questions regarding trial strategy. He was staring at a fiasco in the making, one that he, and Obama, would own.

Johnson pulled Murphy aside for a private conversation. Swann and his team would have to go, Johnson said.

Murphy resisted. Like his predecessor, Moe Davis, Murphy knew the Military Commissions Act contained provisions intended to protect the chief prosecutor from interference. He reminded Johnson that he could not be ordered to fire his staff.

Right, said Johnson, but I can fire you. He dismissed Murphy and, later that summer, decided to put, for the first time, a general officer in the chief prosecutor's slot: Brigadier General Mark Martins, a former aide to General David Petraeus who had worked on the Obama administration's detainee task force. On paper, Martins was a cut above his predecessors, a graduate of West Point and Harvard Law School, a Rhodes Scholar. Martins knew the troubled reality of the commissions experiment; in late 2005, while doing research at the National War College, then-Colonel Martins had visited the commissions office to inquire about the Hamdan case and met Stu Couch, then the trial prosecutor. When Couch wanted to organize a focus group to test jury results for the Hamdan case, Martins provided the entrée to the National War College, where the exercise was held.

Like Bill Lietzau, Martins was both revered and resented by rank-and-file JAGs. Many considered him destined someday to become the judge advocate general of the Army, a three-star general who headed the JAG Corps. Instead, he accepted a billet that had brought so many careers to an end. Rather than challenge that fate, he accepted it up front, deciding that he would retire from the Army on completing his assignment as chief prosecutor.

As had some of his predecessors, Martins began a publicity campaign to win support for commissions, delivering speeches and granting news media interviews to stress the new system's fairness. Unwittingly echoing what the first chief prosecutor, Fred Borch, had said in 2004, Martins urged observers and legal authorities to give commissions the benefit of the doubt, promising they would be impressed by the way a trial actually functioned. "If students and other observers withhold their judgment of the reformed military commissions until they observe a trial firsthand or read these materials," Martins told an audience at Harvard Law School in April 2012, "I believe that they will see a system that is fair and legitimate, and deserving of their confidence."

Stu Couch respected Martins. The general had contacted Couch after taking on the chief prosecutor post, recalling their meeting years earlier on Hamdan. "Great to hear from you—and flattered you remembered our meetings so long ago," Couch replied by email. "I am so thankful that you are at the helm of OMCP at this critical time. The military commissions effort has always needed someone of your experience and reputation to get some respectability."

AT GUANTANAMO ON MAY 6, 2012, Martins took the first chair at the prosecution table when KSM and his codefendants were brought in for arraignment. To the general's right sat Bob Swann; Martins had decided to keep him on board, along with a supporting cast of Bush era staffers

The military judge now hearing the case, Colonel James Pohl, directed Martins to the lectern.

"Your Honor, this military commission is convened by Convening Order No. 12-02, dated 4 April 2012, and referred capital"—that is, seeking the death penalty—"and for a joint trial as reflected on the charge sheet," Martins began, reading from the script the procedures directed. "As to Khalid Sheikh Mohammed, the prosecution caused a copy of the charges in English and Arabic, a language the accused understands, to be served on the accused."

In federal court and courts-martial, arraignment is a pro forma proceeding, a simple reading of the charges to put the accused on notice. But as with every prior military commissions proceeding, there was no room for the routine. The defense immediately discarded the government's narrative, refusing to acknowledge the venue's legitimacy, insisting that even threshold questions—such as whether the defendant wished to be represented by his lawyer—could not be addressed without first assessing the impact of confinement, abuse, and military interference with attorney-client communications prior to the hearing. KSM's lawyer, David Nevin, questioned whether, by wearing a judicial robe, Pohl had prejudged one of the central issues—"the legitimacy of the structure of the court itself," something that had never come up in any case in Nevin's career.

"You will have every opportunity to challenge the structure, the basis of this commission," Pohl said. "If somehow walking through that door with a black robe means I've made up my mind on every legal issue that is going to come up, the answer is no."

"Do you believe or accept that the rights under the United States Constitution, the individual rights, apply in these proceedings?" asked another defense attorney, James Harrington.

"I think it's an open question," Pohl said.

The defiance ranged from the serious to the absurd. Ramzi Binalshibh left his chair, knelt on the floor, and prayed as guards looked on helplessly, awaiting instructions from the judge that never came. Another defendant, Walid bin Attash, removed his shirt to show scars where he said guards had injured him. Defense attorney Cheryl Bormann, dressed in an *abaya*, the black full-body covering worn by many observant Muslim women, complained that female members of the prosecution office were immodestly dressed. She asked the military judge to direct Martins to require "appropriate dress" of his staff, "so that our clients are not forced to not look at the prosecution for fear of committing a sin under their faith."[11]

The defendants refused to wear headphones for simultaneous translation of the proceedings and ignored the military judge.

A defense attorney, Captain Michael Schwartz, began to explain. "The reason for that is the—" is as far as he got, before a military censor cut the audio feed transmitted to an audience of journalists and relatives of 9/11 victims.

"You know the rules," Pohl said. "There is certain material that is not to be disclosed in a public forum unless it has been publicly cleared." Schwartz should know "where those lines are."

"I know that it looks like the line right now is embarrassment to the government," Schwartz retorted. The censored word was *torture.*

Once again, with news media from around the world as witness, military commissions, and their latest prosecutor, were themselves on trial, accused simultaneously of denying fundamental rights while being too inept even to maintain order in the courtroom. Once again, the crimes alleged against the defendants all but vanished from the stage, as the legal experiment itself took star billing. It was the defendants themselves who threw the 9/11 conspiracy back into the spotlight.

Exasperated, exhausted after a raucous day, Pohl set a tentative trial date of May 5, 2013—a year and another presidential term away—and prepared to adjourn. It was nearly 6:30 p.m., and one routine question remained to be addressed.

"Does any accused desire the charges be read?" Pohl said. Normally—virtually always, in fact—defendants waive the formal reading of full charges at arraignment, not merely to save time but to deny the prosecution a chance to lay out its case without response from the defense.

"Your Honor, Mr. bin Attash requests that the charges be read," said one defense lawyer.

"Mr. Binalshibh requests they be read also," said another.

"Mr. Hawsawi requests that the charges be read," a third chimed in.

"In twelve years of being a judge, this is the first time I've heard counsel wanting them to be read," Pohl said. Looking at the clock, Pohl first tried to put off the reading until another pretrial hearing, a month or more away. The defense refused. After a recess so the defendants could pray, the reading began at eight o'clock.

In his charge sheets, Martins had spared no details in laying out the scope of the 9/11 conspiracy. The document was eighty-seven pages long. Now the defendants forced him to stand and recite the dramatic conspiracy he had alleged, transforming the high-security Guantanamo courtroom into something like a marathon staged reading, an involuntary performance lasting two and a half hours.

Martins stood at the lectern and read for thirty minutes, at which point Bob Swann relieved him, followed by a procession of other prosecutors. The defendants enjoyed putting the government through its paces, so much so as to annoy Colonel Pohl.

"Captain Schwartz, you asked for these charges to be read, and all you've done is talk with your client and ignore this," he said. "If you want them read, show the courtesy of listening."

Schwartz made no apologies for putting the government through such contortions.

"It's my client's right," he said.

Epilogue

"Do it right the first time!"
—*Rear Admiral John Duncan Bulkeley, USN*

SO READS THE DEDICATORY plaque at Bulkeley Hall, the headquarters building at Guantanamo Bay, named for the base commander who stood down Castro after the Cuban missile crisis. Whatever else might be said about the military commissions experiment at Guantanamo, it certainly has defied Admiral Bulkeley's command. As 2013 begins, commissions are in their third iteration since they were conceived in the feverish hours following 9/11. With an array of legal challenges and practical problems still facing the project, further revisions are all but inevitable.

After the Supreme Court invalidated President George W. Bush's Military Order of November 2001, the Military Commissions Acts of 2006 and 2009 added several procedural protections for defendants, including a right of appeal to the federal courts. But all three versions create a fundamental difference between military commissions and other trial systems, courts-martial as well as the federal and state courts. Only aliens can be tried by military commission; American citizens, no matter the war crime or terrorist act alleged against them, are exempt from commissions jurisdiction.

That is one of several distinctions between the Bush-Obama commissions and those of prior conflicts, where military jurisdiction was established by the *allegation*—violation of the laws of war—rather than the birthplace or national identity of the defendant. It also creates a significant legal vulnerability under an American legal system whose headquarters, the Supreme Court, carries the inscription "Equal Justice Under Law" on its pediment. Bush administration officials said they excluded Americans from commissions jurisdiction because the potential, however remote, of US citizens haled before military tribunals would provoke an uproar on Capitol Hill and likely doom the project.

But those are the very reasons that the Constitution, as well as international instruments America once championed, such as the Geneva Conventions and the Universal Declaration of Human Rights, frown on different standards of justice based on identity. Moreover, the Supreme Court has required special scrutiny for government classifications that target politically powerless or unpopular groups, on the grounds the majority's reasons for disfavoring such individuals inherently are suspect. Here, there can be little question that the reason is prejudice, however understandable, against aliens suspected of attacking America, or at least of supporting such attacks. But animus against aliens, in contrast to delivering just verdicts or protecting national security, is difficult to square as a legal principle. The Geneva Conventions, likewise, require that enemy prisoners be tried according to the same standards as the capturing nation's own forces —a rule intended to prevent victor's justice.

For the United States, more than principle is at stake. By legitimizing differential treatment based on nationality, the Military Commissions Acts invite reciprocal action by hostile governments. Should a CIA agent be arrested in, for instance, Iran or North Korea, their regimes could invoke identical grounds as has Washington for trying them by a military tribunal with jurisdiction only over enemy aliens. Under the United States' own definition, such an agent could be an unlawful combatant—a spy or saboteur who violated the laws of war by not wearing a uniform.

Of course, federal law, like the laws of many nations, does sometimes treat aliens differently than it does citizens. In the most obvious sense, citizens have a right to live and work in the United States while aliens do not. Courts have upheld some surveillance programs that target noncitizens overseas when warrants would be required to wiretap an American. But when constructing a system that can execute an alien on flimsier evidence than a US citizen, problems emerge.

Consider two co-conspirators arrested while trying to pull off a crime together, with identical evidence against both. If one is a US citizen and the other an alien, the first would be entitled to the protections of the Bill of Rights and the federal court system; the other could be executed by a military commission that, in the government's view, need respect no constitutional limits.[1]

This is not merely a hypothetical. As described in chapter 13, in 2002, a pair of suspected al Qaeda operatives, Jose Padilla and Binyam Mohamed, were detained together while trying to leave Pakistan and later moved into US military custody. Mohamed, an Ethiopia-born British resident, was slated for trial by military commission. But authorities determined that the intelligence information that led to Padilla, a US citizen born in Brooklyn, could not be introduced in federal court. Nor could the statements Padilla gave interrogators during more than three years in military custody. Padilla eventually was transferred to the civilian system for trial on terrorism-related offenses separate from the supposed "dirty bomb" plot that triggered his capture. He was sentenced to seventeen years and four months' imprisonment and sent to the federal "supermax" penitentiary in Florence, Colorado.

Binyam Mohamed faced preliminary hearings at military commissions on charges that carried a potential life term. But London had requested the return of all British citizens and residents, so without public explanation, the Bush administration dropped those charges and cleared Mohamed for release in January 2009. He returned to Britain, where the government granted him permanent residency and paid him approximately $1.5 million to settle allegations that British authorities were complicit in torture he suffered in the CIA's rendition program.[2]

There also were lenient outcomes for most of the other commissions defendants. After his transfer to an Australian prison, David Hicks was released in December 2008. He promptly flouted his plea bargain by publishing a memoir, *Guantanamo: My Journey*, that sold more than thirty thousand copies and was shortlisted for an Australian literary prize.[3] The Australian government's effort to seize the proceeds ended with humiliation in July 2012, when authorities dropped their lawsuit and were ordered to pay Hicks's court costs.

"In a way, I feel that this has cleared my name and I hope now that the Australian government acknowledges that Guantanamo Bay and everything connected with it is illegal," Hicks said at the courthouse.[4]

The Pentagon initially had described Ibrahim al-Qosi, another of the four original commissions defendants, as an al Qaeda financier who "signed checks on behalf of Osama bin Laden."[5] When his case finally went before a commission in 2010, however, prosecutors had dropped all references to terrorist financing. Instead, in a plea bargain, Qosi admitted only that he had been "in charge of the kitchen at the [Star of Jihad] compound" near Jalalabad and that at other times he worked as a driver, as a bodyguard, and on a mortar crew.[6]

Officially, Qosi was sentenced to fourteen years' imprisonment. In fact, his attorneys had made a secret side deal providing for his release and repatriation to Sudan within two years.[7] In July 2012, he arrived in Khartoum.

Of the inaugural defendants, only Ali al-Bahlul, the al Qaeda propagandist, received a severe sentence. Bahlul effectively asked for it, refusing to contest the charges and ordering his defense attorney to stay silent during the trial.

"We have fought and we fight and will fight any government that governs America," he told the commission. He waved a boat and an airplane he had made from paper and recited "The Storm of the Airplanes," his poem glorifying 9/11.[8] After this diatribe, the military commission sentenced him to life imprisonment. Yet even this was more lenient than he might have expected from civilian justice; unlike a federal court, the military commission could not foreclose the possibility, however remote, of parole or repatriation.

Salim Hamdan, meanwhile, has been free in Yemen since early 2009.

That, in practice, a new system intended to deal harshly with aliens ended up being far more forgiving than the existing federal courts points out another issue affecting commissions: Their lack of experience, expertise, and established legitimacy has led to erratic and even counterintuitive results. Even plausible convictions will remain clouded for years, through mandatory appeals through the new Court of Military Commission Review, the DC Circuit, and, ultimately, the Supreme Court. Dozens of legal issues that long have been settled in the federal courts and courts-martial remain unresolved by the terror courts, meaning that appellate judges will have to revisit rights, rules, and procedures established by the existing justice systems and determine their application, if any, to the commissions experiment.

At the same time, the commissions project has proven no solution to the dilemma created by American detainee practices following 9/11: providing a venue for prosecuting defendants whose cases are infected by government misconduct. The Bush military order of November 13, 2001, authorized introduction of evidence obtained even through torture if a "reasonable person" would find the information "probative." Yet even under so permissive a standard, military prosecutors like Stuart Couch found that another open-ended provision of Bush's order—that trials be "full and fair"—precluded them from bringing cases built on prisoner abuse. Confounding the expectations of their political superiors, deeply held precepts of professional ethics, military honor, and legal obligations prevented such officers from casting aside traditional principles of law in favor of rough justice.

Trial standards grew successively higher under the Supreme Court's *Hamdan v. Rumsfeld* decision in 2006, the first Military Commissions Act passed in its wake, and the further revisions President Obama obtained through the Military Commissions Act of 2009. The result has meant continuing limbo for detainees subjected to the harshest abuse, including two Guantanamo prisoners Defense Secretary Rumsfeld authorized for special interrogation plans. Nothing has happened in the case of Mohammed al-Qahtani, the alleged Twentieth Hijacker, since commissions Convening Authority Susan Crawford rejected his prosecution in 2008. The "torture" US interrogators inflicted on Qahtani "has tainted everything going forward," Crawford said, and she applied the standard remedy when government misconduct pervades a criminal case: dismissal of charges.[9] Crawford acknowledged that her action posed a dilemma for the incoming president, Barack Obama. "What do you do with him now if you don't charge him and try him? I would be hesitant to say, 'Let him go,'" she said.[10]

Meanwhile, the second such prisoner, Mohamedou Ould Slahi, has sought freedom through a habeas corpus petition in federal court. In April 2010, a federal district court ordered him released.

"The government's problem is that its proof that [Slahi] gave material support to terrorists is so attenuated, or so tainted by coercion and mistreatment, or so classified, that it cannot support a successful criminal prosecution. Nevertheless, the government wants to hold [Slahi] indefinitely, because of its concern that he might renew his oath to al-Qaida and become a terrorist upon his release. That concern may indeed be well-founded," wrote Judge James Robertson, but a court "may not permit a man to be held indefinitely upon suspicion, or because of the government's prediction that he may do unlawful acts in the future."

In November 2010, however, the DC Circuit vacated Robertson's opinion and sent the case back to the district court for further fact-finding.

A SEISMIC BLOW CAME JUST as this book was going to press. On October 16, 2012, the DC Circuit vacated Salim Hamdan's conviction, ruling that a military commission lacked jurisdiction over the charge against him, material support for terrorism. The decision immediately placed in jeopardy every military commission conviction since the experiment began. All seven defendants had been charged with material support, including David Hicks, against whom it was the only charge.

Writing for a unanimous three-member panel, Judge Brett Kavanaugh adopted an argument that Hamdan's lawyer, Lieutenant Commander Charlie Swift, had raised before Colonel Brownback's military commission in 2004: that material support for terrorism simply was not a war crime. Since the military commission had no jurisdiction over civilian offenses, it could not try Hamdan on the charge.

"When Hamdan committed the conduct in question," from 1996 to 2001, "the international law of war proscribed a variety of war crimes, including forms of terrorism. At that time, however, the international law of war did *not* proscribe material support for terrorism as a war crime," Kavanaugh wrote, and, as the executive branch acknowledged, it still didn't. The US Military Commissions Act of 2006 listed material support for terrorism as a war crime, and that might establish it as a punishable offense going forward. But federal statutes in effect before Hamdan's capture relied on international law to determine the scope of war crimes and thus "did *not* authorize prosecution for material support for terrorism."

Kavanaugh observed that the Military Commissions Act itself declared that the statute codifies "offenses that have traditionally been triable by military commissions" and "does not establish new crimes that did not exist before its enactment." The statement, the court said, reflected Congress's understanding that "the US Constitution bars it from enacting punitive ex post facto laws," that is, laws that punish people for conduct that was lawful when undertaken. But "Congress believed that the Act codified no new crimes and thus posed no ex post facto problem."

Kavanaugh made no aside regarding that obviously disingenuous congressional gambit. But even accepting the legislative declaration at face value, "Congress's premise was incorrect," he wrote. The statute does codify some new war crimes, including "material support for terrorism."

Hamdan's name already denoted a landmark Supreme Court decision reining in excesses of executive power. Now it also stood for the policy failures of establishing the military commission apparatus altogether, an experiment that has cost the nation hundreds of millions of dollars, untold focus from other priorities, and continuing damage to its international reputation. For material support for terrorism already was a crime under domestic law when Hamdan worked for Osama bin Laden, and federal prosecutors could have charged him with it in US District Court—as they did John Walker Lindh, who received a twenty-year sentence after pleading guilty to a far briefer association with the Taliban. By insisting on trial by military commission, the Bush administration destroyed its chance of punishing Hamdan at all.

Yet the DC Circuit's decision implicated more than Salim Hamdan, more than the other material support convictions. It also cast a cloud over another charge filed against every commissions defendant: conspiracy.

Hamdan had been acquitted of conspiracy, so in his case there was no need for the DC Circuit to rule on its validity as a war crime. But the same reasoning that invalidated material support largely applied as well to conspiracy, which long had been disfavored as a criminal charge under the international law of war. In the Supreme Court's 2006 *Hamdan* decision, a four-justice plurality held that conspiracy was *not* a valid war crime; a fifth justice, Anthony Kennedy, reserved the question for a future case. That case could come sooner rather than later. Ali al-Bahlul was appealing his military commission conviction, which included a charge of conspiracy.

The appeals court decision, quickly dubbed *Hamdan II,* had resonance beyond its actual holding. First was the fact that it came from the DC Circuit—a court famous for the extraordinary deference it had paid to the Bush and Obama administrations over terrorism-related questions. So conservative was the DC Circuit's reputation that architects of the Military Commissions Act made it the exclusive forum for appealing convictions from the commissions system, displacing the US Court of Appeals for the Armed Forces, which heard appeals from other military courts.

The circuit judges who voted with Hamdan all were dyed-in-the-wool conservatives. Two were Reagan appointees, Douglas Ginsburg and David Sentelle. The third was Brett Kavanaugh, who had been associate White House counsel and staff secretary to George W. Bush before joining the appeals court in 2006. Kavanaugh wrote the opinion vacating Hamdan's conviction.

■

Courts-martial developed as a mechanism for maintaining discipline in the ranks by swiftly punishing soldiers for transgressions in the field. Military commissions, to the extent that they differed from courts-martial, historically were ad hoc tribunals convened to dispense similar justice to enemy prisoners proximate to the theater of war. Until 2001, they never were envisioned as a permanent element of the American justice system. In World War II, for instance, Axis war criminals captured by the Allies were quickly tried by military commissions. But commissions were considered an expedient necessitated by wartime conditions, not a preferred form of justice. They were discontinued by the 1950s, and Nazi suspects later discovered in hiding were tried for their crimes in federal court.[11]

Following 9/11, none of the government agencies responsible for fighting terrorism—including the CIA, the FBI, the Justice Department, and the Defense Department—contended that the existing court system was unequipped to prosecute terrorists or sought establishment of a permanent, parallel justice system offshore. All of the Guantanamo detainees prosecuted by commission could also have been tried in federal court, and the federal judiciary's track record suggests that they likely would have been convicted more rapidly and received stiffer sentences. In effect, today's military commissions are the legal equivalent of a war of choice.

During the Bush administration, commissions were conceived and championed by officials whose primary motive was redistributing powers from the legislative and judicial branches to the executive.

Commissions were an expression of that ideology rather than a pragmatic response to an irresolvable problem.

Barack Obama hardly shared that agenda, and nothing in his record suggests that he would have instigated commissions had he been president on 9/11. But Obama was persuaded that his political capital was better spent on other priorities—health care, economic recovery, the Iraq drawdown—than on dismantling the legal infrastructure Bush's lawyers had labored to create. The Obama administration apparently believed that blessing commissions would pave the way to advance more important parts of its agenda. Deciding that adjustments to their procedures would make commissions sufficiently just, Obama gave the terror courts a bipartisan imprimatur that virtually ensures they will be a fixture of American law for years to come.

The military justice system, however, was not designed for criminal conspiracies or high-stakes national security cases, and few of the JAGs who serve as its attorneys and judges have experience in such matters. The government has attempted to mitigate that shortcoming by seconding a massive team of Justice Department lawyers and FBI agents to assist commissions, but the different cultures and inherent competition between two very different institutional cultures creates yet another obstacle for the offshore legal experiment. The inexperience of military judges adds another level of uncertainty to the Guantanamo proceedings. Their unfamiliarity with the complex legal questions regularly raised before them may increase the chance for errors that could mar convictions. At the same time, the military judges are acutely aware that federal courts, international authorities, and the legal establishment are scrutinizing their courtrooms for signs of unfairness. In the 9/11 case and others, that concern may have resulted in indulgence toward defendants, if not outright leniency, that a federal judge would never show in a similar case.

It's too late, as Admiral Bulkeley would have insisted, to do commissions right the first time. The question remains whether they can be done right at all.

■

After completing his three-year billet at the Office of Military Commissions, in 2006 Lieutenant Colonel Stuart Couch moved on to serve three years on the Navy–Marine Corps Court of Criminal Appeals. While receiving high marks as a judge, he was passed over for promotion twice and, under the Marine Corps' up-or-out system, that meant the end of his military career. He hung up his uniform and returned to North Carolina, taking a job at a law firm in Charlotte.

This was Couch's second experience in private practice, and he liked it no more than the first. His greatest satisfaction had come as a judge, but he lacked the political connections to get on the short lists even for the lowest rungs of the state or federal judiciaries. Moreover, he was a Republican, and both the governor and the president were Democrats. But along the way, Couch had found some admirers—including Neal Katyal, who had been his adversary when Couch was prosecuting Salim Hamdan.

Katyal now had a senior position in the Obama administration —he would become acting solicitor general—and on his recommendation Attorney General Eric Holder appointed Couch a judge of the US Immigration Court for North Carolina.

When Couch finished his service in the Office of Military Commissions, he received a medal, as is typical for officers when they complete an assignment. On the wall of his small office in Charlotte, Couch hung the citation he received along with it.

"Lieutenant Colonel Vernon S. Couch, United States Marine Corps, distinguished himself by exceptionally meritorious service as Senior Prosecutor, Office of Military Commissions," it reads. "Colonel Couch's outstanding professional skill and ceaseless efforts resulted in major contributions to the development of cases against al Qaida members detained at Guantanamo Bay, Cuba, and furthered the United States' objectives in the Global War on Terrorism. Colonel Couch served as lead military commission prosecutor in United States v. Hamdan and was the primary liaison with the Solicitor

General and Department of Justice attorneys involved in the historic Hamdan v. Rumsfeld United States Supreme Court decision. His judgment, organizational ability, and moral clarity resulted in major contributions to the national security of the United States." In sum, it concluded, his service "exemplified the Marine Corps core values of 'Honor, Courage, and Commitment.'"

It was signed: Donald Rumsfeld.

Notes

Unless otherwise noted, quotations in this book were relayed by a source with direct knowledge or obtained from materials reviewed by the author.

Prologue

1. Richard W. Stewart, *The United States Army in Afghanistan: Operation Enduring Freedom, October 2001–March 2002* (Washington, DC: US Army Center of Military History, 2004), 23–25.
2. See also Steve Coll, "A Secret Hunt Unravels in Afghanistan," *Washington Post*, Feb. 22, 2004.
3. See also findings of fact by Capt. Keith Allred, Military Judge, *U.S. v. Hamdan*, Dec. 17, 2007.
4. Translation of letter read by US official to author.
5. Carol Rosenberg, "Army Officer Recounts Chauffeur's Capture," *Miami Herald*, Dec. 7, 2007.
6. Hamdan affidavit, Feb. 9, 2004.
7. Lawrence Wright, *The Looming Tower* (New York: Knopf, 2006), 154.

1. Tater

1. The P. & P. Chair Company continued making Kennedy Rockers until going out of business in 2008, at which point a rival manufacturer acquired rights to the design and began producing them in Troutman, NC, seventy-five miles away. "Troutman Chair Acquires Kennedy Rocker," *Furniture Today*, Feb. 17, 2009.
2. Joe Killian, "Alcohol Comes to Asheboro," *News and Record* (Greensboro, NC), July 30, 2008.
3. Jeffrey E. Stern, "For God and Country," *Duke* magazine, September–October 2007.
4. Ibid.
5. "Marine Leaves Brig After Serving Time in Stolen Arms Case," Associated Press Newswires, June 23, 2000.

6. Epictetus, *The Enchiridion* 35, trans. Elizabeth Carter, Internet Classics Archive, http://classics.mit.edu//Epictetus/epicench.html.

7. Richard A. Serrano, "Marine Gets 6 Months in Gondola Case," *Los Angeles Times,* May 11, 1999.

8. "Allegations of Deception About Flaws in Marine V-22 Osprey," *60 Minutes,* CBS News, Jan. 21, 2001.

9. In December 2000, a Marine general had told a news conference that 73.2 percent of Ospreys were clear to fly. The real maintenance logs showed the true percentage was 38.

10. Mary Pat Flaherty, "Marines Charged in Falsifying Records," *Washington Post,* Aug. 18, 2001.

2. Military Order

1. Dana Milbank, "White House Counsel Office Now Full of Clinton Legal Foes," *Washington Post,* Jan. 30, 2001.

2. Jane Mayer, "The Hidden Power," *New Yorker,* July 3, 2006.

3. Jess Bravin, "Judge Alito's View of the Presidency: Expansive Powers," *Wall Street Journal,* Jan. 4, 2006.

4. Alexander Hamilton, Federalist No. 70. The essay is largely an argument against a "plural" executive as in the ancient Roman Republic, where two consuls were elected annually to run the government, or the structure of some American colonies where an executive council administered affairs of state. Some states, such as Massachusetts and New Hampshire, still have executive councils that exercise some executive powers alongside the governor. Elsewhere, in Federalist No. 69, Hamilton argues that the American president would be no king, explaining various ways in which his power would be far more limited than that of the British crown.

5. See, e.g., Peter Slevin, "Scholar Stands by Post-9/11 Writings on Torture, Domestic Eavesdropping," *Washington Post,* Dec. 26, 2005.

6. John C. Yoo, "What Education?" *Harvard Crimson,* June 8, 1989.

7. John C. Yoo, "Just Say No to a Class Gift," *Harvard Crimson,* Apr. 12, 1989.

8. John H. Richardson, "Is John Yoo a Monster?" *Esquire,* May 12, 2008, online interview transcript.

9. John C. Yoo, Editorial Dissent, *Harvard Crimson,* Dec. 9, 1987; "Freeing Our Arms in Honduras," *Harvard Crimson,* Mar. 23, 1988; "To the Gulf Station: Use It or Lose It," *Harvard Crimson,* Oct. 29, 1987.

10. John C. Yoo, Editorial, *Harvard Crimson,* Mar. 7, 1988. Yoo told the author that he was assigned to write the editorial.

11. Richardson, "Is John Yoo a Monster?"

12. Ruth Bader Ginsburg was a 1980 Carter appointee to the DC Circuit. President Bill Clinton elevated her to the Supreme Court in 1993.

13. Richardson, "Is John Yoo a Monster?"

14. Paul M. Barrett, "A Young Lawyer Helps Chart Shift in Foreign Policy," *Wall Street Journal,* Sept. 12, 2005.

15. Jess Bravin and John D. McKinnon, "If History Is a Guide, Gore's Latest Tactic May Be a Long Shot," *Wall Street Journal,* Nov. 28, 2000.

16. John Yoo, "Bush Has a Federal Case," opinion article, *Wall Street Journal,* Nov. 16, 2000. Should a judicial stalemate emerge, Yoo scouted another route to the White House: the Florida legislature, controlled by Republicans, could ignore the vote tally and appoint the presidential electors itself.

17. See *Reynolds v. Sims,* 377 U.S. 533 (1964).

18. John C. Yoo, "The Continuation of Politics by Other Means: The Original Understanding of War Powers," *California Law Review,* March 1996.

19. Louis Fisher, *Military Tribunals and Presidential Power* (Lawrence: University Press of Kansas, 2005), 15.

20. Richardson, "Is John Yoo a Monster?"

21. It cited the touchstone of Congress's assertion of authority over armed conflict, the War Powers Resolution, adopted in 1973 over President Nixon's veto. That legislation, passed to prevent presidents from unilaterally launching wars, put limits on executive authority to send troops into combat abroad and required their withdrawal within ninety days absent congressional authorization. The Bush administration, like all administrations before it, considered the War Powers Resolution unconstitutional. Nevertheless, out of "comity" with another branch of government—and fear of a constitutional showdown that could end with the Supreme Court setting the precise limits of executive authority— presidents grudgingly had followed its guidelines. The 9/11 measure declared itself "consistent with" the War Powers Resolution rather than compliant with it.

22. The Tonkin Gulf Resolution, adopted August 7, 1964, authorized US assistance only to members and "protocol states" of the Southeast Asia Treaty Organization, a now-defunct NATO-like regional defense pact including the United States, Cambodia, Laos, New Zealand, Pakistan, the Philippines, South Korea, South Vietnam, and Thailand, along with former colonial powers Britain and France. The Tonkin Gulf Resolution

was more limited than the 9/11 Resolution in other ways as well: it cited the United Nations Charter as a source of authority and set conditions for its own termination, including by congressional vote.

23. In a signing statement, Bush himself underscored this point. The resolution recognizes "the authority of the President under the Constitution to take action to deter and prevent acts of terrorism against the United States," the document said. "In signing this resolution, I maintain the longstanding position of the executive branch regarding the President's constitutional authority to use force, including the Armed Forces of the United States." George W. Bush, Statement on Signing the Authorization for Use of Military Force, Sept. 18, 2001.

24. John Yoo, "The President's Constitutional Authority to Conduct Military Operations Against Terrorists and Nations Supporting Them, Memorandum Opinion for the Deputy Counsel to the President," Office of Legal Counsel, Sept. 25, 2001.

25. Richard W. Stevenson and Adam Liptak, "Cheney Defends Eavesdropping Without Warrants," *New York Times,* Dec. 21, 2005.

26. Memorandum for Alberto R. Gonzales, Counsel to the President, and William J. Haynes, II, General Counsel, Department of Defense, from John C. Yoo, Deputy Assistant Attorney General, and Robert J. Delahunty, Special Counsel, *Re: Authority for Use of Military Force to Combat Terrorist Activities Within the United States* (Oct. 23, 2001).

27. Louis Fisher, *Nazi Saboteurs on Trial,* 2nd ed. (Lawrence: University Press of Kansas, 2005), 35.

28. Ibid., 42.

29. Ibid., 80.

30. Memorandum for Alberto R. Gonzales, Counsel to the President, from Patrick F. Philbin, Deputy Assistant Attorney General, *Re: Legality of the Use of Military Commissions to Try Terrorists* (Nov. 6, 2001).

31. Philippe Sands, *Torture Team* (New York: Palgrave Macmillan, 2008), 95.

32. The Marine Corps, which is part of the Navy Department, has a similar position called the staff judge advocate to the commandant. Unlike the other services, the Marines do not have a separate Judge Advocate General's Corps, and according to recruiting literature, Marine lawyers "do not like to be called Marine JAGs." Nevertheless, herein the term *JAGs* is used to refer broadly to uniformed lawyers in all military branches.

33. See Vanessa Blum, "Pentagon Aims at JAG Corps," *Legal Times,* June 16, 2003.

34. Shiffrin testimony, Senate Armed Services Committee, June 17, 2008.
35. "Options for Bringing Criminal Prosecutions in Federal District Courts," Draft, Sept. 26, 2001. Reviewed by author.
36. The district judge, Leonard Sand, had a long history with such issues. In 1957, Sand was working in the solicitor general's office when the Eisenhower administration lost a Supreme Court case called *Reid v. Covert*, involving a woman who killed her husband, a US Air Force sergeant stationed in England. The Court initially sided with the government, ruling that Mrs. Clarice Covert could be tried by court-martial without benefit of the Fifth and Sixth Amendments. But the justices then agreed to reconsider the case and came out the other way. On second thought, Justice Hugo Black wrote, "we reject the idea that when the United States acts against citizens abroad it can do so free of the Bill of Rights."

    Forty-three years later, the embassy bombing trial gave Sand the chance to reduce Black's opinion to near irrelevance. While the Fourth Amendment technically might protect defendant Wadih el-Hage, a Lebanese-born American citizen who had been living in Nairobi, Sand found it per se unreasonable to expect US agents operating overseas to obtain warrants. That effectively freed federal agents from many of the rules that govern domestic investigations. "Imposition of a warrant requirement in the context of foreign intelligence searches conducted abroad would be a significant and undue burden on the Executive," Sand wrote.
37. Formal government documents usually transliterated bin Laden's first name as *Usama* rather than the *Osama* favored in the popular press. *UBL* was the typical government shorthand for the al Qaeda leader.
38. Barton Gellman and Jo Becker, "Angler—The Cheney Vice Presidency: 'A Different Understanding with the President,'" *Washington Post*, June 24, 2007.
39. Alberto R. Gonzales, "Waging War Within the Constitution," *Texas Tech Law Review*, 2010.
40. Barton Gellman and Jo Becker, "Angler—The Cheney Vice Presidency."
41. Jess Bravin, "Bush Signs Executive Order Establishing Military Tribunals to Try Terror Suspects," *Wall Street Journal*, Nov. 14, 2001.
42. Transcript, "Vice President Cheney Speaks to Chamber of Commerce," *Market Coverage-Morning*, CNNfn, Nov. 14, 2001.
43. David Glazier, "Precedents Lost: The Neglected History of the Military Commission," *Virginia Journal of International Law*, Fall 2005.

44. Yoo, "Politics by Other Means."

45. Office of Professional Responsibility, Department of Justice, *Investigation into the Office of Legal Counsel's Memoranda Concerning Issues Relating to the Central Intelligence Agency's Use of "Enhanced Interrogation Techniques" on Suspected Terrorists,* July 29, 2009.

46. *Henry V,* act 4, scene 7. In 2010, however, Henry was convicted of war crimes by a panel of Supreme Court justices and federal circuit judges participating in an annual mock trial exercise at the Shakespeare Theatre Company in Washington. "We applied the 'evolving standards of decency that mark the progress of a maturing society,'" said Justice Samuel Alito, who delivered the opinion. Jess Bravin, "Supreme Night Court," *Wall Street Journal,* Mar. 14, 2011.

47. Coke's significance to Anglo-American law is evident, literally, to all who pass through the Supreme Court's bronze doors: He is depicted in the doors' bas-reliefs illustrating the evolution of justice. In his scene, "England's Lord Chief Justice Coke bars King James I from the 'King's Court,' making the court, by law, independent of the executive branch of government." "The Bronze Doors," Information Sheet, Office of the Curator, US Supreme Court, May 4, 2010.

48. Sir Edward Coke, *The Selected Writings and Speeches of Sir Edward Coke,* ed. Steve Sheppard, vol. 3 (Indianapolis, IN: Liberty Fund, 2003), available at http://oll.libertyfund.org/title/913/62278.

49. *Reid v. Covert,* 354 U.S. 1 (1957)

50. Glazier, "Precedents Lost"; James Hutson, "Nathan Hale Revisited," *Library of Congress Information Bulletin,* July/August 2003.

51. Glazier, "Precedents Lost."

52. Alan C. Cate, *Founding Fighters* (Westport, CT: Praeger Security International, 2006), 116.

53. Glazier, "Precedents Lost."

54. *Jecker v. Montgomery,* 54 U.S. (13 How.) 498 (1851).

55. House committee report, quoted in Glazier, "Precedents Lost."

56. Quoted in Fisher, *Military Tribunals,* 38.

57. Quoted in Glazier, "Precedents Lost."

58. Fisher, *Nazi Saboteurs,* 120.

59. Jess Bravin, "What War Captives Faced in Japanese Prison Camps, and How U.S. Responded," *Wall Street Journal,* Apr. 7, 2005.

60. Tim Maga, *Judgment at Tokyo* (Lexington: University Press of Kentucky, 2001), 96.

61. Michael Ratner, "Moving Toward a Police State (Or Have We Arrived?):

Secret Military Tribunals, Mass Arrests and Disappearances, Wiretapping and Torture," *CounterPunch*, Nov. 20, 2001.

62. Pam Belluck, "Hue and Murmur Over Curbed Rights," *New York Times*, Nov. 17, 2001.

3. Welcome to the Dungeon

1. Lloyd Cutler, "Lessons on Tribunals—From 1942," opinion article, *Wall Street Journal*, Dec. 31, 2001.

2. *Coffin v. United States*, 156 U.S. 432 (1895).

3. *Black v. State*, 1 Tex.App. 368 (1876).

4. In 2006, the mean elapsed time from sentence to execution was 135 months, according to the US Bureau of Justice Statistics, http://www.ojp .gov/bjs/pub/html/cp/2006/tables/cp06st17.htm.

5. "Providing a fair trial" had to be weighed against other "important objectives," Douglas Feith, the Pentagon policy chief, said in response to follow-up questions.

   Jim Haynes was asked why the administration was creating a parallel trial system instead of using existing procedures. "The cynical interpretation out there is that the main difference between this and the UCMJ is that the UCMJ allows people to appeal up to the Supreme Court," a reporter said.

   "That would be a cynical interpretation," Haynes replied.

6. This outcome wasn't sufficiently dramatic for the television series *NCIS*. In its adaptation of the case, titled "Hung Out to Dry" and first aired September 23, 2003, a Marine paratrooper on a night jump fatally falls through the roof of a car containing two young lovers on a date.

7. David S. Cloud and Neil King Jr., "U.S. Seeks to Question Senegal Detainee Concerning Ties to Alleged Terror Plot," *Wall Street Journal*, Jan. 28, 2000.

8. Christopher J. Chipello, "Canada Probes Possible Link to Tunisian Synagogue Blast," *Wall Street Journal*, May 2, 2002.

9. "Two Jailed Over Tunisia Bombing," BBC News, Feb. 5, 2009.

10. Ralph Blincoe, "Mark Fallon Farewell," Feb. 28, 2008. Unpublished speech by NCIS deputy director.

11. Craig Whitlock, "Probe of USS *Cole* Bombing Unravels," *Washington Post*, May 4, 2008.

12. 9/11 Commission testimony, Apr. 8, 2004.

13. The distant Pacific islands, acquired during America's nineteenth-

century expansion or in the aftermath of World War II, were a different story. Under laws establishing the federal court system, Midway, Wake, and other Pacific islands fell within the District of Hawaii. That meant a federal district judge in Honolulu could try to assert jurisdiction over a prison there. Because Hawaii was in the Ninth Circuit, whose San Francisco–based appellate court was considered the most liberal in the federal judiciary, the Ninth Circuit was the last place Yoo wanted to see Bush administration policies tested.

14. It is unclear who first proposed Guantanamo as a prison location. The base was mentioned by various officials as different agencies and task forces, often walled off from communication with one another, assembled administration policy. See, e.g., Karen Greenberg, *The Least Worst Place* (New York: Oxford University Press, 2009), 6.

15. Lease reprinted in Michael Ratner and Ellen Ray, *Guantanamo: What the World Should Know* (White River Junction, VT: Chelsea Green, 2004), 97.

16. Quoted in Edward C. Keefer, Charles S. Sampson, and Louis J. Smith, eds., *Foreign Relations of the United States, 1961–1963*, vol. 11: *Cuban Missile Crisis and Aftermath* (Washington, DC: GPO, 1966), archived at www.state.gov.

17. M. E. Murphy, *The History of Guantanamo Bay, 1494–1964*, http://www.nsgtmo.navy.mil/history/gtmohistorymurphyvol1ch21.htm.

18. At home, folk singer Pete Seeger had a hit in 1966 with "Guantanamera" ("the girl from Guantanamo"), which set a traditional island tune to a poem by José Martí, the nineteenth-century Cuban revolutionary. Seeger, blacklisted during the McCarthy era, never was invited to perform at the Cold War outpost. See also Murphy, *History of Guantanamo Bay*.

19. See also Jonathan S. Landay, "U.S. Forces in Cuba Accused of Abuse," *Christian Science Monitor*, Feb. 16, 1995.

20. Memorandum for William J. Haynes II, General Counsel, Department of Defense, from Patrick F. Philbin, Deputy Assistant Attorney General, and John C. Yoo, Deputy Assistant Attorney General, *Re: Possible Habeas Jurisdiction over Aliens Held in Guantanamo Bay, Cuba* (Dec. 28, 2001).

21. Jess Bravin, "Guantanamo Bay Detainees Seek Hearings; Lawyers Question Holding Suspected Terrorists Without Offering Legal Case Against Them," *Wall Street Journal*, July 3, 2002.

22. Douglas J. Feith, *War and Decision* (New York: Harper, 2008), 159.

23. Ivan Roman, "Prisoners Face Hard Time in Cuba," *Orlando Sentinel*, Jan. 10, 2002.

24. Sue Anne Pressley, "Preparing for Role in War on Terror; Navy Base in Cuba to House Taliban, al Qaeda Detainees," *Washington Post,* Jan. 10, 2002.

25. Tony Winton, "In Guantanamo Bay, Prison Camp for War Prisoners from Afghanistan Goes Up amid Massive Security," Associated Press Newswires, Jan. 9, 2002.

26. Carol Rosenberg, "A New Alcatraz Rises—Guantanamo Ready for Taliban," *Miami Herald,* Jan. 10, 2002.

27. Angus MacSwan, "Chain-Link Cells await Taliban, al Qaeda Prisoners," Reuters News, Jan. 9, 2002.

28. Jess Bravin, "U.S. Dismisses Queries About Cuba Detainees," *Wall Street Journal,* Jan. 23, 2002.

29. William Lowther and Carol Rosenberg, "Horror of Camp X-Ray; First Pictures Show Use of Sensory Deprivation to Soften Up Suspects for Interrogation," *Mail on Sunday,* Jan. 20, 2002. There was nothing "exclusive" about an official photograph the Pentagon distributed to news organizations and posted on its own website for anyone to see.

30. Andy Rudd, "Cuffed, Masked and Humiliated," *Sunday Mirror,* Jan. 20, 2002.

31. Kamal Ahmed and Peter Beaumont, "Blair Warns Bush on Taliban Suspects," *Observer* (London), Jan. 20, 2002.

32. Jess Bravin, Jackie Calmes, and Carla Anne Robbins, "Status of Guantanamo Bay Detainees Is Focus of Bush Security Team's Meeting," *Wall Street Journal,* Jan. 28, 2002.

33. Jess Bravin and Keith Johnson, "Military-Tribunal Plan for Terror Suspects Runs into Resistance from Allies, Congress," *Wall Street Journal,* Nov. 26, 2001.

34. Jess Bravin, "Judge Won't Hear Case of Prisoners Being Held in Cuba," *Wall Street Journal,* Feb. 22, 2002.

35. *Johnson v. Eisentrager,* 339 U.S. 763 (1950).

36. Jess Bravin, "Group to Ask OAS to Step in to Change U.S. Treatment of Prisoners Held in Cuba," *Wall Street Journal,* Feb. 25, 2002; Bravin, "Panel Says U.S. Policy on Detainees in Cuba Breaks International Law," *Wall Street Journal,* Mar. 14, 2002.

37. Jess Bravin, "U.S. Army Has 30 Ways to Convince al Qaeda Prisoners to Talk, Maybe," *Wall Street Journal,* Apr. 26, 2002.

38. Dana Priest and Barton Gellman, "U.S. Decries Abuse but Defends Interrogations," *Washington Post,* Dec. 26, 2002.

39. Jess Bravin and Gary Fields, "How Do U.S. Interrogators Make a

Captured Terrorist Talk?" *Wall Street Journal*, Mar. 4, 2003; Peter Finn, Joby Warrick, and Julie Tate, "How a Detainee Became an Asset," *Washington Post*, Aug. 29, 2009.

40. Nevertheless, the Bush administration had refused to acknowledge the existence of secret CIA prisons or provide access to the International Committee of the Red Cross or any other human rights monitor to detainees held there. The Red Cross was present at Guantanamo, but not because the administration wanted them there; a JAG colonel, getting no clear instructions from Washington, had followed traditional military protocols and invited the Geneva monitors to Guantanamo when the prison opened in January 2002. Greenberg, *Least Worst Place*, 62.

4. Survival, Evasion, Resistance, and Escape

1. US officials often based such claims on a document seized in 2000 by British police called the Manchester Manual. "The 18th chapter focuses on how detainees should conduct themselves while imprisoned or held captive . . . [including] various statements such as 'the brothers must insist on proving that torture was inflicted on them before a judge.'" Shanita Simmons, "Manchester Manual: The Code of Conduct for Terrorism," Joint Task Force Guantanamo Public Affairs, US Department of Defense, Aug. 14, 2007. According to one analysis, however, the Manchester Manual was not an al Qaeda document intended for terrorists targeting Western targets but rather produced in the early 1990s by Egyptian Islamists opposed to the regime of Egypt's then-president, Hosni Mubarak. The manual did not advise making false claims of torture, it contends, but rather offered guidance for resisting the actual torture militants likely would face if arrested by Egyptian security agents. Kurt Eichenwald, *500 Days* (New York: Touchstone, 2012), 544.

2. The song "Bodies" by the heavy metal band Drowning Pool often was employed by interrogators. US Department of Justice, Office of the Inspector General, *A Review of the FBI's Involvement in and Observations of Detainee Interrogations in Guantanamo Bay, Afghanistan, and Iraq*, May 2008, 124 n96. Drowning Pool drummer Mike Luce later expressed surprise. "If you write a song, you never in your wildest dreams think someone is going to use that song to inflict pain on another human being," he said. Even so, in 2009 Drowning Pool accepted a Defense Department invitation to entertain troops at Guantanamo. "Those guys

just wanted to see some rock 'n' roll," he said. "I mean, come on. Nobody's solving the world's problems here." S. I. Rose, "How Rock Bands Got Backstage at Gitmo Prison," *AOL News,* June 27, 2010. "Bodies" also was a favorite of Jared Loughner, who in a January 2011 mass shooting killed six, including US District Judge John Roll, and wounded thirteen, among them Congresswoman Gabrielle Giffords, in Tucson, Arizona. J. Freedom du Lac, "In Arizona Case, a Chillingly Familiar Song," *Washington Post,* Jan. 11, 2011.

3. Senate Committee on Armed Services, *Inquiry into the Treatment of Detainees in U.S. Custody,* Nov. 20, 2008, 103. The instructors were John Rankin and Christopher Ross.

4. Many of the details previously had been reported, as Bowden acknowledged, in such newspapers as the *New York Times, Sunday Times* of London, *Wall Street Journal,* and *Washington Post.*

5. Jess Bravin, "U.S. Army Has 30 Ways to Convince Al Qaeda Prisoners to Talk, Maybe," *Wall Street Journal,* April 26, 2002.

6. Like teachers anywhere, Huachuca faculty members compared the current crop of students unfavorably to generations past. "All they know is hip-hop and Nintendo," said Sergeant First Class Anthony Novacek. "They don't know how to initiate a conversation, or make small talk," said Sergeant First Class Kelly Sanders.

7. Haynes testimony, Senate Armed Services Committee, June 17, 2008.

8. Mark Mazzetti, "Ex-Pentagon Lawyers Face Inquiry on Interrogation Role," *New York Times,* June 17, 2008.

9. Shiffrin testimony, Senate Armed Services Committee, June 17, 2008.

10. Ogrisseg, Baumgartner testimony, Senate Armed Services Committee, June 17, 2008.

11. Although this memorandum remains classified at publication date, it is referenced in a redacted Aug. 4, 2004, memorandum to OLC from the CIA, released under a Freedom of Information Act lawsuit filed by the American Civil Liberties Union.

12. Included in email from Mark Fallon to Sam McMahon, Oct. 28, 2002.

13. *Rochin v. California,* 342 U.S. 165 (1952).

14. John Goetz et al., trans. Christopher Sultan, "The Career of Prisoner No. 760," *Spiegel Online International* (Hamburg), Sept. 10, 2008, http://www.spiegel.de/international/world/from-germany-to-guantanamo-the-career-of-prisoner-no-760-a-583193-4.html.

15. Ibid.

16. Transcript, Combatant Status Review Tribunal for Mohamedou Ould

Slahi, US Department of Defense, Dec. 8, 2004 (hereafter cited as Slahi CSRT).

17. Josh Meyer, "Border Arrest Stirs Fear of Terrorist Cells in U.S.," *Los Angeles Times,* Mar. 11, 2001.

18. Transcript, Administrative Review Board for Mohamedou Ould Slahi, US Department of Defense, Dec. 15, 2005 (hereafter cited as Slahi ARB).

19. Sheikh Bekaye, "Officials: Man Suspected of Terror Links Detained in Mauritania," Associated Press Newswires, Jan. 28, 2000.

20. Slahi CSRT.

21. Estanislao Oziewicz, "Suspected Bomber Got Easy Entry to Canada," *Globe and Mail* (Toronto), May 16, 2000.

22. David Johnston, "Evidence Is Seen Linking Bin Laden to Algerian Group," *New York Times,* Jan. 27, 2000.

23. "Mauritanian Islamist Denies Links with Bin-Ladin," text of report by *Al-Sharq al-Awsat,* Arabic-language newspaper (London), BBC Monitoring Middle East—Political, Feb. 22, 2000.

24. Slahi ARB.

25. Bekaye, "Officials: Man Suspected of Terror Links."

26. Slahi ARB.

27. "Mauritanian Denies Plotting Bomb Attacks Against U.S.," Associated Press Newswires, Mar. 3, 2000.

28. "Terror Investigation Suspect Released in Mauritania," Associated Press Newswires, Feb. 20, 2000.

29. "Al Qaeda Online for Terrorism," *CNN: Live Today,* Mar. 6, 2002.

30. Slahi ARB.

31. Goetz et al., "Career of Prisoner No. 760."

32. "Al Qaeda Online for Terrorism."

33. Slahi ARB.

34. Ibid.

35. John Carreyrou and David Gauthier-Villars, "Rough Justice: French Judge Makes Enemies in Pursuit of Global Terrorists," *Wall Street Journal Europe,* Oct. 18, 2001.

36. Ronan Bennett, "Ten Days to War," *Guardian* (London), Mar. 8, 2008.

37. Created decades earlier by Robert McNamara, another defense secretary who preferred to have his own intelligence apparatus, the DIA remained a letter behind its famous rival and guarded what prerogatives it had. The DIA unit responsible for interrogations was known as DHS, which suddenly had become a confusing acronym in March 2003, when a post-9/11 law brought the cabinet-level US Department of Homeland

Security into existence. The DIA's DHS was an acronym within an acronym, standing for Defense HUMINT Service, the middle term being Pentagon shorthand for "human intelligence."

38. Slahi ARB.

39. Contradictorily, Jordan also sought a reputation as the Arab country most concerned with human rights. The Hashemite prince Zeid Ra'ad Zeid Al-Hussein, Jordan's permanent representative to the United Nations and, later, ambassador to the United States, was a leader in the movement to establish the International Criminal Court and the first president of its Assembly of States Parties. Jordan is the only Arab country to ratify the Rome Statute of the International Criminal Court, placing itself under the court's jurisdiction.

40. Account from "a former Jordanian detainee," cited by Human Rights Watch release, Dec. 4, 2008.

41. Jess Bravin, "The Conscience of the Colonel," *Wall Street Journal*, Mar. 31, 2007.

42. *Review of the FBI's Involvement*, 296n199.

43. Slahi ARB.

44. *Review of the FBI's Involvement*, 298n200.

45. Ibid., 122.

46. Ibid., 298.

47. Some details of the Slahi interrogation plan were published in *Inquiry into the Treatment of Detainees in U.S. Custody*, 135–143; and in *Review of the FBI's Involvement*, 122–128.

48. Approval timeline in *Inquiry into the Treatment of Detainees in U.S. Custody*, 135–138.

49. Memo from Michael Gelles, Psy.D., *Review of JTF-GTMO Interrogation Plan Detainee 063 dtd November 21, 2002* (Nov. 22, 2002), cited in ibid., 137.

50. Ibid., 138.

51. US Department of Defense, *Investigation into FBI Allegations of Detainee Abuse at Guantanamo Bay, Cuba, Detention Facility* (Schmidt-Furlow Report), Apr. 1, 2005 (Amended June 9, 2005), 22.

52. *Review of the FBI's Involvement*, 124n96.

53. Schmidt-Furlow Report, 24.

54. Ibid., 25.

55. *Review of the FBI's Involvement*, 123.

56. Schmidt-Furlow Report, 26.

57. Bravin, "Conscience of the Colonel."

58. Schmidt-Furlow Report, 25.
59. *Inquiry into the Treatment of Detainees in U.S. Custody*, 139.
60. Bravin, "Conscience of the Colonel."
61. Schmidt-Furlow Report, 25.
62. *Review of the FBI's Involvement*, 123.
63. Ibid., 127.
64. Slahi ARB.
65. *Inquiry into the Treatment of Detainees in U.S. Custody*, 140.
66. Schmidt-Furlow Report, 25.
67. Slahi ARB.
68. *Inquiry into the Treatment of Detainees in U.S. Custody*, 140.

5. London Calling

1. Rory McCarthy, "Inside Bin Laden's Chemical Bunker," *Guardian* (London), Nov. 17, 2001; Nick Fielding, "Network Studied Oklahoma-Style Bomb," *Sunday Times* (London), Nov. 18, 2001. The 9/11 Commission reported that the camp was not directly controlled by al Qaeda but run by a fellow traveler, Abu Zubaydah, who "had an agreement with Bin Ladin to conduct reciprocal recruiting efforts whereby promising trainees at the camps could be invited to join al Qaeda." *The 9/11 Commission Report*, 500n5.
2. Moazzam Begg with Victoria Brittain, *Enemy Combatant* (New York: New Press, 2006), 87; Tim Golden, "Jihadist or Victim: Ex-Detainee Makes a Case," *New York Times*, June 15, 2006; Daniel Foggo and Simon Trump, "Benefit Fraud Ring Funds Islamic Terrorists," *Daily Telegraph* (London), Nov. 17, 2001; Daniel Foggo, "Briton Facing US Trial in Cuba Was Arrested by MI5," *Sunday Telegraph* (London), July 6, 2003; Lisa McCarthy, "New City Terror Link," *Evening Mail* (Birmingham), July 25, 2003; "Yemen Turns Back Relatives of British Suspects," Reuters News, Feb. 4, 1999. A former FBI agent said that he knew in 2000 that Begg had sent money to Abu Zubaydah. Ali H. Soufan with Daniel Freedman, *The Black Banners* (New York: W. W. Norton, 2011), 143.
3. Tim Golden, "Jihadist or Victim: Ex-Detainee Makes a Case," *New York Times*, June 15, 2006.
4. Philip Johnston, "MI5 Defies US over al-Qa'eda Trial," *Daily Telegraph* (London), July 11, 2003.
5. Alistair Self, "The Teacher Accused of Batting for al Qaeda," *Mail on Sunday* (London), Mar. 2, 2003.

6. Affidavit of Solicitor Gareth Peirce, *Begg v. Bush,* Mar. 9, 2004.

7. US Department of Justice, Office of the Inspector General, *A Review of the FBI's Involvement in and Observations of Detainee Interrogations in Guantanamo Bay, Afghanistan, and Iraq,* May 2008, 270.

8. The Pentagon apparently did not acknowledge that it held any prisoners, as it would describe John Walker Lindh as the sole prisoner in US custody. See Chip Cummins, "Afghan Forces Have Captured Taliban Officers," *Wall Street Journal,* Dec. 11, 2001.

9. Jess Bravin, "John Lindh Faces Four New Charges," *Wall Street Journal,* Feb. 6, 2002; see also Jane Mayer, "Lost in the Jihad," *New Yorker,* Mar. 10, 2003.

10. *Meet the Press,* NBC News, Dec. 9, 2001.

11. U.S. Const., art. 3, sec. 3.

12. Press conference, Dec. 4, 2001.

13. Alberto R. Gonzales, "Martial Justice, Full and Fair," op-ed, *New York Times,* Nov. 30, 2001. Likewise: "This isn't a threat to the civil liberties of Americans," George Terwilliger, deputy attorney general under Bush's father, said on the PBS *NewsHour,* Nov. 14, 2001.

14. Siobhan Roth, "Band of Brothers," *Legal Times,* Aug. 18, 2003.

15. Because Lindh was a US citizen arrested abroad, the Justice Department had a choice of where to file charges: Washington, DC; San Francisco, whose federal district court covered Lindh's last home address; or wherever he happened to reenter the United States. That was an easy choice, as both Washington and San Francisco were liberal cities with jurors more likely to be skeptical of the Bush administration.

16. Jess Bravin, "Ashcroft Proposes Less Serious Charge Against John Walker," *Wall Street Journal,* Dec. 20, 2001.

17. Ibid.

18. Richard T. Cooper and Robert L. Jackson, "Legal Status Unclear for U.S. Talib," *Los Angeles Times,* Dec. 5, 2001.

19. Bravin, "Ashcroft Proposes Less Serious Charges."

20. Walter Pincus, "Bush Seeks Legal Strategy for Captured Combatants," *Washington Post,* Dec. 22, 2001.

21. Begg, *Enemy Combatant,* 194ff.

22. *Review of the FBI's Involvement,* 275.

23. Ibid. Begg repeatedly has denied involvement in terrorism and said that inculpatory statements he made in captivity were coerced.

24. "Background Briefing on Military Commissions," transcript, US Department of Defense, July 3, 2003.

25. "A Grave Injustice," editorial, *Observer* (London), July 6, 2003.

26. Nicholas Watt and Vikram Dodd, "MPs' Fury at Secret U.S. Trials of 'Terror' Britons," *Guardian* (London), July 8, 2003.

27. Ibid.

28. Ibid.

29. S. 709, 108th Cong.

30. David Cracknell and Dipesh Gadher, "Lockerbie-Style Trial Bid for Cuba Suspect," *Sunday Times* (London), July 13, 2003.

31. Christopher Hudson, "Lord Goldsmith: The War Lord," *Independent on Sunday* (London), Oct. 17, 2004.

32. Martin Bright et al., "Army Chiefs Feared Iraq War Illegal Just Days Before Start," *Observer* (London), Feb. 29, 2004; Jon Silverman, "Peter Goldsmith: The Silk Who Holds the Secrets," *Independent* (London), Feb. 26, 2005.

33. Jess Bravin, "Guilty Pleas Expected at Tribunals," *Wall Street Journal*, Aug. 11, 2003.

34. Lizette Alvarez, "Marchers in London Denounce Bush Visit," *New York Times*, Nov. 21, 2003.

35. In March 2004, the United States began shipping its Guantanamo Britons home. Begg and Abbasi were in the January 2005 batch. They were arrested on arrival and taken to a police station for questioning. The next day, they were released without charge. Sam Greenhill, "Guantanamo 4 Free," *Daily Mail* (London), Jan. 27, 2005; "Ex-Guantanamo Detainees Walk Free from British Prison," Agence France-Presse, Jan. 26, 2005.

36. Jess Bravin, "White House Lawyers Weigh Classifying al Qaeda Membership as a War Crime," *Wall Street Journal*, Mar. 5, 2002.

37. Reviewed by author.

38. Emphasis in original.

39. Jeffrey K. Walker, "Prosecuting al Qaeda," Crimes of War Project, crimesofwar.org, Dec. 14, 2001; Anthony Dworkin, "Trial, Detention or Release?" Crimes of War Project, crimesofwar.org, May 17, 2002. The Allies had declared the Gestapo a criminal organization, but the Nuremberg Tribunal refused to convict any defendant for membership alone.

6. The Ides of March

1. That's how it was spelled in the script. But, as Professor Michael D. Cooperson of UCLA observes, the Arabic word would be pronounced

more like *muhandis,* and means "engineer." "Architect" would need an additional modifier and would be pronounced *muhandis mi'maari.* *Mohandese* is the Persian cognate. Because al Qaeda is a Sunni Muslim organization, it's unlikely that its leaders would be speaking Persian, the language of Shiite Muslim Iran.

2. US Department of Defense Inspector General, *Report of Investigation: Project: Milcom,* Apr. 30, 2004, 29.

3. Jane Sutton, "Al Qaeda Media Chief Stands Mute at Guantanamo," *Reuters News,* Oct. 27, 2008.

4. David McFadden, "Witness: Guantanamo Prisoner Believes All U.S. Citizens Should Be Targeted for Attacks," Associated Press Newswires, Oct. 29, 2008.

5. Jane Sutton, "Guantanamo Yemeni Claims al Qaeda's 'Best' Video," *Reuters News,* Oct. 29, 2008.

6. Although the attack killed seventeen sailors, it fell short of destroying the vessel, which was repaired and recommissioned in 2002.

7. Sutton, "Qaeda's 'Best' Video."

8. Carol Rosenberg, "Guantanamo War Court Shows Martyrdom Video," *Miami Herald,* Oct. 29, 2008.

9. In two years of proceedings, Denson built an exhaustive record of Nazi crimes at the Dachau, Buchenwald, Flossenburg, and Mauthausen death camps, winning every case. But in the late 1940s, Cold War Washington's priorities shifted from punishing atrocities committed by a defeated former enemy to gaining an advantage over the rising Soviet adversary. American officials eager to curry favor with the Germans secretly commuted the sentences. Under pressure from Chancellor Konrad Adenauer, all the Nazi prisoners Denson convicted were released by 1958, many going on to resume their prior roles in the German establishment. Joshua M. Greene, *Justice at Dachau* (New York: Broadway Books, 2003), 354.

10. *Project: Milcom,* 17.

11. Ibid., 19.

12. Ibid.

13. The closest thing to controversy Haynes's nomination had generated involved which side of the Potomac he called home. The vacant seat traditionally went to a Virginian, and Haynes lived in the District of Columbia. That provoked a few harrumphs from Virginia's two Republican senators, John Warner and George Allen, but they took solace in Haynes's promise to move to their state. Peter Hardin,

"Nominee's Bio Draws Questions," *Richmond Times-Dispatch,* Oct. 1, 2003; Hardin, "Untraditional Choice for Bench," *Richmond Times-Dispatch,* Oct. 13, 2003.

14. Senators Richard J. Durbin of Illinois and Russell D. Feingold of Wisconsin voted no.

15. *Project: Milcom,* 2.

16. Ibid.

17. In February 2004, Couch had spoken with an FBI agent investigating a Saudi graduate student at the University of Idaho suspected of running jihadist websites with Montreal links. The agent wanted Slahi as a witness. See, e.g., Stewart Bell, "Charges Laid over Jihad Web Site," *National Post* (Toronto), Jan. 13, 2004; Paul M. Barrett, "Radical Politics: Idaho Arrest Puts Muslim Students Under Scrutiny," *Wall Street Journal,* May 28, 2003. The student later was acquitted and deported. See Richard B. Schmitt, "Acquittal in Internet Terrorism Case Is a Defeat for Patriot Act," *Los Angeles Times,* June 11, 2004.

18. Jean S. Pictet, ed., *Commentary: I Geneva Convention* (Geneva: International Committee of the Red Cross, 1952; reprint ed., 1995), 50.

19. Ronald Reagan: "Message to the Senate Transmitting the Convention Against Torture and Inhuman Treatment or Punishment," May 20, 1988. Online by Gerhard Peters and John T. Woolley, *The American Presidency Project,* http://www.presidency.ucsb.edu/ws/?pid=35858.

20. An internal Pentagon report into abuses at Guantanamo concluded that the "threats" made to Slahi "do not rise to the level of torture as defined under U.S. law" but did violate the Uniform Code of Military Justice. The Pentagon declined to explain how it reached that conclusion. Lieutenant General Randall Schmidt, the report's director, testified that interrogator Dick Zuley and a JAG officer who worked with him "lawyered up" and would not cooperate with the abuse investigation. A Defense Department spokesman declined to say what discipline, if any, Zuley received, other than that he was not court-martialed. Jess Bravin, "The Conscience of the Colonel," *Wall Street Journal,* Mar. 31, 2007.

21. *Nardone v. U.S.,* 308 U.S. 338 (1939).

22. Eugene Archer, "Emil and the Detectives," movie review, *New York Times,* Dec. 24, 1964.

23. U.S. Const., art. 6, sec. 2.

7. The Nuremberg Defense

1. Severin Carrell, "I Was Shackled, Beaten, Suffocated by a Plastic Bag and Deprived of Sleep," *Independent on Sunday* (London), Jan. 30, 2005.

2. Vanessa Gezari, "Army Probes Deaths of 2 Afghans in U.S. Custody," *Chicago Tribune*, Mar. 5, 2003.

3. Jane Mayer, "The Memo," *New Yorker*, Feb. 27, 2006.

4. Ibid.

5. Alberto Mora, Memorandum for Inspector General, Department of the Navy: Statement for the Record: Office of General Counsel Involvement in Interrogation Issues, July 7, 2004.

6. US Department of Justice, Office of Professional Responsibility, *Investigation into the Office of Legal Counsel's Memoranda Concerning Issues Relating to the Central Intelligence Agency's Use of "Enhanced Interrogation Techniques" on Suspected Terrorists,* July 29, 2009, 75.

7. According to the Justice Department's ethics office, John Yoo "committed intentional professional misconduct when he violated his duty to exercise independent legal judgment and render thorough, objective, and candid legal advice" in drafting memorandums on interrogation practices. *Investigation into the Office of Legal Counsel's Memoranda.* Reviewing those findings, a senior Justice Department official wrote that "I fear that John Yoo's loyalty to his own ideology and convictions clouded his view of his obligation to his client and led him to author opinions that reflected his own extreme, albeit sincerely held, views of executive power while speaking for an institutional client" and that he apparently "failed to appreciate the enormous responsibility that comes with the authority to issue institutional decisions that carried the authoritative weight of the Department of Justice." Although it was a "close question," the official overruled the Office of Professional Responsibility's recommendation to refer the matter to the bar association for possible discipline, citing uncertainty over whether Yoo "set about to knowingly provide inaccurate legal advice to his client or that he acted with conscious indifference to the consequences of his action." Memorandum for the Attorney General from David Margolis, *Memorandum of Decision Regarding the Objections to the Findings of Professional Misconduct in the Office of Professional Responsibility's Report of Investigation into the Office of Legal Counsel's Memoranda,* Jan. 5, 2010.

   Nevertheless, once publicly disclosed, many of the memos were disavowed by both the Bush and Obama administrations. Numerous opinions containing certain "propositions . . . do not reflect the current views of the Office of Legal Counsel and should not be treated as authoritative for any purpose." Steven G. Bradbury, Principal Deputy Attorney General, Office of Legal Counsel, *Memorandum for the Files: Re: Status of Certain OLC Opinions Issued in the Aftermath of the Terrorist Attacks of September 11, 2001,* Jan. 15, 2009. See also Executive Order 13491—Ensuring Lawful Interrogations, Jan. 22, 2009.

8. Jess Bravin, "Pentagon Report Set Framework for Use of Torture," *Wall Street Journal,* June 7, 2004.

9. *Investigation into the Office of Legal Counsel's Memoranda,* 79.

10. Parentheses in original.

11. Addington testimony, US House Judiciary Committee, Subcommittee on the Constitution, Civil Rights, and Civil Liberties, June 26, 2008.

12. 542 U.S. 466 (2004).

13. See, e.g., Anthony Lewis, *Freedom for the Thought That We Hate* (New York: Basic Books, 2007), xiv. Ginsburg cited the late Harvard law professor Paul Freund for the observation.

14. Justice Stevens asked the question in *Hamdi v. Rumsfeld,* 542 U.S. 507 (2004), argued the same day as *Rumsfeld v. Padilla,* 542 U.S. 426 (2004). *Rasul v. Bush,* 542 U.S. 466 (2004), was argued Apr. 20, 2004.

15. Clement continued: Although the Bush administration contended that courts were powerless to enforce treaties, that "doesn't mean that it's not a binding treaty, doesn't mean that it's not going to constrain the actions of the executive branch . . . I wouldn't want there to be any misunderstanding about this. It's also the judgment of those involved in this process that the last thing you want to do is torture somebody or try to do something along those lines. I mean . . . if you did that, you might get information more quickly, but you would really wonder about the reliability of the information you were getting. So the judgment of the people who do this as their responsibility is that the way you would get the best information from individuals is that you interrogate them, you try to develop a relationship of trust."

16. 541 U.S. 36 (2004).

17. Jess Bravin, "U.S. Navy Lawyer Files Suit over Tribunal Policy, Practices," *Wall Street Journal,* Apr. 7, 2004.

18. Craig Jarvis, "Appeal Puts Army's Case on Trial," *News and Observer* (Raleigh, NC), Mar. 22, 2004.

19. The US Court of Appeals for the Armed Forces, a civilian panel that reviews decisions of the uniformed services' justice systems, later

affirmed the Army appellate court. *U.S. v. Kreutzer,* 61 M.J. 272 (C.A.A.F. 2005). In 2009, Kreutzer was sentenced to life in prison. Drew Brooks, "Kreutzer Gets Life in Prison," *Fayetteville Observer* (NC), Mar. 25, 2009.

20. John D. Altenburg to the Judge Advocate General of the Army, "Recall to Active Duty, COL Peter E. Brownback, III," July 1, 2004.

8. The Man from al Qaeda

1. Jess Bravin, "As War Tribunal Opens, Legality Is Challenged," *Wall Street Journal,* Aug. 25, 2004.

2. Jane Sutton, "War Crimes Hearings to Begin for 4 Guantanamo Prisoners," Reuters News, Aug. 22, 2004.

3. Paisley Dodds, "Bin Laden Chauffeur Declines to Enter Plea in Guantanamo While Defense Challenges Impartiality of Panel," Associated Press Newswires, Aug. 24, 2004.

4. Jess Bravin, "War-Crimes Defense Lawyers Say They Lack Resources," *Wall Street Journal,* Aug. 9, 2004.

5. *U.S. v. Hamdan,* trial transcript, Aug. 24, 2004.

6. *U.S. v. Hicks,* trial transcript, Aug. 25, 2004.

7. Leigh Sales, *Detainee 002* (Carlton, Australia: Melbourne University Press, 2007), 13ff.

8. Toni Locy, "Australian Pleads Not Guilty at Guantanamo Hearing," *USA Today,* Aug. 26, 2004.

9. Ahmed al Haj, "Bin Laden Media Expert Faces Gitmo Hearing," Associated Press Newswires, Aug. 23, 2004.

10. 422 U.S. 806.

11. Because it "departed from common-law traditions" and "specialized in trying 'political' offenses, the Star Chamber has for centuries symbolized disregard of basic individual rights," Justice Stewart wrote. Recent Supreme Court decisions had buttressed the right to counsel with *Gideon v. Wainwright,* in 1963, requiring the state to provide free lawyers for indigent defendants. "But it is one thing to hold that every defendant, rich or poor, has the right to the assistance of counsel, and quite another to say that a State may compel a defendant to accept a lawyer he does not want," he continued. "Whatever else may be said of those who wrote the Bill of Rights, surely there can be no doubt that they understood the inestimable worth of free choice."

12. The Sudanese-born Fadl had lived in the United States, where he was recruited for jihad at a Brooklyn mosque. *The 9/11 Commission Report,*

62. Back in Sudan, he worked with Qosi at Taba Investments. Unlike Qosi, it seemed, Fadl also managed to embezzle $110,000. When bin Laden found out, he responded with surprising leniency, asking only restitution. But Fadl figured he was worth more to the Americans. He fled to the US embassy in Eritrea and turned himself in. Fadl gave the FBI detailed information about al Qaeda's structure and regularly turned up as its key witness at terrorism-related trials. Jess Bravin and Glenn R. Simpson, "Suspected Bin Laden Aides to Face U.S. Tribunals," *Wall Street Journal,* Feb. 25, 2004.

9. Habeas Corpus

1. "Many Issues Raised in First Week of Commissions Hearings," American Forces Information Service, Aug. 27, 2004.
2. Toni Locy, "Tribunal Struggles with First Hearings," *USA Today,* Aug. 30, 2004.
3. Glenn Kessler, "Kerry Would Drop Detainee Commissions," *Washington Post,* Sept. 1, 2004.
4. 10 U.S.C. § 603. Pentagon lawyers were assigned to research whether the two-year term necessarily ran from the date of appointment, expiring 730 days later or, better still, could be calculated by counting only the actual hours spent on commissions business, meaning that Rumsfeld's instant generals could retain their stars for many years into the future.
5. After discovering the emergency appointment statute, some officials, particularly Pentagon intelligence chief Stephen Cambone, recommended taking fuller advantage of it to bypass the Senate confirmation process. But members of the Senate, protective of their constitutional prerogative to confirm presidential nominees, were furious. Within days of the press release announcing the instant generals, Rumsfeld received a staff memo reporting "Senate concerns regarding the expanded use" of the emergency appointment power. "Wider use, such as that suggested by USD (I) [undersecretary of defense for intelligence], could offend the Senate and generate a change in statute to require Senate confirmation" for emergency appointees. To "alleviate these concerns," Rumsfeld sent the Senate a letter stating that the emergency appointment power would only be used for the military commissions review panel. See David S. C. Chu to Secretary of Defense, Action Memo, "Authority to Appoint General Officers (Military Review Panels)," Dec. 31, 2003.

6. Walter F. Naedele, "Bucks Judge on Terror Panel a Longtime Rumsfeld Friend," *Philadelphia Inquirer*, Feb. 2, 2004.

7. Edward Fitzpatrick, "R.I. Chief Justice to Hear Appeals by Terror Suspects," *Providence Journal*, Dec. 31, 2003.

8. Ibid.

9. Williams had a gavel that he said was made from the floorboards of Lincoln's office. In August 2001, he posed for the *Wall Street Journal*'s Workspaces column, showing off his ornate chambers with their marble fireplace, brass chandeliers, and oriental rugs. Nancy D. Holt, "Workspaces," *Wall Street Journal*, Aug. 29, 2001.

10. *U.S. v. Quintanilla*, 56 M.J. 37 (C.A.A.F. 2001).

11. Appointing Authority Decision No. 2004-001, Office of Military Commissions, US Department of Defense, Oct. 19, 2004.

12. John J. Lumpkin, "Top Officer in Guantanamo Hearings Dismisses Three Panelists Accused of Possible Bias," Associated Press Newswires, Oct. 21, 2004.

13. Jess Bravin, "Defending the Enemy: Critics of Tribunals Gain Unlikely Allies: Lawyers in Uniform," *Wall Street Journal*, March 18, 2004.

14. In its 2009 rankings of 184 accredited law schools, *U.S. News and World Report* put the University of Memphis at 143, tied with seven other schools, in the fourth and lowest tier. Umberg's law school, Hastings, tied for twenty-fourth place with seven other schools.

15. Umberg was then running for his old seat in the California State Assembly. Soldiers on active duty aren't permitted to campaign, so back home in his Orange County district, his wife, Robin, did it for him, carrying a life-size cardboard cutout of Umberg to political events. He won.

16. April 22, 1971. At the hearing, both the committee chairman, J. William Fulbright, Democrat of Arkansas, and the ranking Republican, Jacob Javits of New York, opposed the Vietnam War and stressed their agreement with Kerry.

17. Paul Shukovsky, "Lawyer Suing Rumsfeld Defends Yemeni Prisoner Held in Cuba," *Seattle Post-Intelligencer*, May 8, 2004.

18. Paul Shukovsky, "Detainee's Case Moves from Seattle to D.C.," *Seattle Post-Intelligencer*, Aug. 10, 2004.

19. Robertson cited a February 2, 2002, memorandum making that point from State Department Legal Adviser William H. Taft IV to White House Counsel Alberto Gonzales.

20. "It is emphatically the province and duty of the judicial department to say what the law is." *Marbury v. Madison*, 5 U.S. 137 (1803).

21. In May 1861, for instance, Chief Justice Roger Taney issued a writ of habeas corpus directing General George Cadwalader to produce a suspected secessionist saboteur he had jailed at Baltimore's Fort McHenry. James F. Simon, *Lincoln and Chief Justice Taney* (New York: Simon and Schuster, 2006), 186. Cadwalader refused, and turned away a marshal Taney sent to Fort McHenry to enforce his order. Taney had no recourse but his quill: "I can only say that if the authority which the constitution has confided to the judiciary department and judicial officers, may thus, upon any pretext or under any circumstances, be usurped by the military power, at its discretion, the people of the United States are no longer living under a government of laws," he fumed. *Ex parte Merryman,* 17 F. Cas. 144 (1861).

10. Mr. Bean

1. Jess Bravin, "Bin Laden Aide Asks High Court to Void Tribunals," *Wall Street Journal,* Nov. 23, 2004.
2. Jess Bravin, "Guantanamo Bay Detainees Seek Hearings," *Wall Street Journal,* July 3, 2002.
3. Natalie O'Brien, "Voyage to the Darkest Side," *Australian* (Sydney), Oct. 25, 2008.
4. Ibid.
5. Mamdouh Habib with Julia Collingwood, *My Story: The Tale of a Terrorist Who Wasn't* (Melbourne: Scribe, 2008), 25.
6. Raymond Bonner, "Australian's Long Path in the U.S. Antiterrorism Maze," *New York Times,* Jan. 29, 2005.
7. Nosair, defended by William Kunstler, was acquitted in state court of the murder charge but convicted of a related weapons offense. In a separate trial, he later was convicted in federal court of conspiracy with the Blind Sheikh.
8. Kara Lawrence and Kim Arlington, "Habib Wrote to Saddam, Gaddafi," *Daily Telegraph* (Sydney), Nov. 29, 2007.
9. James Madden, "Habib 'Said He Met Osama,'" *Australian* (Sydney), Dec. 5, 2007; Bonner, "Australian's Long Path"; Tom Allard and Mike Seccombe, "Tortured Truth," *Sydney Morning Herald,* Feb. 19, 2005.
10. Rod McGurk, "Australian Terror Suspect Reportedly Tried to Recruit Muslims for Holy War," Associated Press Newswires, July 19, 2004.
11. Hall Greenland, "Trial by Jihad," *Bulletin* (Sydney), May 24, 2005.
12. Allard and Seccombe, "Tortured Truth"; see also Habib, *My Story,* 82ff.

13. "The Trials of Mamdouh Habib," SBS Current Affairs Transcripts, Special Broadcasting Service (Australia), July 7, 2004.

14. O'Brien, "Voyage to the Darkest Side"; Tom Allard, "ASIO Tried to Recruit Me as a Spy, Says Habib," *Age* (Melbourne), Dec. 17, 2007.

15. Bravin, "Guantanamo Bay Detainees Seek Hearings."

16. In his memoir, Habib writes that he was "standing in the kitchen" of a Kabul guesthouse "when someone rushed in to tell me that the USA had been attacked. Everybody around me was excited, but none of us had any idea as to exactly what had happened." He then telephoned his wife seeking more information about the attack, but she said she had heard nothing about it. The conversation became "an important piece of 'evidence' much later for the American charge that I had known in advance of the 9/11 attacks" and was "played back to me later in a cell in Egypt." Habib, *My Story*, 78–79.

17. US Department of Justice, Office of the Inspector General, *A Review of the FBI's Involvement in and Observations of Detainee Interrogations in Guantanamo Bay, Afghanistan, and Iraq*, May 2008, 194.

18. Ibid.

19. "Trials of Mamdouh Habib"; "Lawyer Says Guantanamo Australian Habib Tortured While in Egypt," *PM*, Radio Australia, May 20, 2004, transcribed by BBC Monitoring Asia Pacific.

20. Tom Allard, "U.S. Tortured Second Australian," *Sydney Morning Herald*, May 21, 2004.

21. Raymond Bonner, "Detainee Says He Was Tortured in U.S. Custody," *New York Times*, Feb. 13, 2005.

22. Roy Eccleston, "Canberra Blamed on Habib," *Australian* (Sydney), Feb. 7, 2005.

23. "Lawyer: Australian Terror Suspect at Guantanamo Bay Compares Life in Detention to Prison Brutality Film," Associated Press Newswires, Aug. 11, 2004.

24. *Habib v. Commonwealth of Australia* (2010), FCAFC 12.

25. Bonner, "Detainee Says He Was Tortured."

26. "Police and the SSIS [State Security Investigative Service] reportedly employed torture methods such as stripping and blindfolding victims; suspending victims by the wrists and ankles in contorted positions or from a ceiling or door frame with feet just touching the floor; beating victims with fists, whips, metal rods, or other objects; using electric shocks; dousing victims with cold water; sleep deprivation; and sexual abuse, including sodomy. There was evidence that security officials

sexually assaulted some victims or threatened to rape them or their family members." US Department of State, *2009 Human Rights Report: Egypt* (Washington, DC, 2010), http://www.state.gov/g/drl/rls/hrrpt/2009/nea/136067.htm.

27. Meriah Foley, "Freed Australian Returns from Guantanamo," Associated Press Newswires, Jan. 28, 2005; Cynthia Banham, "Welcome Home from Family Who Never Deserted Habib," *Sydney Morning Herald*, Jan. 29, 2005.

28. Glenn Kessler, "Rice Defends Enhanced Interrogations," *Washington Post*, Apr. 30, 2009.

29. Tim Golden, "U.S. Is Examining Plan to Bolster Detainee Rights," *New York Times*, Mar. 27, 2005.

11. A Twentieth Hijacker

1. In the George H. W. Bush administration, Roberts had held Paul Clement's post, principal deputy solicitor general, and then was nominated for the DC Circuit. But the nomination expired before the Senate acted, and Roberts repaired to the firm Hogan & Hartson. During the 2000 election dispute, Roberts operated behind the scenes, joining John Yoo to brief Florida Governor Jeb Bush in the legal fight against Al Gore and later helping Ted Olson prepare for his Supreme Court argument in *Bush v. Gore*. In May 2001, when President Bush held an East Room ceremony to introduce his first judicial selections, Roberts was one of eleven nominees standing with him. See, e.g., Marc Caputo, "Roberts Had Larger 2000 Recount Role," *Miami Herald*, July 27, 2005; and Mary Ellen Klas, "Nominee John Roberts' 2000 Recount Role Gets Spin but No Traction," *Miami Herald*, July 31, 2005.

2. Steve LeVine, "U.S. Believes bin Laden Aide Murdered Pearl," *Wall Street Journal*, Oct. 21, 2003.

3. Yosri Fouda and Nick Fielding, *Masterminds of Terror* (New York: Arcade, 2003).

4. Statement of Jose E. Melendez-Perez to 9/11 Commission, Jan. 26, 2004.

5. Philip Shenon, "Panel Says a Deported Saudi Was Likely '20th Hijacker,'" *New York Times*, Jan. 27, 2004.

6. Tim Golden and Don Van Natta Jr., "U.S. Said to Overstate Value of Guantánamo Detainees," *New York Times*, June 21, 2004.

7. See Substitution for the Testimony of Mohammed Manea Ahmad al-Qahtani, Defendant's Exhibit 944, *U.S. v. Moussaoui* (2006).

8. Substitution for the Testimony of Khalid Sheikh Mohammed, Defendant's Exhibit 941, *U.S. v. Moussaoui* (2006).

9. Substitution for the Testimony of Mustafa Ahmed al-Hawsawi, Defendant's Exhibit 943, *U.S. v. Moussaoui* (2006).

10. The Abu Zubaydah interrogation is recounted in US Department of Justice, Office of the Inspector General, *A Review of the FBI's Involvement in and Observations of Detainee Interrogations in Guantanamo Bay, Afghanistan, and Iraq,* May 2008, 67ff., 321ff.

11. Golden and Van Natta, "U.S. Said to Overstate Value of Guantánamo Detainees."

12. Jane Mayer, *The Dark Side* (New York: Doubleday, 2008), 195.

13. Shiffrin testimony, Senate Armed Services Committee, June 17, 2008.

14. Haynes testimony, Senate Armed Services Committee, June 17, 2008.

15. *Review of the FBI's Involvement,* 81.

16. Ibid., 82.

17. Matthew Purdy and Lowell Bergman, "Unclear Danger: Inside the Lackawanna Terror Case," *New York Times,* Oct. 12, 2003.

18. Jess Bravin, "Who's Held at Guantanamo? Detainees Tell Their Stories," *Wall Street Journal,* Nov. 1, 2004.

19. Jason Felch, "The Closer: An al-Qaeda Recruiter in the United States," Oct. 16, 2003, *Frontline* online extra, www.pbs.org.

20. Ibid.

21. Ibid.

22. Carol Rosenberg, "Ex-U.S. Jihadists Testify at Guantánamo Terror Trial," *Miami Herald,* Oct. 30, 2008.

23. Purdy and Bergman, "Unclear Danger." The administration's war council viewed the Lackawanna Six as a threat significant enough to trigger imposition of military law within the United States. In an October 2001 memo, John Yoo further elaborated his theories of executive supremacy. "The President's *constitutional* authority alone enables him to take military measures" after 9/11, "without regard to location." In another memorandum, Yoo explained that not even Congress could stop Bush from jailing American citizens as "enemy belligerents." The memo, in effect, secretly nullified the Non-Detention Act, which prohibited imprisonment of US citizens without express congressional assent. The 1971 law, inspired by the World War II internment of Japanese-Americans, "does not, and constitutionally could not, interfere," Yoo wrote. See Memorandum for Alberto R. Gonzales, Counsel to the President; William J. Haynes II, General

412   NOTES TO PAGES 261–264

Counsel, Department of Defense, from John C. Yoo, Deputy Assistant
Attorney General; Robert J. Delahunty, Special Counsel, *Re: Authority for
Use of Military Force to Combat Terrorist Activities Within the United
States* (Oct. 23, 2001); Memorandum for Daniel J. Bryant, Assistant
Attorney General, Office of Legislative Affairs, from John C. Yoo, Deputy
Assistant Attorney General, *Re: Applicability of 18 U.S.C. Sec. 4001(a) to
Military Detention of United States Citizens* (June 27, 2002).

24. Nevertheless, the naval brig near Charleston, South Carolina, already hold-
    ing Brooklyn-born enemy combatant Jose Padilla, readied a new wing for
    additional US citizens the president selected. See Jess Bravin, "More Terror
    Suspects May Sit in Limbo," *Wall Street Journal,* Aug. 8, 2002.

25. After 9/11, the field office had obtained Indiana University records of all
    3,200 foreign students who recently took English-as-a-second-language
    courses. Later, under a directive to question young men from Muslim
    countries, agents identified thirteen students who looked suspicious but
    located only four. See Holly Johnson, "Indiana U. Student Names Given
    to FBI," *Indiana Daily Student* (via U-Wire), Oct. 23, 2001; Rex W.
    Huppke, "Federal Authorities Question Four IU Students Regarding
    Terrorist Attacks," Associated Press Newswires, Dec. 12, 2001.

26. Reached by a reporter, the county airport manager tried to be
    reassuring. The plane was authorized and working with air traffic
    control but, due to the "very sensitive situation," he said he could
    provide no details. The important point, he stressed, was that "people
    should not be alarmed by this aircraft." "Small Plane in Indiana Doing
    Police Work," AP Online, Feb. 27, 2003.

27. "FBI Uses Plane to Watch for Signs of Terrorist Connections," Associated
    Press Newswires, Feb. 28, 2003.

28. Ruth Holladay, "FBI's Surveillance in Bloomington Stirs Big Brother
    Fears," *Indianapolis Star,* Mar. 4, 2003.

29. "FBI Uses Plane to Watch for Signs of Terrorist Connections," Associated
    Press Newswires, Feb. 28, 2003.

30. Jumah al-Dossari, "A Voice from Gitmo's Darkness," opinion article, *Los
    Angeles Times,* Jan. 11, 2007.

31. James Risen and Eric Lichtblau, "Spying Program Snared U.S. Calls,"
    New York Times, Dec. 21, 2005.

32. Jess Bravin, "Old Episode Could Haunt Gonzales," *Wall Street Journal,*
    May 16, 2007.

33. Bravin, "Who's Held at Guantanamo?"; Dan Herbeck and Lou Michel,

"Suspected al-Qaida Recruiters Center of Probe," *Buffalo News*, May 19, 2003.

34. Jumah al Dossari, "I'm Home, but Still Haunted by Guantanamo," *Washington Post*, Aug. 17, 2008.

35. Jane Wardell, "Britain's Brown Meets with Saudi Ex-Guantanamo Detainees as He Tours Rehab Facility," Associated Press Newswires, Nov. 2, 2008.

36. Ali H. Soufan with Daniel Freedman, *The Black Banners* (New York: Norton, 2011), 339.

37. Tim Golden, "In U.S. Report, Brutal Details of 2 Afghan Inmates' Deaths," *New York Times*, May 20, 2005.

38. Corsetti later was acquitted of all charges. See Alicia A. Caldwell, "Army Private Acquitted of All Charges in Prisoner Abuse Case," Associated Press Newswires, June 1, 2006. Nevertheless, he later expressed contrition. "I firmly believe it was torture and unfortunately I took part in it," he said. See Michelle Shephard, "Going Through Motions at Khadr's Gitmo 'Trial,'" *Toronto Star*, Jan. 19, 2009.

12. The Marble Palace

1. Will Dunham, "Pentagon Names New Chief Guantanamo Defense Lawyer," Reuters News, July 19, 2005.

2. Jess Bravin, "White House Will Reverse Policy, Ban Evidence Elicited by Torture," *Wall Street Journal*, Mar. 22, 2006.

3. Jess Bravin, "Solicitor General's Tricky Shoals," *Wall Street Journal*, June 15, 2007.

4. Jess Bravin and David Rogers, "High Court to Hear a Key Challenge to Tribunal Policy," *Wall Street Journal*, Nov. 8, 2005.

5. "'War on Terror' Trials Could Allow Evidence Obtained Through Torture," Agence France Presse, Mar. 1, 2006.

6. Carol Rosenberg, "Hearings May Consider Torture," *Miami Herald*, Mar. 2, 2006.

7. Bravin, "White House Will Reverse Policy."

8. Tony Mauro, "Scalia's Remarks Raise Recusal Questions," *Legal Intelligencer*, Mar. 28, 2006.

13. The Vampire Killers

1. Rives's predecessor, Tom Fiscus, was demoted to colonel and forced out of the Air Force for making sexual advances and having affairs with more than a dozen women, including six active duty JAGs. Nicole Gaudiano and Lisa Zilka Chavez, "Fallen Star: How the Air Force's Judge Advocate General Lost His Two-Star Career Over His Own Misconduct," *Air Force Times*, Jan. 24, 2005.

2. Carol Rosenberg, "War Crimes Trial to Begin, Despite Challenge," *Miami Herald*, Mar. 1, 2006.

3. Beth Gorman, "U.S. Prosecutor in Khadr Case Blasts Sympathetic Views of Canadian Teen," Canadian Press, Jan. 10, 2006.

4. Paul Koring, "Khadr Threatened with Gang Rape, Guantanamo Hearing Told," *Globe and Mail* (Toronto), May 7, 2010.

5. Ali H. Soufan with Daniel Freedman, *The Black Banners* (New York: Norton, 2011), 452.

6. Soufan envisioned using Hamdan as a witness in federal counterterrorism prosecutions, and worked with David Kelley, the federal prosecutor in New York, to draft a plea bargain in exchange for his testimony. Ibid., 457.

7. Peter Finn, "Bin Laden Used Ruse to Flee; Moroccans Say Guard Took Phone at Tora Bora," *Washington Post*, Jan. 21, 2003; Soufan, *Black Banners*, 346.

8. "U.S. Hands Over Five Moroccan Guantanamo Suspects," Reuters News, Aug. 2, 2004.

9. Carol Rosenberg, "War-Crimes Hearings Resume in Controversy," *Miami Herald*, Jan. 15, 2006.

10. Jess Bravin, "As Justices Weigh Military Tribunals, a Guantanamo Tale," *Wall Street Journal*, Mar. 28, 2006.

11. For accounts of the Rutledge-Stevens connection, see Joseph T. Thai, "The Law Clerk Who Wrote *Rasul v. Bush*," *Virginia Law Review*, 2006; Craig Green, "Wiley Rutledge, Executive Detention, and Judicial Conscience at War," *Washington University Law Review*, 2006; and Richard Brust, "Setting Precedent in Two Wars," *ABA Journal*, Sept. 1, 2007.

12. Justice Douglas himself had joined the 1973 opinion overruling the strict geographical limit that his own decision in *Ahrens* placed on habeas petitions. *Braden v. Thirtieth Judicial Circuit Court of Kentucky*, 410 U.S. 484 (1973).

13. None of the eight participating justices agreed with the position John

Roberts had taken when he had heard the case as an appellate court judge on the DC Circuit, upholding the Bush military commissions in their entirety. In contrast, the Supreme Court dissenters did not deny Hamdan any right to seek relief in federal court but instead argued that such a claim should not be heard before Hamdan was tried and convicted by a military commission.

14. Emphasis added.

14. The Kangaroo Skinner

1. Anne Plummer Flaherty, "Bush, Republican Rebels Agree on Detainee Interrogation," Associated Press Newswires, Sept. 21, 2006.
2. "U2's Bono Calls for Repatriation of Terror Suspect to Australia from Guantanamo Bay," Associated Press Newswires, Nov. 7, 2006.
3. Carol Rosenberg, "'Tent City' to Host Guantánamo Trials," *Miami Herald*, Sept. 6, 2007.
4. Bob Woodward, "Detainee Tortured, Says U.S. Official," *Washington Post*, Jan. 14, 2009.
5. Rosenberg, "'Tent City' to Host Guantánamo Trials."

15. Material Supporter

1. Jess Bravin, "The Conscience of the Colonel," *Wall Street Journal*, Mar. 31, 2007.
2. Jess Bravin, "Pentagon Forbids Marine to Testify," *Wall Street Journal*, Nov. 8, 2007.
3. Peter Finn, "New Leaders for Detainee Trials," *Washington Post*, Mar. 23, 2010.
4. Mike Melia, "U.S.-Produced Al-Qaida Movie Played at Gitmo Trial," Associated Press via *USA Today*, July 28, 2008.
5. Carol Rosenberg, "Reporter's Notebook: Gitmo Sentence a Shocker," *Miami Herald*, Aug. 10, 2008.
6. Carol Rosenberg, "Gitmo Jury Sentences Driver to 66 Months," *Miami Herald*, Aug. 7, 2008.
7. Jess Bravin, "Hamdan Jury Felt Evidence Didn't Back U.S. Claim," *Wall Street Journal*, Aug. 11, 2008.
8. Jess Bravin, "9/11 Defendants Get Day in Court," *Wall Street Journal*, June 6, 2008.
9. Jess Bravin, "A Nose Job for Khalid Sheikh Mohammed?" *Wall Street Journal*, June 6, 2008.

10. Jess Bravin, "Key Sept. 11 Defendants Want to File Guilty Pleas," *Wall Street Journal*, Dec. 9, 2008.

11. *Brady v. United States*, 397 U.S. 742 (1970).

16. Turning the Page

1. Barack Obama, *The Audacity of Hope* (New York: Three Rivers Press, 2006), 78.

2. Peter Finn and Anne E. Kornblut, "How the White House Lost on Guantanamo," *Washington Post*, Apr. 24, 2011.

3. Daniel Klaidman, *Kill or Capture: The War on Terror and the Soul of the Obama Presidency* (New York: Houghton Mifflin Harcourt, 2012), 147.

4. U.S. Const., amend. VI.

5. Klaidman, *Kill or Capture*, 148.

6. Charlie Savage, "Holder Defends Decision to Use U.S. Court for 9/11 Trial," *New York Times*, Nov. 19, 2009.

7. Jess Bravin and Gary Fields, "New Venue Likely for Terror Trial," *Wall Street Journal*, Jan. 30, 2010.

8. Carol J. Williams and Geraldine Baum, "U.S. Civilian Court Acquits Ex-Guantanamo Detainee of All Major Terrorism Charges," *Los Angeles Times*, Nov. 18, 2010.

9. Chad Bray, "Embassy Bomber Gets Life in Prison," *Wall Street Journal*, Jan. 26, 2011.

10. Jess Bravin, "Mukasey Fears Attacks on New York During Trial of 9/11 Defendants," *Wall Street Journal*, Nov. 13, 2009.

11. Jess Bravin, "Guantanamo Judge Grapples with Disruptive Terror Suspects," *Wall Street Journal*, May 6, 2012.

Epilogue

1. Jess Bravin, "New Rift Opens Over Rights of Detainees," *Wall Street Journal*, June 29, 2009.

2. Christian Gysin, "Going Out Shopping, the Terror Suspect Who Pocketed a Million," *Daily Mail* (London), Oct. 31, 2011.

3. Jamie Walker, "Hicks Book in Line for $15,000 Prize," *Australian* (Sydney), Aug. 23, 2011.

4. Louise Hall and Paul Bibby, "Bid to Seize Profits from Sale of Hicks Memoir Fails," *Sydney Morning Herald*, July 25, 2012.

5. Jess Bravin, "U.S. Works With Sudan on Gitmo," *Wall Street Journal*, Aug. 12, 2010.

6. Jess Bravin, "Guantanamo Panel Turns to Trial of Juvenile," *Wall Street Journal*, Aug. 10, 2010.

7. The Sudanese government, whose president, Omar al-Bashir, was wanted for genocide by the International Criminal Court, used its willingness to accept Qosi and other detainees as leverage with the United States. In a letter to Secretary of State Hillary Rodham Clinton, the Sudanese foreign minister said that "Sudan is ready to cooperate with President Obama in his effort to close down the Guantanamo facility" by accepting detainees. Bravin, "U.S. Works with Sudan on Gitmo."

8. Carol Rosenberg, "Bin Laden Propagandist Convicted of War Crimes," *Miami Herald*, Nov. 3, 2008.

9. Bob Woodward, "Guantanamo Detainee Was Tortured, Says Official Overseeing Military Trials," *Washington Post*, Jan. 14, 2009.

10. The Convention Against Torture requires that a signatory government such as the United States conduct "a prompt and impartial investigation, wherever there is reasonable ground to believe that an act of torture has been committed in any territory under its jurisdiction" and "make these offences punishable by appropriate penalties which take into account their grave nature." There is no indication the United States has followed this treaty obligation, despite Crawford's finding that US officials committed torture—and the fact that the US government possesses comprehensive documentation of those acts and their perpetrators. While Qahtani is an unsympathetic victim, the laws prohibiting torture contain no exceptions even for the most loathsome of individuals.

11. John Bickers, "Military Commissions: No Longer a Useful Strategy," JURIST—Forum, Dec. 19, 2011, http://jurist.org/forum/2011/12/john-bickers-military-commissions.php. Bickers, then an Army officer, was a member of the tiger team assigned to commissions in late 2001.

Acknowledgments

I FIRST GOT WIND OF THE military commissions experiment in October 2001, when I arrived in Washington to cover the legal aftermath of 9/11. I knocked on many doors over the years that followed, and wasn't always turned away.

Some who answered, not perhaps without trepidation, include John Altenburg, Bill Barr, Bob Bauer, John Bellinger, Brad Berenson, Stuart Bowen, David Bowker, Louis Caldera, Phillip Carter, Paul Clement, Bill Coleman, Mark Corallo, Gregory Craig, Dan Daugherty, Moe Davis, Mark Fallon, Tom Fiscus, Tim Flanigan, Eric Freedman, John Goetz, Lindsey Graham, Tom Hemingway, Eric Holder, Mark Jacobson, Timothy James, Jeh Johnson, Neal Katyal, David Kaye, David Kelley, Harold Hongju Koh, Scott Lang, Bill Lietzau, Britt Mallow, Mark Martins, Newton Minow, Dan Mori, Larry Morris, Michael Mukasey, Mary Ellen O'Connell, Michel Paradis, Rob Preston, Michael Ratner, Jack Rives, John Rizzo, Tom Romig, Donald Rumsfeld, Harry Schneider, Stephen Sheppard, Clive Stafford Smith, Ali Soufan, John Paul Stevens, Cully Stimson, Tim Stone, Ronald Sullivan, Phil Sundel, Charlie Swift, Will Taft, Tom Umberg, Keith Urbahn, Matthew Waxman, Ruth Wedgwood, Kevin Winters, and John Yoo. They, and many others whom I am unable to name, have my gratitude. To those I inadvertently have omitted, and doubtless there are some, apologies.

A special word must go to V. Stuart Couch, someone who cannot fairly be described as anything less than an authentic American hero. Stu was reluctant at first to relate his experiences, stemming from a sense of personal humility and, more significantly, a real uncertainty over whether the nation and its Marine Corps would be served by their publication. Supported by his extraordinary wife, Kim, Stu, and not for the first time, took a leap of faith. Once he did, good Marine that he is, he was all in.

According to the pre-electric Bob Dylan, the chimes of freedom flash for the warrior "whose strength is not to fight." They flash, too, for the prosecutor who, when justice requires, finds the strength not to prosecute.

Of course, neither Stu nor anyone else mentioned here can be presumed to agree with how I have told this story, nor are they responsible for mistakes it may contain.

NEITHER MY DAILY REPORTING on commissions nor this book could have happened without the indulgence of my editors at the *Wall Street Journal,* including the current and previous Washington bureau chiefs, Jerry Seib and John Bussey. Many news editors worked closely with me on signal stories over the past decade, but particular thanks are due the former deputy bureau chief, Nikhil Deogun, and his successor, Matthew Rose, who were pivotal in bringing to life the breakthrough story headlined "The Conscience of the Colonel"—the first documented instance in which the torture of a Guantanamo detainee derailed a 9/11-linked prosecution.

For research support beyond the daily news cycle, I thank the University of California, Berkeley, whose Institute of Governmental Studies and Graduate School of Journalism jointly awarded me the John Jacobs Fellowship. Professor Bruce Cain, former director of the UC Washington Center, became this project's academic godfather, providing steady advice and comfortable space to work over many years.

Several readers helped me turn a sprawling story into something more readable. At early stages, Jan Herman, Peter Sagal, and my brother, Nick Bravin, gave sobering critiques. Emma Hughes, professor of criminology at California State University, Fresno, took time from completing her own book to scour my pages for obvious flaws, and Professor David Glazier of Loyola Law School, Los Angeles, critically reviewed my discussion of military law. For eleventh-hour proofreading, I thank the rock 'n' roll writer and editor Abigail McGanney Nolan, a friend since elementary school, and Winston Wood, the sage of Paris, Virginia.

There were moments when it seemed this story might never see publication. Several people stepped in to overrule that fate, including the director of Yale University Press, John Donatich, and the manuscript's once-anonymous outside evaluator, Joe Margulies of Northwestern University Law School, himself an old Guantanamo hand. Once upon a time, Bill Frucht, now Yale's executive editor, helped initiate this book. Years later, after our paths long had parted, Bill returned like a mythic hero to effect its rescue. Bill's assistant, Jaya Chatterjee, cheerfully undertook the doomed mission of attempting to keep me to deadline. Meanwhile, some four hundred miles south of New Haven, in an antebellum home outside Richmond, Yale satellite editor Laura Jones Dooley delivered an actual book from a gestating manuscript.

No author could have a better champion than Sandra Dijkstra, my literary agent for nearly twenty years. More than once has Sandy saved my authorial aspirations from ruin, an effort hardly repaid by a productivity of approximately one book per decade. Sandy's expert and equally indefatigable staff, including Elise Capron, Andrea Cavallaro, and Elisabeth James, never left my corner.

The long process of writing this book tried the patience of my family, from whom I disappeared into the solitary world of writing and research far more frequently than was fair. I thank my grandparents, Jack and Helen Brodman, and my parents, Ben and Sjon Bravin, and promise to call and visit more frequently. No one found the writing experience more painful than my wife, Anne Marie Chaker, with whom I shared a move to Washington, the collapse of our roof, and the birth of our daughter, Juliette, before this book came to fruition. I hope it was worth it.

Index